REPEALING
NATIONAL
PROHIBITION

REPEALING NATIONAL PROHIBITION

DAVID E. KYVIG

The Kent State University Press
Kent, Ohio, & London

©2000 by The Kent State University Press, Kent, Ohio 44242
All rights reserved.
Library of Congress Catalog Card Number 00-032713
ISBN 0-87338-672-8
Manufactured in the United States of America

Second edition.
First edition published by the University of Chicago Press, 1979.

05 04 03 02 01 00   5 4 3 2 1

Library of Congress Cataloging-in-Publication Data
Kyvig, David E.
Repealing national prohibition / David E. Kyvig.—[2nd ed.].
p.   cm.
Includes bibliographical references and index.
ISBN 0-87338-672-8 (pbk. : alk. paper)∞
1. Prohibition—United States. I. Title.
HV5089K95 2000
363.4'1'0973—dc21
00-032713

British Library Cataloging-in-Publication data are available.

for Jennifer and Elizabeth

CONTENTS

LIST OF ILLUSTRATIONS

PREFACE TO THE FIRST EDITION

In an outburst of civic righteousness at the end of World War I, the United States banished alcoholic beverages by adopting the Eighteenth Amendment to its Constitution. Zealous advocates of the reform persuaded an overwhelming majority of federal and state legislators to support this method of abolishing the use of intoxicants which, they insisted, would greatly uplift and vastly benefit the society. Not all Americans agreed, however. Some came to regard national prohibition, as the liquor ban was known, as a threat to cherished liberties and political traditions, and thirsted for a return to what they considered more righteous arrangements. Others simply thirsted. This book examines the reaction to national prohibition, particularly the response of those who led the successful crusade to overturn the Eighteenth Amendment. It seeks to explain the circumstances and reasons for the sole instance in American history of the repeal of an amendment to the United States Constitution.

Eliminating the use of alcoholic beverages throughout the United States seems, to most late-twentieth-century observers, an impossible task. Indeed many find it difficult to take national prohibition seriously. They think of prohibition not as a determined, principled, widely supported attempt at fundamental social reform, but rather as a quixotic experiment. Prohibition is best remembered for generating bootleggers, bathtub gin, and bloody gang wars. Americans in large numbers, it is recalled, drank beer, wine, and distilled spirits before, during, and after the ban on their manufacture and sale. Any effort to prevent such behavior was doomed to fail. Repeal of the law, in other words, was inevitable. In light of its own foolishness, the overtaking of its rural, conservative political backers by a new, more tolerant and pluralistic urban majority, the pressures of a great economic depression, and the policies of an incoming liberal administration, national prohibition simply withered and was cast aside by general consensus as the country moved on to more complex, interesting, and important matters.

Such an offhanded assessment of national prohibition and its repeal is as inadequate as it is commonplace. The prohibition episode deserves more careful and thoughtful attention for several reasons. In the first place, the legal ban on alcoholic beverages represented one of the most significant measures adopted during the early-twentieth-century outburst of reform known as the Progressive Era. A nation undergoing rapid modernization was wrestling with perplexing fundamental questions: What were the acceptable limits of behavior in an interdependent, highly technological, industrial society? What was the proper balance between protecting society and respecting individual rights? What was the suitable role for government when community supervision and restraint was giving way to the anonymity and autonomy of mass, urban society? Nineteenth-century answers appeared increasingly inadequate. Progressives expressed great faith in the potential for "social engineering,' assuming that humankind could and should be improved by intelligent analysis of social problems followed by corrective legislation. In prohibiting alcoholic beverages, the federal government intervened in the everyday activities of individual citizens in an unprecedented fashion and to an unprecedented extent. Experience with prohibition provoked reconsideration of progressive assumptions and approaches.

Secondly, national prohibition took the form of a constitutional amendment, reflecting both the contemporary importance attached to it and the measure of support it achieved. It is difficult to dismiss as a trivial aberration a provision inserted in the Constitution with the approval of more than two-thirds of the members of Congress and the legislatures of forty-five states. Only very rarely has the basic design of the United States government been altered through the formal mechanism provided by the Founding Fathers. More frequently the Constitution evolved in small steps as the result of legislative or executive practices or Supreme Court decisions. Since the ratification of the first ten amendments, the Bill of Rights, in 1791, the Constitution had only been amended seven times. The early national period produced two clarifying amendments, Reconstruction generated three civil-rights amendments, and finally two progressive reforms were added in 1913. Furthermore, no amendment which accumulated the broad support necessary for ratification had ever been rescinded. To do so required an almost total political turnabout. Once adopted, therefore, national prohibition was thought to be firmly entrenched, regardless of opposition. Yet within fifteen years of its ratification, the Eighteenth Amendment was repealed. This rare alteration of the frame of government, followed so soon by the unprecedented recanting of the reform, reveals important shifts in political attitudes of the time and illuminates the process of constitutional change.

Third, the struggle to overturn the Eighteenth Amendment became a political battle of great consequence. Throughout the 1920s and early 1930s, political institutions which had once bent to the Anti-Saloon League found themselves confronted by single-issue pressure groups of an opposite persuasion. The rise of such organizations as the Association Against the Prohibition Amendment is fascinating in itself in light of widespread assumptions that revision or repeal of the Eighteenth Amendment was impossible. Prominent citizens, many of whom had not previously engaged in political activity, articulated their values and beliefs regarding society, reform, and government. At the outset, prohibition was a nonpartisan issue, but the major political parties responded differently to repeal demands, with considerable effect on their fortunes. The Republicans, as the party in power during the 1920s, became identified with the law's enforcement. Meanwhile, the Democratic party was influenced and substantially rewarded by committed antiprohibitionists during its unsuccessful 1928 campaign and its rise to sweeping victory in 1932. Interestingly, this occurred in the face of considerable resistance from the 1932 Democratic presidential nominee, Franklin D. Roosevelt. The ultimate success of the repeal crusade in 1933 affected judgments about acceptable limits to legislative reform, the political influence of antiprohibition leaders, and, thereafter, the course of the New Deal.

Historians have never adequately explored the reasons for the Eighteenth Amendment's reversal nor the process by which it occurred, much less the rapidity with which repeal took place. Preoccupied with the simultaneous unfolding of the depression and New Deal, they have accepted explanations offered by the losing side or based on insufficient research and analysis. Such views, incorporated into textbooks and general histories, have become the conventional wisdom regarding repeal.

When the Twenty-first Amendment, repealing the Eighteenth, was ratified in December 1933, contemporary observers generally credited national Democratic party leaders together with single-issue pressure groups, most notably the Association Against the Prohibition Amendment, with sensitivity to popular preferences and responsibility for the result. Before long, however, prohibition sympathizers cast repeal in a different light. In particular, in a 1940 book entitled *The Amazing Story of Repeal: An Exposé of the Power of Propaganda,* Fletcher Dobyns, a Chicago attorney and ardent prohibitionist, charged that repeal had been engineered by a small group of wealthy men solely for their own financial betterment. This tiny, unrepresentative, but powerful clique, Dobyns maintained, mounted a successful propaganda and political campaign through the Association Against the Prohibition Amendment and satellite organizations of their wives, sons, and lawyers. They acted only "to save themselves hundreds of millions of dollars by substituting for an income tax a liquor tax to be paid by the masses."[1] Ernest R. Gordon soon reinforced Dobyns' argument in *The Wrecking of the Eighteenth Amendment.*[2] Gordon had long since made his sympathies evident in his book *When the Brewer Had the Stranglehold.*[3]

Dobyns and Gordon based their case on testimony from a 1930 Senate Judiciary Committee hearing on lobbying. This hearing produced a slashing partisan attack on Democratic national chairman and AAPA supporter John J. Raskob by Republican senators eager to divert attention from embarrassing revelations that their own national party chairman functioned also as a paid lobbyist for a regional development association. Held in the midst of a deepening depression which had prompted antiprohibitionists to begin suggesting repeal as a device to create jobs, reduce government expenses, and increase revenues, and at a time when advocates of the liquor ban were launching increasingly shrill attacks on their advancing opponents, these hearings exaggerated economic considerations and minimized other sources and aspects of hostility to prohibition. Nevertheless, the testimony later gave disappointed prohibitionists a convenient, plausible, and perhaps even comforting explanation for their defeat. A loss to political manipulators was less devastating than popular rejection. The characterization of repeal leaders as a powerful, wealthy, and selfish cabal gained credibility as Franklin Roosevelt at the height of his popularity in 1936 labeled these same individuals, some of his most vocal opponents, "economic royalists" and representatives of "entrenched greed." Dobyns' extremely negative account became a standard interpretation of the repeal movement's leadership.[4]

A more benign view presented repeal as a reflection of societal change and the irresistible expression of democratic will. This interpretation found roots in the belief that prohibition was a reactionary attempt by conservative, rural, Protestant America to hold onto a disappearing cultural pattern. For instance, Richard Hofstadter, in a widely admired and quoted analysis of populist and progressive reform, characterized prohibition as "a pseudo-reform, a pinched, parochial substitute for reform . . . not merely an aversion to drunkenness and to the evils that accompanied it, but to the immigrant drinking masses, to the pleasures and amenities of city life, and to the well-to-do classes and cultivated men."[5] Such an assessment was not unique with Hofstadter by any means, having been offered as early as 1928 in a classic study of the Anti-Saloon League,[6] advanced again in an important 1963 analysis of the Women's Christian Temperance Union,[7] and used frequently in discussions of urban-rural conflict during the early twentieth century. From such a perspective, repeal hardly seems manipulated or even surprising; rather, the abolition of prohibition seems natural, uncomplicated, predictable. As Andrew Sinclair argued in his much-admired history of prohibition: "The old order of the country gave way to the new order of the city. Rural morality was replaced by urban morality, rural voices by urban voices, rural votes by urban votes."[8] Even more sophisticated analyses, such as Norman H. Clark's 1976 *Deliver Us from Evil: An Interpretation of American Prohibition,* imply that basic social changes rendered repeal practically inevitable.

The repeal of the Eighteenth Amendment involved far more than such explanations allow. It could not merely be manipulated by a cabal, nor was it fated to occur. Constitutional change, in 1919 and 1933 as at other times, required very widespread political acceptance. On the other hand, the startling reversal of public opinion within fifteen years did not assure political action. The amendment process is intricate, and the obstacles to change were intended by the Founding Fathers to be formidable. Fletcher Dobyns provided a useful insight by arguing that skillful leadership was essential to repeal, even if he did not fully understand that leadership's history, motives, or function.

Widespread and increasing disregard of the prohibition law during the 1920s, a phenomenon noted by every alert social commentator from that day to this, provided an important measure of public attitudes toward the liquor ban, but in itself could not reverse the constitutional provision of 1919. Breaking the law was by nature an individualistic and covert act. Mobilizing protest against the law in such proportions as to bring about its repeal required coordination and publicity. Leadership and organization were demanded for the prodigious task of obtaining support from two-thirds of Congress and three-fourths of the states. The network of suppliers of illicit liquor represented the only organization among the law's violators. No one was less likely to seek publicity or agitate for repeal than a bootlegger who was profiting from the existence of prohibition. Leadership for a repeal movement would have to come from elsewhere.

Organized, single-issue pressure groups with a wide range of arguments had generated and channeled broad support crucial to the passage of the Eighteenth Amendment. The same would be true in converting dissatisfaction with national prohibition into a successful movement for repeal. Foremost among repeal groups was the Association Against the Prohibition Amendment. Opposition to growing federal power and unhappiness with prohibition's social consequences motivated the AAPA and later appearing groups: the New York–based Voluntary Committee of Lawyers, a young men's society known as the Crusaders, and the very active, influential, million-member Women's Organization for National Prohibition Reform. These single-purpose voluntary associations, abetted by labor unions, trade and bar associations, medical societies, and veterans' groups, retrieved the idea of repeal from the realm of assumed impossibility and made it a serious matter of public discussion. Also, they shaped the debate over the law, focusing attention on certain issues and thus influencing public opinion. Finally, in part through determined effort and in part through chance, they produced circumstances in which actual or assumed public opinion could be brought to bear at crucial points in the political process.

This effort to explain prohibition repeal will necessarily begin with an examination of the passage of the Eighteenth Amendment. Constitutional revision occurred in the early twentieth century when the long-standing temperance argument that intoxicating beverages undermined the health, prosperity, and morals of America interacted with the progressive belief that modern, urban, industrial society could and should be uplifted through the implementation of proper laws. Opposition to such views provoked the creation of the Association Against the Prohibition Amendment, the first organized hostile response to national prohibition from outside the affected industry. The procedure by which the antiliquor amendment was installed in the Constitution also influenced attitudes toward it.

The next essential will be to examine how national prohibition functioned, what was done to enforce the law, and how its operation was perceived. The reaction against prohibition had much to do with its image, the evolving perception that the law was ineffectual and threatened the rights and safety of the American people. The motives for challenging the Eighteenth Amendment stem from the liquor ban's implementation as well as its conception.

Mass public response to prohibition is, of course, a crucial factor in its overturn. Precisely how popular opinion divided on the issue between 1919 and 1933 is extraordinarily difficult to establish. Exactly why the citizenry felt as it did is even harder to determine. Contemporary popular motives for supporting or opposing prohibition were never adequately surveyed or measured. Nervous political leaders had trouble gauging mass attitudes and acted on the basis of unscientific assessments or pressure group agitation. Historians have little more to go on. The best that can currently be done is to describe quantitative shifts in mass opinion as these were reflected in the few, crude public opinion polls of the time, scattered state referendums, and the one nearly nationwide test of prohibition's popularity, the 1933 vote in thirty-seven states on ratification of the Twenty-first Amendment. If precinct or county level voting data for 1933 were gathered (which has never been done) and quantitatively analyzed, our picture of the dimensions of the repeal landslide would improve, but probably not our understanding of the manner in which it developed. For the motives behind repeal, one must look at the arguments of an articulate leadership, recognizing that they may not always mirror mass opinion.

The study of repeal must focus principally on the leadership of the repeal movement. The organized antiprohibitionists were the crucial as well as the most visible element in the process of constitutional change. In particular, they converted popular attitudes into effective political force strong enough to alter the Constitution. Since the appearance of Fletcher Dobyns' work nearly forty years ago, no careful, detailed examination of the repeal leadership has been undertaken. In the meantime, the records of many participants have become available, most recently the Voluntary Committee of Lawyers Papers at Wesleyan University and the extensive files of Pierre S. du Pont at Eleutherian Mills Historical Library. The latter provide much new information about the Association Against the Prohibition Amendment and the Women's Organization for National Prohibition Reform. Old sources of information, many neglected by Dobyns, as well as newly accessible materials make it possible now to trace the evolution of the antiprohibition movement from its origins, to analyze its motives, to see its maturation by the late 1920s, to assess the impetus for repeal provided by the Great Depression, and to appreciate its role in the politics of the period. The result is a new view of prohibition repeal and many suggestions for reconsideration of other aspects of the era in which it took place.

The drive to rescind the Eighteenth Amendment represented much more than the desire to take a legal drink or shed a tax burden. From the first, repeal advocates objected to prohibition's philosophy of active, authoritative federal government. Concern grew that prohibition, unpopular and frequently violated, was fostering criminal behavior, causing the government to take increasingly repressive enforcement action, and breeding disrespect for all government and law. Fear of social disintegration became widespread long before the onset of the great depression generated additional claims that the liquor ban had proven economically burdensome. Progressive hopes for social uplift through banishment of intoxicants were dashed, leaving national prohibition with too few advocates to fend off attack. The nature of the reform coalition which had carried prohibition into the Constitution in the first place became more apparent than ever as specific complaints were raised and support for the law unraveled.

Anxiety, even alarm, brought men and women into organizations campaigning against the Eighteenth Amendment. To them, American society appeared critically unstable. Furthermore, the federal government seemed ill-equipped to cope with the threat. The membership of the major repeal associations belies views of the prohibition struggle pitting old-stock American against an urban, immigrant working class. Prosperous and well-established men and women generally assumed to be satisfied with social and governmental arrangements, particularly during the late 1920s, were uneasy enough to become involved by the thousands in a political crusade regarded as the longest of longshots. This suggests conventional views of a placid and complacent middle- and upper-class society during the twenties need revision.

The prohibition issue became an important factor in the partisan battles and realignments of the 1920s and 1930s, often in ways difficult to quantify through electoral analysis. Ultimately, voter reaction to Al Smith's antiprohibitionism in 1928 was less significant than the alliance then forged between repeal organizations and the Democrat party or Smith's placing his party's national headquarters for the next four years in hands determined to end prohibition. Maneuvering and leadership decisions which fixed a wet label on the Democrats and a dry one on the Republicans took place coincidentally but fatefully as party fortunes rose and fell because of the depression. The rapid achievement of repeal seems to have been both a cause and effect of changing national voting patterns.

The reaction against national prohibition did not set any clear direction for subsequent reform efforts, offering more of an indication of what was unacceptable. Enthusiasm for using the Constitution to achieve reform goals waned rapidly. The Nineteenth Amendment, mandating women's suffrage, was ratified a few months after the Eighteenth took effect. Thereafter, however, proposed amendments to abolish child labor and guarantee equal rights for women languished despite early manifestations of strength. Four amendments had been ratified between 1913 and 1920. The next three decades, in contrast, were barren of constitutional reform except for prohibition repeal and a minor change reducing the period between national elections and the start of presidential and congressional terms. The ineffectiveness and unpopularity of national prohibition heightened consciousness of the limits of what could be achieved by legislative edict, especially at the federal level. The experience was reflected in the cautious nature of New Deal reform, its focus on institutional rather than direct personal solutions to social problems, and its hesitancy to move beyond what appeared acceptable to a broad spectrum of opinion.

A study of constitutional change can illuminate many facets of the nation's past. Shifting values, needs, and aspirations are reflected in the deliberate modification of governmental structure. Political processes and power distributions become clearer as do the influences of special interests. The rise and fall of national prohibition in a span of twenty years from first proposal to final collapse represents an extraordinary episode in the history of American constitutional change and thus an unique opportunity for examining social and political ideas and practices. The second thoughts which led Americans between 1919 and 1933 to reverse a major commitment to reform deserve attention in any consideration of the possibilities and limitations of American government and society.

The completion of this work testifies to the spirit of cooperation and generous support which a historian encounters in the course of such an undertaking. I could hardly have produced this book alone. In the course of the project, I have attempted to express my appreciation to those who aided me. Here I would like to acknowledge publicly the valuable assistance they rendered.

Any historian of modern America owes a debt to the many archivists who have gathered, cared for, and made accessible enormous collections of records pertaining to the past century. Wherever I went, I received gracious and informed assistance from directors to junior staff archivists. Though I dealt primarily with administrators and reference specialists, I am acutely aware that I owe as much to unseen archivists who acquired, arranged, and described the records which I used. I specifically wish to acknowledge the help of the archival staffs of Columbia University, Eleutherian Mills Historical Library, Herbert Hoover Presidential Library, University of Kentucky, Library of Congress Manuscripts Division, Maryland Historical Society, Michigan Historical Collections, New York Public Library, National Archives, Ohio Historical Society, Princeton University, Franklin D. Roosevelt Presidential Library, Wesleyan University Collection on Legal Change, and Wisconsin State Historical Society. In addition, librarians at the University of Akron, Library of Congress, and Northwestern University rendered considerable assistance.

Several scholars read and commented on all or portions of the manuscript during its long gestation. Though I did not accept all their suggestions, I thought about and benefitted from them. In particular, I wish to thank David Burner, Norman H. Clark, David H. Culbert, Nuala Drescher, H. Roger Grant, J. Stanley Lemons, Richard W. Leopold, Daniel Nelson, Robert H. Wiebe, George Wolfskill, Clement E. Vose, and Robert L. Zangrando.

Northwestern University supported the early stages of my research. The Eleutherian Mills-Hagley Foundation provided a grant which enabled me to examine the Pierre S. du Pont papers during the summer of 1973. On several occasions the University of Akron faculty research fund made possible further research and time for writing. I am deeply grateful to each for the financial assistance and the expression of faith in this project.

While I could not have completed this manuscript without the assistance of the individuals and institutions mentioned, I accept full responsibility for all judgments and interpretations.

PREFACE TO THE
SECOND EDITION

A book is like a child. While they gestate as well as later, as they mature, children and books heighten their progenitors' awareness of the environment into which they are being introduced, stir dormant concerns, and arouse altogether new interests. Once delivered into the world, books as well as children take on lives of their own. Both acquire friends with whom their authors and parents may not even be familiar. Likewise, both display unexpected strengths and reveal unintended weaknesses. Finally, just as the greatest joy of parenthood involves watching a child grow to maturity, make his or her own way in the world, and achieve independent success, the pleasure of authorship includes seeing a book gain a reputation and exercise an influence beyond what could have been anticipated at the time of its conception or birth.

Repealing National Prohibition has encountered every one of those experiences since its delivery in late 1979. The book was conceived as a doctoral dissertation to explore the reaction during the 1920s and early 1930s against Progressive era social reform. It grew into a study of the attempt to end American use of intoxicating beverages by embedding a prohibition on their manufacture, sale, and transportation in an amendment to the U.S. Constitution. The reaction against prohibition culminated in the abandonment of what only fourteen years before had been an extraordinarily popular measure. The reversal would not have been complete without the adoption of another constitutional amendment. My inquiry into the reaction against national prohibition led me to realize that its peculiar situation as a constitutional reform profoundly influenced its entire course. That circumstance, I gradually came to understand, molded the thought of both proponents and opponents, defined their behavior, and shaped perceptions of the episode's meaning. The heart of the book I delivered in 1979 was a detailed examination of the social and political context as well as the process of constitutional development.

At the time I did not fully appreciate how distinctive and substantial had been the influence of national prohibition on the process of constitutional change. My curiosity regarding the place of amendments in the overall American constitutional and political system had, however, been aroused. I found myself turning away from my preoccupation with drink, drawn instead to devote my principal attention during the next two decades to examining the vastly broader topic of the amending process over the whole course of American history. The results of my desire to place the prohibition amendments in a larger context included *Explicit and Authentic Acts: Amending the U.S. Constitution, 1776–1995* (Lawrence: University Press of Kansas, 1996), and an edited collection of essays, *Unintended Consequences of Constitutional Amendment* (Athens: University of Georgia Press, 2000).

As I went off to explore the interests it had stirred, *Repealing National Prohibition* made its own way in the world. I had not abandoned it, but it gained a measure of independence from me. It quickly acquired a group of companions its own age; together they demonstrated the truth of the old adage "strength in numbers." Unknown to me, several historians had simultaneously been working on other aspects of the temperance and prohibition movement. Their books appeared at the same time as *Repealing National Prohibition*, too late, unfortunately, to have any influence on my writing. Collectively, however, they significantly expanded knowledge and interest regarding the history of American drinking. These books called attention to patterns of heavy alcohol use in the United States during the early nineteenth century as well as efforts at various times to craft a public policy that would deal satisfactorily with alcohol problems. These works included Jack S. Blocker, Jr.'s edited volume, *Alcohol, Reform, and Society: The Liquor Issue in Social Context* (Westport: Greenwood, 1978); Larry Engleman's *Intemperance: The Lost War Against Liquor* (New York: Free Press, 1979); Ernest Kurtz's *Not-God: A History of Alcoholics Anonymous* (Center City, Minn.: Hazelden Educational Service, 1979); W. J. Rorabaugh's *The Alcoholic Republic: An American Tradition* (New York: Oxford University Press, 1979); Ian R. Tyrrell's *Sobering Up: From Temperance to Prohibition in Antebellum America* (Westport: Greenwood, 1979); and Elliott West's *The Saloon on the Rocky Mountain Mining Frontier* (Lincoln: University of Nebraska Press, 1979).

The cohort of books emerging together at the end of the 1970s was followed not many years later by a further outpouring of significant works on various aspects of alcohol history. Once again attention focused on the pre–World War I culture of drink and efforts—especially by women—to restrict or eliminate it. Among the most notable volumes to appear were Ruth Bordin's *Woman and Temperance: The Quest for Power and Liberty, 1873–1900* (Philadelphia: Temple University Press, 1981); James Kirby Martin and Mark Edward Lender's *Drinking in America: A History* (New York: Free Press, 1982); Thomas J. Noel, *The City and the Saloon: Denver, 1858–1916* (Lincoln: University of Nebraska Press, 1982); Perry R. Duis's *The Saloon: Public Drinking in Chicago and Boston, 1880–1920* (Urbana: University of Illinois Press, 1983); Robert S. Bader's *Prohibition in Kansas* (Lawrence: University Press of Kansas, 1986); Jack S. Blocker, Jr.'s *"Give To The Winds Thy Fears:" The Women's Temperance Crusade, 1873–1874* (Westport: Greenwood, 1985); and K. Austin Kerr's *Organized for Prohibition: A New History of the Anti-Saloon League* (New Haven: Yale University Press, 1985).

While popular accounts of bootlegging during the 1920s were published from time to time, only one scholarly study during the 1980s focused on the era of national prohibition. Lawrence Spinelli's *Dry Diplomacy: The United States, Great Britain, and Prohibition* (Wilmington, Del.: Scholarly Resources, 1989) offered an unusual and enlightening examination of the role of the intoxicating beverage ban on U.S. foreign relations. Toward the end of this period of broadening and deepening study of alcohol and temperance, two books sought to sum up what had been learned. Jack S. Blocker, Jr.'s American *Temperance Movements: Cycles of Reform* (Boston: Twayne, 1989) provided an excellent overview of the rise and fall of the temperance movement. Meanwhile, John C. Burnham's *Bad Habits: Drinking, Smoking, Taking Drugs, Gambling, Sexual Misbehavior, and Swearing in American History* (New York: New York University Press, 1993) placed prohibition in the context of attempts to regulate all varieties of "minor vices." With the exception of these two works, both sympathetic to my own, the scholarship of the 1980s generally left the demise of prohibition unexamined.

The outpouring of sophisticated historical studies related to alcohol that began in the late 1970s—a veritable population explosion of such work—brought many of the authors together at a series of encounters that resembled parent-teacher association meetings, gatherings of proud parents eager to learn from each other and work together to create a better environment for their offspring. The fiftieth anniversary of the repeal of prohibition in 1983 led the Eleutherian Mills-Hagley Foundation of Greenville, Delaware, the repository of an important collection of prohibition-related papers, to sponsor a scholarly conference highlighting new perspectives on the prohibition episode. Much of the conference's attention focused on the effect of national prohibition, both in its operation and its aftermath. In addition to a core of historians, participants included sociologists, political scientists, public health scholars, and lawyers interested in prohibition history for what it could contribute to their considerations of contemporary alcohol and drug policy. I had the privilege not only of participating in the conference but also editing many of the presentations into a book, *Law, Alcohol, and Order: Perspectives on National Prohibition* (Westport: Greenwood, 1985).

Not long thereafter, a larger group of alcohol scholars gathered for a January 1984 Berkeley, California, conference on the social history of alcohol (which, to my lasting regret, I was unable to attend). The Berkeley meeting led to the formation of the Alcohol and Temperance History Group, a scholarly association that has since grown to nearly two hundred members around the world and which publishes *The Social History of Alcohol Review*. By the time that the Alcohol and Temperance History Group (through the efforts of its then president, Jack Blocker) held an International Congress on the Social History of Alcohol in London, Ontario, in May 1993, a rich, vibrant, and diverse international scholarship on the history of alcohol had emerged in dissertations, scholarly articles, and books. Every issue of *The Social History of Alcohol Review* contained a substantial bibliography of new works. My book, now in its mid-teens, had acquired a large, lively, and diverse set of companions.

By the 1990s *Repealing National Prohibition* and its contemporaries had been around long enough to be joined by a new generation of alcohol scholarship. After having long been on the periphery of scholarly activity that centered on the pre-prohibition era of rising temperance agitation, my book gained more attention. A number of young historians were present at the London conference; two of the most impressive, Richard F. Hamm and Catherine Gilbert Murdock, were engaged in examining issues upon which I had touched but had not studied extensively. Hamm was giving the first detailed attention by a well-trained legal historian to the manner in which the Eighteenth Amendment was constructed. His work would soon appear as *Shaping the Eighteenth Amendment: Temperance Reform, Legal Culture, and the Polity, 1880–1920* (Chapel Hill: University of North Carolina Press, 1995). Murdock, who was examining women's drinking as well as their important role in prohibition repeal, would challenge gender stereotypes of women as uniformly committed to temperance in *Domesticating Drink: Women, Men, and Alcohol in America, 1870–1940* (Baltimore: Johns Hopkins University Press, 1998). When their books appeared, both Hamm and Murdock considerably enriched our understanding of the rise and fall of American constitutional prohibition.

Not all new arrivals on the scholarly scene took part in the gatherings of the Alcohol and Temperance History Group, although they undoubtedly benefited from the accumulation of scholarship. Three studies, two closely related to each other in their focus, elaborated as had Hamm and Murdock on matters to which I had been able to give too little attention. Two—Kenneth M. Murchison's *Federal Criminal Law Doctrines: The Forgotten Influence of National Prohibition* (Durham, N.C.: Duke University Press, 1994), and John J. Gutherie, Jr.'s *Keepers of the Spirits: The Judicial Response to Prohibition Enforcement in Florida, 1885–1935* (Westport: Greenwood, 1998)—explored the significance impact of prohibition enforcement on evolving American criminal law enforcement. Another—Kenneth D. Rose's *American Women and the Repeal of Prohibition* (New York: New York University Press, 1996)—extended awareness of women's critical role in ending the federal liquor ban. The appearance of these volumes, besides making me feel a bit like a scholarly grandparent, improved understanding of the operation of prohibition and the multifaceted opposition to it that had arisen by the early 1930s. Meanwhile Madelon Powers's *Faces Along the Bar: Lore and Order in the Workingman's Saloon, 1870–1920* (Chicago: University of Chicago Press, 1998); John E. Hallwas's *The Bootlegger: A Story of Small-Town America* (Urbana: University of Illinois Press, 1998); and Thomas R. Pegram's *Battling Demon Rum: The Struggle for a Dry America, 1800–1933* (Chicago: Ivan R. Dee, 1998) continued to enlarge understanding of drinking culture, both legal and illegal, and the temperance crusade from beginning to end.

One element of *Repealing National Prohibition* that was undernourished at the outset and remains neglected as an opportunity for meaningful inquiry is the impact of prohibition repeal on subsequent U.S. alcohol policy. Ernest Kurtz's 1979 book on Alcoholics Anonymous and the 1983 Hagley conference on the fiftieth anniversary of repeal only scratched the surface of this important topic. The post-1933 treatment of alcohol in American society, a subject of great social, political, economic, and cultural significance, still awaits the careful attention it deserves.

Neglect of the history of post-repeal U.S. alcohol policy may be explained, at least in part, by the popular image of national prohibition as a complete and utter failure and public policies to regulate drinking as politically risky and futile. Popular images of the 1920s as a "lost weekend" during which bootleggers flourished and through which flowed an unchecked river of booze simply ignore the findings of John Burnham and others that prohibition reduced alcohol intake by more than half. The endlessly repeated myths about a flood of alcohol in the 1920s have overwhelmed the more complex historical reality. A typical recounting of the dominant myth occurred in a 1998 British Broadcasting Corporation three-hour documentary of prohibition. Burnham and I were interviewed at length, but all of his and most of my observations ended up on the cutting room floor while the biography of Chicago bootlegger Al Capone was highlighted along with the flamboyant, but hardly commonplace, reminiscences of a former New York chorus-line dancer. The post-1933 treatment of alcohol in the United States offers a fascinating case study of the power of historical myths as well as an example of the complicated process of public policy formation.

What I least expected when *Repealing National Prohibition* first appeared was the interest that would be shown in it by readers concerned about American drug policy. The history of drug prohibition was a relatively unstudied topic when I was first examining alcohol prohibition and its repeal. At the time, I was not drawn to make comparisons, though on reflection the absolutist nature of the official American commitment to drug prohibition bore more resemblance to the constitutional ban on alcohol than I acknowledged. My focus on the constitutionalized issue of alcohol helped steer me away from legal barriers to drug use that were created and maintained by other means.

As public policy matters, both alcohol and drug prohibition deserve further consideration based on historical understanding instead of popular myth. To argue that alcohol prohibition failed utterly to limit drinking and that, therefore, restrictions on drug use are unworkable is to proceed from a false premise to an ungrounded conclusion. At the same time, to argue that absolute prohibition is the only responsible public policy is to ignore the costs of that approach. During the 1920s the maintenance of alcohol prohibition required the expansion of police forces; the toleration of new policing practices that eroded the privacy of the home, automobile, and telephone; and the expansion of prisons. The consequences of the attempt to define as criminal alcohol production, transportation, and sale for the ultimate purpose of use as a beverage included the rise of a socially unsettling image of widespread lawlessness. Whether or not a social policy objective justifies such social costs is a difficult question to answer, but historical understandings may help illuminate the consequences of alternative responses, if not provide indisputable conclusions.

The unbending absolutism of prohibition advocates once the Eighteenth Amendment had been adopted bears particular notice. Holding firmly to a belief in the righteousness of their position, dry leaders were completely unwilling to strike a compromise to allow beer and wine in order to preserve and render more manageable the ban on far more potent distilled liquors. Such intransigence ultimately encouraged many of their opponents to abandon hope for a moderate solution, a toleration of low-powerful alcoholic beverages, and to seek instead the complete overthrow of constitutional prohibition. This outcome bears consideration in light of present-day resistance to proposals to legalize marijuana in order to undermine the appeal of more potent substances, not to mention other suggestions for more widespread drug reform. Drug control is clearly a public policy issue deserving of further attention. Ultimately it involves philosophical choices, but these can be clarified by improved perceptions of the relevant past. It is my hope that the rebirth of *Repealing National Prohibition* in this paperback edition will contribute to the dialogue that should take place on this difficult and important matter.

This book was born later in the same decade that saw the arrival of my two daughters. All have done well on their own. I hope that all three will age gracefully and none too rapidly. Trusting that this will be so, I dedicate the new edition of the book, not to their mother as I did its predecessor, but to Jennifer and Elizabeth, my greatest pride and joy.

REPEALING
NATIONAL
PROHIBITION

INTRODUCTION

On the morning of December 12, 1927, eighteen middle-aged men, many of them prominent in American business or politics, met at the home of ex-United States senator James W. Wadsworth in northwest Washington, D.C., to discuss launching a political campaign which most contemporary observers considered a hopeless folly. The group which gathered at 2800 Woodland Drive included Pierre S. du Pont, retired chairman of the board of both General Motors and E. I. du Pont de Nemours Company; Charles H. Sabin, president of Guaranty Trust Company of New York; Senators Walter E. Edge of New Jersey and William Cabell Bruce of Maryland; Edward S. Harkness, philanthropist and heir to one of the nation's largest fortunes; and World War I Assistant Secretary of War Benedict Crowell. All that day and part of the next these men talked about their common desire for what seemed impossible: repeal of the Eighteenth Amendment to the United States Constitution.[1]

The amendment, which prohibited the manufacture, sale, or transportation of intoxicating beverages, had been adopted less than nine years earlier. Although frequently criticized and often violated, national prohibition apparently enjoyed widespread public support and, even more important, an impregnable constitutional position. "Drys," as defenders of national prohibition were termed, appeared numerous, ardent, and highly organized, while "wets," opponents of the law, though of uncertain number, seemed definitely less fervent and not at all well organized. The host of the meeting, for instance, had recently lost his New York Senate seat for opposing national prohibition. Several of Wadsworth's guests had devoted years to seeking repeal without making noticeable progress. Among them were leaders of the lone national organization publicly advocating repeal, the Association Against the Prohibition Amendment, and two state repeal societies, the Constitutional Liberty League of Massachusetts and the Moderation League of New York. All three groups appeared stagnant. In 1927 the prospects of repeal seemed, at best, extremely remote.

Prohibitionists had waged a tremendous effort to install their reform in the Constitution, believing that if they succeeded, it would be impossible to dislodge. The ban on alcoholic beverages, they felt, would become an unchallengeable permanent feature of American law. A confident Anti-Saloon League leader explained why.

> There is but one way of changing the Constitution of the United States, consequently there is but one way of changing or repealing the Eighteenth Amendment to the Constitution. Two-thirds of the members of each of the two houses of Congress would first of all have to submit a proposed change in the Eighteenth Amendment to the several states. After such a submission three-fourths of the states would need to ratify such a proposal before any such change or repeal could be made, Therefore, so long as thirteen of the forty-eight states stand firm for the Eighteenth Amendment there can be no repeal of that portion of the Constitution. The leaders of the opposition understand full well that there is not the slightest hope of securing the repeal of the Eighteenth Amendment.[2]

A reversal seemed most unlikely indeed. The Eighteenth Amendment had passed the test of wide acceptability devised by the Founding Fathers for additions to the nation's basic law. Between 1917 and 1922, after all, two-thirds of Congress approved and forty-six state legislatures ratified the new amendment. Much less support was needed thereafter to keep the amendment in place. For instance, the thirteen smallest states in 1920 had a combined population of only about five million, less than five percent of the nation's total, yet under the constitutional system they possessed sufficient power to stymie a repeal attempt. Consequently, one of the amendment's authors, Texas senator Morris Sheppard, had reason for boasting: "There is as much chance of repealing the Eighteenth Amendment as there is for a humming-bird to fly to the planet Mars with the Washington Monument tied to its tail."[3] Even as thirsty an observer as President Warren Harding concluded that the amendment would never be repealed.[4]

The men who met in December 1927 to discuss a campaign for repeal fully recognized the enormity of the task facing them. However, they regarded national prohibition as the foremost public issue of the day. The Eighteenth Amendment, they felt, raised larger and more disturbing public policy questions than merely the control of alcoholic beverages. To them prohibition represented a major expansion of the scope of federal government activity, particularly in regard to individual behavior, and it was based on assumptions which might logically lead to further growth of federal authority. Concurrently, widespread violation of the liquor ban was creating an image of a government unable or unwilling to enforce its statutes. Support for the government appeared to be eroding, and a dangerous social instability seemed to be developing.

Wadsworth and his colleagues were so aroused that they waved aside all advice that their efforts would be futile. In their two-day December meeting and a subsequent session on January 6, 1928, they agreed to revive and reorganize the Association Against the Prohibition Amendment. A single-purpose bipartisan organization to publicize objections and generate pressure for reform seemed to them the most likely device for bringing about a change. Their commitment to such a battle for repeal proved to be an important turning point in the long struggle over national prohibition.

Not even the greatest optimist at the Wadsworth home that December day, AAPA founder William H. Stayton, would have predicted that one week short of six years later the Eighteenth Amendment would be abolished. However, in February 1933, Congress, by a better than two-thirds vote, approved a new amendment, the Twenty-first, overturning the old, and by December 5, more than three-fourths of the states had ratified it in popularly elected conventions. Stayton, Wadsworth, Pierre du Pont, and the others who in December 1927 prepared to battle national prohibition could not foresee the outcome, much less the social, political, or constitutional consequences of the struggle. They could not know, of course, that the Eighteenth Amendment would fall even more abruptly than it rose.

In hindsight, abolition of the Eighteenth Amendment appears inevitable, the logical outcome of a foolish, unpopular reform. The group which gathered at the Wadsworth home in Washington hardly viewed the situation that way, and rightly so. National prohibition had gained wide support as a righteous effort to deal with the serious social problem of alcoholic overindulgence. Even after experience demonstrated the inadequacies and attendent liabilities of this solution, the obstacles of constitutional amendment appeared to prevent change. Repealists, however, proved as determined and resourceful as prohibitionists. Their thirst for restoration of what they considered social and constitutional righteousness combined with an effective political effort and fortunate timing to produce the constitutional reversal of 1933, one of the most improbable and unexpected political events of its time—and one of the most significant.

1 ADOPTING NATIONAL PROHIBITION

The crusade to abolish the use of alcoholic beverages through an amendment to the Constitution hit the United States like a whirlwind in the second decade of the twentieth century. In November 1913 the Anti-Saloon League of America first publicly appealed for a prohibition amendment. By January 1919, scarcely five years later, Congress had approved and forty-four state legislatures had ratified the Eighteenth Amendment, which proclaimed:

1. After one year from the ratification of this article the manufacture, sale, or transportation of intoxicating liquors within, the importation thereof into, or the exportation thereof from the United States, and all territory subject to the jurisdiction thereof for beverage purposes is hereby prohibited.

2. The Congress and the several States shall have concurrent power to enforce this article by appropriate legislation.

3. The article shall be inoperative unless it shall have been ratified as an amendment to the Constitution by the legislatures of the several States, as provided in the Constitution, within seven years from the date of the submission hereof to the States by the Congress.

A tremendously significant social reform affecting the lives of millions had suddenly become part of the nation's rarely altered basic law.

Proponents of the so-called dry law faced little organized resistance as they marched to their triumph. Only brewers, distillers, and other commercial interests made strenuous efforts to block the reform. Individuals and groups offended by the challenge to their ethnic cultural traditions or by the limitation of their right to choose what to drink objected to the national liquor ban, but they lacked the channels and agents to give their protest focus and strength. New opposition to the Eighteenth Amendment began to form, however, in the midst of the prohibitionist victory in response to the law itself, the manner of its adoption, and the political assumptions upon which it was based. The reaction against this important constitutional innovation, therefore, can only be understood in light of the circumstances of national prohibition's creation.

The Eighteenth Amendment was the product of a century-long temperance crusade, the early-twentieth-century progressive environment, and a temporary spirit of wartime sacrifice. Various historians of the reform have tended to emphasize one or another of these factors.[1] However, it is hard to imagine national prohibition being adopted without all three interacting.

X   The temperance movement's long and rich history began early in the nineteenth century as clergymen, politicians, business leaders, and social reformers became concerned about American society's increased drinking.[2] They appealed for moderation in the use of intoxicants in the interests of health, morality, and economic well-being. From the start, evangelical Protestant churches stood in the forefront of the antiliquor movement. These churches felt that intemperance seriously interfered with their soul-saving mission because it destroyed man's health, impaired his reason, and distracted him from the love of God. Intemperance also undermined society by producing poverty, crime, and unhappy homes; this conflicted with the church's obligation to create a Christian social order. Finally, sobriety was considered to be the foundation of economic success and political liberty—visible signs of God's grace. For all of these reasons, evangelical Protestants became increasingly militant temperance agitators as the nineteenth century wore on. X

In the mid-1820s the Reverend Lyman Beecher and others started urging total abstinence. They had come to believe that even moderate use of liquor started people on the downward path to drunkenness. The argument that intemperance was a disease preventable only by complete avoidance of spirits became a crucial article of the prohibitionist faith. Never again would moderate liquor consumption satisfy most temperance reformers; the complete elimination of intoxicants became their goal.

By the 1840s, temperance advocates had been disappointed several times by the results of crusades to win individual abstinence pledges, and they began asking for statutory curbs. Initial efforts in Massachusetts to confine the sale of alcoholic beverages within taverns and in New York to establish local option—the right of a community to ban the sale of intoxicants within its boundaries—proved unsuccessful. Next came the first attempt at state-wide prohibition, the Maine law of 1851 which outlawed the manufacture or sale of "spiritous or intoxicating liquors." A dozen states quickly followed suit, but for the moment the movement had abated. The Maine law and others imitating it were repealed before the end of the 1850s. Then, for a time, the turmoil of the Civil War diverted reformers.

A new wave of temperance agitation began with the formation of the Prohibition party in 1869 and the Women's Christian Temperance Union in 1873, two organizations which put prohibition at the top of a list of desired social and political reforms. By the 1880s their efforts had helped make prohibition a vital issue in many states and territories. Five states adopted prohibitory legislation during the eighties, though only Maine, Kansas, and North Dakota retained their laws for long. The rising tide of populism soon overshadowed and pushed aside the antiliquor crusade. Although once again aborted, the crusade for enforced temperance at this time recorded one significant achievement: the creation in 1893 of the Anti-Saloon League.[3]

The Anti-Saloon League proved the most single-minded and politically effective of all dry organizations. Established by men willing to confine their efforts solely to temperance reform, the league operated as a nonpartisan pressure group. Recognizing that whenever two political parties or two factions of the same party competed with approximate equality the support of a relatively small unattached group could be crucial, the league sought to demonstrate that it controlled enough votes to make the difference between election and defeat, thereby gaining candidates' acceptance of its program in return for its endorsement. Drawing its support primarily from the evangelical Protestant churches, the Anti-Saloon League became a political force to be reckoned with by the early twentieth century.[4]

Prior to 1913 the Anti-Saloon League and its allies in the temperance campaign concentrated on winning local option elections and obtaining state statutes or constitutional amendments barring liquor sales. Nine states and many communities by then had adopted some sort of prohibition, though generally their laws allowed the continued sale of beer and wine and often permitted residents to mail order distilled spirits for their own use from outside the dry district. (Only half of the twenty-six states which instituted prohibition laws before 1920 went "bone-dry," banning alcoholic beverages totally.) Encouraged by such signs of progress as six state prohibition laws since 1907 and congressional passage early in 1913 of the Webb-Kenyon Act, a long-sought federal statute against transporting liquor into states that wished to block its entry, the Anti-Saloon League declared in November 1913 that it would seek a federal constitutional amendment providing for nationwide prohibition.

An amendment to the Constitution obviously appealed to temperance reformers more than a federal statute banning liquor. A simple congressional majority could adopt a statute but, with the shift of a relatively few votes, could likewise topple one. Drys feared that an ordinary law would be in constant danger of being overturned owing to pressure from liquor industry interests or the growing population of liquor-using immigrants. A constitutional amendment, on the other hand, though more difficult to achieve, would be impervious to change. Their reform would not only have been adopted, the Anti-Saloon League reasoned, but would be protected from future human weakness and backsliding.

"Although the Eighteenth Amendment would probably never have materialized except for the [Anti-Saloon] league," observed James H. Timberlake, a perceptive historian of the prohibition movement in the 1910s, "it is equally certain that the league would never have attained its success had not temperance reform been caught up in the progressive spirit itself."[5] Progressivism and prohibition were, in his view, closely related middle-class reform movements seeking to deal with social and economic problems through the use of governmental power. They drew on the same broad base of support and moral idealism, and they proposed similar solutions to society's ills. Examinations of temperance campaigns in such varied states as Texas, Washington, Tennessee, New Mexico, Virginia, California, and Missouri support Timberlake's conclusion that "prohibition was actually written into the Constitution as a progressive reform."[6]

Progressivism, the reform spirit which gripped the United States in the early twentieth century, involved a variety of impulses, some parochial, some national, some complementary, some independent, some innovative, and some conservative. The various strands of progressivism were united, however, at the level of basic assumptions. Sensitive to the upheavals caused by the rapid industrialization and urbanization of America, progressives rejected the populist response of opposing modernization and instead sought to impose an order on the emerging society which would be consistent with their own values and interests. Far more optimistic than the preceding generation about man's capacity to solve problems and mold a satisfactory world, progressives believed that their goals could be reached by creating the proper laws and institutions. Whether the particular task into which they plunged was raising the quality of life for the urban working class, conserving natural resources, establishing professional societies and standards, improving governmental morality, democracy, and services, or controlling business practices, progressives repeatedly displayed their unshakable confidence that legal and bureaucratic instruments could be found which would permanently uplift that aspect of their environment.[7] "They believed," as Ralph H. Gabriel put it, "that man, by using his intellect can re-make society, that he can become the creator of a world organized for man's advantage."[8]

From the progressive viewpoint, temperance arguments made sense. In a modern society, liquor both reduced men's efficiency and spawned a multitude of social, political, and economic evils. Such a phenomenon should be reformed or outlawed for the common good. It is wrong, suggests Paul A. Carter, to think of prohibition as "exclusively the work of moralizing Puritans compensating for the repressions of their own harsh code in a spurious indignation at the pleasure of their neighbors." In his study of progressivism within the Protestant churches, the so-called Social Gospel movement, Carter found "thousands of sincere and not particularly ascetic folk who believed that they fought liquor, not because it has made men happy, but because it has made men unhappy." He concluded that "the dry crusade spoke the language of social and humanitarian reform—and had the profoundest kinship with the Social Gospel."[9]

Arguments in behalf of national prohibition by the Reverend Charles

Stelzle, a Presbyterian Social Gospeler and ardent prohibitionist, suggest some reasons why liquor reform appealed to many progressives. Stelzle, in a 1918 book, *Why Prohibition!*, held that banishing alcohol was essential for the material advancement of American society. Drinking, he asserted, lowered industrial productivity and therefore reduced wages paid to workers; it shortened life and therefore increased the cost of insurance; it took money from other bills and therefore forced storekeepers to raise their prices in compensation; and it produced half of the business for police courts, jails, hospitals, almshouses, and insane asylums and therefore increased taxes to support these institutions.[10]

Stelzle held that the burden of these social and economic costs for the whole society outweighed any individual right to use intoxicants and legitimized the restriction of personal liberty. "There is no such thing," he wrote, "as an absolute individual right to do any particular thing, or to eat or drink any particular thing, or to enjoy the association of one's own family, or even to live, if that thing is in conflict with the law of public necessity." Antiprohibitionists would charge drys with insensitivity to individual rights and liberties, but this was not the case. Prohibitionists simply felt that social betterment outweighed other factors. "The first consideration," Stelzle argued, "is not the individual, but society. Therefore, whatever injures society is not permitted." Small sacrifices of personal liberties may significantly enhance the common good. Therefore, he concluded, "You may exercise your personal liberty only in so far as you do not place additional burdens upon your neighbor, or upon the State."[11]

In insisting that the requirements of modern life necessitated an end to the use of alcohol, Stelzle reflected the position of many progressive advocates of prohibition in the 1910s. The doctrine of environmentalism pervading much of progressive thought held that poverty, child neglect, crime, vice, and other social evils largely resulted from the unfavorable setting in which an individual lived. Corrupt urban political machines, for instance, relied upon saloons as bases of operations and election-day recruitment centers where drinks bought votes. The solution of a wide variety of problems lay in the improvement of the environment, usually by legislative action. Outlawing saloons would allow the political system to function more democratically. Calling alcohol "the mother of felony," a writer in *The American Journal of Sociology* argued that

> in its use and traffic alcohol appears as a powerful antisocial force. Especially is it a social menace with respect to crime. The results of the most cautious research show that it is a producer of criminals and of crime on an enormous scale. What else could one expect. Has not the scientific laboratory proved that the habitual use of alcohol, in whatever quantity, disintegrates the moral character? It impairs the

judgment, clouds the reason, and enfeebles the will; while at the same
time it arouses the appetites, inflames the passions, releases the
primitive beast from the artificial restraint of social discipline.[12]

The only responsible course, he concluded, was to close the saloon and ban
the use of alcoholic beverages. Many social workers and economists of a
progressive inclination joined the chorus of voices demanding suppression of
the saloon and adoption of prohibition for the health of society.[13]

Businessmen and manufacturers often favored prohibition in the belief
that it would increase industrial efficiency and reduce accidents. They felt
that drinking even a small quantity of alcohol impaired a worker's mental
and physical faculties, made him more careless, and lessened his productivity. Following the lead of the railroads, a number of firms, including the
Henry C. Frick Company and the American Sheet and Tin Plate Company,
forbade their employees to drink alcohol either on or off the job. Other
companies strictly prohibited drinking during working hours.[14] Inevitably,
many businessmen turned from their individual efforts to enforce sobriety to
the attempt to achieve abstinence through law. Their enthusiasm for prohibition had a deep tint of self-interest but clearly shared the progressive
attitude that rational men should use the power of the state to promote the
general good as they understood it.

Not all progressives felt it wise to banish intoxicants. In particular, eastern
urban progressives who represented alcohol-using ethnic groups opposed
antiliquor legislation. Yet for the most part, prohibition drew upon the same
broad base of support as other progressive reforms. Most progressives in
Congress voted to pass the Webb-Kenyon Act over President William
Howard Taft's veto in February 1913.[15] The pattern continued when the
Anti-Saloon League began asking for constitutional action.

Congress first took up the amendment question in December 1914. The
resolution won a narrow majority in the House of Representatives, but not
the necessary two-thirds for submission of an amendment to the states for
their approval. During the next two years the resolution failed to come to a
vote. In 1916 considerably more supporters of constitutional prohibition
were elected to Congress, and drys became more optimistic.

The entry of the United States into World War I produced an atmosphere
in which enthusiasm for prohibition accelerated. The need to sacrifice individual pleasure for the defense and improvement of society became a constant theme. The war centralized authority in Washington, loosening
restraints on activity by the federal government. The importance of conserving food resources became apparent, and drys seized the opportunity to
emphasize the waste of grain in the production of alcoholic beverages.
Finally, the war created an atmosphere of hostility toward all things German, not the least of which was beer.

Called into special session to declare war in April 1917, the new Congress adopted temporary wartime prohibition as a measure to conserve grain for the army, America's allies, and the domestic population. The Lever Food and Fuel Control Act of August 1917 banned the production of distilled spirits for the duration of the war. The War Prohibition Act of November 1918 forbade the manufacture and sale of all intoxicating beverages of more than 2.75 percent alcohol content, beer and wine as well as hard liquor, until demobilization was completed. Although some regarded these measures merely as ploys to speed the imposition of national prohibition, they reflected the depth of concern generated by the war and the prevailing belief that alcoholic beverages ought to be sacrificed under the circumstances.[16]

In the midst of the wartime emergency, Congress took up the proposal for constitutional prohibition. The brief debate over the prohibition-amendment resolution repeated long-standing arguments and centered around four issues: revenue, property rights, the effectiveness of statutory prohibition, and the wisdom of increasing the power of the federal government. The debate proceeded along conservative-progressive lines. Opponents of the amendment argued that an end to liquor taxes would eliminate about a third of the federal government's revenues and cause a corresponding increase in general taxation. Proponents pointed to the existing prosperity and the new federal income tax to undercut this argument. Destroying the value of liquor-industry property without compensation was criticized as unjust and as setting a bad precedent. Drys replied that property injurious to society's health and welfare had long been subject to confiscation. Besides, they pointed out, the liquor industry would have one year to liquidate its property, between the amendment's ratification and the date it took effect. Skeptics questioned whether people accustomed to drinking would obey the law, but prohibition advocates argued that violations of criminal laws had never been a sufficient reason for abandoning them and that, furthermore, the overwhelming sentiment for prohibition would make the law enforceable. Some southern conservatives expressed concern about the growing power of the federal government and the intervention of that government into local affairs. Prohibition supporters generally ignored this argument, although they tried to blunt it somewhat by conceding that state governments would have concurrent enforcement powers. Clearly, the debate changed few minds.[17]

By 1917 so many congressmen were prepared to vote for a constitutional amendment that the doubters found themselves brushed aside. On August 1, 1917, by a vote of 65 to 20, the Senate approved an amendment prohibiting the manufacture, sale, transportation, import, or export of intoxicating liquors. The House, after revising the resolution to specifically grant state and federal governments concurrent power of enforcement, approved it 282 to 128 at the end of one afternoon's discussion on December 17. Senate acceptance of the House alterations on December 22 sent the proposed Eighteenth Amendment to the state legislatures for their consideration.[18]

Partisanship was notably absent from congressional action on prohibition in 1917. The Anti-Saloon League had asked legislators, whatever their positions on other issues, to endorse national prohibition in return for its support. This pressure apparently influenced many individual congressmen without having any noticeable effect on either major political party. In the Senate, 29 Republicans and 36 Democrats voted for the resolution; 8 Republicans and 12 Democrats voted against it. In the House, 137 Republicans, 141 Democrats, and 4 independents supported the proposed amendment, while 62 Republicans, 64 Democrats, and 2 independents stood opposed. More than a decade would pass before the major parties adopted distinguishable positions on the liquor question.

Some Senate opponents of the amendment, rather than attacking it outright, had sought to sabotage the proposal by requiring that it be ratified by the states within seven years. They assumed that the twenty-six states which by then had adopted total or partial prohibition laws would not be joined by ten other states in ratifying the amendment within that time span. This proved a major miscalculation. By January 16, 1919, little more than a year after the amendment was placed before the state legislatures, it had been fully ratified.

The lop-sided vote of Congress in submitting the resolution, and the rapid ratification of the Eighteenth Amendment by state legislatures provides an indication of the wide acceptance of the prohibition concept. In only thirteen months, forty-four state legislatures gave the proposal their endorsement, making it one of the most rapidly approved of all amendments. The absence of a direct national referendum or reliable public opinion survey makes it impossible to judge precisely the degree of popular support for the new law. Yet the very requirements for a constitutional change—approval by two-thirds of each house of Congress and ratification by the legislatures of three-fourths of the states—suggests that the assent of a major portion of the body politic and not just the enthusiasm of an aroused minority was involved. Confirmation can be found in the results of referendums on statewide prohibitory measures held in twenty-three states during the five years preceding ratification of the Eighteenth Amendment. The issues voted upon differed in detail, as did the circumstances surrounding each election. Nevertheless, only in California and Missouri did voters persistently reject prohibitory legislation by wide margins, in both states doing so more than once. In three close elections, Ohio voters twice turned down and then adopted statewide prohibition. In Iowa and Vermont state prohibition was narrowly defeated. But in eighteen other states, majorities ranging from 52 percent in Colorado up to 73 percent in Utah and 76 percent in Wyoming approved varying degrees of prohibition.[19] While votes on state measures ought not to be considered as identical to endorsement of a national law, these returns provide impressive evidence that liquor bans enjoyed broad support in the 1910s.

The adoption of the Eighteenth Amendment did not complete the creation of national prohibition. One of the most critical steps followed. The constitutional decree needed enforcement legislation to become effective. Congress in 1919 approved a strict enforcement act drafted by the Anti-Saloon League's general counsel, Wayne Wheeler, but known by the name of its sponsor, the chairman of the House Committee of the Judiciary, Andrew J. Volstead of Minnesota. The Volstead Act established procedures and agencies for enforcement and, in its most controversial section, defined intoxicating beverages as any containing more than one-half of one percent of alcohol. The .5 percent provision—advocated by the Anti-Saloon League and other militant drys—surprised considerable numbers of persons who assumed that, as had been the case with many state laws, only distilled spirits would be banned. Even beer and wine were outlawed under the terms of the Volstead Act.

President Woodrow Wilson, a temperance advocate but an opponent of prohibition, maintained an absolute neutrality toward the Eighteenth Amendment as it progressed through Congress and the state legislatures. Wilson disliked the drys' use of the continuing technical state of war as an excuse to implement prohibition even before the amendment was due to become effective on January 17, 1920, and gave this as his reason for vetoing the Volstead Act on October 27, 1919. Only a month before, however, the president had collapsed while campaigning for the Versailles peace treaty, and he was in no condition to fight for his beliefs regarding prohibition even if he had been willing to risk his little remaining political capital in such a battle. Congress immediately overrode the presidential veto by a vote of 176 to 5 in the House and 65 to 20 in the Senate. The Volstead Act, with its extreme program for implementing national prohibition, became law.[20]

A brief summary can only hint at the rich history of the crusade which led to the passage of the Eighteenth Amendment and the Volstead Act. Nevertheless, it should make several points apparent. The idea of incorporating prohibition into the Constitution to protect against a legislative reversal arose only in the final stages of temperance agitation. The banning of liquor had long been discussed, trials had been undertaken on the local and state level in many parts of the country, and extensive support had accumulated. Progressive attitudes regarding the purpose and possibility of reform reinforced earlier temperance notions and created new sympathy for a dry law among those who previously had little interest in it. A wartime atmosphere of self-sacrificing patriotism provided a final boost. A righteous spirit of reform carried national prohibition into the Constitution of the United States.

As soon as the Eighteenth Amendment was adopted, some troublesome legal and philosophical questions which earlier had been glossed over began to surface. Several important challenges to the national dry law came before the Supreme Court just as the law was taking effect. Although the high court's reaction further demonstrated the support which national prohibition initially enjoyed, the arguments and decisions in these cases drew attention to some disturbing implications of this major constitutional innovation. Even as the adoption of the law received final confirmation by the Court, its popularity began to erode.

At almost the same time that the Volstead Act was being passed, a controversy erupted over Ohio's ratification of the Eighteenth Amendment which undermined the image of substantial majority support for the liquor ban. In November 1917 Ohio voters, at the same election in which they narrowly approved a statewide prohibition law, adopted overwhelmingly (508,282 to 315,030) a state constitutional amendment reserving to themselves the power to review the general assembly's action on federal amendments. This plan, placed on the Ohio ballot by opponents of national prohibition, stipulated that no ratification of a federal amendment by the legislature should go into effect for ninety days. During that time, a petition signed by six percent of the state's voters could be filed to force a referendum, and the assembly's ratification would then not take effect unless approved by a majority of those voting.[21]

On January 7, 1919, the Ohio General Assembly, by a vote of 20 to 12 in the senate and 85 to 29 in the house, ratified the national prohibition amendment. Governor James M. Cox forwarded the joint resolution to Secretary of State Robert Lansing, who counted Ohio among the thirty-six states having ratified when he proclaimed the Eighteenth Amendment adopted as of January 16, 1919. On March 11, 1919, opponents of national prohibition filed a referendum petition with Ohio Secretary of State Harvey C. Smith. Thereupon Smith ordered a referendum at the November 1919 general election on the state's ratification of national prohibition.

George S. Hawke, a Cincinnati attorney and prohibitionist, immediately sought an injunction to prevent Smith from spending public funds for a referendum which, said Hawke, was unconstitutional. The Ohio courts refused Hawke's request. On November 4, 1919, Ohio voters rejected the national prohibition amendment by the slender margin of 500,450 to 499,971. The first state referendum ever held to consider ratification of a federal constitutional amendment had overturned the action of the state legislature, or so it appeared.[22]

Had Ohio ratified the national prohibition amendment? George Hawke immediately asked the United States Supreme Court which was valid: the Ohio General Assembly's "yes" or the voters' "no." When the Court heard the case on April 20, 1920, Hawke and his attorneys, including Wayne Wheeler of the Anti-Saloon League, argued that the legislative ratification should stand and that the referendum was unconstitutional. Article V of the U.S. Constitution specified that amendments proposed by Congress were valid "when ratified by the legislatures of three-fourths of the several states, or by conventions in three-fourths there of, as the one or the other mode of ratification may be proposed by the Congress." Ohio could not, they asserted, impose any limitation upon the ratification process set forth in the federal Constitution.[23]

Defenders of the Ohio referendum contended that the Constitution did not require states to have any particular form of legislature. Indeed the people of a state had the right, if they wished, to abolish their representative assemblies and take all legislative matters into their own hands. Or more practically, the people had the power, affirmed by the Supreme Court in another case brought by Ohio in 1916, to suspend legislative acts pending a referendum vote to accept or reject them. In other words, the argument ran, the term "legislature" included the entire legislative power of the state, not only the two houses of the general assembly but also the popular will as expressed in a referendum.[24]

Wets and drys alike awaited the outcome of *Hawke v. Smith* with great interest. Referendums on national prohibition had been sought in other states besides Ohio. In Maine and Oregon, courts had refused to sanction them, while in California a referendum bill failed in the legislature. In Washington state, wets obtained a mandamus order from the state supreme court ordering acceptance of a referendum petition on the legislature's unanimous ratification of the Eighteenth Amendment, but all went for naught as the secretary of state then found the petition lacking sufficient signatures to place the question on the ballot. If the Supreme Court upheld the Ohio referendum, antiprohibitionists indicated they would probably seek referendums in several states in the hope of invalidating enough legislative ratifications to bring the total below the required three-fourths of all states. Encouraged by the referendum defeat of national prohibition in Ohio, even though by only 479 votes, wets felt they might still overturn the Eighteenth Amendment.[25]

On Tuesday, June 1, 1920, a unanimous Supreme Court upheld the ratification of the Eighteenth Amendment by the Ohio General Assembly:

> Ratification by a State of a constitutional amendment is not an act of legislation within the proper sense of the word. It is but the expression of the assent of the State to a proposed amendment. . . . It is true that the power to legislate in the enactment of the laws of a State is derived from the people of the State. But the power to ratify a proposed amendment to the Federal Constitution has its source in the Federal

Constitution. The act of ratification derives its authority from the
Federal Constitution to which the State and its people have alike
assented.[26]

In the opinion of the Court, when the Congress stipulated that a constitutional amendment be ratified by state legislatures, it neither authorized nor
permitted a referendum. Six days later the Supreme Court firmly reiterated
its view that state referendum provisions could not constitutionally be applied to the rectification process.[27]

  Regardless of the logic and legal soundness of the Supreme Court's ruling
in *Hawke v. Smith,* the Ohio referendum controversy left an impression in
some minds that national prohibition had been foisted on an unwilling
American people by a crafty, well-organized minority using undemocratic
means. Will Rogers, the widely read humorist, wrote, "Ohio was voted wet
buy the people and dry by their misrepresentatives."[28] The image of a reform
achieved by undemocratic means would fester and grow. The validity of
legislative ratification in other states would be brought into question by the
disparity between the lopsided general assembly action and the close but
contrary popular vote in Ohio. The results of many earlier referendums on
state prohibition in other states would be largely forgotten, as would the fact
that the Eighteenth Amendment had been ratified by the same procedure as
all previous constitutional amendments. Instead people would remember
that the Eighteenth Amendment became part of the Constitution without a
direct popular vote in most states and despite a hostile majority in its only
test of public acceptability.

  Brewers, distillers, and liquor distributors desperately challenged the
legality of the Eighteenth Amendment and the Volstead Act in the courts.
Employing some of the best legal talent in the country, these opponents of
prohibition questioned the constitutionality of the amendment as well as the
validity of the Volstead Act. The Supreme Court, reflecting the widespread
support for national prohibition, peremptorily rejected their plea on all
counts.

  The strength of the Court's defense of prohibition can best be appreciated
by examining the details of the appellant's arguments and of the Court's
judgments. The first challenge to the law came from a New York brewer,
Jacob Ruppert, who sought an injunction to restrain the federal government
from enforcing, prior to the effective date of the Eighteenth Amendment,
the wartime prohibition sections of the Volstead Act which forbad the
manufacture and sale of beer with a 2.75 percent alcohol content. On
January 5, 1920, the Supreme Court upheld the act as within the government's war powers and, very significantly, affirmed the right of Congress to
limit the alcoholic content of beer by defining as intoxicating all beverages of
more that one-half percent alcohol. The opinion was considered so

broad as to leave little hope that other objections to prohibition would be sustained.[29]

The Supreme Court issued its most sweeping decision concerning the Eighteenth Amendment in June 1920. Seven cases, each raising fundamental questions concerning the constitutionality of the amendment, were consolidated by the Court and labeled the *National Prohibition Cases*. A host of highly regarded attorneys, including Elihu Root, William D. Guthrie, and Levy Mayer, as well as Herbert A. Rice and Thomas F. McCran, attorneys general for Rhode Island and New Jersey respectively, represented the appellants. The oral arguments lasted for five days, an unusually long time for even the most important cases.

Attorney General Rice began by arguing that the amendment invaded the sovereignty of Rhode Island and her people, an invasion not contemplated by the amending clause of the Constitution. Rhode Island had not ratified the Eighteenth Amendment. The amending power, Rice contended, was provided to allow for the correction of errors in the fundamental instrument of government. The first ten amendments were adopted to insure against the encroachment by the federal government upon state functions and powers. If the amending power were to be construed as to allow any type of amendment, the boundary between federal and state authority could be shifted at will, and the people of a state would be at the mercy of others in matters of political institutions and personal rights. Attorney General McCran, arguing along the same lines, stressed that the Tenth Amendment reserved all unenumerated powers to the states and to the people. The right to surrender such rights and powers, McCran contended, belonged exclusively to the people themselves and not their legislative representatives.[30]

The argument of Elihu Root attracted the most attention. The former Secretary of War, Secretary of State, and senator represented a New Jersey brewer. Drys jested that "Hires Root Beer" had been changed to "Beer Hires Root," but they were clearly worried about the impact this distinguished attorney might have on the Court. Root asserted that the Eighteenth Amendment was simply unconstitutional. The substantive portion of the so-called Eighteenth Amendment, he said, did not relate to the powers or organization of government, as constitutional provisions ordinarily do. Rather, it was a direct act of legislation. He denied that the amending provision of the Constitution, Article V, authorized this type of amendment. Root pointed out that if the validity of the prohibition amendment were to be upheld, its repeal could perpetually be prevented by a minority. Repeal could be accomplished only by the passage of another constitutional amendment which, of course, would require the approval of three-fourths of the states. He distinguished between a constitutional amendment which granted the Congress power to prohibit the use of intoxicating liquors and an amendment which required such a prohibition. An amendment of the former sort would leave the question within the control of a majority of the people, but one of the latter type, such as the current amendment, thwarted the democratic process. Finally, Root contended, the Eighteenth Amendment undermined a fundamental principle of the federal system by directly invading the police powers of the states and encroaching upon the right of local self-government. If the amendment were upheld, he told the Court, the states would no longer be indestructible and the federal system of government could be completely subverted.[31]

Root from the outset opposed the form, spirit, purpose, and effect of the Eighteenth Amendment. He told friends that its denial of personal liberty, its potential for eroding respect for law, and its alteration of the balance between local and national government alarmed him.[32] Most members of the bar, however, did not share Root's belief that the amendment was unconstitutional. Even his colleague William D. Guthrie thought his argument weak.[33] But Root gave a memorable peroration:

> If your Honors shall find a way to declare this so-called Amendment to the Federal Constitution valid, then the Government of the United States as it has been known to us and to our forefathers will have ceased to exist. Your Honors will have discovered a new legislative authority hitherto unknown to the Constitution and quite untrammelled by any of its limitations. You will have declared that two-thirds of a quorum of each House of the Congress, plus a majority of a quorum of each of the two Houses of the Legislatures of three-fourths of the States, may enact any legislation they please without any reference to the limitations of the Constitution, including the Bill of Rights itself. In that case, Your Honors, John Marshall need never have sat upon that bench.[34]

Neither Root's reasoning nor his emotional oratory moved the Court. On June 7, 1920, it rejected every argument of the appellants in the *National Prohibition Cases.* Unanimously upholding the constitutionality of the Eighteenth Amendment, the justices also approved the method by which the state legislatures had ratified it. They held that the prohibition embodied in the amendment was within the power to amend reserved by Article V of the Constitution, and that therefore the amendment must be respected and observed. Commenting upon the role of the states under the amendment, the Court declared that the phrase "concurrent power to enforce" did not include the power to defeat or frustrate prohibition. Concurrent power did not mean joint power or divided power, nor did it require that congressional legislation to enforce the amendment be approved by the states. The power to prohibit granted to Congress was not exclusive; it could be exercised by the states as well, but the law did embrace the entire territory of the United States and could not be avoided by any state.[35] The *National Prohibition*

Cases decision, therefore, resoundingly endorsed the new and untried law.

The announcement of the Supreme Court decisions of June 1920 completed the process of embedding national prohibition in the law of the United States. Drys, as they won victory after victory in the Congress, in the state legislatures, and in the Supreme Court, easily brushed all opposition aside with compelling arguments about the benefits to be obtained from the reform. The prohibitionist success seemed total and permanent. Elihu Root had pointed out to the Supreme Court that once the amendment was emplanted in the Constitution, removing it would probably be impossible. No amendment to the Constitution, once adopted, had ever been repealed. Both supporters and critics of the law recognized this. To its advocates, the reform brought joy. Their arguments appeared to have the support of legislatures, courts, and the masses. To opponents of prohibition, the loss seemed irrevocable. Their objections had been ignored; their influence appeared nonexistent.

National prohibition took effect at midnight, January 16, 1920, one year after ratification of the Eighteenth Amendment. America entered the new age quietly, accepting the law as a great step forward or as a *fait accompli* and in either case believing that its reversal was quite out of the question. The following morning the *New York Times* reported, "John Barleycorn Died Peacefully At The Toll of 12." Had Mr. Barleycorn been in a position to reply, he might have chosen Mark Twain's famous response, "The reports of my death are greatly exaggerated."

2 AMERICA SOBERS UP

When the Eighteenth Amendment took effect on January 17, 1920, most observers assumed that liquor would quickly disappear from the American scene. The possibility that a constitutional mandate would be ignored simply did not occur to them. "Confidence in the law to achieve a moral revolution was unbounded," one scholar of rural America has pointed out, explaining that "this was, after all, no mere statute, it was the Constitution."[1] The assistant commissioner of the Internal Revenue Service, the agency charged with overseeing the new federal law, predicted that it would take six years to make the nation absolutely dry but that prohibition would be generally effective from the outset. Existing state and federal law enforcement agencies were expected to be able to police the new law. Initial plans called for only a modest special enforcement program, its attention directed to large cities where the principal resistance was anticipated.[2] Wayne Wheeler of the Anti-Saloon League confidently anticipated that national prohibition would be respected, and estimated that an annual federal appropriation of five million dollars would be ample to implement it. The popular evangelist Billy Sunday replaced his prohibition sermon with one entitled "Crooks, Corkscrews, Bootleggers, and Whiskey Politicians—They Shall Not Pass."[3] Wartime prohibition, which only banned further manufacture of distilled spirits and strong beer (with an alcohol content exceeding 2.75 percent) had already significantly reduced consumption.[4] Few questioned the Volstead Act's capacity to eliminate intoxicants altogether. Americans accustomed to a society in which observation and pressure from other members of a community encouraged a high degree of conformity did not foresee that there would be difficulties in obtaining compliance with the law. They did not realize that the law would be resented and resisted by sizable elements in an increasingly urban and heterogeneous society where restraints on the individual were becoming far less compelling.[5]

Within a few months it became apparent that not every American felt obliged to stop drinking the moment constitutional prohibition began. In response to consumer demand, a variety of sources provided at first a trickle and later a growing torrent of forbidden beverages.[6] Physicians could legally prescribe "medicinal" spirits or beer for their patients, and before prohibition was six months old, more than fifteen thousand, along with over fifty-seven thousand pharmacists, obtained licenses to dispense liquor. Grape juice or concentrates could be legitimately shipped and sold and, if the individual purchaser chose, allowed to ferment. Distributors learned to attach "warning" labels, reporting that United States Department of Agriculture tests had determined that, for instance, if permitted to sit for sixty days the juice would turn into wine of twelve percent alcohol content. The quadrupled output and rising prices of the California grape industry during the decade showed that many people took such warnings to heart.[7]

Other methods of obtaining alcoholic beverages were more devious. Some "near-beer," which was legally produced by manufacturing genuine beer, then removing the three to five percent alcohol in excess of the approved one-half percent, was diverted to consumers before the alcohol was removed. In other instances, following government inspection, alcohol was reinjected into near-beer, making what was often called "needle beer." Vast amounts of alcohol produced for industrial purposes were diverted, watered down, and flavored for beverage purposes. To discourage this practice, the government directed that industrial alcohol be rendered unfit to drink by the addition of denaturants. Bootleggers did not always bother to remove such poisons, which cost some unsuspecting customers their eyesight or their lives.

Theft of perhaps twenty million gallons of good preprohibition liquor from bonded warehouses in the course of the decade, as well as an undeterminable amount of home brewing and distilling, provided more palatable and dependable beverages. By 1930 illegal stills provided the main supply of liquor, generally a high quality product. The best liquor available was that smuggled in from Canada and from ships anchored on "Rum Row" in the Atlantic beyond the twelve-mile limit of United States jurisdiction. By the late 1920s, one million gallons of Canadian liquor per year, eighty percent of that nation's greatly expanded output, made its way into the United States. British shipment of liquor to islands which provisioned Rum Row increased dramatically. Exports to the Bahamas, for example, went from 944 gallons in 1918 to 386,000 gallons in 1922. The tiny French islands of St. Pierre and Miguelon off the coast of Newfoundland imported 118,600 gallons of British liquor in 1922, "quite a respectable quantity," a British official observed, "for an island population of 6,000."[8] Bootlegging, the illicit commercial system for distributing liquor, solved most problems of bringing together supply and demand. Government appeared unable—some claimed even unwilling—to halt a rising flood of intoxicants. Therefore, many observers at the time, and increasing numbers since the law's repeal, assumed that prohibition simply did not work.

Did national prohibition fail? Answering this question is a bit like deciding whether a glass is half-full or half-empty. One's response depends on certain value judgments regarding the relative importance of the degree of progress toward an objective versus the extent to which the advance falls short of the goal. Views differ as to what constitutes success or failure. National prohibition substantially reduced, but did not altogether eliminate, the use of alcoholic beverages. Thus, depending on their own values, observers at the time and later drew differing conclusions regarding the dry law's success. In order to understand both positive and negative reactions to national prohibition, it is important to examine the manner in which the law functioned, the extent to which it reduced the consumption of intoxicants, and the image of the law's operation derived by the contemporary public. What people thought was happening with national prohibition proved at least as important as what actually took place.

Laws, it is important to remember, seldom enjoy absolute compliance, and indeed a society expects a certain rate of violation of its behavioral codes. Communities create law enforcement agencies in anticipation that laws occasionally will be disregarded. The degree of coercive enforcement varies among societies, just as does the law-making authority. Yet to a considerable degree in every society public acceptance and voluntary compliance determine a law's success. Coercive power has limits; if enough dissenters refuse to obey a law, it cannot be imposed upon them. The acceptable limits of coercion vary, of course, from one society to another and one law to another. In the United States, where hostility to official coercion has a long history, a fairly high degree of voluntary compliance is usually regarded as necessary to a law's success. Thus the question of whether prohibition succeeded or failed involves more than simply determining whether more people obeyed than violated the law. It requires assessing the law's effect in relation to expectations, society's view of an acceptable level of violation, and the tolerable limits of enforcement to produce compliance.

The Volstead Act specified how the constitutional ban on "intoxicating liquors...for beverage purposes" was to be enforced.[9] What the statute did not say had perhaps the greatest importance. While the law barred manufacture, transport, sale, import, or export of intoxicants, it did not specifically make their purchase or use a crime. This allowed continued possession of intoxicants obtained prior to prohibition, provided that such beverages were only for personal use in one's own home. Not only did the failure to outlaw use render prohibition harder to enforce by eliminating possession as *de facto* evidence of crime, but also it allowed the purchaser and consumer of alcoholic beverages to defend his own behavior. Although the distinction was obviously artificial, the consumer could and did insist that there was nothing illegal about his drinking, while at the same time complaining that the failure of government efforts to suppress bootlegging represented a breakdown of law and order.

Adopting the extreme prohibitionist view that any alcohol whatsoever was intoxicating, the Volstead Act outlawed all beverages with an alcoholic content of .5 percent or more. The .5 percent limitation followed a traditional standard used to distinguish between alcoholic and nonalcoholic beverages for purposes of taxation, but that standard was considered by many to be unrealistic in terms of the amount of alcohol needed to produce intoxication. Wartime prohibition, after all, only banned beer with an alcohol content of 2.75 percent or more. Many did not associate intoxication with beer or wine at all but rather with distilled spirits. Nevertheless, the only exception to the .5 percent standard granted by the Volstead Act, which had been drafted by the Anti-Saloon League, involved cider and fruit juices; these subjects of natural fermentation were to be illegal only if declared by a jury to be intoxicating in fact. The Volstead Act, furthermore, did permit the use of intoxicants for medicinal purposes and religious sacraments; denatured industrial alcohol was exempted as well.

The Eighteenth Amendment specified that federal and state governments would have concurrent power to enforce the ban on intoxicating beverages. Therefore the system which evolved to implement prohibition had a dual nature. Congress, anticipating general compliance with the liquor ban as well as cooperation from state and local policing agencies in dealing with those violations which did occur, created a modest enforcement program at first. Two million dollars was appropriated to administer the law for its first five months of operation, followed by $4,750,000 for the fiscal year beginning July 1, 1920. The Prohibition Bureau of the Treasury Department recruited a force of only about fifteen hundred enforcement agents.[10] Every state except Maryland adopted its own antiliquor statute. Most state laws were modeled after the Volstead Act, though some dated from the days of state prohibition and several imposed stricter regulations or harsher penalties than did the federal statute.[11] State and local police forces were expected to enforce these laws as part of their normal duties. Critics at the time and later who claimed that no real effort was made to enforce national prohibition because no large enforcement appropriations were forthcoming need to consider the assumptions and police practices of the day.[12] No general national police force, only specialized customs and treasury units, existed. Furthermore, neither federal nor state officials initially felt a need for a large special force to carry out this one task. The creators of national prohibition anticipated only a modest increase in the task facing law-enforcement officials.

Most Americans obeyed the national prohibition law. Many, at least a third to two-fifths of the adult population if Gallup poll surveys in the 1930s are any indication,[13] had not used alcohol previously and simply continued to abstain. Others ceased to drink beer, wine, or spirits when to do so became illegal. The precise degree of compliance with the law is difficult to determine because violation levels cannot be accurately measured. The best index of the extent to which the law was accepted comes from a somewhat indirect indicator.

Consumption of beer, wine, and spirits prior to and following national prohibition was accurately reflected in the payment of federal excise taxes on alcoholic beverages. The tax figures appear reliable because bootlegging lacked sufficient profitability to be widespread when liquor was legally and conveniently obtainable. The amount of drinking during prohibition can be inferred from consumption rates once alcoholic beverages were again legalized. Drinking may have increased after repeal; it almost certainly did not decline. During the period 1911 through 1915, the last years before widespread state prohibition and the Webb-Kenyon Act began to significantly inhibit the flow of legal liquor, the per capita consumption by Americans of drinking age (15 years and older) amounted to 2.56 gallons of absolute alcohol. This was actually imbibed as 2.09 gallons of distilled spirits (45 percent alcohol), 0.79 gallons of wine (18 percent alcohol), and 29.53 gallons of beer (5 percent alcohol). In 1934, the year immediately following repeal of prohibition, the per capita consumption measured 0.97 gallons of alcohol distributed as 0.64 gallons of spirits, 0.36 gallons of wine, and 13.58 gallons of beer (4.5 percent alcohol after repeal).[14] Total alcohol consumption, by this measure, fell by more than 60 percent because of national prohibition. Granting a generous margin of error, it seems certain that the flow of liquor in the United States was at least cut in half. It is difficult to know whether the same number of drinkers each consumed less or, as seems more likely, fewer persons drank. The crucial factor for this discussion is that national prohibition caused a substantial drop in aggregate alcohol consumption. Though the figures began to rise almost immediately after repeal, not until 1970 did the annual per capita consumption of absolute alcohol reach the level of 1911-15. In other words, not only did Americans drink significantly less as a result of national prohibition, but also the effect of the law in depressing liquor usage apparently lingered for several decades after repeal.

Other evidence confirms this statistical picture of sharply reduced liquor consumption under prohibition. After the Volstead Act had been in force for a half dozen years, social worker Martha Bensley Bruere conducted a nationwide survey of drinking for the National Federation of Settlements. Her admittedly impressionistic study, based upon 193 reports from social workers across the country, focused on lower-class, urban America. Social workers, who generally favored prohibition, perhaps overrated the law's effectiveness. Nevertheless, Bruere's book provided probably the most objective picture of prohibition in practice in the mid-1920s.

The Bruere survey reported that adherence to the dry law varied from place to place. The Scandinavians of Minneapolis and St. Paul continued to drink. On the other hand, prohibition seemed effective in Sioux Falls, South

Dakota. In Butte, Montana, the use of intoxicants had declined, though bootleggers actively plied their trade. Idaho, Oregon, and Washington had generally accepted prohibition, and even in the West Coast wet bastion, San Francisco, working-class drinking appeared much reduced. The Southwest from Texas to Los Angeles was reported to be quite dry. The survey cited New Orleans as America's wettest city, with bootlegging and a general disregard of the law evident everywhere. In the old South, prohibition was said to be effectively enforced for Negroes but not whites. Throughout the Midwest, with some exceptions, residents of rural areas generally observed prohibition, but city dwellers appeared to ignore it. In the great metropolises of the North and East, with their large ethnic communities—Chicago, Detroit, Cleveland, Pittsburgh, Boston, New York, and Philadelphia—the evidence was overwhelming that the law was neither respected nor observed.[15]

Throughout the country, Bruere suggested, less drinking was taking place than before prohibition. Significantly, she reported the more prosperous upper and middle classes violated the alcoholic beverage ban far more frequently than did the working class. Illicitly obtained liquor was expensive. Yale economist Irving Fisher, himself an advocate of prohibition, claimed that in 1928 on the average a quart of beer cost 80¢ (up 600 percent from 1916), gin $5.90 (up 520 percent), and corn whiskey $3.95 (up 150 percent) while average annual income per family was about $2,600.[16] If nothing else, the economics of prohibition substantially reduced drinking by lower-class groups. Thus prohibition succeeded to a considerable degree in restraining drinking by the very social groups with whom many advocates of the law had been concerned. The Bruere study, therefore, offered cheer to drys. Yet her report also demonstrated that acceptance of prohibition varied with ethnic background and local custom as well as economics. Community opinion appeared more influential than federal or state laws or police activity. People in many parts of the United States voluntarily obeyed the Eighteenth Amendment, but elsewhere citizens chose to ignore it. In the latter part of the decade, violations apparently increased, both in small towns and large cities. In Detroit it reportedly became impossible to get a drink "unless you walked at least ten feet and told the busy bartender what you wanted in a voice loud enough for him to hear you above the uproar."[17]

Any evidence to the contrary notwithstanding, national prohibition rapidly acquired an image, not as a law which significantly reduced the use of alcoholic beverages, but rather as a law that was widely flouted. One Wisconsin congressmen, writing to a constituent after a year of national prohibition, asserted, "I believe that there is more bad whiskey consumed in the country today than there was good whiskey before we had prohibition and of course we have made a vast number of liars and law violators through the Volstead Act."[18] In part this commonly held impression stemmed from the substantial amount of drinking which actually did continue. Even given a 60 percent drop in total national alcohol consumption, a considerable amount of imbibing still took place. Yet the image also derived in part from the unusually visible character of those prohibition violations which did occur.

Drinking by its very nature attracted more notice than many other forms of law-breaking. It was, in the first place, generally a social, or group, activity. Moreover, most drinking took place, Bruere and others acknowledged, in urban areas where practically any activity was more likely to be witnessed. Bootleggers had to advertise their availability, albeit carefully, in order to attract customers. The fact that the upper classes were doing much of the imbibing further heightened its visibility. Several additional factors insured that many Americans would have a full, perhaps even exaggerated, awareness of the extent to which the prohibition law was being broken.

The behavior of those who sought to profit by meeting the demand for alcoholic beverages created an indelible image of rampant lawlessness. National prohibition provided a potentially very profitable opportunity for persons willing to take certain risks. "Prohibition is a business," maintained the best known and most successful bootlegger of all, Al Capone of Chicago. "All I do is supply a public demand."[19] Obtaining a supply of a commodity, transporting it to a marketplace, and selling it for an appropriate price were commonplace commercial activities; carrying out these functions in the face of government opposition and without the protections of facilities, goods, and transactions normally provided by government made bootlegging an unusual business. Indeed bootleggers faced the problem—or the opportunity —that hijacking a competitor's shipment of liquor often presented the easiest and certainly the cheapest way of obtaining a supply of goods, and the victim of such a theft had no recourse to regular law enforcement agencies. Nor, for better or worse, could bootleggers expect government to restrain monopolistic practices, regulate prices, or otherwise monitor business practices. Consequently, participants in the prohibition-era liquor business had to develop their own techniques for dealing with competition and the pressures of the marketplace. The bootlegging wars and gangland killings, so vividly reported in the nation's press, represented, on one level, a response to a business problem.

Certain activities beyond the pale of the law, but for which there existed a substantial consumer demand—gambling, prostitution, and narcotics in particular—had been organized in a businesslike fashion well before the 1920s. Those involved in these fields were reluctant to risk their positions in new ventures. Those who became important bootleggers tended to be persons who had obtained some low-level experience in such criminal businesses and aspired to advance. Bootleggers tended to be young men from recent immigrant groups, Italians, Poles, and Jews especially, who were looking for economic opportunity and found traditional routes, legal or criminal, blocked by established entrepreneurs. Of 58 leaders of bootlegging organizations in ten major cities in 1931, after eleven years of prohibition, two-thirds (39) were still under forty years of age, and several were still in their twenties. Al Capone was only thirty-two when he went to prison for income-tax evasion in 1931. Many of these aggressive young men had belonged to youth gangs in New York or elsewhere. They were willing to engage in any profitable activity and to defend their interests by violent means if necessary. National prohibition offered them an unparalleled opportunity.[20]

Violence was commonplace in establishing exclusive sales territories, in obtaining liquor, or in defending a supply. In Chicago, for instance, rival gangs competed intensely. Between September 1923 and October 1926, the peak period of struggle for control of the large Chicago market, an estimated 215 criminals died at the hands of rivals. In comparison, police killed 160 gangsters during the same period. Although by conventional business standards the violence level in bootlegging remained high, it declined over the course of the 1920s. Consolidation, agreement on markets, regularizing of supply and delivery all served to reduce turbulence. John Torrio and Al Capone in Chicago, Charles Solomon in Boston, Max Hoff in Philadelphia, the Purple Gang in Detroit, the Mayfield Road Mob in Cleveland, and Joseph Roma in Denver imposed some order on the bootlegging business in their cities. The more than a thousand gangland murders in New York during prohibition reflect the inability of Arnold Rothstein, Lucky Luciano, Dutch Schultz, Frank Costello, or any other criminal leader to gain control and put an end to (literally) cut-throat competition in the largest market of all.[21]

The nation's press drew a vivid picture of a disregarded law. Newspapers constantly carried reports of police raids on stills and speakeasies. Such stories, along with reports of the many gangland killings in New York, Chicago, and elsewhere, of course represented legitimate news, but their impact far outweighed the statistical evidence of reduced drinking nation-wide. The exploits of prohibition enforcement agents, particularly a few colorful figures in the early years of prohibition, received considerable press attention. New York City's Izzy Einstein and Moe Smith proved masters of disguise, which allowed them to infiltrate speakeasy after speakeasy to obtain evidence and make arrests. Their imaginative and colorful tactics (for example, dressing as wagon drivers to gain entry to working class bars or appearing in outlandish garb representing their idea of Texas ranchers in order to claim to be out-of-towners looking for a place to get a drink) contributed to their success and made them good news copy as well. Izzy and Moe's efforts were so widely reported that they were forced to keep changing their ploys, and by 1925 they were compelled to retire.[22]

Magazines such as *Literary Digest, The New Yorker,* and H. L. Mencken's *American Mercury* frequently referred to drinking by the Eastern upper classes and, by assuming that what could be observed of one class in one region was equally true for all social strata throughout the country, exaggerated the overall level of prohibition violation. Mencken, whom Walter Lippman called "the most powerful influence on this whole generation of educated people,"[23] in particular pictured prohibition as a futile attempt to prevent drinking. Prohibition provided a central example for his endlessly repeated argument that a puritanical and hypocritical rural Protestant "boobus Americanus" was seeking to block the development of sophisticated, cosmopolitan society in the United States. Prohibitionists were attempting, as Mencken put it, "to punish the other fellow for having a better time in the world."[24]

Motion pictures, already popular by the start of the 1920s, became even more so after "talkies" began to appear in 1927. By 1930 an average of ninety million tickets a week were being sold to a population of 123 million Americans.[25] Films helped shape perceptions of what was taking place in American society beyond the individual's immediate experience, contributing among other things to the impression of widespread prohibition violation. Although few films in the early twenties dealt with drinking or bootlegging, by mid-decade movie-goers were being subjected to a wave of films on uninhibited, youthful, jazz-age "flapper" society. "No such picture would be considered properly finished," commented a *New York Times* film reviewer, "without a number of scenes depicting the shaking up and drinking down of cocktails and their resulting effect on those who partake of them."[26] A content analysis of 115 films, a representative sample for 1930, found liquor referred to in 78 percent and drinking depicted in 66 percent. A further examination of 40 of these same films revealed that while only 13 percent showed male villains drinking and 8 percent female villains doing likewise, in 43 percent the heroes drank and in 23 percent the heroines used intoxicants.[27]

A spate of gangster films, most set in New York or Chicago, overtook more old-fashioned murder mysteries by the early 1930s. Bootlegging provided the background for *The Doorway to Hell, The Widow from Chicago, Little Caesar, City Streets, Public Enemy, The Secret Six, Enemies of the Law, Scarface: Shame of a Nation*, and other pictures. In such films, criminal figures invariably came to a bad end—indeed the Motion Picture Producers and Distributors of America practically demanded it—but some nevertheless portrayed bootleggers as honorable, even noble characters. Alcohol became the engine of personal ruin in social melodramas from *Prodigal Daughters* (1923) and *Wine of Youth* (1924) to *Young Man of Manhattan* (1930) and *Are These Our Children* (1931). Despite the overt message of moral condemnation in cinematic treatments of liquor, films conveyed an image of a society which frequently used alcohol and patronized bootleggers.[28]

Ironically, the federal government in its efforts to enforce national prohibition often contributed to the image of a heavily violated law. Six months after the Eighteenth Amendment took effect, for example, Jouett Shouse, an Assistant Secretary of the Treasury whose duties included supervising prohibition enforcement, announced that liquor smuggling had reached such proportions that it could no longer be handled by the 6,000 agents of the Customs Bureau. Shouse estimated that 35,000 men would be required to guard the coasts and borders against the flood of liquor pouring into the country. The Assistant Secretary attributed the problem to an unlimited market for smuggled whiskey and the 1,000 percent profits which could be realized from its sale.[29]

During the 1920 presidential campaign, Republican nominee Warren G. Harding pledged to enforce the Volstead Act "as a fundamental principle of the American conscience," implying that the Wilson administration had neglected its duty.[30] Despite his known fondness for drink, Harding attracted dry support with such statements while his opponent, the avowedly wet James A. Cox, floundered. Once inaugurated, President Harding tried to fulfill his campaign promise but met with little success. He explained to his wet Senate friend, Walter Edge of New Jersey, "Prohibition is a constitutional mandate and I hold it to be absolutely necessary to give it a fair and thorough trial."[31] The president appointed the Anti-Saloon League's candidate, Roy A. Haynes, as commissioner of prohibition and gave the corpulent, eternally optimistic Haynes a generally free hand in selecting personnel to wage battle against bootlegging. Harding began to receive considerable mail from across the country complaining about the failure of the dry law. As reports of prohibition violations increased, Harding became more and more disturbed. Never much of a believer in prohibition himself, Harding had, nevertheless, been willing as a senator to let the country decide whether it wanted the Eighteenth Amendment, and now as president he deplored the wholesale breaking of the law. In early 1923, having gradually realized the importance of personal example, Harding gave up his own clandestine drinking.[32] In a speech in Denver just prior to his death, Harding appealed vigorously for observance of prohibition in the interest of preventing lawlessness, corruption, and collapse of national moral fiber. "Whatever satisfaction there may be in indulgence, whatever objection there is to the so-called invasion of personal liberty," the president asserted, "neither counts when the supremacy of law and the stability of our institutions are menaced."[33] Harding's rhetoric, although intended to encourage compliance with prohibition, furthered the image of a law breaking down.

A report by Attorney General Harry Daugherty to President Calvin Coolidge shortly after Harding's death suggested the extent to which the Volstead Act was being violated in its early years of operation. Daugherty indicated that in the first forty-one months of national prohibition, the federal government had initiated 90,330 prosecutions under the law. The

number of cases had been rising: 5,636 were settled in April 1923, 541 more
than in the initial six months of prohibition. The number of new cases
doubled between fiscal 1922 and fiscal 1923. The government obtained
convictions in 80 percent of the terminated cases. These figures showed, the
attorney general argued, that prohibition enforcement was becoming increasingly effective.[34] They could just as well be seen, however, as an indication of an enormous and increasing number of violations.

The prohibition cases brought into federal court most certainly represented only a small fraction of actual offenses. They nevertheless seemed to
be more than the court and prison system could handle. In 1920, 5,095 of the
34,230 cases terminated in the federal courts involved prohibition violation;
during 1929, 75,298 prohibition cases alone were concluded. In 1920, federal
prisons contained just over 5,000 inmates; ten years later they contained over
12,000, more than 4,000 of whom were serving time for liquor violations.
The courts were so overworked that they frequently resorted to the expedient
of "bargain days." Under this system, on set days large numbers of prohibition violators would plead guilty after being given prior assurance that they
would not receive jail sentences or heavy fines. By 1925, pleas of guilty,
without jury trials, accounted for over 90 percent of the convictions obtained
in federal courts. The legal system appeared overwhelmed by national prohibition.[35]

As president, Calvin Coolidge found prohibition enforcement to be the
same headache it had been for his predecessor. Like Harding, Coolidge was
constantly under pressure from Wayne Wheeler and other dry leaders to
improve enforcement. He received hundreds of letters deploring the rate of
Volstead Act violations and urging forceful action. Coolidge merely acknowledged receipt of letters on the subject, avoiding any substantial response.[36]
As it did with many other issues, the Coolidge administration sought to avoid
the prohibition question as much as possible. Other than seeking Canadian
and British cooperation in halting smuggling, and holding White House
breakfasts for prestigious drys, few federal initiatives were taken while Coolidge remained in office.[37] The picture of rampant prohibition violation
stood unchallenged.

Congress, once having adopted the Volstead Act and appropriated funds
for its enforcement, assumed its job was done and avoided all mention of
prohibition during the law's first year of operation. Evidence of violations,
however, quickly provoked dry demands that Congress strengthen the prohibition law. Whenever Congress acted, it drew attention to the difficulties of
abolishing liquor. When it failed to respond, as was more frequently the
case, drys charged it with indifference to law breaking. Whatever it did,
Congress proved unable to significantly alter prohibition's image.

After Harding's inauguration, Congress learned that retiring Attorney
General A. Mitchell Palmer had ruled that the Volstead Act placed no limit

on the authority of physicians to prescribe beer and wine for medicinal purposes.[38] Senator Frank B. Willis of Ohio and Representative Robert S. Campbell of Kansas moved quickly to correct this oversight by introducing a bill that would forbid the prescription of beer and rigidly limit physicians' authority to prescribe wine and spirits. Only one pint of liquor would be permitted to be dispensed for a patient during any ten-day period, under their plan. Well-prepared dry spokesmen completely dominated the hearings on the Willis-Campbell bill, insisting that this substantial source of intoxicants be eliminated. Physicians and pharmacists protested that beer possessed therapeutic value and that Congress had no right to restrict doctors in their practice of medicine. Nevertheless, in the summer of 1921 the bill passed the House by a vote of 250 to 93, and the Senate by 39 to 20.[39] The Willis-Campbell Act reflected congressional determination to shut off the liquor supply, but like the Volstead Act, it did not resolve the problem of imposing abstinence on those willing to ignore the law in order to have a drink.

For years, Congress continued to wrestle with the problem of creating and staffing an effective federal enforcement organization. The Volstead Act delegated responsibility for implementing national prohibition to an agency of the Bureau of Internal Revenue in the Department of the Treasury. The act exempted enforcement agents from civil service regulations, making them political appointees. The Anti-Saloon League, through its general counsel, Wayne B. Wheeler, relentlessly pressed Harding and Coolidge to name its candidates to positions in the enforcement agency. The prohibition unit, beset by patronage demands and inadequate salaries, attracted a low caliber of appointee and a high rate of corruption. By 1926 one out of twelve agents had been dismissed for such offenses as bribery, extortion, solicitation of money, conspiracy to violate the law, embezzlement, and submission of false reports. A senator who supported prohibition argued lamely that this record was no worse than that of the twelve apostles, but he could not disguise the enforcement unit's very tarnished reputation.[40]

Even if the agency had been staffed with personnel of better quality, its task would have been overwhelming. It received little cooperation from the Department of Justice, with which it shared responsibility for prosecuting violators. Furthermore, the prohibition unit lacked both the manpower and the money to deal with the thousands of miles of unpatrolled coastline, the millions of lawbreaking citizens, and the uncountable hordes of liquor suppliers. The agency focused its efforts on raiding speakeasies and apprehending bootleggers, but this task alone proved beyond its capacity and discouraged a series of prohibition commissioners.

Congress steadily increased enforcement appropriations but never enough to accomplish the goal.[41] In 1927 prohibition agents were finally placed under civil service, and in 1930 the Prohibition Bureau was at last transferred to the Justice Department.[42] As useful as these congressional steps may have been, they came long after the enforcement effort had acquired a dismal reputation and doubts as to whether prohibition could possibly be effective had become deeply ingrained.

Early in 1929 Congress made a determined effort to compel greater adherence to national prohibition. A bill introduced by Washington senator Wesley L. Jones drastically increased penalties for violation of the liquor ban. Maximum prison terms for first offenders were raised from six months to five years, and fines were raised from $1,000 to $10,000.[43] The Jones "Five-and-Ten" Bill, as it was called, passed by lopsided majorities in Congress and signed into law by Coolidge days before he left office, did not improve prohibition's effectiveness but strengthened its reputation as a harsh and unreasonable statute.

During the 1920s the Supreme Court did more than either the Congress or the president to define the manner in which national prohibition would be enforced and thereby to sharpen the law's image. As a Yale law professor, and earlier as president, William Howard Taft had opposed a prohibition amendment because he preferred local option, disliked any changes in the Constitution, and felt national prohibition would be unenforceable.[44] But when the Eighteenth Amendment was ratified, Taft, a constant defender of the sanctity of democratically adopted law, accepted it completely and even became an advocate of temperance by law. He condemned critics of national prohibition, saying, "There isn't the slightest chance that the constitutional amendment will be repealed. You know that and I know it."[45] As chief justice from 1921 until 1930, he sought to have the prohibition laws strictly enforced and took upon himself the writing of prohibition decisions.[46] The opinions handed down by the Taft Court during the 1920s greatly influenced conceptions of the larger implications of the new law as well as the actual course of prohibition enforcement.

In 1922 the Supreme Court heard the case of Vito Lanza, who had been fined for manufacturing and transporting liquor in violation of a Washington state prohibition law and who was now being prosecuted for the same act under the federal statute. Lanza's attorneys argued that such a prosecution violated the Fifth Amendment guarantee against double jeopardy. The Court held that while the Eighteenth Amendment established prohibition as a national policy, the "concurrent power to enforce" clause gave each state the right to exercise an independent judgment in adopting measures to enforce prohibition as long as such laws did not contradict the federal statutes. The rights of states did not derive from the Eighteenth Amendment, but from powers originally belonging to them; the concurrent power provision merely insured that this power would not be denied. The state and the federal government each possessed an independent authority to punish prohibition violations as offenses against its peace and dignity, Chief Justice Taft explained. The Fifth Amendment only barred repeated proceedings by the federal government and did not apply to a situation of this sort. Therefore the Court unanimously upheld the second prosecution of Vito Lanza.[47] Since nearly every state in the union either had a state prohibition law prior to the adoption of the Eighteenth Amendment or had passed one immediately after ratification, the *Lanza* decision meant that prohibition violators could be indicted and punished twice for almost every offense.

Next the court sought to strike a blow at bootlegging. In December 1921, federal prohibition agents patrolling the highway between Detroit and Grand Rapids, Michigan, stopped an automobile driven by George Carroll and John Kiro. Two months earlier the agents had arranged to buy whiskey from Carroll and Kiro, but the two suspected bootleggers had failed to reappear with the liquor. When they recognized the car, the agents admittedly had no evidence that it carried liquor; indeed, they had not anticipated seeing Carroll and Kiro. The agents nevertheless proceeded, without a warrant, to search the car. They found sixty-eight bottles of whiskey and gin concealed behind the upholstery. When Carroll and Kiro were convicted, their attorneys appealed, claiming that the evidence used against them had been seized in violation of the search and seizure provision of the Fourth Amendment. The Supreme Court noted that the Fourth Amendment prohibited only "unreasonable" searches and seizures and held that this case did not involve such an unreasonable act. Speaking for the Court, Taft explained that, since a vehicle could depart before a warrant could be obtained, in order to protect the public interest, officers having reasonable cause could legally search an automobile without a warrant. The defense protested that the officers lacked sufficient grounds for conducting a search since the car did not appear to be carrying liquor and since the agents had never actually purchased liquor from the defendants. The Court, however, held the officers' suspicions reasonable and the obtaining of a search warrant impracticable. By a vote of seven to two, the justices upheld the conviction.[48] The *Carroll* decision of March 2, 1925, greatly expanded the search and seizure powers of prohibition enforcement agents and indeed of all police dealing with automobiles.

Objections by the medical profession to the restrictions of the prohibition laws increased with the 1921 passage of the Willis-Campbell Act. Physicians continued to claim that the Eighteenth Amendment did not permit Congress to interfere with the practice of medicine. In June 1924, however, the Supreme Court unanimously upheld the right of Congress to proscribe the medicinal use of beer.[49] Even more significant was the Court's response to a suit brought by a group of prominent New York physicians led by the Dean Emeritus of the College of Physicians and Surgeons of Columbia University, Dr. Samuel W. Lambert. In 1923 Dr. Lambert obtained a District Court injunction forbidding the local prohibition director from interfering with his prescription of wines and spirits. He claimed that the Willis-Campbell Act's prescription limitation of one pint in ten days for any patient was arbitrary and interfered with his constitutional rights as a physician to treat his patients according to his judgment and training. In 1926 the Supreme Court, by a five to four vote, ruled the power to limit medicinal use of liquor a legitimate part of the power to enforce the prohibition against the beverage use of alcohol. In the Court's view, the one-pint-in-ten-days limitation was not arbitrary; it reflected the opinions of many physicians as to the marginal value of liquor as medicine. Furthermore, the Court held the right to practice medicine to be subordinate always to the police power of the state. Dissenting justices asserted that the Eighteenth Amendment placed a prohibition only on beverage alcohol and could not properly be applied to medicinal liquor, but they were outvoted. [50] The *Lambert* case represented an almost even division of opinion within the Court, but as did earlier decisions, it strengthened the government's hand in enforcing prohibition.

The last major Supreme Court decision concerning prohibition enforcement became in many ways the most controversial and significant. It grew out of a 1925 case in the state of Washington where Roy Olmstead, a major smuggler of Canadian liquor, and seventy-four other persons were convicted on the basis of evidence obtained by tapping their telephones. The wiretaps had been made without trespassing upon any property of the defendants. However, a state statute made wiretapping a misdemeanor. In appealing the case to the Supreme Court, the defense argued that the evidence had been criminally obtained and that telephone tapping violated the rights granted by the Fourth and Fifth Amendments against unreasonable search and seizure and self-incrimination. [51] Led by Chief Justice Taft, who had no sympathy for lawbreakers and whose crusade for stricter enforcement of prohibition reached its zenith in this case, a majority of the Court disagreed. Taft declared that, since no trespass was involved and since no material things were searched or seized, the Fourth Amendment had not been infringed. Nor had the Fifth Amendment guarantee against self-incrimination, since the defendants had not been compelled to talk over the telephone but had done so voluntarily. Finally, under the common law, the admissibility of evidence was not affected by the fact it had been illegally obtained. [52]

Justices Holmes, Brandeis, Stone, and Butler vigorously dissented from the *Olmstead* decision. Brandeis argued that wiretapping, although dressed in the garb of new technology, remained illegal search and seizure. Any unjustified intrusion by the government upon the privacy of the individual, by whatever means, violated the right of privacy guaranteed by the Fourth Amendment. Holmes and Brandeis both protested the use of evidence obtained by a criminal act. Holmes stressed that the government should not foster crime as the means to obtain evidence regarding other crimes. Brandeis declared that the government must observe the same rules as the citizen if it expected to command respect. In one of his most ringing and oft-quoted dissents, Brandeis concluded,

In a government of law, existence of the government will be im-
perilled if it fails to observe the law scrupulously. Our Government is
the potent, the omnipresent teacher. For good or for ill, it teaches the
whole people by its example. Crime is contagious. If the Government
becomes a lawbreaker, it breeds contempt for law; it invites every man
to become a law unto himself; it invites anarchy.[53]

Despite the dissenters' warnings, a majority of the Court upheld the use of
wiretapping. The opinions of Holmes and Brandeis upset Taft, who saw
automobiles and telephones as new and powerful weapons in the hands of
criminals. The Chief Justice felt that to adopt the position taken by Holmes
and Brandeis would be to facilitate crime and furnish immunity from
conviction. The Court, in Taft's opinion, must support the efforts of law-
enforcement officials in combating criminal activity.[54]

Throughout the 1920s the Supreme Court clearly followed Taft's line of
thought. The Court's opinions substantially strengthened the machinery for
enforcing law and order and upholding the Eighteenth Amendment. When
implementation of the new amendment conflicted with the apparent restraints of older ones, a majority of the justices preferred to see the recent
addition well launched. Court decisions and dissents made those who paid
attention aware that prohibition would have far-reaching ramifications on
legal rights. The image of a government prepared to engage in more aggressive and intrusive policing practices than ever before in order to enforce a
particular law was being created by *Lanza, Carroll, Lambert,* and *Olmstead*
at the same time that the impression was being generated of widespread
disregard for that law.

While in reality national prohibition sharply reduced the consumption of
alcohol in the United States, the law fell considerably short of expectations.
It neither eliminated drinking nor produced a sense that such a goal was
within reach. So long as the purchaser of liquor, the supposed victim of a
prohibition violation, participated in the illegal act rather than complained
about it, the normal law enforcement process simply did not function. As a
result, policing agencies bore a much heavier burden. The various images of
lawbreaking, from contacts with the local bootlegger to Hollywood films to
overloaded court dockets, generated a widespread belief that violations were
taking place with unacceptable frequency. Furthermore, attempts at enforcing the law created an impression that government, unable to cope with
lawbreakers by using traditional policing methods, was assuming new powers
in order to accomplish its task. The picture of national prohibition which
emerged over the course of the 1920s disenchanted many Americans and
moved some to an active effort to bring an end to the dry law.

3 NEW CRITICS

Opposition to prohibition existed from the moment liquor bans were first proposed. Brewers, distillers, brewery workers, and hotel and saloon keepers fought hard to protect their financial interests against the passage of laws which would devastate them.[1] When the federal amendment was nevertheless adopted, the economic self-defense opposition quickly withered. What had proven ineffective earlier seemed utterly pointless now. Overturning a constitutional amendment appeared impossible. Even the distinguished lawyer Elihu Root, who represented brewers before the Supreme Court in their last desperate attempt to block imposition of prohibition, conceded that once in place, the amendment would never be repealed.[2] Yet at the moment when the Eighteenth Amendment was being established and discouraged veteran opponents were abandoning the fight, a new antiprohibition movement began to emerge, unrelated to the old, motivated by quite different concerns, and remarkably undaunted by either the seemingly insurmountable obstacles to be confronted or the apparent futility of initial efforts to overturn the law. It would play a central role throughout the fifteen-year struggle to win repeal.

Prior to 1919 the temperance movement faced no organized public opposition except from brewers' and distillers' trade associations. Consumers were inherently difficult to organize, one prohibition scholar suggested, particularly since they assumed that the liquor industry, with its wealth and apparent influence, could easily protect itself.[3] The United States Brewers' Association, founded during the Civil War to seek tax relief, had quickly achieved its initial goal and continued to press its interests. Other industry groups followed suit, organizing, lobbying, participating in congressional election campaigns, and publishing defenses of drinking.[4] The liquor industry, however, weakened its own defenses by failing to reform much-criticized saloon practices and by allowing itself to be caught in compromising positions. In 1916 and 1917, brewers pleaded *nolo contendre* to charges of attempting to corruptly influence elections in Texas and Pennsylvania.[5] Even more damaging, the German-American Alliance, a nationwide organization financed by brewers, was found in 1916 to have been engaging in pro-German activities since 1914. This revelation upset most

Americans, who either preferred neutrality or supported England in the European war. With America's entry into World War I, Pabst, Schlitz, Busch, Blatz, Miller, and other German brewers seemed even more an enemy within the gates despite their ostentatious purchases of war bonds. In July 1918 Congress revoked the charter of the German-American Alliance. In September, Alien Property Custodian A. Mitchell Palmer charged brewers with subsidizing the pro-German press, attempting to influence politics, and generally engaging in unpatriotic activities. A Senate subcommittee substantiated the charges.[6]

Liquor industry impotence in the face of the prohibition crusade resulted not only from their own improprieties and the coincidence of World War I, but also the lack of unity between brewers and distillers. They considered each other business competitors, rather than allies against a common adversary. Anticipating a ban on distilled spirits only, some brewers expected prohibition would actually benefit them. When the Lever Food Control Act of 1917 banned production of spirits for the duration of the war to conserve grain, the United States Brewers' Association quickly pointed to the law's distinction between spirits and beer and asserted that beer was a "wholesome product" related to light wines and soft drinks rather than to hard liquor.[7] Fraternal back-stabbing undermined opposition to the Eighteenth Amendment and failed to deflect the blow of prohibition from any part of the liquor industry.

Brewers and distillers continued to resist as the prohibition amendment made its way through Congress, state legislatures, and the courts. They argued to Congress that national prohibition violated principles of home rule and states' rights. The Distillers' Association of America carried the fight to the states, sought referendums in fourteen of them, and asserted that legislative ratification was improper. The United States Brewers' Association submitted a petition and brief against the Volstead Act to President Wilson. A New Jersey brewery sponsored the final appeal to the Supreme Court.[8] Whatever arguments they used, liquor industry opponents of the Eighteenth Amendment could not avoid the appearance of economic self-interest.

Organized labor provided the only other important resistance to the demand for national prohibition. Brewery workers led the union opposition, with support from bartenders, hotel and restaurant workers, cigarmakers, tobacco workers, glass workers, coopers, and musicians. All realized that the destruction of the liquor industry would eliminate many of their jobs. They also resented prohibition as class legislation, a hypocritical attempt by employers to eliminate working-class drinking in order to obtain greater profits. Many union members, of course, simply enjoyed a drink and visit to the saloon—"the poor man's social club"—and objected to interference with their customs.[9]

The problems that plagued unions opposing prohibition were the same as those facing brewers and distillers: the appearance of economic selfishness, wartime charges of lack of patriotism, and internal conflict. The American Federation of Labor long avoided taking a position on prohibition because of its divided membership. Several unions, anticipating economic benefits and improved industrial safety, favored the Eighteenth Amendment as strongly as the brewery workers opposed it. The hazards of their work led the Brotherhood of Railway Engineers, for instance, to endorse prohibition in 1916. Samuel Gompers, himself opposed to prohibition, worried foremost about dividing his growing organization and determined to put off taking a stand for as long as possible. Not until June 1919 did Gompers, under pressure from increasingly militant antiprohibition member unions, allow an AFL annual convention to state an official position. A resolution introduced by the brewery workers declared that prohibition would destroy the livelihood of many workers, cripple their unions, and was principally intended to deprive workers of a glass of beer following a day's toil. Beer with a modest 2.75 percent alcohol content, they argued, should be exempted. The mild nature of the resolution suggests that it was an executive council compromise. The convention vote, closely representative of membership attitudes, was 24,475 for, 3,997 against, and 1,503 not voting. Public demonstrations, held to express union opposition to prohibition, came too late. Divided opinion within its ranks and weak, last-minute action destroyed the effectiveness of organized labor's stand.[10]

Shortly before the adoption of national prohibition, scattered opposition from other sources also surfaced. Imminent ratification stirred some members of the press and professional groups to speak out. Although a majority of the nation's newspapers favored prohibition, the New York press became strongly critical. A few bar associations attacked provisions of the amendment on legal grounds, without discussing the wisdom of prohibition itself. Several physicians complained that the Volstead Act restricted their practice of medicine.[11] These objections were neither sufficiently widespread nor sufficiently coordinated, however, to be of any consequence.

Following their failure to prevent adoption of national prohibition, the liquor industry declined to fight further, while organized labor put up only limited resistance. Brewers and distillers, resigned to their fate, either competed for the small near-beer and medicinal spirits market, converted to other products such as soft drinks, ice cream, cheese, and malt extract, or went out of business altogether.[12] The Brewery Workers and Hotel and Restaurant Employees (mainly bartenders) unions saw their membership and income decline sharply and with it their ability to carry on the struggle.[13] The AFL showed little enthusiasm for pursuing the potentially divisive issue, though it did continue to propose legalization of 2.75 beer.

For a brief period, the most prominent opposition to the liquor ban came from the Association Opposed to National Prohibition, organized in late

January 1919 by a group of New York hotel owners and real estate men who hoped to stimulate a nationwide hotel industry protest. They complained that the closing of hotel bars was ruining their business, yet somewhat inconsistently announced plans to exclude from their association everyone with a direct financial interest in repeal of the Eighteenth Amendment. Adoption of a platform identical to that of the brewers and distillers, and acknowledgment that their leaders had given 5 percent of gross 1918 alcoholic beverage receipts to the state liquor dealers' antiprohibition campaign fund tarnished the organization's claim of independence. Although the association reorganized to improve its image, it went quickly into eclipse.[14] Once again opposition based upon narrow economic self-interest proved incapable of enlisting wider support for a battle to overturn the alcohol ban.

At the moment when it appeared that all organized opposition to national prohibition was collapsing in futility, new resistance appeared from an unexpected quarter. Not involved with the liquor industry, not intimidated by the difficulty of changing the constitution, this new antiprohibition movement offered arguments and developed political tactics which eventually enabled it to take advantage of growing antipathy toward the Eighteenth Amendment. Although the antiprohibition movement was always broader than any single group, its eventual success depended to a large degree on the arguments presented and political support generated by this one organization, the Association Against the Prohibition Amendment, founded by Captain William H. Stayton.

Stayton, a white-haired, square-jawed lawyer, businessman, and former naval officer working in Washington for the Navy League of the United States, watched with growing alarm the inexorable progress of the Eighteenth Amendment through Congress and the state legislatures. He believed ardently in the rights of states and local communities to make independent decisions. Also he was deeply troubled by progressive notions about reform and by the growing concentration of power in the hands of the federal government. A sincere and uncomplicated man, fifty-eight years old in 1919, Stayton had no financial interest in liquor nor personal political aspirations. He was willing, as events of the next decade and a half demonstrated, to labor ceaselessly to defend what he regarded as abstract righteous principles and what others might term governmental status quo. His ideas did not differ from those of many of his generation who objected to the rapid changes taking place in an increasingly complex and impersonal America. As a result of his commitment and energy, he became the guiding spirit of the AAPA and a central force in the prohibition repeal movement.

Stayton was born March 28, 1861, on a farm near the tiny community of Leipsic, Delaware.[15] The Staytons, of Swedish descent, had lived in Delaware for generations. Despite his father's indifference to education, Stayton as a boy walked several miles each day to attend the nearest school in

William H. Stayton, c. 1920   Eleutherian Mills Historical Library

Smyrna. Eventually, due to his mathematical ability, he won a competitive examination for appointment to the United States Naval Academy at Annapolis. The naval academy offered Stayton a much-desired escape from the farm, and he made the most of the opportunity, making many friends (he later was elected president of the Naval Academy Alumni Association), learning social graces as well as academic skills, graduating thirteenth in the 75-man class of 1881, and successfully wooing the commandant's daughter.[16]

Stayton's strong opinions on government and national defense were formed at Annapolis. One of his teachers, an ardent believer in states' rights, influenced him deeply, Stayton told his friend H. L. Mencken in 1932.

> He told us that the division of powers between the nation and the States was not arbitrary, but that its necessity should be obvious to all reasonable men. He said that everyone who had a home knew that its regulation must be based upon the character and tastes of the people living in it, and that it would be manifestly absurd to ask the President of the United States, or any other functionary at Washington, to manage it. He went on to say that local communities, in their way, were like larger homes, and that States were still larger ones. They had, to be sure, much business in common, and that business could be undertaken in common, but they also had their special interests and desires, and it was essential that they have freedom in dealing with them.
>
> I thought of this often in my days in the navy, cruising up and down the coasts of the United States. I found that even naval officers, in the pursuit of their duties, must consult local and States authorities quite as often as Federal authorities, though they are Federal officers themselves. I began to read the Constitution and to admire it immensely. But at the same time I began to see that there was a growing tendency in America to centralize authority, and I concluded that if it went on there would be grave danger to our experiment in democratic government.[17]

Anything that happened to Stayton thereafter seems only to have reinforced his uncomplicated viewpoint.

After graduation from Annapolis, Stayton served fourteen months on the *U.S.S. Tennessee* in the North Atlantic, then nearly three years as a Marine Corps officer on the *U.S.S. Hartford,* which was based in San Francisco and spent much of its time off the coasts of Chile and Peru. In 1887 he married, and his career took an important turn. He was assigned to the Navy Judge Advocate General's Office in Washington so that he could attend Columbian (now George Washington) University Law School. After earning an LL.B. in 1889 and a master's degree the following year, Stayton resigned his commission in 1891 to practice law in New York. For a time, he represented Hetty Green, the eccentric heiress whose shrewd stock investments and difficult personality earned her the nickname "The Witch of Wall Street." By 1898, however, Stayton was suing Mrs. Green for nonpayment of a $50,000 fee.[18] Increasingly, he specialized in admiralty law, though he took time out to join the New York State Naval Militia, to volunteer for naval duty in the Spanish-American War, and to speculate unsuccessfully in a scheme to develop natural rubber plantations in Mexico. In the first years of the new century, Stayton established a law practice in Baltimore and gradually shifted into the steamship business. He purchased a large, three-story white brick home in Smyrna; this would be home ever after even though Stayton spent much of his time in Baltimore, Washington, and elsewhere.

Captain Stayton (he attained the rank during his brief return to duty in 1898 and proudly used it the rest of his life) was an energetic, restless man who found work totally absorbing. According to his granddaughter, he would begin his labors as early as four A.M. and have a day's work prepared for his secretary by the time she arrived at eight. He was indifferent to what he regarded as nonessentials: he would, for instance, buy six custom-made suits and a dozen ties at a time, all identical; being well-dressed mattered, variety did not. Each spring when he began to itch and fidget, he had to be reminded to take off his winter underwear. Stayton's work habits left him plenty of time for men's clubs, an enormous circle of friends, and a succession of causes.

Early in the twentieth century, Stayton became active in the Navy League of the United States, an organization of New York Naval Militia members, naval academy alumni, businessmen, and others formed in 1902 to agitate for stronger naval defenses. He soon became one of the league's largest contributors and served on its governing board. From April 1916 to January 1918, he served as the league's executive secretary and chief spokesman. He campaigned for more naval building and, after the United States entered World War I, for production speedups opposed by shipyard workers' unions, as well as for federal assistance for expansion of the American merchant marine. Through the league, Stayton met many American business leaders, such as John J. Raskob, treasurer of the Du Pont Company, and Henry Bourne Joy, president of Packard Motor Company, and learned techniques of organizing campaigns to influence public policy.[19]

Nineteen-eighteen found Captain Stayton watching the progress of the prohibition amendment when he was not speaking in Indianapolis, Omaha, or Akron on behalf of more and faster ship building. He criticized congressional support for union efforts to prevent speedups despite the wartime emergency.[20] Much of what he encountered in Wilsonian Washington disturbed him. "Discussions about controlling the public morals, and even the birth and education of children through federal agencies were more frequent and, to many...more interesting than the matter of providing ammunition for the men on the firing lines," he told Mencken. "I found myself particularly alarmed," he went on, "by two movements that were running parallel; one, to procure the passage of a child-labor amendment, so that the management of the family would be taken out of the control of parents, and, second, an effort to pass a Federal prohibition amendment."[21] Such progressive initiatives seemed to him unnecessary and dangerous. To Stayton military defense and defense of existing governmental arrangements went hand in hand.

His military concerns led Stayton to excuse many aspects of the war's effect of concentrating power in federal hands. But matters unrelated to fighting the war did not, in his mind, require a unified, centrally directed program. The loss of individual community decision-making power distressed him deeply. "The Constitution," Stayton insisted to an interviewer in the 1930s, "is the creation of the states, and the federal government exists only to perform those functions which have been delegated to it by the states for their convenience." He continued, "The Constitution is no place for prohibition. That is a local question." His interviewer concluded that Stayton's preoccupation with protecting traditional constitutional arrangements was genuine, single-minded, and unswerving.[22]

The captain frequently met a half dozen friends for lunch at the Shoreham Hotel. In the spring of 1918, Stayton told the group of his opposition to the current proposal for national prohibition. The liquor problem, he said, was a state and local matter which had nothing to do with the federal government; a prohibition amendment would produce discontent and strife. Stayton suggested that they should all write influential people they knew to protest the amendment and, furthermore, form some sort of antiamendment organization. Another of the group, Gorton C. Hinckley, pointed out that President Wilson had asked war workers not to interfere in government affairs. Agreeing that their efforts might be misconstrued, the others preferred to drop the matter for the war's duration. Stayton reluctantly assented, but on November 12, 1918, he once again urged his friends to form an association to prevent adoption of the prohibition amendment. Hinckley, who had worked with Stayton in the Navy League, now enthusiastically supported his proposal. The group agreed and decided to name their organization the Association Against the Prohibition Amendment.[23]

In the weeks that followed, Stayton sought support for the fledgling organization. "As my associations had been largely in the navy," he later recalled, "it was natural that in this first group I sought conferences with navy people, and I think that every man with whom I talked for the first few weeks was an old navy man."[24] Stayton found his initial contacts sympathetic, but the founders of the association recognized the need to attract wider support. They decided that, in order to determine whether they were justified in going ahead, Stayton should undertake to enlist members from the general public. If one hundred members could be obtained in Baltimore,

they agreed, they would continue. Stayton proceeded to enroll local businessmen and members of his Baltimore clubs. Soon the association began to
attract wider notice. Membership applications arrived from Annapolis, New
York, and as far away as Wisconsin. The hundred-member goal was soon
reached. Thus encouraged, Stayton and his colleagues pressed on with the
quest for support and started writing letters or visiting states where the
amendment was under consideration, explaining their objections to ratification.[25]

Suddenly, the futility of the group's limited and late-starting efforts
became evident. During 1918 fifteen state legislatures had ratified national
prohibition. January 1919 saw legislatures, many of which were just beginning biennial sessions, rush to ratify. Within that month, twenty-nine
states approved the amendment, putting it firmly into the Constitution. The
Association Against the Prohibition Amendment had been unable to mount
an effective resistance and engage in extensive debate with their opponents,
but had almost immediately been confronted by a *fait accompli*. Stayton
ruefully admitted, "I do not think that we had the least influence in per-
suading any single legislator in the United States to vote against... ratification."[26] For the moment the antiprohibition group abandoned its efforts as
hopeless. After all, never had a constitutional amendment, once adopted,
been dislodged.[27]

In the months following ratification, Captain Stayton, who was still working for the Navy League, sought the advice of numerous friends. Most urged
him to persevere with the antiprohibition organization and to keep the name
originally coined for it.[28] After six months had passed, the association's
founders got together again and agreed that Stayton should write to six
hundred friends throughout the country testing sentiment for a fight against
the Eighteenth Amendment. The October 2, 1919, letter explained the
group's belief that while "prohibition accomplishes much that is good, and
that it merits dignified treatment and serious consideration, yet we also
believe that the recent prohibition amendment to our Federal Constitution is
improper and dangerous.... Prohibition should, we think, be dealt with
locally, and not in violation of the fundamental principles of home rule
under which our country has grown to greatness." The letter went on: "The
climate of Alaska requires one diet, while Louisiana demands another, and
to so legislate that many citizens in every part of the country feel that what
they may eat or drink is being dictated to them by citizens of other parts of
the land (living under entirely different conditions) is to sow the seeds of
antagonism and to start crops of dissensions and perhaps of future civil
war."[29] Objection to a federal takeover of a state and local function lay at the
heart of Stayton's complaint, though he also deplored the method by which
the amendment had been ratified, saying that most voters never had an
opportunity to express an opinion on the measure.

Some three hundred persons answered Stayton's October 2d letter. His states' rights argument struck a responsive chord; many replies contained small contributions. Encouraged, Stayton and Hinckley drew up rules for the organization: there should be minimal annual dues of $1 for ordinary members and $10 for sustaining members, officers would receive no pay, and no person formerly involved in the liquor trade would be accepted except as a nonvoting member. [30]

For the next year, Stayton and his colleagues proceeded cautiously and uncertainly. They printed some literature and sought to enlist more support. Conscious of the millions spent by drys to achieve national prohibition, these foes of the law evidently wanted to test the strength and nature of opposing sentiment. Then came an immensely encouraging windfall. John A. Roebling, the son of the builder of the Brooklyn Bridge, somehow learned of Stayton's activities and wrote him, asking for references. Roebling said he approved the effort but did not want to involve himself with people who would spend his money unwisely. Stayton suggested that Roebling speak to a New Jersey neighbor, a retired admiral who knew Stayton from his navy days. Shortly thereafter, the mail brought Roebling's check for $10,000. The antiprohibition group's confidence and determination soared. [31]

By December 1920, Stayton and his allies were sufficiently convinced of backing for their cause to incorporate the Association Against the Prohibition Amendment in the District of Columbia. Stayton, Hinckley, and Louis Livingston, a former Navy League clerk, signed the certificate of incorporation, announcing:

> The particular business and objects of the Association shall be to educate its members as to fundamental provisions, objects, and purposes of the Constitution of the United States; to place before its members and before the American citizens information as to the intentions and wishes of those who formulated and adopted the Federal Constitution; to publicly present arguments bearing upon the necessity for keeping the powers of the several States separated from those of the Federal Government, and the advisability of earnest consideration before further yielding up by the several States of those powers which pertain to local self-government. [32]

The conservative concern with constitutionalism and the defense of local self-government which Stayton first articulated thus remained at the heart of the new antiprohibition movement in 1919 and 1920, as support increased and the organization defined its position. Resistance to the expansion of the powers of the federal government would continue to be fundamental to the program of the Association Against the Prohibition Amendment throughout its existence. The AAPA's objections to national prohibition went beyond the question of alcoholic beverages, distinguishing it from earlier opponents of the reform and sustaining it in the discouraging years to come.

Stayton's association faced resistance from two large groups, the millions of people who supported prohibition and those who believed repeal impossible even if it was desirable. The AAPA sought to win converts by demonstrating both the error of national prohibition and the political viability of opposing the amendment. To achieve these purposes, Stayton originally patterned his organization after the Anti-Saloon League. In the twenty-five years since its founding in 1893, the single-minded, nonpartisan league proved much more adept at achieving its goal than its much older ally, the Prohibition party, which only attracted a small fraction of the vote in direct competition with Democrats and Republicans. The Anti-Saloon League recognized that the support of a relatively small group of voters could represent the difference between victory and defeat wherever the major parties were evenly balanced. Candidates would often be willing to embrace the league program when they perceived that it would enhance their chances of attracting a bloc of voters who would cast their ballots on the basis of a single issue.[33] Many antiprohibitionists attributed the passage of the antiliquor amendment solely to the skillful use of such tactics. The AAPA determined to function as a nonpartisan, nonsectarian society open to all men and women, except those involved in the liquor trade. Every member would pledge to vote only for congressional or state legislative candidates who promised to support repeal of the Eighteenth Amendment. The association would not reveal names of members without their consent but would publish the number of pledged voters in a state or election district. Thus AAPA leaders initially assumed that by enrolling enough members they, like the Anti-Saloon League earlier, could obtain a balance of power in elections and force favorable action.[34]

The first order of business for the AAPA was a quest for members. From a nucleus of the few hundred who responded to Captain Stayton's initial letters and personal appeals in 1918 and 1919, the rolls reportedly swelled to several thousand by June 1920. In the spring of 1921, the AAPA claimed 100,000 members. An enthusiastic Stayton predicted a membership of two million by the 1922 elections.[35]

By November 1922, however, Stayton reported a membership of only 457,000, and fifteen months later the total had fallen to 400,000. Growth then resumed. The AAPA in mid-1926 announced a membership of 726,000 scattered fairly evenly across the United States but with the greatest numbers in New York, Ohio, Illinois, and California.[36]

The association's membership claims during these years appear exaggerated, though by how much it is impossible to determine. Financial contributions provide the best index, since most took the form of $1 annual dues payments. The AAPA received few large contributions, none for several years after Roebling's $10,000 gift, then beginning in 1923 (when persons involved in the liquor industry were allowed to contribute up to five percent of the association's income), a handful of $500 and $1,000 donations. The association's financial difficulties stemmed in part from its refusal to accept industry support. Ironically, the effort to remain untainted did not keep the impression from spreading that the AAPA was a front for liquor interests. Captain Stayton, a man of some means, supported the organization for five years at the rate of $1,000 a month. In 1926 Stayton reported that national and state AAPA offices had collected altogether about $800,000 in five years. This sum suggests either that membership figures were inflated or that many people on the rolls had not given even a dollar to the association. In any case, it seems unlikely that the association had anywhere near three-quarters of a million members in 1926.[37]

Growing membership led the AAPA to adopt a more elaborate organizational structure. Beginning in 1921, whenever the leaders felt that enough members had been enlisted, a state division was established to take over local recruitment, solicitation of contributions, and election campaigning. State divisions were asked, but often failed, to turn over one-fourth of their receipts to the national headquarters, from which Stayton and Hinckley ran the publicity campaign against prohibition. The first state division was apparently organized in Pennsylvania. A division created in Maryland the same year began with 14,000 members. By 1922 the New York state division was active enough to support a separate women's committee. A California branch established in 1922 claimed 25,000 members within two years and had active local chapters in Los Angeles, San Francisco, San Jose, and Sacramento. In a few cases state AAPA divisions were created by absorbing independent local antiprohibition organizations, such as the Constitutional Liberty League of Massachusetts and the Moderation Leagues of Minnesota and Ohio. By 1926 the AAPA claimed divisions in twenty-five states, nearly every state outside the South not perceived as hopelessly dry.[38]

Besides creating state divisions, the association developed small groups, called voluntary committees, within the ranks of unrelated organizations or as independent groups. The first such group, the Voluntary Committee of the New York Yacht Club, was founded in 1922 by Stayton's close friend William Bell Wait, a New York attorney. For several years, voluntary committees proved a fruitful source of contributions and endorsements of the AAPA. At one point more than eighty of these committees were said to be operating throughout the country.[39] Stayton also made at least one attempt to set up an ostensibly independent national committee of prominent individuals which would study the operation of prohibition and then condemn its evils.[40] This, like the voluntary committees, was clearly an attempt to strengthen the image of widespread antiprohibition agitation and confer upon the AAPA respectability by association.

Although the Association Against the Prohibition Amendment was almost entirely male, listing only men among its directors, it did create separate

women's organizations, known as Molly Pitcher Clubs, in some of the largest
state divisions, most notably New York and Pennsylvania. The Molly Pitcher
Clubs sought to spread the antiprohibition message among women's societies
and also engaged in some lobbying efforts in Albany and Washington. Only
a few hundred women joined the Molly Pitcher Clubs, perhaps because they
were so obviously nothing more than auxiliaries of the AAPA. By 1928 the
clubs had disappeared, although a small, meagerly financed New York
group led by Miss M. Louise Gross continued under a series of different
names: Women's Committee for Modification of the Volstead Act, Women's
Committee for Repeal of the 18th Amendment, and the Women's Moderation Union. None had any noticeable impact.[41] Not until the end of the
decade would an important women's antiprohibition organization appear,
and then it would be largely independent of the AAPA.

Stayton gradually abandoned talk of gaining a balance of power at the
polls, of making the AAPA a reverse image of the Anti-Saloon League, after
early attempts to duplicate the league's size and tactics proved unsuccessful.
In 1920 the association asked all congressional candidates to espouse repeal
if they desired its support. However, when the AAPA refused to disclose the
size of its membership, most candidates ignored its request. In the next two
national elections, the AAPA asked congressional candidates their position
on prohibition, then published the names of approved candidates and
occasionally sponsored rallies in their behalf. If opposing candidates took
the same position, the association remained impartial. The Anti-Saloon
League quickly counterattacked, opposing office-seekers on the AAPA list.
To the embarrassment of the association, a number of the 249 candidates
supported in 1922 and the 169 approved in 1924 repudiated its endorsement.[42] Without a massive membership, the AAPA found few ways to put
pressure on candidates. Ousting incumbents during a period of general
prosperity and contentment was hard enough without having to persuade
their challengers to take up a cause of uncertain popularity. The tactics
initially employed by the AAPA had little chance to succeed unless far greater
strength could be manifested or the country's general political situation
changed.

Rather than simply seeking to enroll as many members as possible, Captain Stayton concentrated increasingly on enlisting persons whose stature
and resources would influence public opinion. When the AAPA quest for
members first got underway, Stayton's friend Judge George Gray of Wilmington, Delaware, urged him to place priority on high quality rather than
great quantity. Gray pointed out that opposition to prohibition was identified with brewers and distillers. It would be wise, he said, to give the new
association an appearance of high purpose and respectability.[43] The elite-
oriented Stayton welcomed Judge Gray's advice. Stayton, the poor farmboy
become naval officer, attorney, business executive, and club man, regarded

upper-class men as the best members. They could make large donations and spare the dissipation of resources inherent in an appeal to the masses for small contributions. At the same time a list of supporters from the higher reaches of the business and social world would demonstrate the inherent soundness of the AAPA, encouraging additional contributions, memberships, and political support.[44] Stayton in 1930 confessed to feeling ill on learning that the membership department intended to solicit members from lists of automobile owners. Automobile owners could be seen any Saturday or Sunday parading on the road from Annapolis to Baltimore in their shirt sleeves! Stayton made it clear that he preferred members who wore coats.[45]

The AAPA enlisted mainly business and professional men. Prominent figures such as the author Irvin S. Cobb; Stuyvesant Fish, president of the Illinois Central Railroad; ex–New York mayor Seth Low; and Charles H. Sabin, president of Guaranty Trust Company of New York, were among the earliest members. After receiving a number of invitations from Stayton, John J. Raskob joined in June 1922. Shortly thereafter, Raskob's business associate, Irénée du Pont, president of the Du Pont Company, became a member. By 1926 Stayton had attracted Irénée's older brother Pierre, former Assistant Secretary of War Benedict Crowell, Pennsylvania Railroad president W. W. Atterbury, Chicago merchant Marshall Field, publisher Charles Scribner, retired Packard Motor Company president Henry Bourne Joy, New York financier Grayson M.-P. Murphy, Senators Thomas F. Bayard of Delaware and William Cabell Bruce of Maryland, Congressman John Philip Hill of Baltimore, former federal judge Henry S. Priest of St. Louis, and Carnegie Institute president Samuel Harden Church.[46] Before 1928 these notables took little action other than to endorse Stayton's efforts, but they were nevertheless moving into the organization's leadership, as well as giving the AAPA the respectable image which the captain sought. They shared the paternalistic sense of social responsibility widespread in the business community during the 1920s.[47] While they espoused democratic principles, in their view of democracy the upper classes bore a particular obligation to defend the interests of all. Consequently, they were willing to campaign for beliefs shared with Stayton.

In the early 1920s an opponent of the Eighteenth Amendment could choose among more than forty antiprohibition societies. Most selected the Association Against the Prohibition Amendment. Some other organizations, such as the cautious Moderation League founded by Elihu Root and other New Yorkers, languished, while even more (the aforementioned Association Opposed to National Prohibition, for instance) disappeared altogether.[48] Its distinctive arguments distinguished the AAPA from other antiprohibition groups. The constitutional critique seems to be what attracted members, particularly influential upper-class figures, to the association.

The AAPA continued to put its complaint simply and directly, as in a 1922 pamphlet: "The Constitution inherited from our Fathers has been amended and mutilated.... Our Constitutional guarantees...have been violated. Sumptuary law (such as national prohibition) grants and withholds privileges upon a difference of religious belief. The right to govern ourselves in local affairs—a right won by our ancestors in three generations of struggle—is ignored."[49] Stayton, repeating the AAPA argument in more down to earth terms to a large crowd in New York's Carnegie Hall in April 1922, called the Eighteenth Amendment "a rotten insult to the American people," a law which says that "we can't be trusted." No one standard for regulating alcoholic beverages could apply to all communities in so large a country. The founding fathers never intended that such state powers be given to the federal government. Mutilation of the Constitution caused reverence for federal law to be replaced by "utter contempt." "This prohibition business is only a symptom of a disease," he continued, "the desire of fanatics to meddle in the other man's affairs and to regulate the details of your lives and mine." The crowd registered its agreement with this straightforward rejection of a progressive reform philosophy by vigorously applauding Stayton's remarks.[50]

Stayton believed that the vital spirit of the Constitution was retention by individual states of power over their individual affairs. "This spirit," he wrote, "has been destroyed by the Eighteenth Amendment, under which the right of local self-government is torn from the individual states, whose people are made subject, even in the small routine affairs of their daily lives, to those living in far distant localities and under other conditions." While he conceded that states might have their own prohibition laws, Stayton felt that national prohibition was no more justified than nationalizing governorships and sending out governors from Washington.[51]

Those who were drawn to the AAPA in the early 1920s shared Stayton's concerns insofar as can be determined from the fragmentary records available. The feeling that prohibition did not belong in the Constitution was widely held. Samuel Harden Church lamented that "we have indolently permitted a well-organized and enormously financed body composed of zealots, fanatics and bigots...to insert a Draconian statute in the great charter of our liberties.... We forget, in this mad endeavor to control the conduct of men whose thoughts or habits differ from our own, that nations cannot be made virtuous or abstinent by acts of Parliament."[52] Judge Priest worried that "Every government that has attempted to legislate for the uplifting of the moral sense of its people or to suppress the vices of its people has inevitably come to grief."[53] Ransom H. Gillett, a former Republican state assemblyman in New York who for a time served as the association's general counsel, told the Economics Club of Boston that prohibition tampered with the delicate balance between national, state, and local government. "We have imperiled the liberties of ourselves and those who will come after us."[54]

During a public debate on prohibition in New York City, Gillett again emphasized the constitutional impropriety of the Eighteenth Amendment. The Constitution had been created to define the powers of government, he said; nowhere in the original document nor in the seventeen amendments adopted in over one hundred years was there any sort of prohibition. The people had been careful not to place too much power in the hands of a centralized government. Then in an excess of zeal, the Eighteenth Amendment was written into the Constitution and the guarantee against tyranny was cast aside. As he had in Boston, Gillett pointed to the Supreme Court's *U.S. v. Lanza* decision, which allowed both state and federal prosecution of a prohibition violation, as a prime example of the threat to traditional American liberties. The essence of the prohibition question, as Gillett saw it, was whether or not the American people were going to "hand over to government the paternalistic power to regulate lives and habits."[55]

Fabian Franklin, a New York author and coeditor of the *Independent,* expressed his concern for the Constitution in his 1922 book, *What Prohibition Has Done to America,* and shortly thereafter joined the AAPA. Franklin had praised the association even earlier in a short-lived journal which he edited until it was absorbed by the *Independent.*[56] The object of a constitution, Franklin wrote, is to establish certain fundamentals of government so that they cannot be changed by mere majority will or ordinary legislative process. The object was not to shackle future generations regarding ordinary practices of daily life but to insure stability for the government and protection of basic personal rights and liberties. "The Eighteenth Amendment seizes upon the mechanism designed for this purpose, and perverts it to the diametrically opposite end, that of *safeguarding the denial of liberty.*" A bad law, placed in the Constitution and recognized by the people as nearly impossible to change, would naturally be resented and disregarded. Not only did the prohibition amendment degrade the Constitution by invading rather than protecting individual rights, Franklin continued, it undermined a cardinal element of national well-being, local authority and decision making. "If we do not hold the line where the line *can* be held, we give up the cause altogether; and it will be only a question of time when we shall have drifted into complete subjection to a centralized government, and State boundaries will have no more serious significance than country boundaries now have.... If there is one thing in the wide world the control of which naturally and preeminently belongs to the individual State and not to the central government at Washington, that thing is the personal conduct and habits of the people of the State.... The Prohibition Amendment is not merely an *impairment* of the principle of self-government of the States; it constitutes an absolute abandonment of that principle."[57] Though Franklin went on to discuss other objections to national prohibition, his basic concern clearly paralleled that of William Stayton.

Those who joined Stayton's association and publicly aired their concerns saw the Eighteenth Amendment as a basic threat to a treasured principle. Time and again, they decried the loss of "the right to govern ourselves in local affairs." Other serious problems—declining respect for law, ineffective law enforcement, loss of traditional rights—inevitably resulted, they believed, from this loss. Members of the AAPA were reacting against fundamental changes occurring in American government, in particular the progressive attempt to stabilize and improve modern society through legislative devices. They resented the decline of local autonomy and the growth of government centralization, which World War I greatly accelerated. While the war was being waged, they had been unable or unwilling to oppose the trend. In the postwar world, vivid manifestations of expanding federal power, in particular the Eighteenth Amendment, the Volstead Act, and supportive Supreme Court decisions, distressed them deeply. Prohibition offered one concrete and immediate issue through which alarmed citizens could strike back at this pervasive and disturbing trend. Stayton found many people who shared his constitutional concerns sufficiently to enlist in his campaign. The only puzzle was how to achieve the reversal they all sought.

4 KICKING A STONE WALL

Having decided to fight, opponents of national prohibition faced the problem of how to conduct the battle. The Eighteenth Amendment appeared as impregnable as a medieval stone fortress to a band of ill-equipped foot soldiers, and complaining about its constitutional deficiencies seemed about as effective as kicking the base of the fortress wall. Initial efforts to breach the walls or circumvent the fortress proved equally futile. After a half dozen years of siege, the fortress remained unshaken, while the attackers found themselves limp from exertion, disheartened by their lack of progress, and searching for new tactics.

Nearly everyone who contemplated trying to overturn the Eighteenth Amendment became discouraged by the political requirements of repeal. Archibald Stevenson, a prominent New York attorney who joined William H. Stayton in objecting to national prohibition as an intrusion on states' rights, came by 1927 to regard as "useless" any effort to repeal the amendment. "The mechanism controlling the amending power of the Federal Constitution," he complained, "is very much like the ratchet on a cog wheel. The wheel may be turned conveniently in one direction, but it cannot be reversed."[1] Three-fourths of the states may effect a change in the Constitution, Stevenson pointed out, even though the remaining one-fourth contain a majority of the population. In 1926 the twelve most populous states contained over sixty-six million residents while the balance, a constitutional majority, had fewer than thirty-one million. Even if a large majority of states had second thoughts, he went on, they could not rescind their action as long as thirteen states objected. The thirteen smallest states could block repeal even though their combined population in 1920 was only five million, less than that of New York City. His mathematics and his assumption that more than enough states would choose to hold onto prohibition convinced Stevenson that a repeal campaign would have no chance of success. He was by no means alone in so thinking.[2]

Clarence Darrow, the famed defense lawyer and civil libertarian, objected strenuously to prohibition, but because of dry strength in many sparsely populated western and southern states, he regarded repeal as out of the question.

By whatever means it was done, and however slight may have been the understanding of the people, the fact is that Prohibition is entrenched today in the fundamental law of the nation, and, what is more important, that there are many men and powerful organizations who feel it to be their duty to enforce it. The impossibility of its complete reversal has only slowly dawned upon the American people. Even to modify the Volstead Act would require a political revolution; to repeal the Eighteenth Amendment is well-nigh inconceivable. Eleven or twelve million voters, properly distributed amongst the States that naturally support Prohibition, will suffice to keep it on the books.[3]

Republican Senator James W. Wadsworth of New York, who had voted against the amendment, shared Darrow's view that it was in the Constitution to stay. Samuel Gompers of the AFL conceded that repeal was "utterly hopeless." "That avenue of reform is closed," agreed Walter Lippmann, a vociferous critic of the dry law. After surveying the situation, the *New York Times* concluded editorially, "The Amendment is beyond effective attack."[4]

In light of the widespread view that the Eighteenth Amendment could never be rescinded, opponents of national prohibition in the early 1920s diverted their attention toward the more modest and seemingly more attainable goal of rendering the law less obnoxious in practice. Eliminating the double jeopardy of state and federal prosecutions and changing the legal definition of intoxicating beverages to allow the use of mild beer became the two most eagerly pursued adjustments. The Moderation League of New York was formed in 1923 to work for the latter purpose. Moderation leagues were also founded in Ohio, Minnesota, and Pennsylvania.[5] Apparently none of these organizations attracted more than a few hundred members, though the New York league enlisted some prominent citizens, such as Elihu Root, but in itself, their emergence alongside the already organized and functioning repeal-minded Association Against the Prohibition Amendment demonstrated the pessimistic attitudes of quite a few committed antiprohibitionists.

Even as determined a constitutional opponent of national prohibition as Captain Stayton appeared in the early 1920s to bow to such discouraging appraisals. Although they never abandoned repeal of the Eighteenth Amendment as an ultimate objective, Stayton and the AAPA devoted far more attention to efforts to soften the definitions and enforcement provisions of the antiliquor laws. In April 1922 Stayton told three thousand supporters in New York's Carnegie Hall that association priorities were, first, legalization of beer and wine for home use; second, amendment or repeal of the Volstead Act; and, only third, repeal of the Eighteenth Amendment.[6] Defending the captain's speech in a letter to the *New York Times,* New York AAPA division treasurer Stuyvesant Fish justified the association's willingness to work for modification of prohibition: "The purging of the Constitution of the prohibition amendment will take time and may have to be left to our children's children to work out.'"[7] In the meantime, modification could be achieved by a simple majority vote in Congress. An association letterhead defending modification efforts proclaimed; "WE ARE NOT FACING A HOPELESS TASK!"[8] The *Times,* responding editorially, encouraged the AAPA's more modest efforts, while dismissing repeal as an unattainable goal: "An association for reasonable prohibition, a society for the modification of the Volstead Act, while it undertakes a mighty task, will find strong support."[9]

Sensitive to views such as those expressed by the *Times,* Stayton did not claim too much for reform or repeal of the Volstead Act. He maintained only that it would be "like getting one step up the stairs." The Volstead Act, he believed, "has produced a very great evil in the country, and I think we would be very bad citizens, so believing, if we did not do all we could to secure an amendment to the Volstead Act." Furthermore, "the repeal of the Eighteenth Amendment will necessarily take years, and I think that no man is required to stand and subject himself to an injury if there is some way of remedying it."[10] Willingness to espouse limited, short-term goals did not cause the AAPA to forget about repeal, but it did spare the association the criticism of being totally unrealistic. Furthermore, the AAPA gained a place on platforms where modification of prohibition was being discussed and won the opportunity to participate in the first successful counterattack on the dry law. This latter development, the 1923 repeal of the New York state prohibition enforcement act, gave fresh hope to all antiprohibitionists at a time of universally gloomy estimates of their prospects.

Nearly every state had adopted its own prohibition enforcement act, either in the days of state prohibition or immediately following the Eighteenth Amendment's ratification. The second clause of the amendment, granting Congress and state legislatures "concurrent power to enforce" prohibition, encouraged duplication. Some states passed laws even stricter than the Volstead Act, barring the possession of liquor legally acquired before the adoption of the Eighteenth Amendment or, as was the case in sixteen states, defining an intoxicating beverage at even a lower alcoholic content than the one-half percent established by the Volstead Act. State law enforcement officers carried much of the burden of policing prohibition.[11]

Antiprohibitionists became particularly upset with concurrent enforcement provisions when in 1922 the Supreme Court announced in *U.S. v. Lanza* that persons could be prosecuted under both federal and state statutes for the same prohibition offense (see chap. 2). An AAPA spokesman declared that the *Lanza* ruling smacked of double jeopardy and undermined Fifth Amendment protections.[12] To end state assistance in enforcing national prohibition, efforts were made to repeal enforcement acts in New York and later in other states. Attacks on state prohibition laws had both symbolic and substantive purposes. A successful assault left the federal law untouched, but reduced resources for its enforcement. Not only would possible double jeopardy under prohibition be lifted, but victory might encourage the view that all antiliquor laws were susceptible to change.

Prohibition became an unusually partisan issue in New York state. In January 1919 a Republican majority in the legislature had ratified the Eighteenth Amendment on a straight party-line vote, despite the plea of newly elected Democratic governor Alfred E. Smith that the question first be submitted to a popular referendum. In April 1920 the legislature passed and Smith signed a bill to allow manufacture and sale within the state of beer with a 2.75 percent alcohol content. The United States Supreme Court soon validated the national .5 percent limit in the *National Prohibition Cases* and, in *Hawke v. Smith,* declared referendums such as the one the governor still advocated constitutionally pointless. Smith, though he ran a million votes ahead of the national Democratic ticket, succumbed to the Harding landslide in November 1920. His successor, Republican Nathan Miller, approved the April 1921 action of an enlarged Republican majority adopting the Mullan-Gage Bill, a state prohibition enforcement law closely patterned after the Volstead Act. In 1922, however, New York Democrats won a sweeping election victory on a platform which, among other things, called for prohibition modification to allow 2.75 beer. The popular Smith easily regained the governorship and in his first message to the legislature endorsed the platform's modification proposal. The legislature, however, went much further, approving on May 3, 1923, a bill introduced by Tammany Hall spokesman Louis Cuvillier to repeal the Mullan-Gage Act.[13]

The legislature's action placed Governor Smith in a quandary. Antiprohibitionists pressed him to follow his personal wet sentiments and sign the Cuvillier bill. Drys, meanwhile, insisted he veto the measure in order to uphold the laws and Constitution of the United States. Smith, who following his 1922 reelection was being seriously discussed as a 1924 Democratic presidential candidate, hesitated for nearly a month. He realized that either choice would antagonize large groups and damage his chances for the nomination. Earlier that spring Smith had been widely criticized after publication of a supposedly off-the-record remark he had made to a group of reporters: "Wouldn't you like to have your foot on the rail and blow the foam off some suds?" The governor realized that the stir would be nothing compared to the uproar which would follow approval of the repeal. Yet many of his faithful supporters expected nothing less. Finally, the hesitant Smith called a public hearing to air the arguments for and against Mullan-Gage repeal.[14]

Ransom Gillett of the New York AAPA led wet forces, which also included the state AFL and the New York Molly Pitcher Club, in an effort to persuade Smith to sign the Cuvillier bill. With Smith presiding over a packed assembly chamber and giving no indication which way he was leaning, Gillett argued that the legislature's repeal vote came from representatives of seventy percent of the state's people and that the governor had no right to ignore this mandate. As long as the Mullan-Gage law was in force, Gillett pointed out, a prohibition violator in New York faced double jeopardy. Finally, he asserted, the concurrent-power clause merely authorized but did not require state action in support of national prohibition. Repeal of the state law would not nullify the Constitution, as drys argued, but would instead force Congress to accept its hitherto avoided full responsibility for enforcement of the federal law. Other proponents of repeal followed Gillett, and a letter of support from Samuel Gompers was read. When their turn came to speak, a series of prohibitionists urged a veto to uphold law enforcement.[15]

On June 1, 1923, the day after the bitter five-hour debate, Al Smith signed the repeal bill. Henry Pringle, Smith's most dependable contemporary biographer, says the governor vacillated until the last minute before giving in to exhortations from Tammany Hall leaders.[16] In a 4,000 word statement defending his decision, the governor echoed the AAPA argument. The concurrent-power clause did not require the state to have an enforcement act, he said. Mullan-Gage repeal would not nullify the federal law in New York, but it would eliminate double jeopardy. Smith, obviously concerned about dry reaction, stressed that state officers would still be obliged to uphold the federal law, the only difference being that now all cases would be tried in federal court. Prohibitionists were not persuaded; they recognized that their cause had suffered a major setback. Meanwhile a jubilant Ransom Gillett exclaimed, "That lifts Governor Smith out of the class of politicians and puts him in the class with statesmen."[17]

The repeal of the Mullan-Gage Act gave antiprohibitionists a tremendous psychological lift. The hitherto invincible forces of absolute and strict prohibition had been politically defeated for the first time. Could not other, and perhaps greater, victories be achieved with more determination and effort? Smith's decision kindled an admiration among the antiprohibitionists that would continue to grow thereafter. Smith became the first major political figure, and for a long time the only one, to jeopardize his own prospects by taking consequential action against prohibition. It was an act that the Eighteenth Amendment's opponents would never forget. AAPA endorsement of Smith's presidential candidacy the following year demonstrated the bond which had been forged.[18]

The New York state enforcement act battle was a unique episode in the early 1920s. Far more frequently, the AAPA found itself involved, along with other antiprohibition groups, in campaigns to revise the Volstead Act's definition of an intoxicating beverage. As soon as the Volstead Act had been introduced, complaints had begun to be registered about the extremism of banning all beverages with more than .5 percent alcohol. Even if repeal of the Eighteenth Amendment was beyond reach, some prohibition critics believed it possible that the alcohol limit could be modified to permit beer

and wine and render the law more tolerable. Changing the statutory definition of an intoxicant appeared constitutionally permissible. Furthermore,
modification could be upheld as consistent with an interest in temperance
and not an abandonment of that goal.

The AAPA was acutely aware of the widespread sympathy throughout the
country for the establishment of temperance and the abolition of the social
evils associated with liquor. Immoderate use of alcohol had indeed, its
spokesmen concurred, ruined too many lives. Millions agreed on the need to
end the abuse of alcohol, even if they differed on whether achieving that goal
required total prohibition. Much initial support for the Eighteenth Amendment clearly stemmed from distaste for the saloon, seen by many as the
encourager of excessive drinking and thereby a prime contributor to poverty,
family neglect, and the success of unsavory political machines. AAPA leaders
emphasized that they favored temperance and were "unalterably opposed to
the saloon." For some time, the association's letterhead bore the slogan,
"Beers and Light Wines *NOW:* But no Saloons *EVER.*[19] These declarations
tacitly acknowledged the impossibility, early in the twenties, of gaining
support for repeal without assurance that the association had no desire for
the return of the saloon and unrestrained drinking.

Urging modest change to legalize mild beer and weak wine provided a
means of demonstrating loyalty to the objective of temperance. Modificationists argued that their proposed reform would lead people away from the
illicit distilled spirits found mainly in speakeasies and toward less potent
beverages which would legally be consumed at home. Those who wished
something to drink would be harmlessly satisfied with beer. We stand just as
much for temperance and law enforcement as the Anti-Saloon League, the
modificationists maintained, but we are more realistic about how to achieve
such goals. "The Volstead Law has been tried,—and convicted."[20]

The campaign for Volstead Act modification to permit beverages with a
2.75 percent alcohol content was begun by the American Federation of
Labor. Samuel Gompers not only feared the loss of jobs with total prohibition, but also thought beer a refreshing, nutritious, nonintoxicating drink
which would satisfy most working men.[21] Preprohibition beer had averaged 5
percent alcohol, and its capacity to intoxicate was debated. Wartime prohibition, supposedly banning all intoxicants, had permitted manufacture
and sale of 2.75 beer. Surely the latter standard would meet the requirements
of the Eighteenth Amendment, labor assumed. The June 1919 AFL convention had asked that 2.75 beer be exempted from the Eighteenth Amendment's provisions. Thereafter, the AFL constantly urged Volstead Act modification. Both the 1921 and 1923 federation conventions called for legalization of 2.75 beer. The president of the photoengravers union, Matthew
Woll, the AFL vice president closest to Gompers and most active in organized
labor's campaign to change the prohibition laws, explained that modification

would give workers "a wholesome and digestible beverage...that they naturally crave" and that, as a result, "that big body of wage earners and citizens will have respect for the law and believe in the enforcement of the law."[22] In other words, workers would be more likely to obey a law which merely took away hard liquor and which allowed them a mild drink they enjoyed. Gompers' cautious successor as AFL president, William Green, held firmly to the same position after he took office in December 1924.[23]

The AAPA began publicly endorsing 2.75 modification in 1922. In an April speech, Captain Stayton identified it as a primary goal, and the association campaigned for it during the fall elections. When they met briefly with President Coolidge in January 1924, association leaders made Volstead modification their principal request. The AAPA called on both major political parties to endorse modification in their 1924 platforms, but to no avail. Nevertheless, the association's public statements continued to stress modification during 1925 and 1926.[24]

A shared interest in modifying the Volstead definition of an intoxicant drew various antiprohibition groups together. During a January 1924 "Face-the-Facts" conference to publicize its objections to national prohibition, the AAPA announced formation of the Joint Legislative Committee, an alliance with the American Federation of Labor, the Moderation League of New York, and the Constitutional Liberty League of Massachusetts to seek modification. The joint committee brought together the largest organizations opposing prohibition, the four-million-member AFL and the three antiprohibition societies who together claimed (with undoubted exaggeration) a million members.[25] This alliance was forged to present a united front to Congress. The joint committee quickly arranged for the first full-scale review of the prohibition situation. Fifty-nine sympathetic congressmen introduced identical bills calling for legalization of 2.75 beverages, and hearings on the proposal were scheduled. The joint committee had little hope for immediate favorable action but sought maximum publicity for its viewpoint.[26] The House Judiciary Committee offered a congenial forum, since chairman Andrew Volstead had been defeated for reelection in 1922 and succeeded by a sympathetic Philadelphia Republican, George S. Graham.[27]

The modification hearings of April and May 1924 provided the first serious congressional consideration of national prohibition since adoption of the Volstead Act. Julian Codman, a Boston attorney who headed the Constitutional Liberty League and served as counsel for the Joint Legislative Committee, marshalled a small army of witnesses favoring modification. Generally, their presentations stressed that existing prohibition laws had proved ineffective in reducing drinking and crime and that they bred corruption and helped create a general disrespect for law. Legalization of 2.75 beer, committee witnesses argued, would improve law observance and reduce public tensions. Codman, in his introductory remarks, made no mention of the constitutional issues involved in national prohibition which so concerned Stayton and others. He presented modification as the cure for undesirable conditions.[28]

Samuel Gompers, a prime witness for the Joint Legislative Committee, asserted that legal mild beer would ween people away from illicit hard liquor and increase their confidence in the country's laws and institutions. The president of the Illinois Federation of Labor argued that working men enjoyed and needed a refreshing glass of beer after work. If allowed 2.75 beer, they would be satisfied and unwilling to violate the law in order to obtain stronger drink. Matthew Woll pointed out that the prohibitionists' appeal for ratification of the Eighteenth Amendment had centered on criticism of saloons and hard liquor and had not foreshadowed the subsequent absolute ban on even mild alcoholic beverages. The Volstead Act's .5 percent limitation violated public trust and stirred popular revolt. Modifying the definition of an intoxicating beverage, said Woll, would restore confidence in government and produce law observance based on a belief in its justice and morality. Modification would foster temperance and morality, which had suffered setbacks with passage of the Volstead Act.[29]

Spokesman for the AAPA, Captain Stayton and Missouri division chairman Henry S. Priest, endorsed modification without concealing their fundamental objections to prohibition. Priest contended that prohibition was being ignored because the public did not recognize the conduct proscribed by the law as criminal. Though he hoped it would not be, he maintained that if the Eighteenth Amendment was retained, its enforcement act should be changed to conform with popular attitudes regarding intoxicants and to carry out the benevolent purposes of the amendment: eliminating saloons and ending intemperance. Stayton pictured national prohibition as destroying both temperance and law observance, and he described modification as a legitimate and helpful corrective.[30]

Women from the Philadelphia Molly Pitcher Club endorsed modification as a means of curbing some evil aspects of national prohibition—growing intemperance, especially among young people, and increasing disrespect for law. The Molly Pitcher Clubs were not abandoning their opposition to the Eighteenth Amendment, they said, but at the moment the question was one of improving conditions under the law. After a series of witnesses had made similar statements, Codman concluded the Joint Legislative Committee's presentation by submitting several documents: legal opinions that 2.75 beverages were not in fact intoxicating and therefore could be constitutionally allowed; medical opinions that 2.75 beer would not be harmful; and letters from ministers, employers, and union leaders saying that modification would make prohibition enforcement easier and would satisfy workingmen.[31]

The joint committee's presentation was sharply disputed by the prohibitionists, to whom the latter half of the hearing was given. They argued that any amount of alcohol was harmful and that any existing problems with prohibition could be eliminated through proper enforcement of the law. The debate did not persuade Congress to take any action, but it did publicize the modification argument throughout the country.[32]

After the 1924 hearings had failed to move Congress, the campaign to modify prohibition languished for nearly two years. The first serious effort to revive it came from New Jersey Senator Walter E. Edge, a good friend of the AAPA. In a major Senate speech on December 15, 1925, Edge lamented the growing failure of prohibition and increasing evidence of alcoholism and crime. While he preferred repeal of the Eighteenth Amendment, he conceded that that would take years. Congress could, however, improve conditions immediately by allowing 2.75 beer.[33] Edge and his colleague and fellow AAPA supporter, William Cabell Bruce of Maryland, then conferred with Captain Stayton. They asked Stayton to present the antiprohibitionist case to a Senate subcommittee. Under Stayton's leadership the Joint Legislative Committee was reorganized early in 1926 to represent the critics of prohibition at the hearings.[34]

The Senate hearings of April 1926 marked the high point of modification efforts. A subcommittee of the Committee on the Judiciary was studying a variety of proposals to amend the Eighteenth Amendment so that states could exempt themselves from national prohibition, to change the Volstead Act's definition of an intoxicating beverage, to allow freer medicinal use of intoxicants, and to hold a national referendum on modification or repeal of national prohibition. Reforms in prohibition enforcement were also being considered. Julian Codman, who again served as the Joint Legislative Committee's spokesman while Stayton remained in the background, concentrated on Volstead Act modification from the outset. Codman asserted that the Volstead Act had exceeded the mandate of the Eighteenth Amendment by defining as intoxicating, beverages which in fact were not intoxicating, and furthermore, that the law had failed to prevent drinking or decrease crime. Rather, he said, the Volstead Act had done incredible harm by promoting bootlegging, destroying the standards of youth, and creating universal contempt for law.[35]

Matthew Woll appeared before the subcommittee to express the AFL's continuing interest in modification. He reported that there was great resentment against the Volstead Act's definition of intoxicants. Workers, he said, regarded the definition as "unsound, illogical, and in contravention of the intent and spirit of the Eighteenth Amendment," and they thought that a beverage of 2.75 percent alcohol content was not an intoxicant "but merely a stimulant." Popular resentment had increased, Woll continued, because safeguards against unjust search and seizure and against double jeopardy had been cast aside by the courts, while at the same time glaring evidence appeared of corruption and malfeasance by public officials. The AFL spokesman saw the Volstead Act rather than the Eighteenth Amendment as the source of the problems, and therefore he felt that modification would provide a solution.[36]

General Lincoln B. Andrews, the Assistant Secretary of the Treasury who supervised prohibition enforcement, strengthened the antiprohibitionist case when he admitted to the subcommittee that prohibition agents had engaged in a considerable amount of bribe-taking, corruption, and intoxication. Furthermore, proper enforcement could not be accomplished with current resources, he maintained. Under questioning by Codman, Andrews admitted his personal belief that modification to allow the sale of light beers, not to be consumed in saloons, would aid in promoting temperance and eliminating the illicit liquor traffic.[37] This startling revelation from the federal government's chief prohibition enforcement officer cheered antiprohibitionists and led the Anti-Saloon League to demand Andrews' dismissal.[38] Emory R. Buckner, U.S. district attorney for the Southern District of New York, buttressed Andrews' much-publicized testimony by telling the senators that the country was being flooded with illegal liquor and that either Congress would need to modify the law or spend incalculable sums to enforce it.[39]

Such statements by high government officials directly involved in law enforcement gave credence to the Joint Legislative Committee's assertions that prohibition was not working and was producing undesirable conditions. The Senate subcommittee, however, was not impressed. It gave both the Eighteenth Amendment and the Volstead Act resounding endorsements.

> We believe this Amendment to be morally right and economically sound.
>
> So long as this Amendment is part of our fundamental law, it is the duty of all officers Legislative, Executive, and Judicial to aid in its enforcement.
>
> The advocates of modification of the present Prohibition Laws propose to weaken the same. They seek to directly or indirectly authorize the manufacture and sale of intoxicating beverages. This is contrary to the spirit and intent of the Eighteenth Amendment.[40]

Thereupon, at the subcommittee's recommendation, all modification proposals were dropped.

Having presented to Congress what they regarded as their strongest case for moderate reform, antiprohibitionists had gotten nowhere. One obvious reason for such total failure had been their inability to convince politicians of either party that prohibition reform had any chance of passage or that its advocacy would attract more votes than it would cost. From his office across the street from the Capitol, Wayne Wheeler continued to cultivate the Anti-

Saloon League's reputation of being able to produce enough votes to sway an election. Therefore, except in clearly wet districts, candidates in 1926, as they had in 1920, 1922, and 1924, generally sought to avoid identification with prohibition repeal or even modification. Perhaps the clearest indication of how politicians assessed the strength of the antiprohibition movement emerged from the national party conventions of 1924.

Four years earlier the new national prohibition law had not been a significant issue at either Republican or Democratic convention. The Republicans in 1920 had adopted a platform containing an innocuous pledge of "unyielding devotion to the Constitution."[41] The Democratic platform committee had preferred to say nothing at all regarding prohibition. The committee and later the full convention had overwhelmingly rejected both William Jennings Bryan's proposal favoring effective enforcement of prohibition and a Tammany counterproposal for Volstead Act modification to allow beer and wine.[42] By 1924, however, national prohibition had become a more serious issue to both parties.

As the party in power, and carrying the burden of the various Harding administration scandals, the Republicans in 1924 were extremely sensitive to criticism of their conduct of government. Though Republicans had not initially advocated national prohibition any more than Democrats had, they had become its custodians by virtue of their holding office since 1920. The Anti-Saloon League, through its Washington representative, Wayne Wheeler, had kept in close touch with the administration, pressing for appointment of its candidates to positions in the Prohibition Bureau and offering regular reminders of the danger of offending the drys. Though reluctant to increase the federal enforcement budget, both the late President Harding and his successor Calvin Coolidge had deemed it appropriate to make speeches urging Americans to uphold the law and expressing their own commitment to that end.

When the 1924 Republican convention met in Cleveland, a series of witnesses from more than twenty organizations urged the platform committee to endorse strict prohibition enforcement. Calling it the president's duty to enforce the law and the platform's responsibility to support his efforts, Wheeler pointed out that the league would work to defeat wet candidates, including modificationists. The only contrary voices among the witnesses belonged to AFL secretary Frank Morrison, advocating 2.75 beer, and Captain Stayton, who decried the need to "bow down and worship one law" and called for Volstead Act modification to make the drastic law more workable. The vote-conscious committee ignored Stayton and adopted a "law and order" plank. Following Wheeler's advice, party draftsmen avoided direct reference to the dry law, but left no doubt as to the Republican position.

We must have respect for law. We must have observance of law. We
must have enforcement of law. The very existence of the Government
depends upon this. The substitution of private will for public law is
only another name for oppression, disorder, anarchy and the mob rule.
    Every Government depends upon the loyalty and respect of its
citizens. Violations of the law weaken and threaten government itself.
No honest Government can condone such actions on the part of its
citizens. The Republican party pledges the full strength of the Government for the maintenance of these principles by the enforcement of the
Constitution and of all laws. [43]

Of course, the platform offered no specifics as to how prohibition might be
enforced, but party leaders judged that there was no prospect of changing
the law and that even to hint at the possibility would offend many supporters
as well as outrage the Anti-Saloon League. The modificationist Joint Legislative Committee had written to every Republican delegate, "The political
party that is tied up with the Anti-Saloon League and its prohibition law that
has spread corruption like a blight across the continent and rocked the faith
of the people in the integrity of their Government will undoubtedly face an
embarrassing situation in November."[44] Clearly, few Republicans placed any
stock in such dire warnings.
    The Association Against the Prohibition Amendment expected better
treatment at the hands of the Democratic convention meeting in New York,
in part because Alfred E. Smith was a leading candidate for the party's
presidential nomination. Even before the Republicans had adjourned,
Charles S. Wood, AAPA Pennsylvania state director, predicted that, although
the association's 500,000 members were about equally divided between
Republicans and Democrats, 90 percent would vote for Smith, should he be
nominated. The association, said Wood, could also support another nominee, such as former Secretary of War Newton D. Baker or Maryland governor Albert Ritchie, who held satisfactory views on prohibition, but they
clearly favored Smith, the hero of Mullan-Gage repeal.[45]
    On the eve of the Democratic convention, the AAPA held a rally in a New
York hotel attended by 1,500 people, including some delegates. Resolutions
adopted termed prohibition a violation of the "liberties of the individual
citizen and the rights of the several states," and a "plainly apparent" failure.
The gathering demanded a change in the Volstead Act, returning enforcement responsibility to the states as the first step toward repeal of the
Eighteenth Amendment. The same day Stayton asserted that the Anti-
Saloon League had come to New York seeking a prohibition-enforcement
plank to hamstring the Democrats. The league, he charged, was allied with
the Republican party.[46]
    Although there was more antiprohibitionist sentiment in the New York

convention than there had been in Cleveland (the AAPA claimed that 135 delegates, 10 percent of the convention's total, were members), dry sympathies dominated. A convention majority sufficiently nativist and fundamentalist to be unwilling to condemn the Ku Klux Klan was not about to take a stand against the Eighteenth Amendment. While platform statements on the League of Nations and especially the Klan prompted fierce battles, the delegates quietly approved a plank representing the same tacit acceptance of prohibition found in the Republican document, a pledge to respect and enforce the Constitution and all laws. The Democratic platform did also include a plank calling for the preservation of states' rights and an end to centralizing tendencies. Stayton immediately hailed the latter plank, saying that it expressed the fundamental principles in the fight against the prohibition tyranny. He made no mention, however, of his disappointment with the law-enforcement plank.[47] Before long the AAPA was claiming that it had influenced the Democrats and the Republicans as well. "Neither party dared to offend the 'wet' vote by any pronouncement in favor of prohibition." These brave words, however, masked considerable disappointment.[48]

The defeat of Al Smith in the epic 103-ballot struggle for the presidential nomination constituted another setback for the antiprohibition cause. Smith represented urban, new immigrant, northern wet Democrats while his opponent, William G. McAdoo, championed rural and small-town, old-stock, conservative, dry Democrats from the South and West. Neither faction had the power to control a convention governed by a two-thirds rule for nomination, but each had the strength to block the other. Antiprohibition sentiment, while present, was insufficient to produce an acceptable platform or nominee at Madison Square Garden in July 1924. The Democrats' compromise presidential selection, John W. Davis, though accused of wet sympathies by the Anti-Saloon League, faithfully defended the party's enforcement plank. Davis's prohibition position may have driven many wet workingmen to support the independent progressive candidacy of Robert La Follette.[49] Disappointed officers of the AAPA announced that since neither party had put forth an acceptable platform or candidate, the association would take no part in the national campaign but would confine its efforts to those congressional elections where the issue was clearly drawn.[50]

Frustration with the unresponsive political system caused some antiprohibitionists to abandon all hope of normal reform and to openly discuss the possibility of ignoring the law. The increasingly firm belief that the Constitution could not be changed was reinforced by the unwillingness of either party even to discuss slight relaxation of the Volstead Act. Wayne Wheeler had called the antiprohibitionists' one modest victory, the repeal of the New York State enforcement act, "attempted nullification of the Constitution" and "a direct encouragement to lawlessness."[51] Before long, some discouraged antiprohibitionists came to feel that real nullification, the simple nonobservance and nonenforcement of a law which remained on the books, offered the only escape from prohibition.

Arthur R. Hadley, president emeritus of Yale University, in a November 1925 *Harper's Magazine* article, published the first serious proposal for nullification of prohibition. Laws were observed, Hadley argued, because the vast majority of people voluntarily accepted them, not because police compelled obedience. "Conscience and public opinion enforce the laws," he said; "the police suppress the exceptions." Voluntary observance of law was an essential of self-government; without it anarchy would result. Hadley saw tyranny replacing democracy when a government went beyond what public sentiment would support and adopted laws at the demand of pressure groups. When an unsatisfactory law could not be removed, the remedy lay with the people. "If any considerable number of citizens who are habitually law-abiding think that some particular statute is bad enough in itself or dangerous enough in its indirect effects to make it worthwhile to block its enforcement, they can do so." Hadley labeled such widespread disobedience "nullification," claiming that the North had nullified the Fugitive Slave Law and the South had nullified the Reconstruction Acts. This was not revolution, Hadley maintained, but rather the members of a community deciding not to obey the laws they regard as bad or inconvenient, while continuing to observe others. "The officials charged with the enforcement of the law simply see that it is beyond their power to secure obedience to it. If those who passed the law or secured its passage are wise," counseled Hadley, "they will acquiesce in this result. If the police look the other way when such a law is broken, its bad effects are avoided without much harm to anybody." It would be better if legislatures avoided enacting bad laws by developing clearer ideas of public opinion and the limits of government, for with nullification, "if a good man breaks a bad law under pressure of necessity, it will encourage another man who is not so good to break several other laws which may not be so bad at all." In the face of unwise legislation, however, nullification was an obvious, indeed sometimes the only, remedy. "It is the safety valve which helps a self-governing community avoid the alternative between tyranny and revolution. It reduces the tension; it gives a warning to those in authority which they disregard at their peril."[52]

Hadley remained vague on such points as the percentage of violations sufficient to turn dangerous lawlessness into acceptable nullification and whether all laws, or only particular ones, could be so overturned. Still, this was not a simple and irresponsible call for lawbreaking. Its distinguished author was seeking a rational escape from the dilemma of a law unpopular with at least a very large minority of the American people and yet apparently beyond change. Other respectable voices soon took up the idea of nullification.[53] Walter Lippmann, for one, thought nullification offered a way out of an impossible situation in which a majority opposed but could not repeal an amendment. "This is a normal and traditional American method of circumventing the inflexibility of the Constitution," he wrote. "When the Constitution has come into conflict with the living needs of the nation, and when amendment was impossible, the method of changing the Constitution has been to change it and then get the very human Supreme Court to sanction it." Lippmann pointed out that the Fourteenth and Fifteenth Amendments had been effectively nullified and Southern majority opinion served by election laws which ignored the Constitution and disfranchised the Negro. The same could be done with prohibition. "A community has not ceased to be essentially law-abiding merely because it refuses to practice literal obedience. There is such a thing as orderly disobedience to a statute, a disobedience which is open, frankly avowed, and in conformity with the general sense of what is reasonable."[54] Clarence Darrow, Brand Whitlock, and others presented similar arguments in their desire somehow to be rid of the unwanted law.[55] Catholic moral theologian Father John A. Ryan did not overtly advocate nullification, but by 1927 he abandoned his earlier position that citizens were obligated to obey laws as long as they were enacted in good faith to achieve a valuable social purpose. Ryan, an influential liberal Catholic scholar, concluded that prohibition lacked public acceptance, excessively restricted individual liberty, proved harmful in practice, and therefore was no longer morally valid or binding.[56]

The rather twisted reasoning of the nullification argument reflected the anguish of those who offered it. People like Lippmann and Darrow earlier in their careers had expressed great faith that law could be an engine of progressive social reform, causing people to behave more nobly than they would otherwise. Nullification took the position that only laws which reflected a social consensus were enforceable. Their willingness to adopt this viewpoint suggests how frustrated they were about the prospects of change through the normal political process and how intensely they felt the need to end national prohibition.

The leaders of the AAPA emphatically rejected the nullification proposal. "I should be greatly alarmed," wrote Stayton, "at any official recognition of the existing unofficial hypocrisy."[57] Julian Codman did flirt with the idea of nullification, which at least partly explains Stayton's growing disenchantment with the Massachusetts attorney.[58] A deep attachment to the idea of law observance, and complaints about an unreasonable, frequently violated law producing disrespect for all laws did not prepare the AAPA to advocate ignoring any law, however offensive. Furthermore, unlike the nullificationists, they were beginning to feel some optimism regarding the possibility of reform. By the end of 1926 several signs that public sentiment was shifting had appeared.

The *Literary Digest* had conducted the first large-scale national opinion survey on prohibition during the summer of 1922. Although unsophisticated by modern standards, the *Digest's* mail poll of its subscribers offered the best available picture at that time of middle-class opinion. Of more than 900,000 ballots returned, 38.6 percent favored enforcement of existing laws, 40.8 percent preferred Volstead Act modification tó allow light wines and beer, and only 20.6 percent favored repeal of the Eighteenth Amendment. A special tally of women's ballots showed a slightly higher portion for enforcement, while a tabulation of factory workers found less than 9 percent for enforcement, nearly 30 percent for repeal, and an overwhelming 62 percent for modification. [59] While the *Digest* poll did not reveal how many of those surveyed had originally favored the Eighteenth Amendment, it suggests that by 1922 a majority accepted the principle of prohibition. They thought the law should be enforced as it stood or, at most, changed to remove the ban on the mildest alcoholic beverages.

Four 1922 state referendums, taken as a group, reflected a similar view. In California a state prohibition-enforcement act was approved by a small majority after having been defeated two years earlier. Ohio voters rejected by a substantial margin a proposal to modify the state prohibition law to legalize beer and wine. In Illinois, on the other hand, a modification referendum carried by two to one, while the Massachusetts voters refused four-to-three to approve an enforcement act. Altogether voters in 1922 divided fairly evenly between enforcement and modification. [60] Presumably some preferred repeal to modification, but a large share accepted prohibition as it stood.

By mid-decade, popular attitudes appeared to be changing. In 1925 *Collier's* magazine interviewed 263,583 men and women across the country regarding prohibition. Asked, "Are you satisfied with conditions as they are?" 68 percent said no and only 32 percent said yes. Thirty-nine percent felt the law was being enforced locally, while 61 percent thought not. Such questions emphasized discontent, while a more neutral query showed that 61 percent considered prohibition enforceable and only 39 percent disagreed. [61] The *Collier's* survey did not inquire directly whether people favored repeal, modification, or continuation of the present law. But a substantial majority of those polled clearly did not approve of current conditions.

In 1926 eight state referendums provided the decade's largest sample of public opinion regarding prohibition. The questions varied, however, and did not always offer a clear indication of support for the liquor ban. In New York nearly two and a half million voters approved by a margin of better than three to one a proposal to legalize beverages above .5 percent alcohol content. In Illinois and Wisconsin similar modification referendums carried easily. Fifty-four percent of Montana voters approved repeal of the state enforcement act. Meanwhile a Nevada referendum calling national prohibition a failure and requesting that Congress call a convention to repeal or amend the Eighteenth Amendment passed three to one. Offsetting these five endorsements of modification or repeal, voters in California, Colorado, and Missouri solidly rejected proposals to repeal state enforcement laws. The contemporary appraisal of these returns—that opponents of prohibition had gained considerable popular backing although they had little support in state and federal legislatures—appears accurate.[62] Public opposition to prohibition would increase greatly in later polls and referendums, but by 1926 signs of a shift away from acceptance of the law, whether as a boon or as a *fait accompli,* had begun to appear.

Some opponents of the dry law, for example, Senator William Cabell Bruce and the judges of a Hearst newspaper contest for the best essay on how to achieve temperance, maintained that modification offered the only attainable solution.[63] But the Association Against the Prohibition Amendment gradually began to shift its course. In part, changes in AAPA activities and tactics may have resulted from a recognition that previous efforts had led nowhere. Citizens' rallys in Carnegie Hall, Brooklyn, Pittsburgh, and elsewhere, a meeting in St. Louis of AAPA representatives from around the nation, two well-attended "Face-the-Facts" conferences in Washington, and cross-country speaking tours by Captain Stayton and others all generated publicity.[64] Neither the arguments presented nor the resulting growth of membership rolls produced any positive revision of the law. In fact, the number of sympathetic congressmen fell in 1924 and again in 1926.[65] Only a few congressmen, such as Representatives Fiorello LaGuardia of New York, Adolph J. Sabath of Chicago, John Philip Hill of Baltimore, and Edward Voigt of Wisconsin, and Senators Walter E. Edge and Edward I. Edwards of New Jersey, James A. Reed of Missouri, William Cabell Bruce of Maryland, and James W. Wadsworth of New York spoke out against national prohibition frequently and loudly.

The attempt to modify the legal alcohol limit and the system of concurrent federal and state enforcement had absorbed much energy and produced only state enforcement-act repeal in New York and Montana. Modification referendums, of course, could have no effect unless Congress acted. Congress in 1926 firmly rejected all proposals for significant relaxation of the Volstead Act. Hopes for a compromise solution based on modification waned even further as it became clear that drinking habits were changing among those Americans who defied the law. Whereas before national prohibition, beer had been the predominant alcoholic beverage of choice, imbibers appeared to be turning increasingly to distilled liquors served in mixed drinks, or as was becoming the fashionable term, cocktails. Doubts increased that those who wanted to drink would be satisfied by weak 2.75 beer.

Those who opposed national prohibition for reasons other than their own thirst saw less and less to recommend modification. Concerns about the rising rate of crime, corruption of government officials, or spreading disrespect for law could not be relieved by either modest reform or the radical step of nullification; these expedients would lead to continued violation of the law. Neither modification nor nullification were at all palatable to those, like Stayton, who regarded the improper presence of the prohibition edict in the Constitution as the real problem.

The leaders of the AAPA gradually came to realize during the middle years of the twenties that only repeal would do. Their own arguments against prohibition pointed to such a conclusion. The task *was* clearly enormous, but little purpose was served by seeking halfway solutions. The organization was gaining new members whose interests, as will be seen, would not be served by mere modification. Both the results of polls and referendums and the evidence of widespread drinking indicated the growing unhappiness of many Americans with prohibition. Frustration with past failures to move the obstacle confronting them, as well as optimism about future prospects for success, caused the AAPA to redirect and intensify its campaign. New resources and a changing national mood encouraged those who continued to attack the hitherto impregnable defenses of national prohibition.

5 THIRSTING AFTER RIGHTEOUSNESS

"This prohibition thing is getting worse every day. It cannot go on this way or the whole government will be disgraced." So wrote United States senator James W. Wadsworth to a friend in March 1926.[1] By the time the Eighteenth Amendment had been in effect for a half decade, a large and growing number of Americans appeared to be disregarding the liquor ban. Many citizens who ignored the preratification debate had now seen enough to form a firm opinion on the law's benefits and drawbacks. While some were convinced that national prohibition helped improve social, economic, and moral conditions in the United States, others concluded, like the Republican senior senator from New York, that the reform was a disaster. Several extremely wealthy prohibition critics, regarding the Association Against the Prohibition Amendment as the best available agent for attacking the law, tried to improve its performance by reorganizing the association and providing it with more funds. Their concerns about national prohibition gave the AAPA its final form, won the association other followers, and did much to set the tone and terms of the battle over retaining or rescinding the antiliquor amendment.

The day national prohibition took effect in 1920, a federal official directly responsible for overseeing it predicted that the law would bring an end to the liquor traffic in six years.[2] For the fiscal year ending June 30, 1926, however, federal agents made approximately 160,000 seizures of fermenting or distilling equipment and confiscated almost thirty-eight million gallons of illegal beer, wine, and spirits! Furthermore, thirty-seven thousand persons were convicted of violating the Volstead Act in fiscal 1926, compared to twenty-two thousand during the law's first eighteen months of operation. Every available index registered growing rates of violation rather than an increasingly effective law, despite Congress's more than doubling its initial prohibition enforcement appropriation by 1926.[3] While many Americans observed the liquor ban, of course, many others broke the law without being apprehended. The rising arrest rate provided a crude reflection of spreading disdain for national prohibition and a parallel growth of alarm on the part of many citizens.

This was "prohibition at its worst," wrote Irving Fisher, a prominent Yale monetary theorist who would become even better known for announcing in early October 1929, "Stock prices have reached what looks like a permanently high plateau."[4] Fisher, an ardent prohibitionist, argued that even with admitted violations the current state of affairs represented a vast improvement over the days prior to the Eighteenth Amendment. Total consumption of alcohol was, Fisher estimated, no more than 10 to 16 percent of the preprohibition rate; arrests of youths for drunkenness had fallen by two-thirds; and the national death rate had declined 10 percent. Meanwhile, public health showed definite improvement; national income had increased by $6 billion, due to prohibition; and because workers' efficiency was not being reduced by drinking, real wages were up 28 percent since 1919. Once the law was properly enforced and people accepted it as a permanent fixture, the economist predicted, there would be a further improvement of conditions.[5]

Not everyone accepted Fisher's statistics or his cheerful assessment. Many attributed the economic and social progress of the twenties to other causes. Among those who disagreed with Fisher were several men who by the middle of the decade were moving to take the lead in the Association Against the Prohibition Amendment. Their ideas are well worth examining in some detail. Their expressed opinions provide the best evidence of the thinking of those most committed to tearing down the Eighteenth Amendment.

Those individuals who would eventually dominate the AAPA and the repeal crusade became actively involved in antiprohibition activities in the mid-twenties because of awakening fears for the health, safety, and righteousness of their society. National prohibition appeared to them to be causing rising crime, lost respect for all law, a breakdown in morality, especially among the young, and corruption in government. No doubt some conditions they attributed to prohibition stemmed from unrelated developments in a rapidly changing society, but to them this one law seemed the principal difficulty.

Beneath their immediate worries about social instability and decay ran another concern. Like William Stayton, most felt deeply threatened by the federal government's growing power during the years of progressive reform. They expressed fear at the loss of local control over what they believed to be essentially community matters, such as the establishment of standards of acceptable behavior. What remained unspoken was crucial: since in many cases they themselves possessed great local influence, they would lose personally if decision-making shifted to the national level. Some certainly worried that increased government regulation of business would follow. They upheld laissez faire capitalism as a philosophical ideal and a practical explanation for social progress and personal success. Federal controls could, they feared, affect their profits and practices and would be difficult for individual companies to influence. Furthermore, growth of federal power carried with it the probability of larger government budgets, the burden of which they would likely be expected to bear. Already, national prohibition was costing a great deal in enforcement expenses and lost tax revenues. Men comfortable with past governmental arrangements came to see prohibition as detrimental in itself and, if permitted to stand, the precursor of other dreadful changes.

In a letter to a Wisconsin newspaper editor who belonged to the AAPA, Captain Stayton recorded reactions he encountered during an April 1926 Detroit meeting with "a group of very serious businessmen, every one of whom had been dry and had contributed to the Anti-Saloon League, and who had originally believed in National Prohibition." One manufacturer in the group had asserted, "The people are not very much interested in the question of wet and dry, but they have become tremendously interested in the question of the form of government under which they shall live. They realize that prohibition is not a real disease, but merely a symptom of a very great and deep-seated disease—the disease of plutocracy, of centralization of government from Washington in public affairs that extends now into the home and to the dinner table." The worried speaker concluded by exclaiming, "If we have five years more of this curse, there will be fighting in the streets of American cities. People will not submit much longer to the impositions to which they are now being subjected." To his amazement, Stayton wrote, not one man had dissented, but rather "the ominous nodding of heads was unanimous."[6]

Detroit autoworkers probably did not share the perceptions of these executives regardless of how much they disliked prohibition. However, business and professional people with whom Stayton had contact often did. Evidence of this can be readily found in the record left by several individuals prominent in the affairs of the AAPA.

Henry Bourne Joy, a retired Packard Motor Company president, who knew Stayton from having served as vice-president of the Navy League, may have been among the Detroit group the captain reported meeting. Joy and his wife had once belonged to the Anti-Saloon League. Appalled by social conditions which they attributed to saloons, they had contributed to and actively supported the movement for national prohibition. After the Eighteenth Amendment took effect, however, Joy gradually lost faith in the reform. He told an old school friend that he had discovered his servants making excellent wine and beer for the entire household except himself and Mrs. Joy. He was shocked further to learn of widespread drinking in the surrounding community. By 1925 Joy decided that prohibition was unenforceable, since perhaps half the population desired to drink. The evils spawned by the law—the drinking of poor quality and often harmful liquor, crime, social antagonisms, and burdensome taxes—far exceeded its benefits.[7]

Privately Joy confided, "I made a mistake. I was stupidly wrong."[8] The same year Joy wrote in the *North American Review* that "America must open its eyes and recognize that human nature cannot be changed by legal enactment." Those who had voted for prohibition must realize, he said, that the law was ineffective, that liquor was available everywhere, and that vast spending on enforcement had not cut off the supply. Rampant crime and jammed courts and jails had resulted. "We might as well legislate against the natural functions of existence as to seek to continue on our present path towards a complete disregard for our laws and for the natural rights of a free people," he concluded.[9] Soon after his views were published, Joy began contributing to the AAPA.[10]

Personal experiences had helped motivate Henry Joy to support the anti-prohibition movement. From his home on the shores of Lake St. Clair, part of the waterway separating southeast Michigan from Ontario, he had watched efforts to halt the illegal importing of Canadian liquor. He had not complained, said Joy, when federal agents shot at smugglers attempting to land on his beach. He had objected, however, in December 1926, when federal agents in civilian dress, refusing to identify themselves until local police were called, had entered and searched his boathouse and seized eleven bottles of beer from the quarters of an aged watchman. Joy felt this sort of act did more harm and caused more resentment of government than prohibition was worth. A year later, agents had returned and, when the watchman was slow to respond to their knock, had broken down his door. In another incident nearby, a prohibition officer standing on shore had hailed a duck hunter in a small boat. Unable to hear the agent over the noise of his motor, the hunter had continued on his way. The officer had promptly shot him dead. Though a murder charge was filed, government attorneys had arranged for the case to be moved to federal court where they had won a light six-months sentence for manslaughter.[11] Not far from Detroit the controversial automobile search had taken place which had resulted in the Supreme Court's *Carroll v. U.S.* ruling, already discussed in chapter 2. Such episodes had deeply upset Joy. "The people live in fear of unlawful search of their homes and their motor cars as they travel, and unlawful shootings and killings by the officers of the Treasury Department."[12] Exposure to violent methods of prohibition enforcement stiffened Joy's opposition to the dry law. His donations to the AAPA increased, and before the end of 1927 he announced that he was abandoning his life-long support of the Republican party because it was upholding prohibition.[13]

Two prominent financiers also became active in the AAPA shortly after the middle of the decade. Grayson Mallet-Prevost Murphy of New York, a West Point graduate, veteran of two wars, and a founder of the American Legion, had built a successful Wall Street investment firm and held directorships in Guaranty Trust, Anaconda, Goodyear, and Bethlehem Steel. Robert K. Cassatt of Philadelphia, the son of a president of the Pennsylvania Railroad, ran an important investment banking company. These two conservative Republicans shared opinions as to the flaws of national prohibition. Murphy told a congressional committee that World War I had accustomed him to rigid, centralized government and that therefore, at the outset, he had fully expected the liquor ban to succeed. He joined Stayton's organization after concluding that the Eighteenth Amendment was "absolutely contrary to the spirit of the rest of the Constitution" and that it led to further contrary acts by the government, such as wiretapping, bribery, and the careless shooting of innocent people by prohibition agents. Respect for the Constitution had been "materially weakened." Furthermore, said Murphy, prohibition produced much crime and furnished the underworld with a large, steady income. Finally, the law interfered with established social customs and deprived the state of an opportunity to regulate the flow of liquor. Cassatt believed, as well, that prohibition was out of place in the Constitution. It seemed to him also that prohibition was leading to infringement of hitherto constitutionally protected personal rights. As did Murphy, he felt the United States too large and the customs too varied for one national law governing personal habits. Neither man liked instability, and both came to regard prohibition as a dangerous unsettling influence on government and society.[14]

James W. Wadsworth, Jr., a U.S. senator from New York, opposed national prohibition at a time when Henry Joy still supported it and Cassatt and Murphy had not yet become concerned. Wadsworth, in fact, had voted against the Eighteenth Amendment when it had come before the Congress, and he had since publicly endorsed the AAPA.[15] Not until his defeat for reelection to the Senate in 1926, however, did Wadsworth take an active role in the antiprohibition organization.

Wadsworth came from a family prominent for generations in the life of the Genesee Valley, southwest of Rochester, and in the affairs of the nation. Among his ancestors he could count an original settler of Connecticut, George Washington's commissary general, a major-general in the War of 1812, and a founder of the Republican party who had run for governor of New York and, as a Civil War general, had died at the Battle of the Wilderness. Wadsworth's father, James, Sr., had managed the family's vast land holdings and had spent twenty years in Congress, serving as chairman of the House Committee on Agriculture for a decade after 1896. The senator's ancestors—from great-great-grand uncle General James Wadsworth, who had opposed ratification of the federal Constitution in 1788, to his father, who in 1906 had suffered a falling out with President Theodore Roosevelt over a federal meat-inspection bill and had as a result lost his House seat— had opposed the growth and concentration of governmental power. Nothing in his own secure, comfortable life had inclined Wadsworth to question, much less reject, the viewpoint with which he had been raised.[16]

The younger James Wadsworth, born in 1877, attended fine boarding schools and Yale University with other sons of the late–nineteenth-century elite. At Yale he earned barely passing grades but was named to Walter Camp's All-American baseball team. Professor William Graham Sumner, the renowned social Darwinist, once had to admonish him for reading a newspaper in class. Nevertheless, Sumner influenced him the most, Wadsworth felt, perhaps because Sumner's view that the most talented persons would naturally rise to the top of a free society affirmed Wadsworth's opinion of himself and his peers. After marrying the daughter of Secretary of State John Hay, Wadsworth entered politics. Elected to the New York state assembly in 1904, he became his party leaders' compromise choice for Speaker the following year. Although Democrats Robert Wagner, James J. Walker, and especially Alfred E. Smith became his friends, Wadsworth remained a regular Republican who chaired the New York delegation to the 1912 national convention and kept it almost solidly for Taft. In 1914 Wadsworth won the Senate seat of retiring Elihu Root, an admired friend. Six years later, having risen to the chairmanship of the military affairs committee, the handsome, popular senator easily won reelection despite opposition from women's suffragists, the American Legion, and the AFL.[17]

Wadsworth voted against both the Eighteenth and Nineteenth Amendments when they were before the Senate. He felt strongly that the Constitution, to him the source and guardian of cherished traditions, should be concerned only with defining and limiting the powers of government. It should not deal with matters properly left to the states, such as the suffrage, nor should it contain statute law, such as prohibition.[18] The rights of states were to be jealously defended, and centralization of power in the federal government strenuously opposed. "I am sure," he told the National Republican Club at a 1923 Lincoln's birthday dinner, "we all dread the establishment, gradual though it may be, of a system of government in this nation which will sap the strength, initiative and sense of responsibility of the citizen and of the community in which he lives."[19] Wadsworth's most thorough biographer regards an "anti-statist" attitude, hostility to government intervention of any sort in domestic affairs, as the constant thread running throughout the New Yorker's career.[20]

Wadsworth worried in advance that unhappiness with prohibition "would result in widespread contempt of law and of the Constitution itself. And if there is one thing above all others that will wreck this republic, it is contempt of the Constitution."[21] By the time constitutional prohibition was three years old, Wadsworth was expressing alarm over violation of the liquor ban, not because of the drinking taking place but because "it is undermining the Constitution of the United States."[22] At the time, he saw little that could be done to alter the Eighteenth Amendment, but he believed that it never would have been adopted had referendums been allowed such as the one in Ohio, which the Supreme Court had overruled in *Hawke v. Smith*. For several years the New York senator agitated for a change in the constitutional amending procedure to allow for referendums or to require state legislatures considering ratification to have been elected subsequent to the submission of proposed amendments to the states.[23] By the mid-1920s Wadsworth had become recognized as one of the Senate's most outspoken critics of national prohibition.

In 1926 Wadsworth faced a difficult contest for reelection, one in which prohibition became the principal issue. A convincing victory, some thought, might win the senator a place on the 1928 Republican national ticket. In the same election, Alfred E. Smith sought a fourth term as governor; his chances for the Democratic presidential nomination two years later were thought to rest squarely on his ability to poll a large vote. Wadsworth and Smith held similar views on prohibition despite their allegiance to different political parties. Rumors circulated that an arrangement had been made to provide each incumbent with a weak opponent and, thereby, an easy victory. When reports of such a deal surfaced in the New York *World* and elsewhere, the Democrats felt obliged to protect Smith by putting up the strongest possible candidate, Judge Robert F. Wagner, who was as wet as Wadsworth. Thereupon the Anti-Saloon League and the Women's Christian Temperance Union, hoping to serve notice on both parties, put forth an independent Republican candidate, Franklin W. Christman, to draw normally Republican dry votes away from the heretic Wadsworth.[24]

During the campaign, Wadsworth spoke out repeatedly on prohibition, even in dry upstate areas. He considered it the crucial issue, one which conscience required he discuss. Furthermore, he said, no audience let him avoid it. The senator talked of the dangers to traditional forms of government posed by a centralizing, civil-liberties threatening, personally interfering national prohibition. He also charged that the amendment produced high enforcement costs, general disregard for law, hypocrisy, and corruption.[25] "Political and social morals are being poisoned to an extent never approached in the history of the country," Wadsworth warned.[26]

Christman's vituperative campaign, which largely ignored Wagner's wet position while vigorously attacking Wadsworth's antiprohibition record, succeeded after a fashion. The two wet candidates polled the vast majority of votes, Wagner edging out Wadsworth by the slim margin of 116,000. Christman, whose votes came almost entirely from heavily Republican upstate counties, drew 232,000. The dry spoiler clearly cost Wadsworth the election and gave him further reason to feel that prohibition was a distorting and damaging influence in American government.[27] An error had been committed in putting a restriction on individual behavior in the Constitution, he wrote a constituent following his defeat, "And we shall continue to suffer just so long as that 'Thou shalt not' remains in the Constitution."[28] Stripped of senatorial rank and sensitive about the cause of his downfall, Wadsworth joined the AAPA campaign against national prohibition. During the next seven years, Wadsworth made, by his own count, 131 speeches throughout the country on behalf of the association.[29]

In contrast to James Wadsworth, the three du Pont brothers of Wilmington, Delaware—Pierre, Irénée, and Lammot—had never been involved in politics. Du Ponts had lived along the Brandywine nearly as long as Wadsworths had lived along the Genesee. To escape the upheavals of the French Revolution, they had moved to Delaware in 1800 and established powder mills. Pierre and his brothers belonged to the fourth American generation of du Ponts and like most of their predecessors were preoccupied with the family business. Their ancestors had achieved enough comfort and prominence to be pleased with America's political, economic, and social system. The du Pont fortune, however, would be vastly expanded through the constant striving of Pierre, his brothers, and cousins. As they prospered, they encountered increasing federal regulation of their munitions business as well as more than one antitrust suit.[30]

The du Pont brothers became so concerned about national prohibition as a threat to governmental and social arrangements they preferred that they too became deeply involved in the AAPA. Pierre, the oldest, was the shrewd businessman who did the most to build modest family wealth into an enormous fortune; his other preoccupations and cautious nature made him the last to take up the antiprohibition crusade. Irénée, who often acted as spokesman for his more shy and reticent brothers and who followed his older brother as Du Pont Company president in 1919, was as outspoken and aggressive on prohibition as other topics. Lammot, the youngest, served as Du Pont Company president after 1925, and his constant involvement in corporate affairs kept him from taking as full a role in the AAPA as did his retired brothers. Nevertheless, Lammot served as a figurehead chairman of the association's finance committee and made financial contributions rivaling those of Irénée and Pierre. The du Pont brothers, along with their close friend and business associate John J. Raskob, became so active in the repeal campaign that they eventually came to personify the antiprohibition association to many outsiders.

Captain Stayton had written to the du Ponts during his early search for members. Pierre expressed some sympathy with the cause but did not join. By the summer of 1922 Irénée and Lammot accepted the invitation, paying the one dollar annual dues. In November Irénée became a Class B sustaining member, giving ten dollars to the association. (Class A sustaining members paid fifty dollars annually.) Apart from renewing his membership each year and contributing ten dollars to the 1924 campaign fund, Irénée did nothing until autumn 1925, when he began to describe in letters to friends how concerned he had become about the prohibition situation. By early 1926 he was helping organize and finance a Delaware division of the AAPA. He not only encouraged friends and business associates to join, but offered to pay the one dollar dues for 5,000 people who wanted to enroll but could not contribute.[31]

Irénée reacted to a *Collier's* article by William Allen White criticizing the antiprohibition movement by setting forth his reasons for entering the campaign so energetically.

First: It is not producing total abstinence but on the contrary is increasing the abuse of liquor, especially among young people.
Second: It is transferring an enormous revenue which could be collected by the Government in the form of a tax to the bootlegger and corrupt dry agent.
Third: It is an infringement on state rights and it is preferable that the several states govern themselves wherever possible.
Fourth: but not last, it is the opening wedge to a breaking down of our whole theory of Government by legislating through the Constitution.[32]

The last two reasons, so like Stayton's, may explain why Irénée originally joined the AAPA; but the first two, which he repeatedly emphasized in statements during the mid-twenties, probably had more to do with his expanded efforts at that time.

National prohibition had become "unworkable, demoralizing, and expensive," Irénée felt.[33] Not only did drinking continue, but the agents supposedly enforcing the law were taking graft, "the cost of which is, of course, paid by the consumer of liquor." He saw the liquor distribution system as little different from one with high-priced licenses to sell liquor, except that "the license fee is paid to the corrupt agent and to the bootlegger instead of to the United States Government or state governments."[34] It upset Irénée that the government received no revenue from the liquor industry, while criminals were richly rewarded. "The corporations of this country are being taxed 13% of their net profits, which is substantially in lieu of the tax on liquor which should flow to the Government."[35] One of the few antiprohibitionists to mention the taxation implications of the prohibition law in the mid-twenties, Irénée clearly felt troubled that legitimate industries were carrying a tax burden avoided and enlarged by bootleggers.

Irénée du Pont professed that he firmly believed in temperance but that he considered national prohibition to have reversed a national trend and to have made drinking fashionable. He expressed alarm at increasing abuse of liquor, especially excessive drinking by young people.[36] "In 1914," he wrote with some exaggeration, "we had become a temperate country; drinking in the upper classes had nearly vanished and was no longer a problem industrially. It was then almost impossible for minors to buy liquor; certainly they didn't do it." In contrast, "today it is notorious that a minor can get all the bootleg liquor he wants without regulation. Prohibition...has driven the saloon off the sidewalk but has put it in the cellar where it is out of sight."[37]

Government insistence that industrial alcohol be denatured revolted Irénée, for it meant "putting poisons into a material which is almost sure to be used somewhere as a beverage, with the resultant blinding or death of the unfortunate." He concluded that, "personally, I would rather a few habitual drunkards die of their own volition by the use of alcoholic beverages than to have one man accidentally killed by the route of denatured alcohol."[38] Prohibition, in sum, discredited government and distorted its purposes by involving it in matters which it should avoid. It cost a great deal in enforcement expense and lost tax revenue, while not producing temperance. Irénée, therefore, was eager to see the liquor ban abolished.

Pierre du Pont took much longer to join the antiprohibition movement than did his brothers, Irénée and Lammot. Indeed, Pierre later recalled having at the time approved the adoption of the Eighteenth Amendment. The Du Pont Company, primarily engaged in the manufacture of explosives and munitions, had for years, as a safety measure, strictly prohibited workers from using alcohol, and Pierre had thought that an end to all drinking would be for the good.[39] After it came, however, Pierre's complete conversion propelled him into the leadership of the repeal movement.

Pierre du Pont had, in the mid-twenties, recently withdrawn from active leadership of two of America's greatest corporations and was turning his full attention to personal interests. In 1923 he stepped down as president of General Motors, having left the same post at E. I. du Pont de Nemours, Inc., four years earlier. By nature a shy man, he had put all his energies into business management. For another year he remained active in GM affairs, and until 1928 he stayed on as chairman of the board of both companies. But after making arrangements for disposal of his vast stockholdings and taking his wife on an extended European tour, Pierre by late 1925 was relatively unburdened for the first time in his adult life.[40]

Born in 1870, Pierre had been orphaned at fourteen when his father was killed in a factory explosion. Thereafter, he became so much the head of the family that even his brothers and sisters called him "Dad." After graduating from the Massachusetts Institute of Technology in 1890 (as Irénée and Lammot would do later), he worked briefly in the family powder company, then invested in street railway companies in Lorain, Ohio, and Dallas, Texas. In cooperation with two cousins, Pierre bought the almost bankrupt Du Pont Company in 1902 and within fifteen years, using astute, innovative financing and management techniques, turned it into a huge, diversified, and very prosperous industrial empire under his control. He and John Raskob then duplicated the feat with General Motors.[41]

Prior to his retirement from business, Pierre found little time for involvement in public affairs. His civic activities had been largely confined to efforts to improve Delaware public education by reforming the state tax system, giving nearly four million dollars to build schools for black children, and donating another two million to improve the state university. Beginning in 1925 he served as the state's school tax commissioner.[42] Freed of his business responsibilities and still vigorous at fifty-five, Pierre in the middle of the 1920s was for the first time in his career both eager and able to address public issues. The process of transferring his stockholdings to relatives, to retain control of the two giant corporations within the family and yet avoid heavy estate taxes, heightened his awareness of tax burdens and government expenses at this time. In letters to a cousin regarding stock transfers, Pierre began in 1924 to complain that the Eighteenth Amendment was under-mining government, encouraging graft, corruption, and "utter disregard of law," yet not discouraging drinking.[43]

Early in 1925, as he recalled it, Stayton asked Pierre du Pont why he had not joined the AAPA along with his younger brothers. Pierre wondered whether the association was not simply "the spokesman for the liquor traf-fic?" Stayton assured him it was not. Still Pierre suspected that the vast majority of Americans favored prohibition and that it might be a good thing for the country. Stayton described the ratification process, in particular the invalidated Ohio referendum rejecting the amendment. He suggested that Pierre look for himself into the question of prohibition's acceptance and of its benefits by writing to both law-enforcement officials and factory managers. Prohibition Commissioner Roy Haynes replied that, except for the city of Detroit, the country was dry. Du Pont Company and General Motors plant managers, on the contrary, wrote of bootlegging and worsening conditions. Pierre, trusting his employees, felt that it was unpardonable that a public official would falsify the situation. Talking to Irénée and reading several books helped convince Pierre to fight the Eighteenth Amendment. By March 1925 he was opposing a Delaware state enforcement bill. In November he began to contribute to the AAPA, and a year later he became a director of the Delaware division.[44]

Pierre du Pont expressed his reasons for entering the antiprohibition crusade in both private correspondence and public statements. Intemper-ance, lawlessness, threats to property rights, and the loss of local decision-making power all concerned him. Initially, he referred frequently to his support for temperance and to the drys' having gone too far. To a defender of national prohibition, he wrote that "the great error in the Prohibition move-ment is failure to distinguish between the moderate use of alcohol and drinking to excess." The WCTU and other dry groups, Pierre complained, "continually dwell upon the evils of alcohol and the curse of drink." Pierre himself failed to see moderate drinking as criminal or even injurious. Tem-perate people are naturally resentful "when the over-zealous become intem-perate themselves and regardless of anything attempt to class the owner of any small amount of wine or stimulant, no matter for what purpose used, in the same class of undesirables as the most chronic drunkard."[45] People neither respect nor observe the liquor ban, he said, but "flout the law, causing national scandal." Consequently, vast sums of money were being turned over to a criminal underworld. A dangerous lawlessness had resulted from the popular revolt against prohibition.[46]

Not only was the prohibition amendment ineffectual in promoting temperance, Pierre du Pont contended, it was undemocratic and unconstitutional. This view he reached after consulting his attorney.[47] The Eighteenth Amendment had been adopted without the people's having had an opportunity to vote on it and, in several instances, in contrast to the expressed will of the state's voters. Furthermore, a federal system of government had been established so that people might choose their own laws in local matters. "If the people of thirty-six states believe they are better off not drinking alcoholic beverages, or if they think they have stopped their drinking simply by prohibiting it, they are welcome to their belief," he wrote. "They have neither moral nor constitutional right to insist that all other states shall pretend to the same view."[48]

The idea that the federal government, in the interest of social reform, could, without compensation, take an action destroying an industry troubled Pierre. "When the Constitution of the United States was amended and the Volstead Act passed, much property invested in the production of alcoholic liquor, in a legal manner, was rendered useless, and there was no thought of recompense to the innocents who suffered." The whole process, he concluded, "has been an outrage to American institutions."[49] Pierre's sensitivity on this point may have been caused by a 1911 antitrust decision forcing a partial splitting up of the Du Pont Company. Or it may have been due to a heavy special tax on profits from sales of gunpowder and other explosives which Congress passed in the summer of 1916 and made retroactive to January 1916; resentment at Du Pont profits from foreign contracts had appeared to prompt the legislation.[50] At any rate, Pierre was quite aware of government's potential for restricting business and wished that government's power to do so could be limited.

At times Pierre's criticisms of national prohibition extended into other areas, but his basic themes of protest did not change.

These then, are the fundamental objections to the Eighteenth Amendment and the Volstead law:

They are failures as a remedy for the drink evil.

They command no respect and scant observation because they disregard the wishes and rights of a very large number of people.

They were brought into being hastily, without proper approval, and it seems to me, by methods that are not constitutional.[51]

Pierre's concern with prohibition ran deep enough to overcome his natural shyness, leading him to plunge into the speaking and writing campaign against the liquor ban.

The person who, along with Pierre du Pont and William Stayton, proved eventually to be perhaps the most significant figure in the AAPA was Pierre's closest business associate, John J. Raskob. The career of the small, quiet, fastidious Raskob, one scholar observed, "could be used as a model for an Horatio Alger tale."[52] Born to poor immigrants, an Alsatian cigarmaker and his Irish wife, in Lockport, New York, in 1879, Raskob was forced by his father's death to support his mother, three younger brothers, and a sister. The ambitious Raskob studied stenography and bookkeeping. Eventually, in 1900 at the age of twenty-one, he obtained a position as secretary to Pierre du Pont. Raskob made himself invaluable to his employer, assisting him in the reorganization and refinancing of the Du Pont Company. The two men, separated by only nine years in age, became warm personal friends as well as lifelong business colleagues.[53]

After becoming corporate treasurer in 1914, Raskob began to invest in a struggling Detroit automobile firm, General Motors. He persuaded Pierre to join him. In 1915, when GM's founder William Durant and a group of bankers who had invested heavily in the firm were fighting for control of the company, Raskob persuaded them to elect Pierre, still a small stockholder, chairman of the board. Thereafter, Raskob urged the Du Pont Company to buy GM stock with some of its huge war profits. Through their holding company, Christiana Securities, the du Ponts eventually acquired a controlling interest in General Motors, nearly thirty-six percent of the firm's common stock. Although Pierre served as GM president from 1920 to 1923, Raskob as treasurer and chairman of the finance committee involved himself more deeply than any of the du Ponts in the automobile firm. Management and finance practices developed at Du Pont were applied to GM. Raskob devised the General Motors Acceptance Corporation to allow installment purchasing of automobiles, an important innovation which allowed many Americans with modest incomes to buy cars or to trade up to more expensive models. The company's sales and profits mushroomed. Raskob acquired a large personal fortune and a reputation as an extremely capable businessman.

An innovative and progressive businessman, Raskob advanced several proposals for improving the lot of workers, while at the same time staunchly defending free enterprise. He advocated a shorter work week both for the workers' benefit and because he felt that, faced with greater leisure, the worker would become more of a consumer. In 1929 Raskob suggested a "workingmen's trust," a scheme whereby workers would regularly invest a small portion of their wages in American industry. These ideas, advanced but not radical for the 1920s, reflected Raskob's view that if left alone by government, those who worked hard would succeed in an American economic system in which corporations had come to recognize their social responsibilities. Prohibition threatened this structure, he warned an Anti-Saloon League official: "If the Prohibition Amendment and laws at present on our books (remember I say 'if') are resulting in a lack of respect for law in our institutions, it is but a short step to such a lack of respect for property rights as to result in bolshevism."[54]

Captain Stayton first wrote to Raskob about the AAPA in the fall of 1919, but the businessman, wrapped up in GM affairs, did not respond immediately. Finally, however, along with Irénée du Pont, Raskob accepted Stayton's invitation to join the association by sending in his dollar in June 1922. Again like Irénée, he began increasing his contributions to the association in mid-decade.[55] He explained his motives in a letter to a prohibitionist in June 1928, which the AAPA reprinted and distributed. "I am not a drinking man (this does not mean I never take a drink), am a director in corporations employing over three hundred thousand workmen and have a family of twelve children ranging in ages from five to twenty-one years," he began. "The thing that is giving me the greatest concern in connection with the rearing of these children and the future of our country is the fact that our citizens seem to be developing a thorough lack of respect for our laws and institutions, and there seems to be a growing feeling that nothing is wrong in life except getting caught." Raskob was devoted to his family. "What impressions are registering on the minds of my sons and daughters," he asked, "when they see thoroughly reputable and successful men and women drinking, talking about their bootleggers, the good 'stuff' they get, expressing contempt for the Volstead Law, etc.?" Although he tried to teach his children temperance, Raskob wondered "what ideas are forming in their young and fertile brains with respect to law and order?"[56]

As a devout Roman Catholic in an age when his church faced frequent attack, Raskob also worried about the intolerance reflected in prohibition. The dry law attempted to regulate conduct in which Catholics had been much more accustomed than Protestants to engage. Dry Protestants had no right, he felt, to impose their will "in matters where no moral wrong is involved and where liberty is curtailed." Government should no more prohibit drinking than deny religious freedom, Raskob said, and the attempt to do so would result in rebellion. He wished instead to see a re-creation of "the atmosphere that gave birth to our Constitution—an atmosphere of brotherly love which spells tolerance and a keen respect for ourselves, for each other, for our laws, institutions and, above all, respect for our God, our liberty and our freedom."[57] To Raskob, reestablishment of tolerance came increasingly to mean an end to the Eighteenth Amendment.

Pierre S. du Pont, 1930   Prints and Photographs Division, Library of Congress

Irénée du Pont (third from left, second row) with members of the AAPA, WONPR, and Crusaders in Wilmington, Delaware, August 1932

Eleutherian Mills Historical Library

John J. Raskob (left) and James W. Wadsworth, Jr. (right), 1928
Wadsworth Papers, Library of Congress

Raskob, the du Ponts, Wadsworth, Cassatt, Murphy, and Joy each described his opposition to national prohibition differently, but all shared an underlying view: federal government intrusion was upsetting their stable, comfortable world. Many of these repeal advocates saw themselves as self-made men. Whether from modest backgrounds, as were William Stayton, John Raskob, or Grayson Murphy, or from comfortable families like the Wadsworths or the du Ponts, they achieved their eminence through personal effort. Understandably, these successful men believed strongly that the traditional American system of individual freedom and circumscribed government worked. Ability, unrestrained by government, would prove itself, they did not doubt. All felt the federal government had gotten into an area where it ought not to be, could not do an effective job, and was causing all sorts of turmoil. Many of these men had been used to drinking alcoholic beverages before national prohibition, and though they kept liquor on hand and served it to their friends, they felt uncomfortable violating the law. Government should not enter, they asserted, where the individual was competent to decide. Clearly, they worried that if government could interfere in such unprecedented fashion in personal habits, it could also intrude more deeply into other matters, such as business affairs. Such power in the hands of a distant central government insensitive to local conditions and impervious to local influence, such as they were used to exercising, alarmed them especially.

Had prohibition succeeded in ending the use of alcohol, at least some would have continued to criticize the law in principal, but government's failure to enforce its declared will caused even more dismay. The American system of government provided a combination of freedom and order which had allowed their ancestors and themselves to acquire and preserve wealth and status. The prospect of a government strong enough to strip them of property and privileged position disturbed them, but no more than the spectre of government too weak to defend them. When they talked about loss of respect for law, they were genuinely concerned that scoffing at prohibition might lead to disobedience to other laws. Government's ability to enforce law was in doubt. They worried that the props might be removed from under their own positions. The Constitution had always symbolized the stability and limitations of government power, but a Constitution provided little protection if it could be radically and (apparently) easily changed or its provisions could not be enforced. Stayton's AAPA expressed the concerns of those to whom the prohibition question became one of constitutional stability.

Those entering the AAPA with articulated objections to prohibition were joined by other well-to-do men enlisting in the repeal campaign without announced motives. Between 1925 and 1927 the association began to receive substantial contributions from, among others, Edward S. Harkness, noted

New York philanthropist whose father had been an early business partner of John D. Rockefeller, Robert T. Crane of Chicago's Crane Company, and Arthur Curtiss James, the principal owner of the Phelps Dodge Corporation and reputedly the largest individual holder of American railroad stocks. Older members such as John A. Roebling and Charles H. Sabin, the president of New York's Guaranty Trust Company, who was a friend of both Wadsworth and Pierre du Pont, increased their donations as well.[58] These men no doubt shared the concerns of those of similar background who did make plain their objections to prohibition.

Men like James Wadsworth and Pierre du Pont, once committed to an enterprise, very quickly became impatient unless visible progress was being made toward their goal. Before long, they concluded that the Association Against the Prohibition Amendment was not effectively organized and had bogged down despite growing opportunities. Several signs confirmed such judgments.

In 1926 two congressional hearings had brought the AAPA new visibility and stature. A senate judiciary subcommittee held hearings in April to consider changes in prohibition. The AAPA and other members of the Joint Legislative Committee not only gained a forum but heard some of their criticisms of the law repeated by federal prohibition enforcement officials.[59] In contrast, Wayne Wheeler's refusal to appear before the subcommittee tarnished the drys' image.[60] Two months later a special Senate committee investigating political campaign irregularities called Captain Stayton to testify. He willingly and candidly answered all questions put to him concerning AAPA organization, methods, and finances and provided a list of all who had contributed one hundred dollars or more since the association's incorporation. On the immediate issue of AAPA support for the allegedly corrupt William S. Vare in a Pennsylvania Senate primary, Stayton explained that the other two candidates had taken unacceptable positions on prohibition. The association appeared single-minded in pursuit of its goal, if not always fortunate in its choice of candidates, and was spared further involvement in the Vare scandals. Several newspapers complimented Stayton on his frank testimony, contrasting it to the hostile, secretive demeanor of Wheeler in his appearance before the committee.[61]

The AAPA did not, however, take advantage of this new visibility by stepping up its efforts. Although membership and contributions were growing, Captain Stayton continued to run the association with the assistance only of Gorton C. Hinckley, the national secretary; Louis Livingstone, the national field secretary; and a small staff. They continued to put forth a steady stream of propaganda—letters, pamphlets, press releases, and posters—emphasizing the evils of prohibition. But Stayton and his aides approached political contests very cautiously, unwilling to risk the AAPA's financial resources unless certain of victory.[62] Thus they failed to take a leading role in the eight state prohibition referendums of 1926.

Two of the most active state AAPA branches differed publicly with national leaders in 1926, and one withdrew from the organization. Prohibition became an issue in a Wisconsin Republican senatorial primary even though the state AAPA had announced that both major candidates had taken acceptable stands. Less than a week before the election, the national AAPA placed a full-page endorsement of progressive Governor John J. Blaine in newspapers throughout Wisconsin. Conservative incumbent Irvine L. Lenroot's position on prohibition, including his votes for the Eighteenth Amendment and the Volstead Act, was described as "evasive and wholly unsatisfactory." Immediately, the state AAPA executive committee repudiated the Blaine endorsement, praised Lenroot, and sought to dismiss their state chairman for his role in the affair. A spokesman said that Stayton knew nothing of internal state affairs and was "highly presumptuous when he comes to Wisconsin and interferes with the rights and duties of our electorate.... Captain Stayton has a personal axe to grind and is wholly without authority to talk for our organization."[63] The AAPA opposition to centralized national authority appeared to have influenced attitudes toward its own leadership. The furor, a by-product of a complex political struggle in Wisconsin, died after Blaine narrowly won the primary.

An even more striking example of discord developed in Missouri, where the state AAPA branch had long been strong and active. In the spring of 1926 the Missouri division, with Stayton's apparent blessing, obtained 50,000 signatures on a petition proposing a November ballot on repeal of state prohibition laws. It hoped to demonstrate that a majority of Missourians disliked prohibition. When both Republican and Democratic state platforms opposed the referendum, Stayton feared a defeat that would set back the repeal cause. He sought to blunt its effect. On September 3 he advised voters to withhold their support, calling the referendum unnecessary since both Senate candidates were wet. The referendum lost almost two to one. The Missouri division head, Judge Henry S. Priest, bitterly charged the national AAPA with reneging on promised financial and publicity assistance. With that aid, he said, the referendum would have carried. "We feel constrained to repudiate your dictatorship and express our indignation at the betrayal of the confidence we reposed in you," Priest wrote angrily to Stayton, "and to withdraw from your organization and to form one of our own to prosecute the worthy cause which we feel your stupid one-horse management is endangering."[64]

Public bickering and defections embarrassed the AAPA, but less obvious troubles plagued it as well. Grayson Murphy wrote Wadsworth after the April 1926 Congressional hearings on modification that he and Julian Codman felt Stayton's health was breaking down. With the burdens of the repeal fight increasing, he continued, the association needed "a keen, well informed political organizer."[65] At the same time, the 65-year-old captain reciprocally developed a strong personal dislike for Codman when he became convinced that the Joint Legislative Committee counsel was trying to take over or split the association.[66] Wadsworth agreed that Stayton was showing strain but confessed uncertainty as to what should be done.[67]

By late 1927 impatience with the tactics of the AAPA and the slow progress of the repeal movement came to the surface. James Wadsworth decided to do more about reorganizing the association than merely discussing it with Codman and Murphy. The former senator agreed to host a meeting of prominent men opposed to prohibition at his Washington home on December 12 to consider what should be done. Wadsworth consulted Stayton on the guest list, and the AAPA staff made the arrangements. Shortly before the meeting, Stayton, perhaps seeking to mollify critics, pledged a vigorous campaign in 1928. At two large dinners in New York in late November, he revealed plans to raise three million dollars and seek a national referendum on prohibition.[68] Wadsworth immediately wrote Murphy that "we shall most certainly discuss his suggestion at our meeting in Washington, and I think we can make it apparent in a perfectly good-natured way that there may be a wiser policy. Thus far, I have found him quite amenable to suggestions, providing they are spoken to him direct."[69] Nothing more would be heard of Stayton's proposals.

Both veterans of the antiprohibition crusade and recent adherents to the cause attended the session which began December 12 and lasted into the following day. AAPA founders Stayton and Hinckley were there along with longtime members Charles H. Sabin and William Bell Wait of New York, E. Clemens Horst of San Francisco, and Sidney T. Miller of Michigan. Austen G. Fox represented the New York Modification League. Congressional sympathizers, Senators Edge and Bruce as well as Representatives H. S. White of Colorado and Charles Linthicum of Maryland, were present along with former representative Thomas W. Phillips of Pennsylvania. Pierre du Pont, Edward S. Harkness, former Assistant Secretary of War Benedict Crowell of Cleveland, Codman, and Murphy rounded out the group. Elihu Root, Henry B. Joy, and Representative James M. Beck of Philadelphia, a former solicitor general, were among those invited who could not attend.[70]

The relatively recent converts in the group, principally Wadsworth and Pierre du Pont, seized the initiative. With Wadsworth presiding, the gathering quickly agreed that national prohibition had failed and an opportune time had arrived to work on a solution. Wadsworth appointed two committees to explore how to proceed. The first, including Wait, Edge, Fox, Stayton, and Wadsworth and chaired by Julian Codman, was to discuss objectives. The second, headed by Pierre du Pont and involving Harkness, Sabin and Stayton, was to consider how the effort should be organized. Codman's committee recommended undertaking an effort to modify the

Volstead Act to ban only distilled liquor. The committee, wishing repeal but seeing no immediate prospect of achieving it, was willing to put off repeal to an uncertain future. They also suggested a decentralization of the antiprohibition campaign, with state committees doing most of the work and money raising. Finally, Codman personally proposed terminating the AAPA, which he felt had alienated modificationists, made enemies, and developed a reputation as being "somewhat futile." He felt a new organization, with a different name, would help the cause.[71] The influence of Codman, one of the more prominent early repeal leaders, clearly was declining, for these recommendations were brushed aside for the quite contrary plans developed by Pierre du Pont's committee.

When the full group met again at Wadsworth's home on January 6, 1928, the du Pont committee submitted a terse four-page report which commended Stayton for his past efforts and proposed that the AAPA be continued under the same name, "as descriptive of our ultimate purpose." At the same time, the report urged a more active effort to repeal both the Volstead Act and the amendment. Most importantly, however, the committee recommended a new pattern of organization. A national board of directors would be chosen for the value of their endorsement of the association. Captain Stayton would serve as chairman of this board. Effective power, however, would be in the hands of a five-to-seven member executive committee of this board. The executive committee would meet frequently, formulate policy, and actively supervise the affairs of the AAPA. An experienced executive would be appointed president of the association to work with Stayton and, like the captain, report to the executive committee. The report proposed that Henry Curran of New York, a friend of Wadsworth's, be offered the presidency. Both Curran and Stayton would be paid from a special fund guaranteed by members of the board so that the general funds of the association could be directed toward the public campaign for repeal and be expended primarily in the locality where they were raised. Finally, a publicity campaign should be launched with the aid of advertising expert Bruce Barton, who had offered his assistance and with whom the committee had met. The report was quickly accepted in its entirety.[72]

Pierre du Pont, fittingly enough, became chairman of the new executive committee. The entire AAPA reorganization showed his strong influence. The pattern of a window-dressing board of directors and a strong executive committee to which the organization's spokesmen and administrators were responsible followed closely the general management systems established at the Du Pont Company and General Motors. In each instance, important policy decisions were discussed and determined by an informed committee rather than by an individual. Being elevated to the chairmanship of the board of directors somewhat displeased Stayton, who wanted his former power and independence. But Pierre du Pont, whose resources could accelerate the campaign, wished to proceed in a fashion he regarded as efficient and productive, so Stayton accepted the changes gracefully. The executive committee originally included, in addition to Pierre, his brother Irénée, Stayton, and four of Wadsworth's good friends: Grayson Murphy, Charles Sabin, Benedict Crowell, and Henry Curran. Edward Harkness was invited to serve, but declined. The following year Wadsworth himself joined, and later Robert Cassatt became a member. Otherwise membership did not grow. The executive committee met often, almost weekly at the outset, and every member participated actively in its deliberations.[73] Whereas earlier Stayton had guided the AAPA with a free hand, after the reorganization, the executive committee, led by Pierre du Pont, clearly directed the association.

The executive committee, at Wadsworth's suggestion, chose Henry H. Curran president of the restructured AAPA. Curran and Wadsworth had been Yale classmates and had worked together for years in New York Republican politics. They shared a mutual dislike for federal power and a desire for a revival of state and local government. Curran, fifty-one in 1928, had been a reporter, a lawyer, a publicity agent, and a reform Republican alderman in New York City. In 1919 he had won an upset election to become borough president of Manhattan, and two years later he lost a race for mayor. Such partisan services earned him appointment in 1923 as commissioner of immigration for the Port of New York, a post he resigned in 1926 to become counsel for the City Club of New York. Curran's facial expression, it was said, was as wooden as Buster Keaton's, but his aggressive, outspoken manner and sharp sense of humor appealed to the association.[74]

After announcing Curran's appointment January 15, 1928, the executive committee began seeking members for the board of directors. Hoping to create a large, distinguished board with members from every state to emphasize the repeal movement's respectability, the committee at first sought fifty men, then rapidly raised its sights. From the nucleus of the executive committee, the board grew to 67 by mid-April, 103 by year's end, and 435 by 1933.[75] With various executive committee members suggesting candidates, and Stayton or Pierre du Pont making most of the contacts, the board came to include notables from various fields—law, education, medicine, organized labor—but, not surprisingly, for the most part from the heights of American business and finance. Among those initially invited to join were Charles M. Schwab of United States Steel, Henry H. Westinghouse of Westinghouse, Paul W. Litchfield of Goodyear, Fred Fisher and Charles F. Kettering of General Motors, Eldridge R. Johnson of Victor Talking Machine Company, R. L. Agassiz of Calumet and Hecla Copper, and W. W. Atterbury of the Pennsylvania Railroad; all but the first three accepted. Longtime AAPA supporters Arthur Curtiss James, Henry B. Joy, and John J. Raskob reinforced the board's business character. Some well-known nonbusiness critics of prohibition were invited to membership: Elihu Root, Columbia University president Nicholas Murray Butler, and former senator Oscar W. Underwood declined; author and editor Fabian Franklin, Carnegie Institute president Samuel Harden Church, and AFL vice-president Matthew Woll accepted. Finally, the heads of AAPA state divisions and all nonlegislators who had attended the Wadsworth meetings were enlisted as well.[76] The board of directors met rarely, performed nominal duties, but, as intended, provided a showcase for prominent advocates of repeal.

The association's reorganization generated additional financial backing. Members of the executive committee and the board of directors contributed large sums of money to the repeal fight. In March 1928 Pierre and Irénée du Pont each offered $15,000 toward the immediate expenses of the expanded AAPA program. By the end of June, they had pledged a further $25,000 apiece for the following twelve months. John Raskob promised $25,000 a year for two years and indicated his intention to continue the contribution for three more years if the association made satisfactory progress. In addition, Pierre, Irénée, and Raskob joined Lammot du Pont, Sabin, Harkness, and Thomas W. Phillips in pledging for five years a special annual donation of $5,000 each to pay salaries of $25,000 to Curran and $10,000 to Stayton. Executive committee members Grayson Murphy and Benedict Crowell contributed lesser, but still substantial sums, as did directors Arthur Curtiss James, Eldridge R. Johnson, John Roebling, Fred Fisher, Robert T. Crane, and William I. Walters.[77]

Although such donations meant that the AAPA was never again impoverished, its leaders still complained continually about insufficient resources. Repeal organizations never possessed more than a minor fraction of the funds that temperance forces had expended in winning passage of the Eighteenth Amendment. National AAPA spending from 1928 through 1933 averaged about $450,000 per year, slightly exceeding income. In the year of its greatest income, 1930, the association was forced to borrow over $100,000 to cover its $818,137 expenditure. AAPA total income during the six years preceding repeal roughly equaled the Anti-Saloon League's annual budget of $2,500,000 during the final stages of its fight for national prohibition.[78] Nevertheless, from 1928 onward the antiprohibition organization possessed enough funds to engage in a vigorous campaign.

The announcement in April 1928 of the AAPA's reorganization and the initial membership of its new board of directors, helped foster an image of the association as a tiny elite. Previously, prohibitionists had charged the AAPA with being a front for brewery interests, pointing to the several thousand dollars Stayton had accepted from Fred Pabst and other brewers. Drys now claimed that the association was nothing more than the creature of a small, wealthy, selfish clique interested in reducing its income taxes.[79] Fletcher Dobyns repeated these charges in his 1940 book on the repeal movement, and they were apparently plausible enough to be accepted by several generations of historians.[80] Association leaders, either because they failed to appreciate the negative consequences of such a reputation or because they did not care, allowed the dry characterization to go unchallenged. Annual reports of the association emphasized the backgrounds of members of the board of directors, and public disclosures of contributions highlighted the small group of large donors.

The AAPA began to file contribution and expense reports with the House of Representatives after passage of the Federal Corrupt Practices Act in 1925. Antiprohibitionists had urged passage of this legislation to expose Anti-Saloon League finances. The league, however, refused to report, claiming to be nonpolitical.[81] The reporting law required identification of the donor and amount of contributions of $100 or more, but only the annual sum of smaller gifts. Quite naturally attention focused on big contributions even when, in 1926, 53 percent of the association's income came from gifts of under $100. As the proportion of these smaller gifts fell to 22 percent of total income in 1928 and 14 percent in 1932, the spotlight shone even more brightly on large donations. The corrupt-practices act reports, which were not always complete, showed that between 1928 and 1932 the three du Pont brothers contributed $113,000, $137,000 and $147,000, respectively, while John Raskob, Robert Crane, Arthur Curtiss James, and Edward Harkness gave from $64,000 to $70,000 apiece. These seven men provided almost 29 percent of the association's income during those five years. Several other directors made substantial donations as well, from $3,000 or $4,000 up to as much as $40,000.[82] Since an outside judgment had to be based only on these reports to the House of Representatives, the image of the AAPA as the tool of a tiny band of very wealthy individuals was understandable, indeed could hardly have been avoided.

A somewhat different impression emerges, however, upon examination of contribution summaries and balance sheets prepared annually for the executive committee. For many years these documents remained buried in the files of Pierre du Pont and his colleagues. Beginning in 1929, the AAPA kept records of the number as well as the amount of contributions. In that year, eighty directors of the association donated $298,938, an average of $3,737 per director; this represented 65 percent of the year's income but less than 1 percent of the number of all donations. During the same time, 7,911 donations of $1 to $25, averaging $5.11, were received. While this amounted to only 9.5 percent of total receipts, it was 83 percent of the number of contributions. Another 1,573 members (16 percent of all donors) gave amounts of more than $25, averaging $74.84.[83] Clearly the AAPA received much broader support than the Federal Corrupt Practices Act reports revealed.

From 1930 on, the association compiled figures for four categories of donations: those from national directors, from state division directors (an inconsequential group which never produced more than 2 percent of income or the numbers of donations), from members giving $100 or more, and from those giving smaller amounts. Each year, the last classification accounted for more than 90 percent of all contributions. During the peak income year of 1930, this represented 21,588 gifts averaging $8.05, or 28 percent of all money received. During the next three years, the number of donors in all categories declined sharply, no doubt because of the depression. Small donors produced only 13 to 15 percent of association income, but they provided 7,952 gifts averaging $8.13 in 1931, 5,163 averaging $8.55 in 1932, and 3,495 averaging $10.74 in 1933. From 1928 through 1933, the years during which the AAPA was supposedly only a front for a handful of rich businessmen, it received contributions from an average of 10,049 individuals a year, more than 9 out of 10 of whom made only modest gifts.[84]

The pattern of support for the association is somewhat further clarified by the few membership figures available. These statistics seem less significant than contribution reports since a person could belong to the AAPA by simply endorsing its position. No dues were required. After the 1928 reorganization, new lists were compiled, and earlier inflated claims dropped. Early in 1930, Curran reported 150,000 members nationwide; at the end of the year, he claimed 360,000. Enrollment reached a peak of 550,000 in 1932.[85] Since only a small portion of these people went even so far as to send the AAPA a dollar, these figures can be regarded as a fairly modest measure of strength. Nevertheless, it is worth noting that over a half million persons did take at least a small step to register their agreement with the association's position.

When all the available evidence is considered, an image of the AAPA emerges which varies considerably from the one painted by its dry opponents. A core of wealthy, enthusiastic leaders did pour large sums of money into the association. None provided the organization with anything like the $350,000 which John D. Rockefeller gave the Anti-Saloon League between 1900 and 1919. Nor did they represent the sole backing for the AAPA, any more than Rockefeller, Henry Ford, and S. S. Kresge did for the Anti-Saloon League. In fact, for the principal organization of both wets and drys, well over 90 percent of all donations were under $100.[86] Thousands of small contributors provided the AAPA a second level of participation, and the large nonpaying membership offered a base of support. Thus, the association appears to have been a political pressure group of fairly normal composition, with an inner circle of dedicated, deeply involved leaders and a much larger, though more modestly engaged, body of sympathizers.

The AAPA attracted an average of ten thousand donors a year and altogether over half a million adherents because of the appeal of its positions. The message of constitutional peril which Stayton began to preach in 1919 drew not only the du Ponts, Wadsworth, and their friends to the association, but many others as well. A sizable group of Americans stood ready by the late

1920s to support an organization which opposed national prohibition as an expansion of federal power. Whether their first concern was uncontrolled crime, lost local influence on political decisions, restrictions of individualism, corruption of youth, possible tax increases, or spreading liquor abuse, they could identify with an organization which preached against prohibition on the basis that it tampered with the Constitution and placed too much authority in the hands of a central government. The leaders and supporters of the AAPA were drawn to common ground which was clearly staked out in a resolution which the new board of directors, as one of its first acts, adopted in the spring of 1928:

> RESOLVED, That we shall work, first and foremost, for the entire repeal of the Eighteenth Amendment to the Constitution of the United States, to the end of casting out this solitary, sumptuary statute, the intrusion of which into constitutional realms has so severely hurt our country. The question of whether prohibition or regulation is the more effective relation of government to the liquor traffic is utterly subordinate to the distortion of our Federal Constitution by compelling it to carry the burden of a task which is an affair for the police power of each of our forty-eight separate and sovereign states, and never should be the business of the Federal Government.[87]

6 FROM THE JAWS OF DEFEAT

In 1928, the year the Association Against the Prohibition Amendment reorganized, national prohibition became a major topic of political debate. The liquor issue loomed large in the presidential contest between the favorite of the drys, Herbert Hoover, and the hope of the wets, Alfred E. Smith. Smith's decisive loss in his quest for the White House represented another in a long series of defeats for antiprohibitionists, yet his candidacy began linking the Democratic party to the repeal cause. Perhaps most crucial, the man Smith selected to chair the Democratic National Committee for the next four years, John J. Raskob, belonged to the AAPA board of directors. By contrast, the campaign as well as the new administration's interpretation of the election results strengthened Republican support for prohibition. Partisan alignment on national prohibition, which would accelerate during Hoover's term and significantly influence repeal, began to take shape during 1928. The AAPA, determined to carry on, and cheered by signs of sympathy among Democratic leaders, quickly dispelled any discouragement it felt about the election returns and launched an aggressive offensive. The repeal movement steadily gathered momentum thereafter.

Prior to 1928 the prohibition issue had cut across party lines. Both parties counted convinced drys and ardent wets among their ranks. Almost equal numbers of Republicans and Democrats had voted for the Eighteenth Amendment when it won congressional approval in 1917. The Republicans, as the party in power after 1920, and therefore responsible for law enforcement, had gradually been taking on more of a prohibitionist cast, although not without objections from many of its most illustrious supporters. Meanwhile, the northern urban wing of the Democratic party opposed prohibition, while the southern and western element of the party favored it. The two branches had fought to a standstill in 1924. The AAPA, steadfastly nonpartisan, drew from both sides. Among its leaders, for instance, William Stayton, Charles Sabin, and Grayson Murphy were lifelong Democrats, while Henry Curran, Irénée and Pierre du Pont, James Wadsworth, and Henry Joy were equally devout Republicans. So long as the platforms and national candidates of both parties continued to skirt the prohibition question, as they had in 1920 and 1924, with pious statements about the need for law enforcement, no connection could be made between victory or defeat and a position on the alcohol ban. Once distinctions began to be drawn between the two, a process in which the AAPA played an important role, conclusions could be and were reached regarding the law's popularity. The affixing of a dry label on the Republicans and a wet label on the Democrats, despite continued division within each party, proved crucial. From 1928 on, a Republican electoral triumph came increasingly to be looked on as a renewed endorsement of prohibition, while a Democratic victory came to be regarded as a mandate for repeal.

In 1928 the prohibition debate erupted first at the Republican convention in Kansas City. Senator Reed Smoot's draft platform called for observance of the Constitution and all laws, but drys led by Senator William Borah demanded a specific pledge of prohibition enforcement.[1] Republican opponents of the law, headed by Columbia University president Nicholas Murray Butler, James Wadsworth, and Henry Curran, urged the platform committee to admit the failure of the Eighteenth Amendment. "We ask this not only for the practical reason that Federal prohibition, after eight years of trial, is doing more and more harm and less and less good—that it just doesn't work —which is a fact that you and I and everybody else knows," said AAPA president Curran. "Our plea rests on higher ground than that. It goes far beyond all questions of liquor traffic. It rests on the safety of the Constitution itself." He explained, "The introduction of this solitary sumptuary statute into our Constitution has already nullified the very spirit of that well-tried instrument. The prohibition amendment is more than a meddling barnacle on the framework of our ship of state. It is a direct puncture in the sound hull of local self-government by our local sovereign states."[2]

A long, stormy debate preceded committee rejection of the Butler plank advocating repeal of the Eighteenth Amendment on states' rights grounds. Instead platform drafters approved Borah's plank, pledging "observance and vigorous enforcement" of the amendment. Butler appealed to the full convention, but won only two to three hundred voice votes from the 1,089 delegates on a motion to table his plank. Returning to New York, Butler declared that the convention's actions had made the Republicans a prohibition party.[3]

The Republican convention's nominee for the presidency, Secretary of Commerce Herbert Hoover, gave substance to Butler's characterization. In his speech formally accepting the nomination, Hoover announced his opposition to repeal of the Eighteenth Amendment and his support for "efficient enforcement of the laws enacted thereunder."[4] Long identified as a progressive, Hoover believed that the path to social improvement lay in the direction of greater cooperative public action and less materialism. Equal opportunity for individual development, to him the central American ideal, occasionally required the sacrifice of self-interest to advance the general good. The commerce secretary felt encouraged that a major step in this direction had been taken with national prohibition. "The crushing of the liquor trade without a cent of compensation, with scarcely even a discussion of it," he wrote in 1922, "does not bear out the notion that we give property rights any headway over human rights."[5] Three years later he gave prohibition credit for "enormously increased efficiency in production" and, together with other recent improvements, for having "raised our standard of living and material comfort to a height unparalleled in our history and therefore of the history of the world."[6] As he sought the presidential nomination in 1928, Hoover found himself pressed by his party's leading dry office-holder, Senator Borah, to again state his views on prohibition. Hoover readily admitted that "grave abuses" had occurred under prohibition but argued that these must not be allowed to break down the Constitution or the laws. He placed great faith in efficient, honest administration of existing statutes to achieve the desired goal, and he rejected Volstead Act modification as an impermissible nullification of the Constitution. He told Borah and repeated in his acceptance speech these oft-quoted and more often misquoted words: "Our country has deliberately undertaken a great social and economic experiment, noble in motive and far-reaching in purpose. It must be worked out constructively."[7] By this statement, Hoover revealed himself as a much more convinced defender of national prohibition than either of the two Republican presidents he was trying to succeed. Ever afterward, he would be remembered as a prohibitionist who considered the Eighteenth Amendment "a noble experiment."

The Democratic convention, which followed its rival by two weeks, took a position on prohibition which was, to say the least, ambiguous. Meeting in Houston, the Democrats chose a dry platform and a wet candidate. Attempts to strike a balance between the dry southern and western wing of the party and the wet northern wing did not entirely succeed. The resolutions committee, having heard from speakers on both sides, including Captain Stayton, considered a subcommittee's compromise plank promising law enforcement but acknowledging the people's right to change the Constitution. After long and heated discussion, the platform committee, to avert a threatened dry floor fight, instead approved a plank which condemned Republican law-enforcement failures during the previous eight years and pledged Democrats "to an honest effort to enforce the Eighteenth Amendment." In presenting the platforms to the convention, the resolutions committee chairman, Senator Key Pittman, stressed that the plank in no way prevented any party member from seeking repeal of the prohibition amendment. Wet and dry spokesmen verified Pittman's interpretation.[8] Such qualifications and the nomination of Alfred E. Smith, well known as an opponent of prohibition ever since the 1923 Mullan-Gage law repeal, diminished the importance of the platform declaration.

Once nominated, Governor Smith telegraphed the Houston convention from Albany that he would defend the Constitution and the laws, changes in which could only be made by the people through their legislative representatives. At the same time, however, he felt it the president's duty to point the way to a solution of unsatisfactory conditions. "Corruption of law enforcement officials, bootlegging, lawlessness are now prevalent throughout this country," Smith charged. He believed fundamental changes should be made in existing provisions for national prohibition, specifically a return to state and local liquor control.[9] Smith's statement, which he repeated in its entirety during his August twenty-second speech formally accepting the nomination, helped identify the Democratic candidate and his party, despite its dry platform, as sympathetic to the wet cause.

Smith quickly strengthened his party's new image by appointing John Raskob to chair the Democratic National Committee. The choice caught the country by surprise. Raskob lacked any prior political experience. His sole Democratic affiliation was a close friendship with Smith, whom he had met in 1926. Indeed *Who's Who* listed the new Democratic national chairman as a Republican who had voted for Coolidge in 1924! Raskob was known to the public only as a business genius, a devout Catholic who contributed heavily to his church, and an outspoken advocate of prohibition repeal.[10] In the spring of 1928 the Association Against the Prohibition Amendment had appointed Raskob, a six-year member, to its board of directors, and only a month before Smith's announcement, the association had distributed 100,000 copies of a Raskob statement vigorously attacking national prohibition.[11] In accepting the chairmanship, Raskob asserted that there were times in the life of a nation when nonpoliticians must take an active interest in government. Praising Smith's stand on prohibition, he left no doubt why he felt a critical moment in American history was at hand.[12] Observers correctly saw the selection of Raskob as an attempt to reassure businessmen and to court their support,[13] but the naming of a prominent AAPA director as national chairman also symbolized a growing Democratic attachment to the antiprohibition cause.

The 1928 campaign itself emphasized emerging partisan divisions on the prohibition issue. While Hoover defended the Eighteenth Amendment, Smith responded by charging that prohibition was a farce that had bred corruption, caused the rise of crime, and encouraged disrespect for all law. The Democratic candidate attacked prohibition during speeches in Albany, Milwaukee, Nashville, Chicago, Philadelphia, and Baltimore, proposing that Congress raise the maximum legal alcohol content and return liquor control to the states.[14]

Smith's stand alienated dry Democrats, yet brought some hitherto independent or Republican repeal advocates into the Democratic fold. John Raskob and Pierre du Pont led the way. Raskob's feelings regarding prohibition motivated him to work tirelessly and to personally contribute $530,000 to the Smith campaign. Privately he told Irénée du Pont, "Personally, I can really see no big difference between the two parties except the wet and dry question, and, of course, some people say the religious question, which I think both of us agree should form no part of politics."[15] As the campaign heated up, Raskob wrote, "There are few things more necessary or expedient to the future welfare and well-being of our country and its people than some modification of existing liquor laws that will restore temperate life. The Republican Administrations have failed to do this and I think have deliberately, through the prohibition enforcement unit, kept the truth with respect to what is happening under our liquor laws, from the people."[16]

Pierre du Pont, who made large political contributions in response to Raskob's appeals, confessed that he found some Democratic positions just as hard to accept as some Republican views, but he insisted on the overriding importance of prohibition repeal.[17] He wrote to Lammot, "Mr. Hoover has put himself in a position where he cannot recommend material changes in the law. Smith undoubtedly will do so." Pierre lectured his Republican-leaning younger brother, "You gloss over the charges against the Enforcement Division under Republican regime. If for no other reason the change should be had."[18] He further revealed his feelings to an Erie, Pennsylvania, correspondent: "While it is a disagreeable thing to desert one's political party, I felt this year that the party had deserted me and I could not stand for their ignoring the Prohibition question and for their methods of enforcing the Volstead Act. The latter especially is an outrage and an insult to our people."[19]

AAPA president Henry Curran announced that, despite twenty years of service in the Republican party and a continuing loyalty to the GOP, he too intended "to vote for Governor Smith to be President, because he is right, and Mr. Hoover is wrong, on the one great issue of this campaign—prohibition."[20] Several normally Republican directors told Stayton they intended to support Smith in 1928 because of prohibition. On the other hand, some influential AAPA board members, James Wadsworth and Irénée du Pont among them, were not ready to abandon the Republican party, saying that since neither platform espoused repeal, other considerations had decided their vote. The association itself remained officially neutral, unwilling to take sides because neither party had completely accepted its position and because its own leaders were not yet fully agreed.[21] Yet the visibility of many prominent AAPA supporters within the Democratic ranks reinforced the party's increasingly wet image.

At the same time, supporters of prohibition lined up behind Hoover's candidacy. Defections from the Democratic column in the South, where much dry enthusiasm was centered, exceeded any election since the Civil War. Bishop James Cannon, head of the Methodist Board of Temperance,

Prohibition, and Public Morals and leading dry spokesman since the 1927 death of Wayne Wheeler, campaigned vigorously throughout the South against Smith.[22] "The greatest moral menace on the present political horizon," proclaimed A. A. Schoolcraft, a minister from Lunenburg, Massachusetts, "is the dripping-wet figure of Governor Smith."[23] Midwestern drys also voiced opposition to the New York governor. Strong objections arose to Smith's Catholicism and his urban, immigrant-family background as well as his stand on the Eighteenth Amendment. Still, Robert Moats Miller's conclusion seems valid: "to millions of Protestants prohibition was truthfully an issue of transcendent importance;...when Protestants said they opposed Smith because of his wetness, they meant precisely what they said."[24]

Many factors besides prohibition and religion influenced voter decisions in 1928, among them contentment with Republican economic policies and high regard for Hoover's long record of extraordinary achievement. "In 1928 Hoover would have won over any Democratic candidate," concluded David Burner in his careful study of the Democratic Party during the twenties. "No Democrat, whatever his faith and whatever his political program, could have vanquished the party that was presiding over the feverish prosperity of the later twenties."[25] Hoover polled 21.4 million votes, or 58.2 percent of the ballots, soundly defeating Smith, who received 15.0 million, or 41.2 percent of the votes. Recent analysts of the returns have correctly attributed the electors' choice to a complex variety of economic, religious, ethnic, party-loyalty, and other motives, and not any single issue.[26]

Nevertheless, in an immediate sense the 1928 election represented disaster for those opposing national prohibition. The wet position was seen as quite unpopular. Even apparently dispassionate contemporary observers announced that Smith's position on prohibition was one of the principal reasons for his downfall. Nor did it escape notice that the new Congress contained more drys than ever before. In the fifty-six House and Senate races where the AAPA had interceded, only nineteen wets won, eleven of them incumbents and five others victors in contests where the association had approved both candidates. Henry Curran ruefully concluded, "In 1928 we were licked."[27]

The incoming administration likewise viewed the returns as signifying approval of national prohibition. In his inaugural address, Hoover confidently urged state and local officials to help enforce the law and called on the public to support government efforts. To do otherwise, he warned, would destroy respect for all law. Citizens had the right to work for prohibition repeal, conceded the new president, but meanwhile their duty was to discourage its violation. Those who felt that repeal was impossible regarded Hoover's statement as a clear endorsement of prohibition. Drys announced their delight with the speech. Newly appointed Secretary of Commerce Robert P. Lamont publicly resigned from the AAPA, finding continued membership incompatible with service in Hoover's cabinet.[28] Partisan distinctions on the prohibition issue might help the repeal cause if the political climate changed, but the 1928 election results were understood to convey the message that prohibition enjoyed broad support.

Al Smith's defeat, while it deeply disappointed wets, strengthened their resolve.[29] The sympathy shown their position by a major, albeit badly drubbed presidential candidate and the elevation of one of their own to a party chairmanship convinced AAPA leaders that repeal was attainable. At the same time, they could not help but be aware of how far they stood from mustering the overwhelming support needed to amend the Constitution. Given the need for such a change to be approved by two-thirds of Congress and three-fourths of the states, most legislators would hesitate to challenge the status quo on this sensitive issue unless they could perceive a substantial political consensus favoring repeal. Neither popular pressure nor political support for reversing the Eighteenth Amendment could be expected until experience or convincing arguments swayed a vast portion of the electorate. The AAPA executive committee determined to pursue a vigorous campaign to influence public opinion.

The prohibition issue had received superficial and emotional treatment during the 1928 campaign. What exactly Hoover intended by his vague talk of law enforcement had gone unquestioned. On the other hand, prohibitionists had vilified Smith for suggesting a return to local liquor control. Both wets and drys had seemed to feel that the validity of their dogmatically proclaimed positions must be self-evident. Exhortations had substituted for rational examination of prohibition's effect on American society. This had merely continued the established pattern of wet-dry debate. While prohibitionists regularly asserted that the law was generally effective and was yielding numerous social benefits, their opponents proclaimed the law unenforceable and warned that it produced crime and the breakdown of constitutional principles. Rarely did the public hear a serious, thoughtful, examination of prohibition and its impact. The handful of private studies drew on limited, inconclusive evidence. The federal government merely compiled arrest and liquor confiscation statistics. In 1926 the Social Science Research Council, finding existing information seriously inadequate, planned, but was unable to fund, a thorough, half-million dollar study of prohibition.[30] Public understanding of prohibition remained low. "It is fair to say that there has been much exaggeration and misrepresentation on both sides," the AAPA executive committee admitted early in 1928. "The dearth of facts is a remarkable manifestation of the fog of controversy which still obscures the study of Prohibition."[31] The association itself bore some responsibility for this state of affairs. Prior to its reorganization, AAPA public statements had frequently retold sensational stories of prohibition violations, publicized every increment, however modest, in the strength of the repeal movement, and proclaimed unconvincingly that "the Anti-Saloon League's grip is broken."[32]

Over the years, Stayton had mobilized a solid core of repeal support with his warnings of constitutional and social disaster. However, there was little chance of creating a political consensus of the magnitude required to achieve repeal on the basis of an abstract philosophy of government and predictions of social decay. The 1928 election helped the executive committee realize that most voters were not convinced of the need for or possibility of repeal. To be moved to demand repeal, they must see varied and impressive evidence of prohibition's ill-effects. Therefore, the AAPA pursued a new publicity campaign which, while reiterating the association's fundamental objections to the law, sought above all to present a wealth of verifiable and persuasive facts unfavorable to national prohibition.

In April 1928 the AAPA executive committee created departments of research and information to investigate and publicize the operation and practical effects of national prohibition, estimate its economic influence, and examine foreign systems of liquor control. New York social worker John G. Gebhart, who had participated in the Social Science Research Council's abortive study and compiled its only report, a survey of information sources, was hired to head the research department. The executive committee gave Gebhart a staff of three full-time and several part-time assistants, including an economist and several field investigators, and an annual budget of $100,000 at first, more later.[33] Between 1928 and January 1931 the department produced thirteen research pamphlets, of which more than 1,100,000 copies were distributed. The pamphlets and summaries prepared by the information department for use as news releases reached a larger audience than the association had ever attracted. According to the AAPA's own estimate, stories dealing with its investigations appeared in over 250 million copies of newspapers, an average of over 18 million copies per pamphlet. The research department, as well as releasing scores of statements, gave considerable assistance to sympathetic authors. In all, the association engaged in a substantial effort to bring new information about prohibition to a wide audience.[34]

The publications of the research department revealed the AAPA's fully developed positions and most broadly distributed arguments. They raised new objections to national prohibition while reinforcing the AAPA's traditional complaints about the law. They suggest the primary concerns of the repeal organization and how its earlier motives were retained and refined in the course of appealing for public support.

The research department first explored prohibition's stimulation of crime and corruption in government. Henry Joy urged investigation of "crime and outrages committed by members of the prohibition unit," while Thomas W. Phillips offered $2,500 to publicize "these outrages...to such an extent that it will make the prohibitionists blush with shame and possibly make Hoover come out and denounce them." Pierre and Irénée du Pont enthusiastically agreed.[35] The Joy-Phillips proposals, made in the midst of the 1928 campaign, bore political overtones, but the pamphlet, *Scandals of Prohibition Enforcement*, did not appear until March 1929, indicating a sustained concern with corruption. Drawing on official reports regarding five major cities, the pamphlet vividly described police department corruption in Philadelphia; Chicago's orgy of murder and bootlegging; graft indictments of the superintendent of police, over twenty policemen, and other officials in Pittsburgh; and Detroit and Buffalo border guard connivance in liquor smuggling. The federal prohibition bureau had dismissed nearly 1,300 employees for improper activities between 1920 and 1928, the report pointed out. Furthermore, Canadian records showed vastly increased liquor exports to the United States. Finally, the pamphlet described other "scandals" such as wiretapping to secure evidence, reckless use of firearms by prohibition agents, and declining judicial and penal standards caused by court and prison congestion.[36] The report cited William Howard Taft's 1915 prediction that national prohibition would transfer the liquor trade to criminals and require a large federal enforcement agency with sinister powers. "The reaching out of the great central power to brush the doorsteps of local communities, far removed geographically and politically from Washington, will be irritating in such states and communities, and will be a strain upon the bond of the national union," Taft had warned before becoming Chief Justice. "It will produce variation in the enforcement of the law. There will be loose administration in spots all over the United States, and a politically inclined national administration will be strongly tempted to acquiesce in such a condition."[37] The evidence in *Scandals of Prohibition Enforcement*, its authors concluded, fulfilled Taft's prophecy and demonstrated that the solution lay in a return to state liquor control.

The research department next emphasized prohibition's economic effect, a theme not frequently heard before, by computing its annual cost. Adding actual appropriations for the Prohibition Bureau and Coast Guard to estimated expenditures of the Customs Service and Justice Department, and deducting the $5,500,000 revenue from fines, produced a net federal enforcement expense of just over $36,000,000 in 1928. The research department also considered lost revenue from liquor taxes. Based on 1918 tax rates and per capita consumption for the final prewar, preprohibition years, 1910–14, 1928 federal liquor tax revenue would have exceeded $850,000,000. States, counties, and cities would have received an additional $50,000,000 at least. Combining enforcement expenses and lost revenue enabled the AAPA to announce in its May 1929 publication, *Cost of Prohibition and Your Income Tax*, that the bill for 1928 was $936,000,000. A second edition one year later set the 1929 total at $951,000,000. In comparison, the pamphlets pointed out, federal revenue from individual income taxes amounted to

$883,000,000 in 1928 and $1,096,000,000 in 1929.[38] The two editions of *Cost* carefully explained the AAPA calculations and avoided rhetorical attacks on the high price of prohibition. They became the most widely distributed of all AAPA research pamphlets, 209,000 copies being printed. Most significantly, estimated newspaper circulation of the cost reports reached nearly 80 million copies.[39] Antiprohibitionist concerns for economy in government would grow in prominence after the onset of the depression, but the *Cost* pamphlets demonstrate that they began even before the Great Crash.

In July 1929 a pamphlet entitled *Canada Liquor Crossing the Border* used Dominion Bureau of Statistics records to show that the United States received 90 percent of its northern neighbor's liquor exports as well as large quantities of passed-through Scotch whiskey and French wine. Over $31,000,000 of liquor was exported to the United States in 1927 alone. Before prohibition, Canada had annually sent about 30,000 imperial gallons of spirits across its southern border. While the figure dropped to 8,600 gallons in 1921, thereafter it rose steadily and since 1926 exceeded a million gallons yearly. American customs agents admittedly seized only 5 to 10 percent at the border. A 1924 treaty to exchange smuggling information did not help, and Canada proved unwilling to take further steps. The AAPA report, careful, detailed, and presented without editorial comment, once again underscored the futility of government efforts to stop the liquor traffic.[40]

Measuring the Liquor Tide, a broader survey of indexes of alcohol consumption, soon followed and became one of the more widely read research pamphlets. The association distributed seventy thousand copies, and stories based on it achieved a combined newspaper circulation of nearly forty-six million.[41] Bureau of Prohibition annual reports were quoted, showing steady increases in seizures of contraband liquor (from 153,000 gallons in 1920 to 32,500,000 by 1928) and distilling equipment (15,000 pieces in 1920; 260,000 in 1928). Census Bureau figures showed decreasing death rates from alcoholism during the war and first year of prohibition, but a steady rise, both urban and rural, thereafter. The 1928 rate, 5 alcoholism deaths per 100,000 population, approached preprohibition levels. Arrests for drunkenness in a group of over five hundred communities fell from 1917 through 1920, then doubled during the next eight years. States which kept such records reported corresponding increases in alcoholic insanity, arrests for drunken driving, and deaths from cirrhosis of the liver.[42] Concentrating on drinking patterns since 1920, *Measuring the Liquor Tide* ignored the question of whether conditions under national prohibition compared favorably with those prior to the passage of state and federal liquor bans. Nevertheless, the pamphlet's stark statistics reinforced the AAPA contention that intemperance had not been halted.

The AAPA investigated deaths resulting from efforts to enforce prohibition. *Canada Liquor* described several shootings of reputable citizens and suspected rum-runners in Minnesota, Michigan, and New York. A few months later, *Reforming America with a Shotgun: A Study of Prohibition Killings* estimated that about 1,000 civilians and officers had lost their lives in the course of Volstead Act enforcement. By comparison the federal government acknowledged 286 such deaths, while the *Washington Herald* claimed 1,360. Using federal reports, court records, and its own investigations, the research department described dozens of fatalities in detail. The emphasis was on unnecessary shootings of innocent victims, rather than deaths of bootleggers or prohibition agents engaged in gun battles. Agents shot at tires, stumbled and accidently discharged their weapons, or otherwise took wild shots which killed a suspect. The survey listed shootings of persons in flight or erroneously thought to have guns, of prohibition agents mistaken for bootleggers, and of innocent bystanders including children and even one United States senator, Frank L. Greene of Vermont (who survived a severe head wound). When states indicted prohibition agents for such shootings, federal attorneys intervened and caused cases to be removed to federal courts, where they generally won acquittals. This procedure was entirely legal, but the report implied that it was used to protect reckless agents. *Reforming America* underscored the AAPA argument that government prohibition-enforcement efforts endangered society.[43]

Justice Department reports provided the evidence for one of the AAPA's final studies, *Prohibition Enforcement: Its Effect on Courts and Prisons*. In 1916, according to the study, federal courts handled 20,432 criminal cases, But by 1929 the number had jumped to 85,328. In 1928 and 1929, prohibition cases accounted for nearly two-thirds of all federal district court criminal cases (as well as over half the civil suits against the government). Since the courts were unprepared for such an increase in slow and costly jury trials, it became necessary to resort to "bargain days" on which defendants agreed to plead guilty in return for a light fine or short sentence. Penal institutions found themselves overwhelmed, although two-thirds of convicted prohibition offenders were merely fined. By 1930 federal prisons held nearly twice their normal capacity, and the overflow crowded state and county jails. The AAPA concluded that the prohibition burden was preventing American courts and prisons from dealing with alarming increases in other forms of crime.[44]

AAPA research pamphlets reflected the association's foremost concern: loss of state and local self-control in government, causing dangerous social and political decay. With evidence compiled from government reports, newspapers, and other independent sources, the AAPA's reports appeared carefully prepared, well-reasoned, and objective. Newspaper wire services carried them as news rather than dismissing them as shrill partisan tracts. The pamphlets effectively documented and broadcast association charges that prohibition had failed in its purpose of stopping intemperance, yet had fostered crime and posed threats to traditional rights. Reflecting the AAPA's narrow view, the pamphlets made no mention of other features of American society—increased urbanization, business leaders' failure to observe laws, and high-level government corruption among them—which might account for increased crime, lost respect for law, and other disquieting conditions. With their shortcomings drawing few comments from anyone other than rabid drys, the pamphlets reflected the increasingly deft campaign of the revitalized association.

Leaders of the Association Against the Prohibition Amendment felt that other nations could show America better ways of encouraging temperance. The research department undertook an extensive examination of foreign systems of liquor control, sending investigators to Canada, Scandinavia, and western Europe.[45] A series of eight original and unusually interesting descriptive pamphlets resulted.

The first foreign study, *The Quebec System: A Study of Liquor Control,* reported glowingly on government-regulated liquor sales. To replace a much-violated prohibition law, Quebec in 1921 had given a government commission a sales and distribution monopoly on wine and spirits. Access to less intoxicating beverages was made comparatively easy, and to the most intoxicating, more difficult. Spirits could be purchased one bottle at a time in government stores for private consumption. The same stores could sell wine in unlimited quantities, and licensed restaurants could serve it with meals. Beer could be purchased in bottles from licensed stores and by the glass in licensed taverns. The plan worked well, the AAPA reported, with "remarkably low" per capita consumption of alcoholic beverages compared to the United States. Beer and wine were noticeably preferred. The law was observed; arrests for drunkenness had declined, except among American tourists; and Quebec received one-fifth of its government revenues from the liquor commission. Subsequent pamphlets described how most Canadian provinces had successfully adopted variations of the Quebec system. Nova Scotia and Prince Edward Island alone were attempting prohibition, and they had experienced increased intemperance, considerable bootlegging, and improper prescription of medicinal liquor. Pleased with much of Canada's locally determined approach to liquor control, the AAPA concluded, "The United States can profit by the record of our Canadian neighbors."[46]

European liquor-control systems also interested the AAPA. Sweden had set up government-supervised, privately financed monopolies to manufacture and distribute liquor. The Swedish plan, developed by Ivan Bratt, a physician, set the profit limit at 7 percent, removing economic incentives to encourage drinking. Beer and wine sales were unrestricted, but spirits were rationed and reduced or cut off altogether for persons who used liquor improperly. Official records showed that since the Bratt system began in 1914, convictions for drunkenness had dropped 57 percent, crimes of violence had declined 48 percent, and annual per capita consumption of spirits fell 35 percent, from 6.9 liters in 1913 to 4.5 in 1927. Meanwhile, Sweden's income from taxes on liquor manufacturing, imports, sales, and profits doubled, providing a sixth of government revenue. England licensed sellers of alcoholic beverages. The AAPA investigation credited reduced liquor consumption and intemperance in England to steady reduction since 1904 in the number of licenses, high excise taxes on intoxicants, and restriction of the hours of public sale. Denmark had reportedly achieved great gains in temperance by doing nothing more than placing very high taxes on spirits. Only Norway and Finland's temperance efforts were deemed failures; both had adopted national prohibition.[47]

The foreign studies received less public attention than did other research department publications. The AAPA published 40 to 80 thousand copies of each, and 187 thousand of *The Quebec System;* but newspaper stories about them never exceeded 15 million circulation and usually fell far short of that. They represented, however, a major AAPA effort at the time to determine, find, and call attention to satisfactory, temperance-promoting alternatives to national prohibition. Association leaders considered it as improper to force any new system of liquor control on the states as it had been to impose the Eighteenth Amendment and Volstead Act on them. Nevertheless, the executive committee spent over a year discussing various options. Pierre du Pont, who had been giving the matter considerable study ever since 1926, when he had first been attracted to the Quebec system, even published his own *Plan for Distribution and Control of Intoxicating Liquors in the United States.* Past abuses demonstrated that public protection required restrictions on intoxicants, he concluded. The guiding principle should be as free an access as could be made consistent with the protection of others. To this end, he was opposed to sale of liquor by the glass, or sale for consumption in a public place, for fear it would bring back the saloon. Furthermore, du Pont proposed that liquor abusers and persons under eighteen be restrained from drinking. Examination and licensing for fitness to purchase liquor appealed to him, as did the Swedish system of a state-regulated, private liquor-sales monopoly. Unrestrained private enterprise, he felt, might encourage drinking and restore the undesirable saloon. The Quebec system he gradually came to distrust, fearing that government employees could be corrupted, and doubting their fitness for commercial activity. The Swedish private monopoly, with prices set and profits regulated by the state, offered, he thought, the advantages of public regulation and efficient operation of the liquor trade.[48]

The foreign studies and du Pont's plan revealed a great deal about AAPA attitudes. Association leaders judged various programs first and foremost on their ability to provide temperance and freedom from crime. As a result, they endorsed the concept of strong governmental regulation. They did not approve of federal control, with decision-making far removed from those affected and not attuned to local variations, but they did accept regulation on the level of a province or small homogeneous nation (the supposed equivalent of a state). Association leaders also supported examination and licensing of individual drinkers, sale of liquor in sealed packages not to be opened or consumed on the premises where sold, strict limitation of private profit in the liquor business, and state price-fixing to keep prices down so as to discourage bootlegging. As they considered alternatives to national prohibition in the late 1920s, AAPA leaders revealed themselves as foes of a powerful, intrusive federal government, but not equally active state governments.

Two separate and substantial government inquiries into the operation of the liquor ban soon followed the AAPA attempt to build its case with well-researched and documented arguments. The furious but unenlightened campaign debate of 1928 and possibly the early AAPA research pamphlets brought recognition of the need for more, and more reliable, information on the effects of prohibition. Investigations by a congressional committee and a presidential commission, although controversial, added to the body of public information regarding the dry law. Furthermore, they appeared to deepen partisan differences and commitments in the controversy.

During the 1928 presidential campaign, Herbert Hoover had pledged to establish a prohibition study commission, and on the day he took office, Congress appropriated funds for the inquiry. In his inaugural address, the new president talked of disregard for law as "the most malign" danger to the country. Ineffective law-enforcement machinery and citizen indifference undermined justice. "To consider these evils, to find their remedy, is the most sore necessity of our times."[49] When he appointed the eleven-member commission in May 1929, Hoover asked it to consider the entire problem of American criminal justice and recommend improvements in the administration of federal laws. Some saw this as an attempt to divert Chairman George Wickersham, a former United States Attorney General, and the other members of the National Commission on Law Observance and Enforcement from focusing too intently on prohibition.[50] But the Wickersham commission, as it quickly came to be known, perceived the study of national prohibition as its principal responsibility. It quietly set about gathering information, engaging academic and professional experts to conduct special research studies on such topics as the causes and cost of crime, the police, juvenile delinquency, the courts, probation, prisons, and parole. The commission took testimony in private, examining representatives of labor unions, the Anti-Saloon League, and the Association Against the Prohibition Amendment. Except for a letter from Wickersham in July 1929 urging more state enforcement support, which New York governor Franklin Roosevelt read to a national governor's conference, and a brief, inconclusive interim report in January 1930 recommending minor changes in enforcement procedures and the transfer of the Prohibition Bureau from the Treasury to the Justice Department, the commission gave no indication for more than a year and half of what it was learning or what it would recommend.[51] One member of the commission became so frustrated by the pace of its work and its domination by the chairman and executive secretary that he submitted his resignation, which Hoover did not accept.[52] Nevertheless, the public presentation of information and the shaping of opinions fell to others during a time when the new administration had hoped to provide more effective enforcement and to build popular support for the law.

Early in 1930 the House Judiciary Committee decided to hold hearings to consider proposals for altering the Eighteenth Amendment. Since the last major congressional inquiry in 1926, prohibition agents had been put under civil service, enforcement appropriations had been increased, and maximum penalties for Volstead Act violations had been raised to five years' imprisonment or a $10,000 fine, or both. The latter legislation, known as the Jones Five-and-Ten Law, for its sponsor, Washington senator Wesley L. Jones, stirred particular controversy. The Judiciary Committee's highly publicized hearings, held between February and April 1930, gave wets and drys alike a chance to present their views on the Jones law, the functioning of the Prohibition Bureau, and the liquor situation in general.

The Anti-Saloon League, the Women's Christian Temperance Union, the Methodist Board of Temperance, Prohibition, and Public Morals, the Association Against the Prohibition Amendment, and lesser groups made their standard dry or wet arguments. Grayson Murphy made a statement typical of the nearly two dozen AAPA officers and directors who spoke: "In the first place, the eighteenth amendment is absolutely contrary to the spirit of the rest of the Constitution.... [This] has led to all sorts of government acts which are contrary to the spirit of the Constitution...[and] more crime, more corruption, more hypocrisy than any other law or set of sumptuary laws I have ever heard of in the world."[53] One of the few fresh approaches came from AAPA research director John Gebhart, who presented an impressive array of evidence on the evil effects of prohibition. He documented increases of drunkenness and crime since 1920, the adverse impact of prohibition on the legal and penal system, and the economic burdens of the law. Gebhart revealed a new study showing rises in both alcohol consumption and liquor prices since 1920. Prohibition had not stopped drinking, Gebhart concluded; it only increased costs to consumers and diverted profits into the hands of criminals.[54] Gebhart's fact-laden presentation, which attracted considerable attention and which drys chose to ignore rather than rebut, represented a major success in the AAPA educational effort, even though the only congressional response was to seek improved prohibition enforcement by finally moving the Prohibition Bureau to the Justice Department.

On January 20, 1931, President Hoover made public the Wickersham commission's long-awaited report on prohibition. In a statement released the previous day, Hoover had announced that while it found current enforcement unsatisfactory, "the commission, by a large majority, does not favor the repeal of the eighteenth amendment as a method of cure for the inherent abuses of the liquor traffic. I am in accord with this view."[55] The two-page statement of conclusions and recommendations, signed by ten of the eleven commissioners, to which Hoover referred, opposed prohibition repeal, return of the saloon, government liquor monopolies, or legalization of beer and wine. It found that enforcement was improving but still inadequate and needing greater federal appropriations. Buried in paragraph ten was the curiously phrased acknowledgement that some members "are not convinced that Prohibition under the Eighteenth Amendment is unenforceable and believe that a further trial should be made with the help of the recommended improvements, and that if after such a trial effective enforcement is not secured there should be a revision of the Amendment," and that others were ready for immediate revision.[56] The president rejected any such suggestions. "My own duty and that of all executive officials is clear—to enforce the law with all the means at our disposal without equivocation or reservation."[57]

A reading of the entire 162-page report, including the results of the commission's prohibition studies and the individual conclusions of each member, made apparent the serious distortions in Hoover's characterization of it. The finding of increased drinking since 1920, widespread bootlegging and official corruption, overburdened judicial and penal systems, lack of state support for enforcement, and damaged respect for law agreed with AAPA analyses. The report conveyed an underlying sense of skepticism as to whether prohibition could ever be made to work. Pierre du Pont thought the association itself could just as easily have written the body of the report. "The facts certainly track your citation of facts, and, in most cases, could not have been put in better words for our purposes," he told Henry Curran. "How the recommendations could have been drawn from the facts is beyond me."[58]

Individual statements which the eleven commissioners attached to the report clearly demonstrated that the "conclusions and recommendations" represented a political compromise, a clear effort at least in some eyes, to avoid embarrassing the Hoover administration.[59] The separate statements had little in common with the supposedly agreed upon summary. A preponderant majority of commissioners found the current system of national prohibition unenforceable or unwise; nine referred to the noticeable lack of public support for the law; and six wanted immediate change. Former Secretary of War Newton D. Baker and Monte M. Lemann of New Orleans (the only member who refused to sign the general report) favored outright repeal of the Eighteenth Amendment and the return of liquor-control responsibility to the states. Commissioner Henry W. Anderson had become so interested in descriptions of the Bratt system that he had traveled to Sweden to investigate personally the government-regulated liquor monopoly. Now he recommended its immediate adoption with slight reservations, technically only modifying the Eighteenth Amendment, but actually, by making liquor again available, repealing national prohibition. Four commissioners agreed completely with Anderson, and two more endorsed his solution if a further trial of prohibition were to prove unsuccessful. A reluctant chairman Wickersham saw problems with the Anderson plan, but he too regarded it as the best alternative if the continued prohibition enforcement he preferred were to fail. Only one commissioner, federal judge William I. Grubb, unequivocally favored further pursuit of prohibition in the hope of achieving better enforcement and public support. [60]

The obvious contradiction between the commissioners' individual views and what Hoover had presented as their shared conclusions caused an uproar. Wets and drys alike hardly knew whether to praise or damn the report. Both sides generally concentrated on portions which favored their cause. Many newspapers and journals noted the confusion which the report had caused and criticized the president for misleading the country about the commission's views. [61] The White House's own confidential analysis of several hundred newspapers, most of them small, found editorial opinion predominantly critical. [62] "What was done," charged Walter Lippmann, "was to evade a direct and explicit official confession that federal prohibition is a hopeless failure." [63] "Is his action either constructive or courageous? Is his treatment of the report in his message of transmittal even honest?" asked *The Nation*. [64] Another writer in *The Nation* more charitably described the president as having emphasized the report's few conclusions with which he could agree. [65] Others, Franklin P. Adams of the New York *World* for one, simply made fun of the commission:

> Prohibition is an awful flop.
>   We like it.
> It can't stop what it's meant to stop.
>   We like it.
> It's left a trail of graft and slime
> It don't prohibit worth a dime
> It's filled our land with vice and crime,
>   Nevertheless, we're for it. [66]

Frivolous oversimplification such as this perhaps most accurately reflected the reception given the report. At any rate, the confusion and controversy it generated ended any hopes that the Wickersham commission could resolve the national prohibition issue.

The Wickersham commission report did draw increased attention to the debate over prohibition. The study of existing conditions, which the AAPA shrewdly emphasized in its efforts to influence public opinion and which the House Judiciary Committee publicized and the Wickersham commission independently confirmed, produced a general agreement that the law was not effective. A majority of Wickersham commission members expressed admiration for the same remedy which appealed to AAPA executive chairman Pierre du Pont, a return of liquor under controlled conditions. Had it not been for the influence of President Hoover, it would have been clearly evident that the thinking of the Wickersham commission ran along the same lines as that of the AAPA.

The circumstances of the Wickersham report's release tied Herbert Hoover more firmly and publicly to the prohibition cause than ever before. While in 1928 Hoover had merely described national prohibition as "an experiment noble in motive and far-reaching in purpose," by 1931 he was saying that he opposed repeal and favored more effective enforcement. "So far as he is able," judged the *New York Times,* he has committed the Republican party to a thoroughgoing and unyielding policy of enforcing prohibition by the full power of the Federal Government."[67] The president unquestionably projected a strong, clear image as a defender of prohibition. Yet by resorting to his favorite problem-solving device, the fact-finding commission of experts, Hoover unwittingly provided ammunition for the dry law's opponents.

The political contest of 1928 had set in motion a new phase of the prohibition debate, one in which conditions under the law were closely examined and partisan positions began to be defined. By January 1931, when the Wickersham commission report was released, lines were drawn more sharply than ever before. While the commissioners assumed that Eighteenth Amendment repeal remained impossible and that a solution would need to be found in modification, however drastic, signs were already beginning to multiply that this might not be so. The encouragement which the Association Against the Prohibition Amendment received from the 1928 Smith campaign was being reinforced by various indications of growing popular and political support.

7 HARD TIMES, HOPEFUL TIMES

After a decade of national prohibition, disobedience, popular dissatisfaction, and organized efforts to overturn the law, all appeared to be on the upswing. Various measures of public opinion, though imprecise, showed a clear turning against the liquor ban by the end of the 1920s. Several important organizations, some old, some newly established for this sole purpose, expressed their members' hostility to prohibition and tried to translate this unhappiness into political change. The appearance of a sizable women's organization opposed to prohibition was particularly important. Meanwhile, dry societies, whether because of complacency, altered attitudes, or several spectacular instances of leadership misbehavior, lost members. Nevertheless, after ten years prohibition remained entrenched, and widespread, deep skepticism persisted, at least outside the ranks of militant antiprohibition organizations, as to the possibility of ever repealing the Eighteenth Amendment. The national economic collapse which began late in 1929 and gradually enveloped every aspect of American life affected the prohibition situation as profoundly as it did all else. The growing malaise of the Great Depression introduced new political and social as well as economic circumstances, greatly accelerating the revolt against prohibition and causing the prospect of repeal to be taken seriously for the first time.

Signs of spreading disenchantment with national prohibition appeared well before the stock market crash. In June 1928, voters in North Dakota narrowly defeated a referendum proposal to repeal the prohibition clause in their state constitution. Of some two hundred thousand ballots cast, 48.3 percent favored repeal. For a state which had entered the union in 1889 with prohibition in its constitution and had maintained a dry reputation ever since, this result astonished onlookers.[1] In November, Montana voters, who two years earlier had repealed their state prohibition enforcement act, refused by a slightly larger margin to reinstate the law. On the same day, three out of five Massachusetts electors voted to direct their state senators to ask Congress to initiate repeal of the Eighteenth Amendment. In contrast, four years earlier 50.5 percent of Massachusetts voters approved passage of a state prohibition law. In both Republican Montana and Democratic Massachusetts, the wet proportion of the vote ran far ahead of that for Alfred E. Smith.

In Montana the antienforcement vote stood at 54.1 percent, compared to 40.5 percent for Smith; in Massachusetts the repeal referendum won 62.6 percent, while Smith received 50.2 percent.[2] Then in April 1929, a month after Congress passed the Jones law and a new president, Herbert Hoover, called for states to enforce prohibition, a hard-fought referendum in Wisconsin produced an unusually heavy turnout and a 63.3 percent majority for repeal of the state enforcement law. The city of Milwaukee, where voting was heavy, chose repeal by a six to one margin, while a lighter vote throughout the rest of the state divided more evenly. In 1926 a higher proportion of Wisconsin voters, 66.3 percent, endorsed modification to permit 2.75 beer, but the 1929 referendum involved a much more advanced wet position.[3] Issues and circumstances varied, and the referendum campaigns differed as well. The Association Against the Prohibition Amendment, for instance, waged active campaigns in Massachusetts and Wisconsin, but did relatively little elsewhere.[4] Yet repeatedly in these four widely scattered and socially dissimilar states, a diverse electorate cast a large antiprohibition vote.

Early in 1930, the *Literary Digest* repeated its 1922 national public opinion survey on prohibition. In by far the largest poll it had ever conducted, the *Digest* reported that only 30.5 percent of all respondents (8 percent fewer than in 1922) supported prohibition, and only 29.1 percent (down 11 percent) favored modification to permit beer and wine. Those favoring repeal had doubled, from 20.6 percent in 1922 to 40.4 percent in May 1930.[5] The 4,800,000 ballots cast represented nearly one-fifteenth of the adult population, discounting possible bias in the *Digest* sampling technique. Interpreters of the poll saw a great shift from dryness to "moistness" and an even greater one from modification to repeal. Proportioning the moist vote between wets and drys and analyzing the results state by state led one statistician to assert that popular majorities in thirty-seven states were now prepared to vote for repeal.[6] The *Digest* poll, the *New Republic* and *Harper's* both stated, destroyed the assumption that at least thirteen states were irretrievably dry and that therefore repeal was impossible.[7]

By 1930 the nation's press both reflected and influenced this shift of public opinion. A *New York Herald-Tribune* survey of editorial policies of 110 daily newspapers in thirty-six states showed dry papers outnumbering wet papers by more than two to one in 1919. By 1930, however, they were evenly divided. More significantly, the average circulation of the wet papers was 100,600 copies, and the dry papers only 28,200. Interestingly the dry to wet shift occurred more frequently among small, nonmetropolitan newspapers. Crime, corruption, and enforcement failure were most frequently cited as reasons.[8] The survey left out such important wet newspapers as the *New York Times, Washington Post,* and the *Herald-Tribune* itself as well as many smaller papers with dry tendencies. Nevertheless, journalistic trends were evident.

Of ultimately greater significance to the repeal campaign than even these expressions of popular and press disenchantment with national prohibition, important new organizations began to join the AAPA crusade. In the past, the AAPA had found it difficult to work with other antiprohibition organizations and looked upon their proliferation as divisive. A group such as the Federal Dispensary Tax Reduction League, founded by a Denver physician, Frederick W. Buck, in 1923 to advocate a complicated plan for a government-operated, high-tax, regulated-sale alcoholic beverage system, attracted only about fifty thousand supporters and a handful of congressmen (principally Adolph J. Sabath of Chicago); Stayton considered it merely a money-making scheme. The FDTRL paid its fund-raisers a 50 percent commission and also supported a headquarters staff. Buck's organization stimulated one 1928 congressional hearing on reforming prohibition but otherwise accomplished little, while diverting resources from other efforts. "I have never known these people to do any actual work," Stayton told Pierre du Pont, "and I have known them to do things which were harmful."[9]

After the 1928 election, however, association leaders recognized the need to expand support for repeal beyond what the AAPA itself could attract, and they selectively encouraged new groups.[10] The rise of additional repeal-minded societies not only mobilized a wider spectrum of opposition, it also intensified lobbying efforts at both federal and state levels, generated more antiprohibition publicity, and helped dispel the impression that wets could never gain enough political support to achieve repeal. Dry claims that only drinkers, the liquor trade, and businessmen seeking tax reductions favored repeal became harder to sustain when large numbers of women, lawyers, and veterans announced their desire to abolish prohibition.

One of the main pillars upholding the idea that the Eighteenth Amendment was unrepealable was the belief that American women, since 1920 fully enfranchised, could be counted upon to support prohibition nearly unanimously. Women had contributed mightily to the passage of the Eighteenth Amendment, with Frances Willard, Anna Gordon, Carry Nation, Ella Boole, and the Women's Christian Temperance Union as prominent as any man or male organization in the dry campaign. Defense of the home, protection of the family, and concern for youth had often been cited as reasons for establishing prohibition and were expected to keep women firmly behind even an imperfect liquor ban. A decade of prohibition produced hardly any evidence to the contrary. The leading antiprohibition groups remained almost entirely male, with only men listed as directors. The AAPA's early attempt to create separate women's divisions, Molly Pitcher Clubs, had never attracted many members and was abandoned prior to the association's reorganization. But in 1929 an independent and effective women's repeal organization, the Women's Organization for National Prohibition Reform, appeared to challenge old assumptions.

The spirit propelling this organization was Pauline Morton Sabin of New York. Not a campaigner for women's suffrage, Pauline Sabin seized the Nineteenth Amendment's opportunities with seldom-matched energy and effect. She had been raised in a political family. Her grandfather, J. Sterling Morton, had been governor of Nebraska and Secretary of Agriculture under Grover Cleveland, while her father, Paul Morton, became Theodore Roosevelt's Secretary of the Navy when she was sixteen. Pauline Morton had been born to wealth and high social position as well. Her father had been vice-president of the Santa Fe Railroad before his cabinet service, and he became chairman of the board and president of the Equitable Life Assurance Society thereafter. Her uncle had developed the "When It Rains, It Pours" salt company. After a stylish but limited education in private schools in the United States and abroad, Pauline Morton made a social debut and then in 1907, at the age of nineteen, married a wealthy New York sportsman, J. Hopkins Smith, Jr. During the next few years, she bore two sons, involved herself in family life, and gave no visible indication of becoming a politically active, independent woman.[11]

In 1914 another side of Pauline Morton Smith began to appear. She divorced her husband and, with another woman, established a profitable interior decorating shop. She gave up this budding business career in 1916 to marry Charles Hamilton Sabin, chairman of the board of Guaranty Trust Company, but soon began to get interested in politics, at first through charitable work. "I found," the new Mrs. Sabin explained, "that on charity boards in New York City you had to have political pull to get things done."[12] Her preoccupation with politics quickly surpassed all else. Although her husband was a Democrat, Pauline Sabin shared her father's allegiance to the Republican party. In 1919 she was giving elaborate lawn parties for Republican organizations at the Sabin estate on Long Island. The same year she joined the Suffolk County Republican Committee and by 1920 had been made a member of the party's state executive committee. Mrs. Sabin helped found the Women's National Republican Club and served as its president from 1921 to 1926, building a membership of several thousand and earning a reputation as an excellent fund-raiser and a skillful organizer. When women were added to the Republican National Committee, as advisors in 1923 and full members a year later, Pauline Sabin became New York's first representative. She was a delegate to the Republican conventions of 1924 and 1928, cochaired Senator James Wadsworth's unsuccessful 1926 reelection campaign, and directed women's activities for the Coolidge and Hoover presidential campaigns in the East.

Pauline Sabin's concern over prohibition grew slowly. Initially she favored the Eighteenth Amendment, explaining later, "I felt I should approve of it because it would help my two sons. The word-pictures of the agitators carried me away. I thought a world without liquor would be a beautiful world."[13]

Gradually, however, intertwined motherly and political concerns caused her to change her mind. Her first cautious public criticism of prohibition came in 1926 when she defended Wadsworth's opposition to the law. By 1928 she had become more outspoken. The hypocrisy of politicians who would support resolutions for stricter enforcement and half an hour later be drinking cocktails disturbed her. The ineffectiveness of the law, the apparent decline of temperate drinking, and the growing prestige of bootleggers troubled her even more. Mothers, she explained, had believed that prohibition would eliminate the temptation of drinking from their children's lives, but found instead that "children are growing up with a total lack of respect for the Constitution and for the law."[14]

In later statements, she elaborated further on her objections to prohibition. With settlement workers reporting increasing drunkenness, she worried, "The young see the law broken at home and upon the street. Can we expect them to be lawful?"[15] Mrs. Sabin complained to the House Judiciary Committee: "In preprohibition days, mothers had little fear in regard to the saloon as far as their children were concerned. A saloon-keeper's license was revoked if he were caught selling liquor to minors. Today in any speakeasy in the United States you can find boys and girls in their teens drinking liquor, and this situation has become so acute that the mothers of the country feel something must be done to protect their children."[16] Finally, she opposed federal involvement in matters of personal conduct.[17] National prohibition, in sum, seemed to Pauline Sabin to be undermining American youth, the orderly, law-observing habits of society, and the principles of personal liberty and decentralized government, all important elements in the world of this conservative, upper-class, politically active woman.

She decided to found a women's repeal organization during a 1928 congressional hearing when Ella Boole, president of the WCTU, thundered, "I represent the women of America!" Sabin recalled remarking to herself, "Well, lady, here's one woman you don't represent."[18] In June 1928 she declared that "a serious burden rests on the men and women who have political responsibility" to state frankly their attitude toward prohibition. Women opposed to the law could, if organized, bring about a change, she predicted.[19] Her own well-developed sense of political responsibility led her to think of guiding such a movement.

After publicly criticizing prohibition, Pauline Sabin nevertheless campaigned for Herbert Hoover. She was a party loyalist and believed that Hoover's campaign promise to appoint a prohibition study commission showed a receptivity to reform. Disillusioned by Hoover's inaugural address and planning to work for a change in the law, Sabin resigned from the Republican National Committee in order to be unhampered by party ties. Within a month, she denounced the Hoover administration for supporting national prohibition.[20]

Pauline Sabin moved quickly to give form to her announced intention. She first enlisted the support of several of her New York friends and social peers, Mrs. Cortlandt Nicoll, Mrs. Coffin Van Rensselaer, Mrs. Caspar Whitney, and others. Then she added other upper-class women from throughout the country, among them Mrs. R. Stuyvesant Pierrepont of New Jersey, Mrs. William Lowell Putnam of Boston, Mrs. Amasa Stone Mather of Cleveland, Mrs. John B. Casserly of San Francisco, Mrs. Henry B. Joy of Detroit, Mrs. W. W. Montgomery of Philadelphia, and Mrs. Pierre S. du Pont of Delaware. During the next two months three organizational meetings were held in New York, and Mrs. Sabin toured parts of the East and Middle West to seek support.[21]

On May 28, 1929, 24 women from eleven states formally launched their endeavor at the fashionable Drake Hotel in Chicago. At an earlier meeting to select a name, the merely awkward Women's Organization for National Prohibition Reform (WONPR) won out over the truly dreadful Women's Legion for True Temperance. The Chicago gathering chose Mrs. Sabin chairman, formed a national advisory council of 125 women from twenty-six states, and reported organizing progress in several states. Despite frequent condemnations of prohibition, the group chose not to propose a specific remedy until more women from more states could come together in a general convention. Despite their caution, the mere fact that such prominent women had met to oppose prohibition drew national press attention.[22]

The WONPR opened a small office in New York. For a month or so, the AAPA paid the office expenses, but thereafter members' donations made the WONPR self-sufficient. Mrs. Sabin made speeches and wrote articles criticizing prohibition for producing more rather than less drinking, endangering youth, corrupting public officials, and breeding contempt for law and the Constitution. She struck a responsive chord, for in less than a year 100,000 members were enrolled and thirteen relatively autonomous state branches were formed. By its first convention, the WONPR had set its direction as a highly visible, nonpartisan, mass-membership, volunteer organization.[23]

Critics of the Women's Organization for National Prohibition Reform characterized it as a puppet of the Association Against the Prohibition Amendment, a new and more effective Molly Pitcher Club. The leaders of the AAPA, recognizing that women were an important obstacle to repeal, "in true Russian fashion, ordered their wives and daughters into the trenches," Fletcher Dobyns later charged.[24] The Anti-Saloon League and, especially, the WCTU wished to maintain the popular assumption that women overwhelmingly supported national prohibition. One dry leader scornfully called the WONPR nothing more than a clever advertising device.[25] Charles Sabin, after all, served on the AAPA executive committee and was the association's treasurer. After the 1928 election, he had participated in executive committee discussions of the need for a women's antiprohibition group.[26] But no

AAPA record reveals any steps having been taken to organize women. In politics, the resourceful and energetic Pauline Sabin always acted independently of her husband, who was an active Democrat throughout the years that she worked so diligently for the Republican party. In the spring of 1929 she appears to have acted independently once again in founding the WONPR. She kept M. Louise Gross and the vestiges of the Molly Pitcher Clubs at arm's length, despite Gross's many suggestions that the WONPR accept her leadership.[27] WONPR membership eventually so far exceeded that of the AAPA, and the family overlap between organizations was so slight, that the dry charge that these women were not acting of their own free will lacks credibility.

The Women's Organization for National Prohibition Reform's first national convention in Cleveland in April 1930 articulated a basic viewpoint regarding prohibition which would remain largely unchanged until the end of the repeal fight. Some elements of the women's critique of prohibition were peculiarly their own, while others were common throughout the organized repeal movement. The WONPR regarded itself as an advocate of temperance and believed that prohibition had reversed a trend toward moderation and restraint in the use of intoxicating beverages. WONPR spokeswomen expressed particular distress at the effects of national prohibition on children and family life. Temperate use of alcoholic beverages had been increasing up to 1918, maintained Mrs. Carroll Miller of Pittsburgh, one of the convention's principal speakers, "But suddenly true temperance was cast aside for a supposedly quick method of reform and Prohibition was inserted into our Constitution with the notion that people could be made better by legislative enactment rather than through precept, education, reason and persuasion." This flouting of the American belief in free will, she continued, had resulted in the law being ignored; crime, political corruption, and misuse of alcohol increasing; and a general disregard for all laws developing. "And because we women value the American home above everything else and because we wish the youth in that home to develop high character and to grow in uprightness toward decent citizenship," Mrs. Miller concluded, "we demand that these prohibition measures which hinder his development and growth, be repealed."[28]

Time and time again, the WONPR expressed concern over the violence, corruption, and alcoholic excesses of prohibition, all of which, they emphasized, had a harmful influence upon American youth. The organization reprinted an article by a New York juvenile court judge blaming national prohibition for increases in child neglect and young people's disrespect for law.[29] "Many of our members are young mothers—too young to remember the old saloon," Mrs. Sabin explained. "But they are working for repeal because they don't want their babies to grow up in the hip-flask, speakeasy atmosphere that has polluted their own youth."[30] The need to protect children and the home became central themes for the women's antiprohibition movement, just as they had been in the temperance crusade.

Also the WONPR shared AAPA distress at the apparent breakdown in the social fabric, the weakening of the ties between citizen and government which disdain for prohibition appeared to produce, and federal involvement in matters of individual behavior. The WONPR considered proposals calling merely for Volstead Act modification inadequate since, they argued, that would eliminate neither federal involvement in liquor control nor the criminal activity of bootlegging. The Cleveland convention unanimously declared:

> 1. We are convinced that National Prohibition is fundamentally wrong. (a) Because it conflicts with the basic American principle of local home rule and destroys the balance established by the framers of our government, between powers delegated to the federal authority and those reserved to the sovereign states or to the people themselves. (b) And because its attempt to impose total abstinence by national government fiat ignores the truth that no law will be respected or can be enforced unless supported by the moral sense and common conscience of the communities affected by it.
> 2. We are convinced that National Prohibition, wrong in principle, has been equally disastrous in consequences in the hypocrisy, the corruption, the tragic loss of life and the appalling increase of crime which have attended the abortive attempt to enforce it; in the shocking effect it has had upon the youth of the nation; in the impairment of constitutional guarantees of individual rights; in the weakening of the sense of solidarity between the citizen and the government which is the only sure basis of a country's strength.[31]

The elderly presiding officer of the Cleveland convention, Mrs. Henry B. Joy, once a prohibitionist like her AAPA-director husband, summarized the broad sweep of the WONPR's opposition to prohibition. After noting increased crime, overcrowded prisons, social and economic distress, and loss of respect for law and the law enforcement system, she concluded, "To my view, the prohibition conditions constitute the greatest menace to our country's welfare which has existed in my lifetime."[32]

The WONPR expanded even more rapidly after its Cleveland meeting. At the second annual convention in Washington in April 1931, Pauline Sabin announced total membership of 300,000 and "live, active organizations in thirty-three states." One year later, 600,000 members and forty-one state branches were claimed. By the 1932 election, membership reportedly had passed 1.1 million, and when repeal was achieved in December 1933, 1.5 million women belonged, it was said. Although membership claims are hard to verify and are probably somewhat exaggerated, on the basis of these figures the women's organization must be deemed by far the largest antiprohibition association, three times the size of the AAPA at its peak.[33]

Pauline Morton Sabin addressing the WONPR convention, Washington, D.C., April 1932   Prints and Photographs Division, Library of Congress

Participants in the third national WONPR convention gathered on the steps of the United States Capitol, April 1932
Eleutherian Mills Historical Library

The WONPR placed great importance on attaining a large membership. If vote-counting politicians were to take the repeal crusade seriously, they must realize that not all women supported prohibition. The national publicity chairman believed that no more important news could be distributed than reports of increased membership, for "it is the only way we have of demonstrating our strength nationally."[34] Branches in New York (where by April 1933, 305,000 women were enrolled), Illinois (214,000), Michigan, Ohio, and Pennsylvania (each about 100,000), California, Massachusetts, Missouri, and New Jersey (between 50,000 and 65,000 apiece), and Connecticut (35,000) became especially significant. Quite a few other states reported several thousand members, and by the end of 1933 only Arkansas, Kansas, Louisiana, Nevada, Oklahoma, and South Dakota lacked any organization. In general, the group grew strongest in the northeast and remained weakest in the states of the old confederacy. Four to 6 percent of the state's women joined the WONPR in Connecticut, Delaware, Illinois, and New York. State branches took considerable pride in announcing that membership had exceeded or doubled or even—in the case of Illinois in 1933—reached thirteen times that of the state WCTU. When national WONPR membership reached 400,000 in December 1931, surpassing the total claimed by the WCTU, it was considered a major milestone in the organization's history.[35] The WONPR's rapid and enormous growth, according to James Wadsworth, "made a lot of men wake up and realize that, 'By heavens, there is a chance of getting repeal if the women are going to join with us!'"[36] Women prohibitionists, not surprisingly, were less pleased. One wrote to Pauline Sabin, "Every evening I get down on my knees and pray to God to damn your soul."[37]

The WONPR assaulted the stereotype of total female support for prohibition in other ways. States branches distributed literature, lobbied legislators, studied liquor control systems, held public meetings and parades, and campaigned for repeal candidates or against prohibitionists.[38] Nationally, the women's organization disputed WCTU claims, based on convention resolutions of the General Federation of Women's Clubs, that all three million federation members endorsed prohibition. Asserting that many of its own adherents also belonged to the federation, the WONPR in February 1932 challenged the GFWC to conduct a membership referendum on prohibition. Although no such poll was ever held, the federation fell silent on the prohibition issue. The WONPR had again undercut claims that women universally favored national prohibition.[39]

Why was the WONPR so successful in attracting support and thereby shattering the image of women as unswerving prohibitionists? Some observers suggested that many women enlisted to improve their social standing, to associate with and emulate the fashionable ladies who led the organization.[40] To some degree, this may have been the case. Scarcely a description of

Pauline Sabin was published which failed to mention her grace and delicate beauty, her fine taste in clothing, and her prominence in New York society. Magazines as diverse as *Vogue, Time, McCall's, Smart Set, Liberty, The New Yorker, Forum,* and *Vanity Fair* all pointed out the high social position of the WONPR leadership.[41] A writer for *Vogue,* in an early article on the women's organization, exclaimed, "It always takes an important lady to set a style, one with considerable manner and chic. Just such ones have started the organized women's movement for prohibition reform."[42]

All too often, however, the efforts of American women have been dismissed as trivial whatever the motives or achievements involved. A common means of discounting women's serious activity has been to attribute it to a mere quest for domestic improvement or social advancement. The women's organization, although largely middle and upper class in composition, drew women of various backgrounds and not only socialites. A noticeably higher percentage of WONPR members were working women than was the case in the population as a whole. A number who took up the repeal issue were regularly involved in politics, while far more participated in charitable or other civic causes.[43] It seems unlikely that such active women were persuaded to join simply to follow fashion. One New York WONPR officer suggested that the importance of the social standing of the organization's leaders lay in the encouragement it gave to concerned but cautious women. "The fact that the published list of sponsors contains the names of some of the most highly respected women in the country," said Mrs. Christian R. Holmes, "inspires confidence in those who have wanted to join us, but did not dare. They are no longer afraid to come into the open and declare themselves."[44]

Undoubtedly, the growth of the WONPR was not inhibited by the desire of some women to follow "chic" social leaders and to share in the considerable acclaim being given this new women's crusade. However, substantive objections to prohibition appear to have weighed heavily on the minds of many who joined the Women's Organization for National Prohibition Reform. Published surveys of female antiprohibitionists, although admittedly quite limited, show them sincerely concerned that prohibition was subverting youth, the home and family, the economy, and respect for all law.[45] The decision of the WONPR to declare the mild goal of "Reform" in its name, despite its commitment to full repeal, may have boosted membership somewhat, but the general outspokenness of the organization suggests that most women knew exactly what they were joining and accepted the WONPR platform. Serious opposition to national prohibition, rather than social climbing, seems to have been the principal reason that, beginning in 1929 and 1930, hundreds of thousands of women aligned themselves with the repeal movement.

In mid-1927 a few prominent New York attorneys formed their own small antiprohibition group. In December they began to speak out against the

Eighteenth Amendment, calling it inconsistent with the spirit and purpose of the Constitution and Bill of Rights. The amendment and the laws enacted thereunder, they charged, confused and hindered the administration of other laws and generally impaired respect for law. By October 1928 the group had established a small office and employed an executive secretary, Helena P. Rhudy.[46] The following January they formally incorporated as the Voluntary Committee of Lawyers (VCL), with Joseph H. Choate, Jr., as chairman of an executive committee and Harrison Tweed as treasurer. Choate, the son of a renowned constitutional lawyer and ambassador to Britain, and Tweed, eventually president of the Bar Association of the City of New York, held partnerships in two of New York's most distinguished law firms. They typified the leaders of the bar who made up the membership of the VCL. The committee never became large, despite Mrs. Rhudy's travels and correspondence to recruit attorneys. At its peak in 1932, it listed only 3,626 members.[47] Choate called it "an odd organization" and explained that "things were run by a vague but able Executive Committee in New York in which everyone did what he thought best."[48] New York City remained the committee's focal point, although Chicago and Philadelphia developed sizable contingents, and eventually 80 percent of all members came from outside New York. The VCL, dependent on small contributions from members, only once, in 1930, enjoyed an annual budget as high as $15,000.[49] Because of the stature of Choate, Tweed, and many of its other members, the influence which the VCL exerted, however, proved disproportionate to its size and budget.

The Voluntary Committee of Lawyers forged strong ideological and personal bonds to the Association Against the Prohibition Amendment. Joseph Choate had belonged to the AAPA since at least 1926. Several other VCL leaders, many of whom knew the du Ponts, Charles Sabin, Grayson Murphy, Raskob, and other association leaders from legal, banking, or corporate contacts, eventually became AAPA directors. Defense of constitutional tradition and a stable society stood uppermost in the minds of both groups. In its incorporation statement, the VCL asserted:

> The Eighteenth Amendment and the Volstead Act violate the basic principles of our law and government and encroach upon the powers properly reserved to the states and the people, [and] the attempt to enforce them has been productive of such evils and abuses as are necessarily incident to a violation of these principles, including disrespect for law, obstruction of the due administration of justice, corruption of public officials, abuse of legal process, resort by the government to improper and illegal acts in the procurement of evidence and infringement of such constitutional guarantees as immunity from double jeopardy and illegal search and seizure.[50]

The essential issue in prohibition, Frederic R. Coudert argued in one of the VCL's few pamphlets, was the constitutional problem of power distribution between the states and nation. The Eighteenth Amendment, he said, subverted the federal system, undermined law enforcement, and destroyed respect for law. "American lawyers must assume the leadership in the struggle for the restoration of our Constitution."[51]

While a few members argued publicly against national prohibition, the Voluntary Committee of Lawyers mainly worked quietly behind the scenes, where its prestigious membership gave it considerable influence with other lawyers. Wherever it gained a hearing, the committee urged the local bar to adopt resolutions opposing the Eighteenth Amendment and the Volstead Act. Between 1928 and 1930, bar associations in New York, Philadelphia, Boston, Detroit, Washington, St. Louis, San Francisco, and Portland, Oregon, as well as the state bars of New Jersey, Nevada, and Virginia declared themselves in favor of returning the regulation of liquor to the states. At the American Bar Association's convention in Memphis in October 1929, members began lobbying for a repeal resolution from the national body. The following July the ABA, conscious that the issue would be brought before its next convention, and eager to avoid a bitter public fight, polled its members on whether to hold a prohibition referendum. When they overwhelmingly agreed, a simultaneous vote on the question of retaining or discarding the Eighteenth Amendment was tabulated. With three-fourths of ABA members voting, 13,779 favored repeal and only 6,340 opposed it.[52] The announcement of these lopsided results in November 1930 dealt national prohibition a severe blow by putting the largest, most inclusive organization in the legal profession on record as rejecting prohibition by a two-to-one margin. The Voluntary Committee of Lawyers had quietly engineered an important victory for the wet cause. Two years later, at a crucial stage of the repeal process, its special expertise and influence would again prove invaluable.

Another antiprohibition society appeared on the scene about the same time as the WONPR and the VCL. In May 1929 a group of young Cleveland businessmen led by Fred G. Clark, a thirty-nine-year-old lubricating oil company president who had worked for Benedict Crowell during World War I, established a local organization known as the Crusaders. Clark later recalled that the St. Valentine's Day Massacre in Chicago, the bloody result of rivalry among bootleggers, moved them to action. The growing power and wealth of gangsters and the decline of law and order in society caused by prohibition concerned them, he said. By January 1930, when they claimed 4,000 members in Cleveland and decided to make the Crusaders a national antiprohibition organization for young men, Clark and his colleagues also held prohibition responsible for the declining economic condition of the country.[53]

The Crusaders set themselves a goal of ten million members, each paying one dollar dues, by 1932. It is doubtful, however, that they even reached the one million members they eventually claimed. Their efforts featured bombastic rhetoric and loose structure. In Mississippi the Crusaders executive committee included a young novelist from Oxford. Twenty-five years later the author, William Faulkner, could barely recall the organization, saying it was probably something he got excited about and signed his name to "one hot summer night over a bottle of gin."[54]

The AAPA sought to cooperate with the Crusaders, especially through an executive committee member, Benedict Crowell, who lived in Cleveland. The sons of several AAPA leaders joined the new society. By mid-1931, however, Henry Curran was beginning to find the Crusaders uncooperative. In September the AAPA president reported that the young men's group was in serious financial trouble, and a year later research director John Gebhart regarded them as insignificant. The Crusaders never became an important voice on the national scene, although they concocted some elaborate publicity stunts and may have had grass-roots influence in some states.[55]

None of the individual or collective unhappiness with national prohibition appeared likely to bring down the Eighteenth Amendment as the 1920s wound to a close. Few Congressmen, even those who disliked prohibition, wished to risk dry wrath by supporting a repeal resolution. Many continued to hope prohibition could be made effective and looked to President Hoover's National Commission on Law Observance and Enforcement to find a way. Wets were unable to muster a third of the Senate or a fourth of the House of Representatives in the February 1929 vote on the Jones Five-and-Ten bill, establishing heavier penalties for prohibition violations.[56] A two-thirds vote of Congress to submit the repeal question to the states clearly was not in prospect. But the stock market crash of October 1929 and the general economic collapse which followed produced a new and unexpected set of circumstances.

Throughout the 1920s, prohibitionists gave the law credit for the prevailing prosperity. Indeed, with enforcement more difficult than expected, they cited prohibition's economic benefits as a major justification for maintaining it. In a book titled *Prohibition and Prosperity*, Samuel Crowther called the liquor ban, "The one great and fundamental change that has taken place in this country during the past ten years." In his view, the dry law "sought to throw a dam across that part of the river of purchasing power which formerly flowed uselessly for liquor and to re-route the stream through turbines which might usefully turn to create wealth. Today the dam is built and the money which formerly went for drink is the motive power of our prosperity."[57] Crowther argued that money spent on liquor was absolutely wasted, while money saved by prohibition was spent on other things and generated more production, more wages, and more profit. Furthermore, preventing workers from drinking increased industrial efficiency. Workingmen were spending less on liquor and gaining the true liberty which could only come with wealth. Only higher income groups who could afford it without reducing their other expenditures now drank, said Crowther.[58] Right up to the moment of collapse, both prohibition advocates and the unsympathetic attributed prosperity to the influence of the liquor ban.[59] Then the tables were turned, and the claims of prohibition's effect on the economy were used against the law.

The Association Against the Prohibition Amendment had occasionally complained of national prohibition's cost, but as the depression deepened, the association began to examine the law's economic aspects in more detail and to dispute claims of its benefits. Prohibition increased government expenditures and reduced revenues, the AAPA proclaimed. Repeal would help alleviate economic distress. Such arguments found an attentive audience in a nation increasingly beset by economic troubles and uncertain about the cause of its misery.

In October 1930 the AAPA research department challenged claims of prohibition's economic benefits in a pamphlet entitled *Does Prohibition Pay?* Unless the nation was realizing a net savings in the expenditure for drink, the pamphlet began, the dry premise must collapse. Estimating domestic liquor production on the basis of annual output of hops, wine grapes, and corn sugar minus the amount of these commodities accounted for by legitimate industry, the association calculated that per capita beer consumption was down three-fourths compared to prewar levels, but wine consumption had doubled, and consumption of spirits was up 10 percent. At current bootleg prices, the annual national liquor bill amounted to $2,848,000,000, nearly a billion dollars more per year than had been spent for intoxicants before the war. Therefore, prohibition had achieved no net savings. New industrial technology, steady employment, the availability of new commodities, and the expansion of credit had accounted for economic growth in the 1920s, the research department concluded.[60]

This widely reported AAPA liquor bill estimate was challenged by prohibitionists, but accepted in other quarters. Some even thought the figure too low. Clark Warburton, a Columbia University economist who assisted Gebhart in his early research but then departed to conduct his own investigation, presented a wealth of evidence supporting the association's claim that prohibition had not contributed to prosperity. Warburton agreed with the AAPA's calculation of liquor consumption. However, his estimate of the annual expenditure on liquor, five billion dollars in 1929 and four billion in 1930, the first year of the depression, considerably exceeded the AAPA's.[61]

The association soon began making vigorous use of an argument first broached in 1929 in *The Cost of Prohibition and Your Income Tax.* A new brochure, *The Need of a New Source of Government Revenue,* maintained that prohibition repeal could wipe out the federal deficit. In the seventeen states considered likely to approve liquor sales, 1918 tax rates would generate over $900,000,000 in federal revenue per year, the association predicted. A later pamphlet reported that the net cost of enforcing prohibition from 1920 through 1931 totaled $310,000,000, and that lost federal liquor-tax revenue for the same period amounted to roughly $11,000,000,000. Without prohibition, the study continued, the federal budget could have been balanced, the national debt substantially reduced, and taxes on incomes and profits decreased. "The present serious financial situation in which our federal government is placed could have been mitigated, if not entirely avoided," the report concluded, "had we not, by adopting national prohibition, abandoned a steady and dependable source of revenue."[62]

When the AAPA raised economic objections to prohibition, drys saw only self-interest. For years they charged that wealthy wet leaders only wanted repeal so that liquor could be taxed and income taxes reduced. The Anti-Saloon League accused Irénée du Pont of saying that "one of his companies would save $10,000,000 in corporation tax if we should have, say, the British tax on beer."[63] In 1926 Captain Stayton had so quoted Irénée. Irénée explained to a friend that he had told Stayton in private that "if liquor were taxed and paid to the Government instead of being taxed double and paid to the bootleggers, the Government could reduce profit and income taxes by 50% which in the case of General Motors Corporation alone would result in a reduction of their taxes by $10,000,000." Irénée had presumed that "this would be paid either to stockholders as dividends or, what is more likely, be distributed in the form of lower prices on motor cars."[64] Drys sought "to discredit anyone who was opposed to them and to disregard the possibility that any of their opponents might be even halfway decent people," he complained. As for himself, he opposed the evil conditions of intemperance, the government's total loss of control over the liquor traffic, and the corruption of law enforcement. He did feel that corporate profits taxes, which furnished the funds formerly supplied by liquor taxes, could be eliminated if the tax on alcohol flowed to the government instead of to bootleggers and corrupt officials.[65] Irénée pointed out that Anti-Saloon League economic motives were just as open to question:

> You evidently believe it is better to tax the profits of a corporation than to tax beer. No tax is levied on beer today. Why do you wish that manufacture be exempt of taxation like church property, and why do you attempt to hold me up as one with ulterior motives for his beliefs?
>
> Have I not got greater grounds for assuming that you are interested in bootlegging and the enormous profits therein by maintaining the present outrageous conditions?
>
> ... I do not make such an accusation, but I think you are misguided and unfair.[66]

Nevertheless, prohibitionists created the impression that the AAPA had acted merely out of financial self-interest.[67]

Undeniably, the economic situation concerned the members of the Association Against the Prohibition Amendment. As did many other people at the time, they saw unwise fiscal policy as the depression's cause. Restoration of a vigorous economy depended, they felt, upon a balanced federal budget trimmed of unnecessary expenditures and upon tax reductions to release more money for private enterprise and profit. They considered it both foolish and unfair not to tax the highly profitable liquor traffic, while disproportionately heavy tax burdens hindered other industries in their recovery. "Americans are sick, as never before, of the squandering of millions of dollars on an exploded experiment while people are clamoring for work and food," Henry Curran wrote. "When we kill Prohibition we not only regain our national self-respect but we give jobs to the unemployed, start the upswing to better business and provide a billion dollars a year to wipe out the government's deficit and prevent heavier taxes."[68]

Yet economics remained only one AAPA concern among several and, at that, as much a concern with national as with personal economic well-being. Association leaders certainly believed that prohibition damaged the economy, but they did not consider economics the overriding reason for their repeal efforts. Years before they made major objections to enforcement costs and tax burdens, antiprohibitionists had complained bitterly about crime, intemperance, and constitutional damage. "Neither my brother nor I," asserted Irénée du Pont, "have any ulterior motive in being opposed to Prohibition and are conscientious believers that it is a mistake to continue the so-called 'experiment.'"[69] The AAPA economic argument did prove persuasive, nevertheless, in winning additional support for repeal.

Others saw the need to reduce government expenses, to increase state and federal revenues, and to provide jobs as good reasons for legalizing the manufacture and sale of alcoholic beverages. The Women's Organization for National Prohibition Reform, for instance, included the AAPA's arguments and figures on the dry law's economic impact in its own publications.[70] In a letter to the president, a loyal Hoover supporter showed how the depression affected attitudes:

> When the nation was enjoying unprecedented prosperity, the huge loss of revenue from liquor taxes might be overlooked, particularly because a good many people believed that there was some connection between prosperity and prohibition. But this supposed connection now appears to be merely an alliterative fallacy. And in the present depression the country simply cannot afford to give away to bootleggers, corrupt officials, and other criminals nearly a billion dollars annually which could be raised by taxing a lawful liquor traffic. This additional

revenue could be used either to eliminate the deficit or to cut corporate and individual income taxes almost in half. The effect in hastening the business recovery would be incalculable. One of the specters that now paralyze industry is the prospect of increased income taxes which must be faced in the coming years, for tax receipts next year will probably be less than this year, leaving another huge deficit. Prohibition reform is the only law-making act which would have an immediate tonic effect economically.[71]

The depression gave organized labor, long opposed to national prohibition, additional reason to complain. Representatives of labor told the Wickersham commission in 1930 that prohibition eliminated jobs and discriminated against workers who could not afford illicit liquor as easily as the upper classes. The dry law, in other words, increased the economic distress. Furthermore, said AFL vice-president Matthew Woll, an AAPA director, union people were developing a dangerous resentment and distrust of government because of prohibition. "They feel if a judge can be bought for liquor, he can be bought for anything else; if a police officer can be quieted by a little money for liquor, he can be quieted for something else." Faith in government's willingness to help workers was evaporating.[72] As the depression grew worse and claims were made that even modification to permit 2.75 beer would create 250,000 jobs,[73] labor became increasingly hostile to the liquor ban.

In January 1931 the American Federation of Labor created a committee to agitate for prohibition reform. The AFL still held to its long-time cautious policy of seeking Volstead Act modification to allow beer and wine, but it was obviously moving toward stronger demands. Matthew Woll became president of Labor's National Committee for Modification of the Volstead Act. The committee held a two-day conference in Philadelphia in April 1931, during which labor leaders heard from repeal advocates such as Pauline Sabin and laid plans among themselves for appeals to Congress. Woll later stressed to a House committee that American workers opposed prohibition as much as did wet millionaires.[74]

The American Legion, a million-member World War I veteran's association, displayed an acute concern over the shattering effect of the depression on many of its members. Having lobbied successfully in the early 1920s for a veteran's pension, the legion, at its September 1931 convention in Detroit, considered a proposal to demand that the bonus be paid immediately. A last-minute personal appearance by President Hoover helped defeat the idea for the time. But the Detroit convention was less willing to respect Hoover's views on prohibition. As the president finished his appeal for patriotic cooperation in the battle against depression, a delegate bellowed, "We want a beer," and the convention erupted in a wet demonstration.[75] The legion had dodged the alcohol issue for years, but during 1931 Henry Curran urged local posts to pass antiprohibition resolutions. Following a debate in which delegates cheered wet speakers and booed drys, the Detroit convention by a vote of 1,008 to 394 declared that "the Eighteenth Amendment...has created a condition endangering respect for law and the security of American institutions." The resolution asked Congress to submit the question of prohibition repeal or modification to the states with the request that they in turn present the issue directly to the voters.[76] Representatives of the other major veterans' organization, the 200,000 member Veterans of Foreign Wars, meeting the same month in Kansas City, unanimously approved a similar resolution.[77] The politically powerful veterans' lobbies spoke emphatically and, for once, in unison.

The onset of a severe depression not only stimulated a reevaluation of the economic impact of national prohibition and brought new critics of the dry law to the fore, it also coincided with a grave blow to the public image of the temperance crusade. For years, wets had sought to undermine support for prohibition by discrediting the law's most prominent advocates. In 1923 the Missouri AAPA exposed the state's Anti-Saloon League superintendent, the Reverend W. C. Shupp, who among other things influenced prohibition officials to grant lucrative medicinal liquor permits to his drug company and to raid bootleggers in competition with others who were paying him bribes. Shupp quickly resigned his league post because of "broken health." The next year a jury convicted New York's Anti-Saloon League superintendent, William "Pussyfoot" Anderson, of forging league financial records to conceal his skimming of contributions. The AAPA called attention to these cases and a similar scandal involving the Kansas league superintendent as indications of the moral bankruptcy of the Anti-Saloon League. Congressmen who had voted dry and then were caught bringing foreign liquor into the country, as three were in 1929, also drew scornful notice.[78] But these incidents seemed to have little impact, especially in comparison to revelations in 1929 and 1930 concerning the country's leading dry spokesman.

Following the death in 1927 of Wayne B. Wheeler, the general counsel and chief Washington representative of the Anti-Saloon League, Bishop James Cannon, Jr., of Virginia, chairman of the Methodist Board of Temperance, Prohibition, and Public Morals, emerged as the most powerful figure in the dry phalanx. H. L. Mencken, with his usual hyperbole, charged that "Congress was his troop of Boy Scouts, and Presidents trembled whenever his name was mentioned."[79] Cannon became a principal organizer and leading spokesman for the dry southern Democratic revolt against Al Smith in 1928 which saw five former confederate states go Republican for the first time since Reconstruction. After this triumph, rumors circulated widely that Cannon would seek election to the Senate. Then, in part through the machinations of his long-time foe, Virginia Democratic senator Carter Glass, Bishop Cannon's image of moral probity and power came apart. First, his extremely profitable stock speculation on margin through a notorious New York securities firm, which had declared bankruptcy and been charged with mail fraud, came to light. To many, such activity bordered on gambling, hardly appropriate behavior for a clergyman, especially one in Cannon's position. Shortly thereafter, Glass gave the press information he had been holding for a decade showing that Cannon, while president of Blackstone College, a small Virginia girls' school, had hoarded flour during World War I and sold it at great profit. By the spring of 1930, Cannon had to defend himself before a Senate committee investigating lobbyists on charges of financial irregularities during the 1928 campaign and before the General Conference of the Methodist Church on charges that his activities had harmed the church. Then in July, newspapers throughout the country carried the sensational report that the bishop, who had just married his secretary, had been carrying on an affair with her since before his first wife's death in 1929. Cannon spent the next three years defending himself before a special church committee, a Senate select committee on campaign expenditures, and a federal court where a grand jury had indicted him for conspiring to violate the Federal Corrupt Practices Law. Although he escaped conviction, the barrage of charges, some well-documented, shattered Cannon's reputation and influence.[80] Dry ranks contained no replacement of equivalent stature or skill. A tarnished reputation together with an economic depression caused a sharp drop in already declining Anti-Saloon League contributions.[81] Thus prohibitionists faced the greatest challenge to their position in a weakened condition.

By the time the United States had spent a year in the grips of an economic crisis, prospects for a change in national prohibition brightened considerably, although the political obstacles remained substantial. The already rising tide of opposition, both individual and organizational, had accelerated noticeably as a result of the depression. The advent of a number of new organizations soliciting contributions for antiprohibition work provided a sure sign of improving wet fortunes. Groups such as the Prosperity Beer League, the Congressional Districts Modification League, the National Committee for the Repeal of the 18th Amendment, Inc., the Blue Cockade, the Companions of the Golden Dawn, and the Anti-Prohibition Battle Fund appeared little more than attempts to raise money to pay salaries to their founders.[82] That the repeal cause attracted such profiteers reflected their view that AAPA contributors and many other people would be willing to support any agency which offered relief from national prohibition. Unlike the AAPA, WONPR, and VCL, these groups quickly disappeared, having done nothing to advance the cause of repeal. The major antiprohibition societies, meanwhile, abetted by the depression and setbacks suffered by the drys, hammered away at the liquor ban. In the circumstances of 1930 and after, their campaign began to overcome long-standing assumptions that the Eighteenth Amendment could never be overturned.

8 TAKING SIDES

The months and years culminating in the national party conventions of 1932 saw the most crucial political battles in the campaign to repeal the Eighteenth Amendment. In 1928 the major presidential candidates had expressed divergent views on national prohibition, but their parties had written similar platforms. At their 1932 conventions, however, Democrats and Republicans produced sharply contrasting planks on the liquor ban, tying the law's fate thereafter to partisan fortunes. Both parties furiously debated the issue between 1928 and 1932, but advantages lay on opposite sides in the two parallel discussions. The dry president who carried the 1928 election for the Republicans dominated his party's councils during the next four years. The losing wet Democrat enjoyed no such control over his party, but he had installed a like-minded party chairman who was willing to fight for his views. In each party strongly divided opinion kept the question alive and the outcome uncertain until the convention voted on the 1932 platform. The major antiprohibition organizations, their ranks swelled by the depression, joined in each struggle and stood ready to label each party's position as satisfactory or unsatisfactory. The June 1932 convention decisions completed a highly publicized process of partisan alignment which had been developing ever since 1928 and which would assume great significance.

The odds against conventional political success seemed so long when two-thirds congressional and three-fourths state approval were required that antiprohibition forces looked hopefully for some way of side-stepping the normal constitutional amendment process. If drys could block change merely by retaining the support of one house of thirteen state legislatures, the only way to end national prohibition, some believed, would be for the courts to declare the Eighteenth Amendment invalid. Wets made their last serious attempt to bring this about in 1930 with a challenge to the constitutionality of the Eighteenth Amendment's ratification.

The United States Supreme Court, in upholding ratification of the Eighteenth Amendment in *Hawke v. Smith* and the *National Prohibition Cases* in 1920, had not answered every question about the amending process. At the time several constitutional scholars questioned whether the amending power could be used to take away state legislative or police functions without the direct assent of the people of the state. If this were possible, they argued, state government could be destroyed by amendments approved by legislative majorities in three-fourths of the states, but not by the people. The possibility of a legislature acting contrary to the popular will could not be dismissed following the Ohio referendum episode which had prompted *Hawke v. Smith*.[1] However, after the Supreme Court ignored these issues, little was heard concerning them for several years.

Late in 1927 the New York County Lawyers' Association began reexamining the Eighteenth Amendment's constitutionality. A committee studied the matter and in March 1930 released a report prepared by one of its members, Selden Bacon.[2] Bacon contended that the Tenth Amendment to the Constitution ("The powers not delegated to the United States by the Constitution, nor prohibited by it to the States, are reserved to the States respectively, or to the people") limited Article V, the amending article. The means of ratifying an amendment—by state legislatures or convention—were to be determined on the basis of rights and powers affected by the proposal, not by congressional whim.

If the amending power was unlimited, Bacon said, Congress and legislative majorities in three-fourths of the states could wipe out all individual rights protected by the first eight amendments, although those eight amendments were assumed when adopted to be beyond the possibility of usurpation by the federal government and subject to surrender only by the people themselves. In *Hawke v. Smith,* however, the Supreme Court had ruled that ratification was a federal function, not subject to any limitation imposed by the people of a state. If so, complained Bacon, all rights guaranteed the individual could be voted away by a state legislature without citizen consent. Clearly the founding fathers had not intended this.

Bacon pointed out that conventions, not state legislatures, had ratified the original Constitution. In a special election the people had conferred specific power upon their delegates to approve this form of government. Concern with limiting federal power over the individual had led to adoption of the first ten amendments. The Ninth Amendment prevented informal expansion of federal powers. The Tenth sought to check their extension through constitutional amendment. State legislatures, contended Bacon, could appropriately ratify only those amendments which merely involved the rights of state governments themselves; popularly elected constitutional conventions must be employed when individual rights were to be affected. Since the Eighteenth Amendment involved individual rights, Bacon concluded, it had been improperly ratified.[3]

The committee issuing Bacon's report urged that a test case be carried to the Supreme Court, but the lawyers' association took no action.[4] Bacon, however, belonged to the Association Against the Prohibition Amendment, and on the evening of March 31, 1930, he and his colleagues met with Henry

Curran, William Stayton, and Pierre du Pont to discuss his report. Association leaders listened enthusiastically to what Bacon told them, for his argument both confirmed their view of the Constitution and offered a possible means of overturning the Eighteenth Amendment. The next day the executive committee voted to print and distribute 25,000 copies of Bacon's report in pamphlet form. Stayton wrote to Henry Joy, "The point raised by [Bacon] is of high importance to the future constitutional history of this country."[5] Within a few months, Bacon's group began a test case, appearing in the Newark, New Jersey, federal district court on behalf of William Sprague, a bootlegger caught transporting beer in clear violation of the prohibition law. Captain Stayton personally attended the trial on October 9, 1930, to hear Bacon's argument, and other AAPA leaders followed the Sprague case with great interest.[6]

On December 16, 1930, Federal Judge William Clark startled the nation by declaring the Eighteenth Amendment void because it had not been ratified by the convention method. He quashed William Sprague's indictment. Clark, a thirty-nine-year-old judge with a reputation for judicial independence, arrived at the same conclusion as Bacon by a slightly different route. Reportedly with advice from constitutional-law professor Edwin S. Corwin of Princeton, Clark held that historical and theoretical principles of local self-government and popular sovereignty required that amendments transferring powers reserved to the states or the people be ratified by the method most closely representing the people. A constitutional convention elected to decide one issue only was satisfactorily representative. The members of a state legislature, elected on a variety of issues, perhaps not even including the proposed amendment, did not necessarily reflect the popular will and thus were not competent to act for the people on such an amendment.[7]

Pierre du Pont and Grayson Murphy, among others, publicly hailed Judge Clark's decision, though they continued their other antiprohibition activities. As expected, within two months a unanimous Supreme Court reversed the Sprague ruling. The Court, hearing arguments on January 21, 1931, and delivering its opinion on February 24, specifically rejected Bacon's and Clark's views, declaring that Article V gave Congress a clear right to choose the method of ratification. Neither the Tenth Amendment nor a reasonable interpretation of Article V placed any limitation on the amending power. The Supreme Court once again emphatically declared that the Eighteenth Amendment had been legally adopted.[8]

Although success eluded the antiprohibitionists in *U.S. v. Sprague,* the case nevertheless proved important. "Even if this opinion meets with a cold reception in the appellate courts," wrote Judge Clark in clear anticipation of the Supreme Court's action, "we hope that it will at least have the effect of focusing the country's thought upon the neglected method of considering constitutional amendments in conventions."[9] Bacon felt that Clark "has so widely advertised the subject that almost any lawyer now who can get a copy of it will really study our brief."[10] Bacon and Clark did draw attention to the significance of the method by which amendments were ratified. In the nearly 150 years since the Constitution had been adopted by state conventions, only the legislative process had been used. *U.S. v. Sprague* served as a reminder that the Article V provision for ratification of amendments by elected state conventions was available as a form of referendum.

A month after Judge Clark's decision and before the Supreme Court ruling, the Wickersham commission, in its report on prohibition, concluded that part of the difficulty in enforcing the law was that "the ratification of the Amendment was given by legislatures which were not in general elected with any reference to this subject." The commission observed,

> In many instances, as a result of old systems of apportionment, these legislative bodies were not regarded as truly representative of all elements of the community. When ratifications took place a considerable portion of the population were away in active military or other service. It may be doubted if under the conditions then prevailing the results would have been any different if these things had not been true, yet these circumstances gave grounds for resentment which has been reflected in the public attitude toward the law and thus raised additional obstacles to observance and enforcement.[11]

Three commissioners, William S. Kenyon, Paul J. McCormick, and George Wickersham, specifically recommended that the people's will regarding prohibition be determined by the only available form of national referendum, a repeal amendment submitted by Congress to popularly elected state conventions. This referendum idea appealed to others as well.[12]

After the *U.S. v. Sprague* ruling, the AAPA and other repeal advocates insisted that conventions be used to accurately represent the public's wishes in ratifying any change in the prohibition amendment. Both the 1919 Ohio fiasco and the overrepresentation of rural, presumably dry, voters in most state legislatures worried wets. Judge Clark's decision persuaded Pierre du Pont, for one, that constitutional guarantees of individual rights could not legitimately be altered except by popular consent.[13] On the other hand, the Supreme Court's treatment of the Sprague case disabused wets of any hope that the courts might settle the prohibition question favorably in the foreseeable future.[14] The Court's decision forced antiprohibitionists to recognize that their goals could only be achieved in the political arena.

By 1931 the route to repeal increasingly appeared to run through the Democratic party. Although neither had resolved the issue, both Republicans and Democrats had taken steps to affirm positions assumed in 1928. The AAPA sought to win support from each, but with very different results.

As the 1932 national elections drew closer, the contrasts became more and more clear.

Herbert Hoover's defense of national prohibition, as he sought nomination and election to the presidency in 1928, and at his triumphant inauguration, disenchanted some Republican wets. As we have seen, Pauline Sabin quickly surrendered her Republican National Committee seat so that, she said, party ties would not hamper her work for repeal. Henry B. Joy made a great show of resigning from the Detroit Republican Club in December 1929, saying that he could not in good conscience support a party which did not oppose prohibition and its evil effects. Newspapers all over the country carried the AAPA director's condemnation of his party's policy. Former senator James Wadsworth announced that he would attend the 1930 New York Republican state convention to fight for a wet platform and candidates, but for the first time in twenty-five years would not be a delegate. He did not want to feel bound by convention decisions, should they prove unsatisfactory.[15]

A prominent Republican congressman and former United States Solicitor General added to the chorus of dissent within the party. James M. Beck epitomized political conservatism in the 1920s. Upon Beck's election to the House of Representatives in 1926, the *Washington Post* called him "the acknowledged leader of those who are opposed to the extension of Federal power."[16] In speeches and books, Beck repeatedly praised individual liberty, dual sovereignty, an independent judiciary, and the checks and balances system as the keystones of the Constitution and American greatness.[17] Prohibition affronted Beck more than any other issue in the twenties. "No amendment has more vitally affected the basic principle of the Constitution viz. Home Rule," he wrote. "That the federal government should prescribe to the peoples of the States what they should drink would have been unthinkable to the framers of the Constitution."[18] As solicitor general under Harding and Coolidge between 1921 and 1925, Beck had often expressed frustration at his obligation to defend federal prohibition and enforcement in court.[19] Once in the House, he felt more comfortable in publicly criticizing the liquor ban.

Beck found himself increasingly estranged from his party's position and allied with the AAPA. In 1930 the Philadelphia congressman, urged on by Stayton and Joy, rose in the House to issue a ringing denunciation of prohibition and Republican support for it. He suggested that Congress simply nullify the law by refusing to appropriate funds to enforce it. Challenging Hoover's pledge to enforce the liquor ban, Beck asserted that government power had limits. Acceptance by the people, he said, gave laws their legitimacy. The Eighteenth Amendment destroyed the basic principle of local self-government and infringed individual rights; current widespread public resistance followed the grand tradition of revolt against oppression. The Whig party's attempt to compromise on the moral issue of the Fugitive

Slave Law had brought that party's destruction, "a sinister omen for the Republican Party even in this day of its great power," Beck preached. "I say it with regret, but I say it as a necessary warning, that the Republican Party cannot longer afford to sell its soul to the fanatical Drys and if it does, and thus becomes the party of Prohibition, it may have a like fate."[20]

Despite Joy, Wadsworth, and Beck's discouragement, by the 1930 elections the AAPA had not abandoned hope of converting the Grand Old Party. That year the Connecticut, New Jersey, New York, Washington, and Wisconsin state Republican platforms endorsed repeal, while Illinois and Rhode Island Republicans pledged to abide by prohibition referendums (which wets subsequently won, 2 to 1 and 3 to 1). This heartened the AAPA. In the New Jersey senatorial primary, Dwight Morrow opened his campaign with an emphatic call for repeal of the Eighteenth Amendment, saying that the federal government could not appropriately exercise a local police function and, furthermore, that a national liquor policy ignored local diversity. The AAPA greeted his declaration with great enthusiasm, reprinting the speech and distributing it widely. Morrow, after all, was certainly one of the country's most distinguished and well-known Republicans, a J. P. Morgan partner, a very successful ambassador to Mexico, and a close friend of Calvin Coolidge, not to mention being Charles Lindbergh's father-in-law. When Morrow won first the primary and then the general election, the AAPA rejoiced that the Republicans were beginning to come to their senses.[21]

Having several of its leaders from the Philadelphia-Wilmington area, the AAPA went to great lengths to persuade Pennsylvania's dominant Republican party to join the state's Democrats in supporting repeal. In 1930 rival Republican factions headed by Gifford Pinchot and William Vare fought for control of the party. Pinchot was adamantly dry, while the Vare machine candidates, though privately wet, took an ambiguous position on prohibition. Therefore the Pennsylvania AAPA, labeling itself the Liberal party, entered its own slate, headed by association director Thomas W. Phillips, in the Republican primary. Phillips polled 281,000 votes, most apparently taken from favored Vare candidate Francis S. Brown. As a result, Pinchot won the gubernatorial nomination by a slim 15,000 votes. The association felt it had demonstrated that it held a balance of power, much as the Anti-Saloon League had once done, and that thereafter Republican candidates would no longer straddle the prohibition issue. The Liberal party eventually gave wet Democratic candidate John Hemphill its gubernatorial nomination. Several prominent Republican AAPA directors, among them Robert K. Cassatt, Samuel Vauclain, president of Baldwin Locomotive, and Pennsylvania Railroad president W. W. Atterbury, a member of the Republican National Committee, endorsed Hemphill as well. Nevertheless, the AAPA clearly hoped to win over Pennsylvania Republicans by the next election.[22] In fact they turned a deaf ear to a proposal by Samuel Harden Church, the president of Carnegie Institute and an AAPA director, that they turn the Liberal party into a full-fledged third party.[23]

After the 1930 campaign, the Republican party's national leadership showed further hostility to the wet cause. Immediately after the election, Senator Simeon D. Fess of Ohio, the new Republican national chairman, warned that the party must clearly stand for prohibition enforcement. To endorse repeal or straddle the issue would prove fatal in the next election. Within two months, President Hoover released the Wickersham commission report. Some close to the president expected him to use the report to free himself from his pledges to maintain prohibition; but when he ignored the individual recommendations of the commissioners and opposed any change whatsoever in the law, he tied himself and his party to the drys more firmly than ever before. Dwight Morrow, who had raised antiprohibitionists' hopes, provided a final disappointment. Once he had entered the Senate, Morrow dutifully supported the president and remained silent on repeal.[24]

While Republicans enlarged their commitment to prohibition enforcement, the Democratic party shifted increasingly toward advocacy of repeal. The wet wing of the party continued to expand, while once-powerful dry convictions faded. No fewer than fourteen state Democratic platforms, including such populous states as Massachusetts, New York, New Jersey, Pennsylvania, and Illinois, endorsed repeal in 1930.[25] In fact, only one congressional race in the country that year, the Senate contest in Montana, pitted a wet Republican against a dry Democrat.[26] National chairman John J. Raskob, who had entered politics mainly because of prohibition and who refused to allow party politicians to duck the issue easily, did much to generate the growing Democratic sentiment.

The Democrat's landslide loss in 1928 brought calls for Raskob's resignation as party chairman.[27] However, since this converted Republican businessman collected or personally contributed more money in 1928 than Democrats ever before had available to wage a national campaign, indeed more than the Republicans for the only time other than in 1912, most party leaders were willing to have him remain.[28] Bitterly disappointed by Smith's defeat, Raskob determined to raise the Democratic party from the ashes. He would "build an organization which parallels, as nearly as conditions will permit, a first rate business enterprise operating all the time, spending money effectively and meeting the real issues at hand."[29]

In the past, the national committee had been active only during presidential campaigns. Raskob recognized that winning elections required a continuous effort. Others had suggested this before, but Raskob first put it into effect.[30] In the spring of 1929 he appointed Jouett Shouse as a full-time executive for the national committee and hired Charles Michelson, formerly the New York *World's* Washington correspondent, to direct publicity. Raskob set Shouse and Michelson about the tasks of building up the party throughout the country and presenting the Democratic side of political issues. He pledged his own continuing financial support so that the effort could be maintained for four years. Even in the depths of the depression, Raskob contributed $15,000 to $30,000 a month.[31] In short, John Raskob personally created a permanent, professionally staffed national organization for the party, an important innovation which has since become the norm for both parties.

Jouett Shouse, the new executive chairman, had worked as a newspaper-man and lawyer before being elected to Congress as a Kansas Democrat in 1914. The Women's Christian Temperance Union was powerful in Shouse's district, and he voted regularly for prohibition legislation, including the resolution proposing the Eighteenth Amendment. A Wilsonian Democrat and enthusiastic supporter of the war effort, Shouse met defeat for reelection in 1918. He subsequently served as an assistant secretary of the treasury under Carter Glass and counted among his duties supervision of the new prohibition enforcement agency. Shouse returned to private life as a lawyer and lobbyist during the 1920s, although he emerged momentarily in 1924 to lead the Kansas delegation to the Democratic national convention, where it supported the dry William G. McAdoo. Raskob asked Shouse to serve on a national advisory committee during Smith's 1928 campaign, and for the first time the former congressman spoke out against prohibition.[32] In selecting Shouse to direct the national committee's day-to-day affairs, Raskob chose an adaptable and unlikely looking partisan warrior. Shouse dressed impeccably, wore a pince-nez, and carried a walking stick. This charming, eloquent gentleman worked tirelessly and effectively, exploiting his connections in all sections of the party.[33] Although it may not have appeared so at first, Shouse also proved a valuable ally to Raskob in the struggle to commit the party to oppose national prohibition. As he grew more acquainted with Raskob, Shouse took up the antiprohibition cause with more and more vigor.

In his first two years as national chairman, Raskob concentrated on fund raising, organization, and publicizing the statements of Democratic office holders. He said little regarding his own political concerns. But his wet views drew wide attention nevertheless. A 1930 Senate investigation of lobbying acutely embarrassed Republicans by revealing that their national chairman, Claudius H. Huston, was also a well-paid lobbyist for the Tennessee River Improvement Association. To divert attention from Huston's improprieties, Republican Senator Arthur R. Robinson of Indiana pointed accusingly to Raskob's AAPA connections. Called to testify, Raskob freely admitted his long membership in the association and contributions of $64,500 since the beginning of 1928. He supported the AAPA's principles and trusted its leaders, Raskob said, but took no personal role in its activities. The national chairman denied having tried to commit the Democratic party on the liquor question. The Senate committee then called Curran and Stayton and subpoenaed the association's records. The investigation disclosed a good deal about the AAPA's activities and views, but discovered nothing scandalous regarding Raskob.[34] In effect, the lobby inquiry principally stressed to the public that considerably more sympathy for prohibition repeal could be found among Democratic leaders than among their Republican counterparts.

After two years as chairman, John Raskob plainly felt the national committee was the legitimate voice of the Democratic party. Al Smith had for the most part abandoned any role as party spokesman following his defeat. Raskob abhorred a leaderless, inarticulate organization. So while Smith remained silent, Shouse and Michelson, under Raskob's watchful eye, guided the party. They labored diligently to restore party harmony, strengthen party machinery throughout the country, and keep up criticism of Republican shortcomings. Aided enormously by an economic collapse during a Republican administration, the Democrats scored tremendous gains in 1930, winning fifty-three additional seats and control of the House and picking up eight seats to come within one seat of a majority in the Senate.

The Ohio Senate race typified the Democratic resurgence. Robert J. Bulkley of Cleveland, a lawyer and, during World War I, a War Department assistant to AAPA leader Benedict Crowell, made prohibition repeal his central theme in a five-way primary and later in his campaign against dry Republican incumbent Roscoe McCulloch. Bulkley ran a well-organized, well-financed campaign with support from both the party and wet organizations. He stressed the standard AAPA complaints that widespread prohibition violation encouraged disrespect for laws generally, that prohibition's economic benefits all went to criminals, and that federal power was encroaching dangerously on state functions. Bulkley won 55 percent of the vote in a state drys called the "mother of prohibition" and the *Chicago Tribune* termed the "stronghold of the drys." The economic climate helped Bulkley carry normally Republican Ohio, but his wet views distinguished him from other Democrats in the primary, which he won by a two-to-one majority over his closest rival, and they continued to attract great attention in the general election.[35] To Raskob, such election victories vindicated his efforts; they also confirmed his view that the national committee should speak out.

Shortly after the 1930 elections, Raskob and Shouse began urging that the national committee issue statements of Democratic positions on important questions. Although it seldom chose to do so, the committee was authorized to recommend policies for the next convention's endorsement. Raskob often asserted that the party should stand for something, not just try to win elections on expedients. Foremost on the chairman's mind was prohibition repeal. Shouse began telling Democratic leaders and audiences that the party must take a definite stance on prohibition. He voiced alarm over the crime and contempt for law engendered by the existing system, and favored a return to state control of the liquor traffic. Raskob, meanwhile, was planning to ask the national committee to recommend publicly that the next party platform support a new constitutional amendment allowing any state to exempt itself from national prohibition. Under this plan, a state could supervise the manufacture, transportation, and sale of alcoholic beverages without federal interference if a majority of voters approved in a referendum. Albeit more carefully worked out, Raskob's "home-rule amendment" resembled plans proposed by Al Smith in 1928 and Pierre du Pont in 1929.[36] His plan sought to disarm opposition by avoiding a straight repeal of the Eighteenth Amendment and protecting states which wanted to remain dry, but Raskob clearly aimed to take liquor control out of federal hands.

While Raskob and Shouse prepared to take up the home-rule amendment with the Democratic national committee, President Hoover released the Wickersham commission's prohibition report, along with his own endorsement of continued enforcement. Shouse and Joseph P. Tumulty urged Raskob to delay action to avoid the risk of dividing Democrats. The Republican position was now so well-known, they argued, that an expression of opposition had become unnecessary. A determined Raskob overcame their objections, and both were soon helping prepare for a discussion of prohibition at a March 5, 1931, meeting of the national committee.[37]

Raskob's desire to repeal prohibition collided with the presidential aspirations of Franklin D. Roosevelt. In 1928 Roosevelt had won the New York governorship while Smith was losing his race for the presidency. Smith considered himself FDR's political patron and expected to play an important role in the new Albany regime. Roosevelt's failure to seek the advice of his predecessor upset Smith. The unconcealed antipathy which arose between Roosevelt and Raskob, Al Smith's close friend and ally, is often assumed to have been a product of the conflicting presidential ambitions of FDR and Smith. Differing economic attitudes are credited as a contributing factor.[38] However, for a businessman in the twenties, Raskob held quite progressive economic views.[39] He remained adamantly conservative only on the need for action to come through state government to protect against distant, excessive federal power. For this reason, unlike Roosevelt, he was very much concerned with prohibition and its implications. Raskob, whose sincere dedication to repeal led him to contribute more than $120,000 to the AAPA between 1926 and 1933, relegated other political issues to secondary importance. "There are few things more necessary or expedient to the future welfare and well-being of our country and its people," he explained privately, "than some modification of existing liquor laws that will restore temperate life."[40] Preoccupied with prohibition, Raskob saw little in the New York governor's record to recommend him on the issue. Roosevelt, on his part, appears not to have appreciated the depth of the national chairman's feelings on prohibition and to have assumed he was simply trying to further the cause of Al Smith.

In fact, although Raskob greatly admired Smith, he was willing to support any candidate with a satisfactory position on prohibition. Indeed, the national chairman encouraged the presidential aspirations of Maryland Governor Albert Ritchie, who, like Smith and unlike Roosevelt, had long opposed the Eighteenth Amendment.[41]

Roosevelt had always hedged on prohibition. In his first campaign, a New York state assembly race in 1910, he had won support from wets and drys alike by supporting local option. His image as a moderate dry who would balance the ticket with the wet James M. Cox had helped him gain the 1920 vice-presidential nomination. In 1923 Roosevelt advised Governor Smith to defend the state prohibition enforcement law, the Mullan-Gage Act, to avoid alienating drys. On the grounds that New York was obligated to assist the federal government in prohibition enforcement, he urged a veto of the legislature's repeal of the law. Roosevelt also suggested that Smith mollify wets by sponsoring new legislation going no farther than to require state authorities, upon request, to assist federal law-enforcement officials. Smith rejected such evasions and approved the Mullan-Gage repeal. In 1928 Smith and Raskob, with great difficulty, convinced the popular Roosevelt to run for governor to strengthen the national Democratic ticket in New York. Roosevelt, not completely recovered from polio and facing some financial burdens, was not eager to return to politics yet. Raskob made a $25,000 donation to the Warm Springs Foundation to free Roosevelt of financial obligations so that he could make the race. In the gubernatorial campaign, Roosevelt avoided the prohibition issue as much as possible despite its importance to the Smith campaign. Such behavior, along with FDR's unconcealed objections to Raskob's appointment as national chairman, hardly increased Raskob's enthusiasm for Roosevelt.[42]

As governor, Roosevelt established an irregular record on prohibition. Initially, he ordered state law-enforcement officials to arrest Volstead Act violators and turn them over to federal courts, since New York had no prohibition law. Then at the 1929 Governors' Conference, he urged that states be delegated full responsibility for prohibition enforcement. The New York Democratic convention in June 1930 included in its platform a call for prohibition repeal. Earlier that spring, Roosevelt had led Smith and Raskob to believe that he would favor, or at least not oppose, such a plank. However, Roosevelt apparently tried to back away from this commitment, avoiding the issue throughout the summer. Finally, on September 9, with the political tide in New York running strongly against prohibition, Roosevelt announced that he favored repeal of the Eighteenth Amendment and its replacement with an amendment giving states the right to sell liquor through state agencies, or to ban it, as the people wished. The Association Against the Prohibition Amendment applauded his stand, however belated, and attributed Roosevelt's overwhelming reelection to it.[43]

Soon after his reelection as governor, Roosevelt began his quest for the 1932 Democratic presidential nomination. He and his advisors wanted to avoid the prohibition issue, seeing it as potentially embarrassing. A declaration for repeal, it was felt, would cost the New York governor much of his extensive southern support, while a defense of prohibition would ruin him with northern urban Democrats. Better, therefore, to ignore the issue, the Roosevelt camp believed. Thus they viewed Raskob's home-rule amendment as a clever tactic to damage their cause by forcing FDR to take a position.[44] Raskob earnestly wanted the party committed to repeal, and the presence of a front-running presidential candidate who was undependable on the prohibition issue could only increase his desire to insure that this was done without delay.

When the Democratic national committee met in Washington, D.C., on March 5, 1931, Raskob spoke of the party's Jeffersonian principles. Recalling that Jefferson recommended limited federal authority and strong local government as bulwarks of liberty, Raskob urged that the party rededicate itself to the spirit of the Constitution by ending unreasonable government interference in business and, especially, by supporting his home-rule amendment on prohibition. Raskob denied that he was seeking commitment to a specific policy, claiming that he merely wished the national committee to refer his proposal to the convention for earnest consideration.[45] Such a national committee request would, of course, have had nearly the effect of a policy statement.

The Roosevelt forces were prepared for Raskob. They arranged to have the New York Democratic committee, on March 2, adopt a resolution denying that the national committee had any right to pledge or advise the party on controversial issues. A copy of this resolution was sent to every national committee member except Raskob and Shouse. Roosevelt's campaign manager, James Farley, aroused southerners. Senators Cordell Hull of Tennessee, Joseph T. Robinson of Arkansas, and Cameron A. Morrison of North Carolina vigorously attacked Raskob and his plan at the March 5 meeting. Recognizing the strength of the opposition, Raskob asked that any decision on his suggestion be deferred.[46] The national committee chairman later confided to Shouse that he was upset with Roosevelt's actions to block what Raskob considered "a constructive thing." Raskob wrote Roosevelt a rather angry letter, criticizing the New York resolution, forcefully defending the powers of the national committee, and insisting that the party squarely face the prohibition issue. Roosevelt made no reply, a sign of the growing rancor on both sides.[47]

Both sides felt they had won a victory, and, in view of their goals, each had. Roosevelt and Farley thought that by blocking a vote they had prevented an erosion of their position. Raskob, on the other hand, considered that progress had been made toward a strong Democratic repeal plank. He

Clifford K. Berryman editorial cartoon, November 30, 1931, calling attention to Franklin D. Roosevelt's discomfort and uncertainty regarding prohibition

Prints and Photographs Division, Library of Congress

told another AAPA director that the proposal would have carried by a vote of about seventy to thirty, but that "in line with good democratic doctrine" he was willing to defer action for several months hoping to "sell the south the fairness of the proposal on prohibition and secure its support and cooperation."[48] Raskob's optimism could only have been reinforced by the widespread, generally favorable notice his effort received in the press.[49] The party was strengthening its antiprohibition image.

Raskob's efforts did not slacken after March 1931. One month later he wrote a lengthy letter to national committee members defending his proposal. The party needed to enunciate the principles for which it stood, he repeated. The national committee bore a duty to recommend policies for the party's consideration. The home-rule amendment was constitutionally legitimate and would restore decision-making to the people. "Can any patriotic citizen *deny the people opportunity to vote* on this important and vital question and properly call himself a Democrat?" he asked.[50] The chairman's letter attracted much attention and considerable praise. Jouett Shouse kept the issue alive by roundly criticizing national prohibition and recommending Raskob's home-rule plan to the Women's National Democratic Club.[51]

In November 1931 Raskob again sought endorsement of his proposal. He wrote to the ninety thousand contributors to the 1928 Democratic campaign, and after attacking the Eighteenth Amendment for expanding federal power, asserted that the party should face the issue and present a plan for reform based on states' rights and local self-government. An accompanying questionnaire asked whether the recipient favored a platform pledging all Democratic congressmen to support a resolution submitting the prohibition question to the people. Raskob also inquired whether the contributors preferred his home-rule plan or straight repeal of the Eighteenth Amendment. "Do you believe," he asked finally, "other economic issues will be so overwhelming in the 1932 campaign that the Democratic platform can successfully ignore the prohibition question *with its economic problems* by remaining silent or by adopting a mere law enforcement plank as was done in the 1928 convention?"[52]

Raskob reportedly planned to present the questionnaire results to the national committee as evidence that it should recommend a prohibition policy to the Democratic convention. The *Washington Post,* however, accused Raskob of splitting the party over prohibition. Leaping to defend his friend, Pierre du Pont asked why the American people should be deprived of a chance to vote on the issue.[53] The Roosevelt camp again saw Raskob's initiative as hostile and began marshalling strength to oppose the chairman at the January 9, 1932, national committee meeting. The motives of the Roosevelt forces were complex. They desired to maintain party harmony by avoiding the prohibition issue. They also wanted to increase FDR's prestige by pinning a defeat on Raskob.[54] Before the meeting, Raskob claimed he was not trying to commit the party to a wet plank with the home-rule plan, but rather was seeking a common ground, based on Jeffersonian principles, on which all Democrats could agree. He felt that delegates should have an opportunity to consider the issue carefully before adopting a platform plank. Raskob then arranged a compromise with Harry F. Byrd and other influential dry Democrats whereby his questionnaire would not be discussed at the meeting and the home-rule plan would be referred to the national convention without recommendation. Observers considered the January 9 national committee meeting a victory for Roosevelt, since discussion of prohibition was forestalled and a Roosevelt candidate was easily elected national committee secretary.[55] But approval without debate of the Raskob-Byrd agreement inched the party still closer to a decision on the wet-dry question. Committing a previously evasive convention to face the issue represented an antiprohibitionist victory. The following month, in a speech in Buffalo, Roosevelt, recognizing the direction of Democratic thinking and wishing to avoid being labeled altogether dry, repeated his 1930 call for the rights of states to choose how to regulate liquor.[56]

As the 1932 national political conventions drew near, pressures on both parties increased. Al Smith publicly endorsed Raskob's home-rule amendment as a way of returning to state liquor control.[57] In the Senate, new hearings on modification and repeal showed the size and number of antiprohibition organizations growing. Steadily worsening economic conditions generated more arguments that repeal would produce new government revenue, reduce taxes, create jobs, and expand demand for agricultural products.[58] In March 1932 House wets mustered enough strength to force the first roll call ever on repeal. The vote came on a petition to discharge from committee a resolution similar to Raskob's home-rule amendment offered by Representatives James Beck and J. Charles Linthicum of Maryland. Beck had drafted the resolution in consultation with AAPA leaders. Although the discharge vote failed 227 to 187, it achieved the wet objective of putting every House member's prohibition position on record just prior to their reelection campaigns. Furthermore, it vividly demonstrated that repeal sentiment in the House was nearing a majority.[59]

Changes in public opinion appeared to be accelerating. A new *Literary Digest* public opinion poll showed a substantial shift in popular attitudes since 1930. Unlike earlier surveys, which had offered Volstead Act modification as an alternative, the spring 1932 poll offered only two choices, continuance of the Eighteenth Amendment or repeal. Of the 4,668,000 votes cast, 73.5 percent favored repeal. Forty-six states registered majorities for repeal. In light of charges that this poll exaggerated wet strength, as well as the disrepute into which *Literary Digest* polls fell after the magazine's famous 1936 prediction that Alf Landon would defeat Franklin Roosevelt, it should be pointed out that this final *Digest* prohibition poll closely reflected repeal voting the following year. The thirty-seven states holding repeal convention delegate elections in 1933 produced a 72.9 percent wet majority. Even with some polling error, the *Digest* results represented a substantial public demand for repeal.⁶⁰

Not only moderates but also formerly committed drys were joining the long-time wets in advocating repeal. Charles Stelzle, a prominent Presbyterian clergyman whose 1918 book *Why Prohibition!* argued persuasively for national prohibition, offered his services in behalf of repeal to Pierre du Pont. "Like many others who sincerely believed in what we advocated at that time, I am personally greatly disappointed in the results obtained through its enactment," he explained, "and I am quite prepared to say so, with the same sincerity that prompted me because of my previous conviction."⁶¹ John D. Rockefeller, Jr., announced a far more spectacular reversal shortly before the Republican convention. Together with his father, Rockefeller had contributed $350,000 to the Anti-Saloon League over the years and had come to be regarded as a leading supporter of the prohibition movement. In a public letter to Nicholas Murray Butler, Rockefeller explained,

> When the Eighteenth Amendment was passed I earnestly hoped—
> with a host of advocates of temperance—that it would be generally
> supported by public opinion and thus the day be hastened when the
> value to society of men with minds and bodies free from the under-
> mining effects of alcohol would be generally realized. That this had not
> been the result, but rather that drinking has generally increased; that
> the speakeasy has replaced the saloon, not only unit for unit, but
> probably two-fold if not three-fold; that a vast array of lawbreakers
> has been recruited and financed on a colossal scale; that many of our
> best citizens, piqued at what they regarded as an infringement of their
> private rights, have openly and unabashedly disregarded the Eigh-
> teenth Amendment; that as an inevitable result respect for all law has
> been greatly lessened; that crime has increased to an unprecedented
> degree—I have slowly and reluctantly come to believe.⁶²

Rockefeller stunned drys and elated wets with his appeal to both parties to support repeal of the Eighteenth Amendment.⁶³

Organizations opposing prohibition also stepped up their efforts to influence both parties as the conventions drew near. They demanded that the public be given a chance to decide the liquor question. The AAPA reminded Congress that the Anti-Saloon League, though now violently opposed, had once asked exactly the same thing. In April, Henry Curran denounced efforts to delay or avoid meeting the issue and called upon each party to provide people an opportunity to vote on the simple question of whether or not to repeal the Eighteenth Amendment. The following month the AAPA president appealed to each Republican delegate by letter to declare for immediate and complete repeal, or at least pledge to submit the issue to popularly elected state conventions. National prohibition had failed, Curran wrote, and three-fourths of the American people wished to abolish it.[64] Pierre du Pont told James Farley that he would not contribute further to the party until it endorsed repeal. The Women's Organization for National Prohibition Repeal addressed a similar request to Democratic delegates. The VCL, meanwhile, sent to Hoover and possible Democratic nominees a resolution signed by fifty-three prominent attorneys. Joseph Choate, emphasizing that repeal mattered more than party allegiance, said, "The question of whether the Republican or the Democratic party shall run the government is subordinate to the question whether our traditional form of government is to continue at all."[65]

On June 7, 1932, the leaders of the four major antiprohibition organizations, the AAPA, WONPR, Voluntary Committee of Lawyers, and Crusaders, together with the American Hotel Association, a national trade association, announced formation of the United Repeal Council to coordinate activities in the fight for repeal.[66] Suggested months earlier, this joint committee proved difficult to establish. Petty jealousies and friction between Henry Curran and Fred Clark of the Crusaders evidently proved stumbling blocks. Matthew Woll's AFL group, Labor's National Committee for Modification of the Volstead Act, participated in organized talks, but for reasons which are not clear declined to join. Pierre du Pont's election as chairman of the council acknowledged AAPA preeminence among antiprohibitionists.[67] The appearance of the URC on the eve of the party conventions intensified interest on forthcoming Republican and Democratic decisions.

Four years of developing partisan polarization over national prohibition culminated in June 1932 in Chicago. Despite the nation's terrible economic distress, prohibition alone stirred intense feelings at both political conventions. Whether because it seemed a simpler problem to solve or offered the hope of economic relief, many of those present felt national prohibition was the crucial question of the moment. When the smoke finally cleared, the two parties had publically committed themselves to contrasting positions on repeal, making a November showdown inevitable.

The Republicans met first. They gathered in a dispirited mood, for the necessity of renominating President Hoover and the difficulty of reelecting him were equally apparent. Quite a few Republicans felt the party's only chance of success lay in endorsing repeal of the Eighteenth Amendment.[68] Others felt that abandoning the law courted disaster at the polls. Hoover rejected all suggestions that he modify his position. His appointments secretary not only turned away a VCL delegation, but earlier he had refused a request from Hoover's own ambassador to Sweden to present a plan for solving the prohibition problem based on the Bratt system.[69] The difficulty of resolving the liquor question added to the convention's pervasive gloom.

Republican wets put considerable pressure on their party. Several months before the convention, the Republican Citizens Committee Against National Prohibition, founded in December 1931 by AAPA directors Raymond Pitcairn, Lammot du Pont, Joseph H. Choate, Jr., Thomas W. Phillips, Henry Joy, and other wets, began urging the party to declare for repeal. In a form letter to contributors to the 1928 GOP campaign, the committee warned that unless it stood for repeal, the party could not win in 1932.[70] Committee chairman Pitcairn, Pauline Sabin, Matthew Woll, Nicholas Murray Butler, and Colonel Robert McCormick of the *Chicago Tribune* repeated the warning at a convention-eve rally of eight thousand antiprohibitionists in the Chicago Coliseum.[71] Throughout the spring of 1932, and especially during the weeks immediately preceding the Republican convention, the volume of White House mail regarding prohibition reached its heaviest level in Hoover's term. A large majority urged modification or repeal, generally on economic grounds, until late May, when many drys, reading newspaper reports that the president favored resubmission of the amendment to the states, wrote urging Hoover to stand firm.[72] On the eve of the convention, H. L. Mencken described the wet Republicans as roaring with confidence. "If platforms were settled in hotel lobbies," he reported from Chicago, "there would be nothing left to do save play 'The Star-Spangled Banner' and open the saloons."[73]

The United Repeal Council urged Republican platform writers to adopt a plank drafted by Curran, Pauline Sabin, and others. It affirmed the people's right to decide the Eighteenth Amendment's fate by pledging Republican congressmen to submit a repeal resolution to state conventions.[74] Pierre du Pont, James Wadsworth, Nicholas Murray Butler, and other wet spokesmen appeared before the platform committee. Meanwhile rumors flew that Hoover and his inner circle had decided upon some middle course between repeal and a law-enforcement plank.[75]

The resolutions committee gave the antiprohibitionists a cold reception. Hoover's representative, Treasury Secretary Ogden Mills, dominated the proceedings and obtained passage of a prohibition plank tailored to the president's preferences.[76] This plank first pledged the party's continued support for law enforcement, then pointed out the prescribed method for amending the Constitution. The Eighteenth Amendment, the plank continued, was not a partisan issue. "Members of the Republican Party hold different opinions with respect to it and no public official or member of the party should be pledged or forced to choose between his party affiliations and his honest convictions upon this question." The party instead should submit a new amendment to popularly elected state conventions. The terms of this proposed amendment revealed the essence of the Republican position.

> We do not favor a submission limited to the issue of retention or repeal, for the American nation never in its history has gone backward, and in

this case the progress which has been thus far made must be preserved, while the evils must be eliminated.

We therefore believe that the people should have an opportunity to pass upon a proposed amendment the provision of which, while retaining in the Federal Government power to preserve the gains already made in dealing with the evils inherent in the liquor traffic, should allow States to deal with the problem as their citizens may determine, but subject always to the power of the Federal Government to protect those States where prohibition may exist and safeguard our citizens everywhere from the return of the saloon and attendant abuses.[77]

This plank offered something to the wets—submission of prohibition reform to a popular vote. At the same time, it promised the drys continued federal liquor control. "The Hoover plank," snorted H. L. Mencken, "at least has the great virtue of being quite unintelligible to simple folk."[78]

Wet Republicans, outnumbered in the platform committee and unhappy with a plank which avoided obligating party office-holders to support even modest changes, carried their fight to the convention floor. When Senator Hiram Bingham of Connecticut offered a minority report recommending immediate repeal of the Eighteenth Amendment, a spontaneous six-minute demonstration erupted. The galleries cheered as Bingham went on to decry prohibition and say that the country had a right to know whether the GOP stood for or against the law. Nicholas Murray Butler also drew applause as he charged that the majority plank denied the people a right to vote on the basic issue of restoring the Constitution to its original form. Booing and jeers from the floor as well as the galleries greeted defenders of the administration plank, but with solid southern support they managed nevertheless to win a roll call on the issue, 690 to 460.[79]

The platform fight marked a new peak in antiprohibitionist strength within Republican ranks, but it demonstrated, to a nationwide radio audience among others, that wets remained a minority at odds with party leaders. "Don't change barrels while going over Niagara" was the general Republican philosophy, concluded a sarcastic *New Republic*.[80] The United Repeal Council quickly condemned the Republican plank for refusing to return the liquor problem to state control. Pierre du Pont insisted that the Eighteenth Amendment's failure could not be remedied on the federal level; unqualified repeal was necessary. Republican AAPA members chose even harsher words. Wadsworth called the plank a fraud, and Curran termed it completely unsatisfactory.[81] Even the staunchly Republican *New York Herald Tribune* lamented, "In some paradise for politicians there may yet be devised a compromise more inclusive and vague than the wet-moist-dry plank.... To date it has no rival."[82] By its action in Chicago, the GOP reaffirmed the image it had been developing for several years and entered the

1932 election campaign identified as the defender of prohibition.

The 1932 Democratic convention was quite unlike its Republican counterpart. Given the party's excellent prospects of regaining the White House after twelve years, the mood was optimistic, the struggle for leadership fierce. The contest for the presidential nomination essentially pitted Roosevelt against a field of challengers, nearly all wetter than FDR. With the economic crisis generating only attacks on the incumbent administration and vague pledges to improve conditions, the Democrats divided principally on whether to endorse repeal or avoid committing themselves, as had the Republicans. The Roosevelt forces held the latter viewpoint, so the platform and presidential contests intertwined.

The battle among Democrats actually began at a meeting of the committee on arrangements in April over the question of convention officers. John Raskob proposed that Jouett Shouse be chosen temporary chairman and keynote speaker to recognize his party service, a suggestion that won much support. The Roosevelt camp objected, fearing that Shouse would seek to block the New York governor's nomination. Shouse had followed Roosevelt's announcement of his candidacy with calls for states to send uninstructed delegations to Chicago, a clear attempt to keep the nomination out of Roosevelt's hands.[83] At the April meeting, a compromise was worked out whereby the Roosevelt candidate, Senator Alben Barkley of Kentucky, would be named temporary chairman and Shouse would be "commended" for permanent chairman. This arrangement was approved over the telephone by Governor Roosevelt, who pointed out that the committee lacked the power to recommend a permanent chairman but could "commend" one.[84] Raskob and Shouse believed Roosevelt was committed to this agreement. Otherwise, Charles Michelson pointed out, they would have fought for the temporary chairmanship, having a good chance to win.[85] Soon after the April 4 meeting, however, the Roosevelt camp announced it would support Senator Thomas J. Walsh of Montana for permanent chairman and denied that "commending" Shouse constituted a binding commitment. This incident added considerably to an already deep distrust of Roosevelt by Raskob and other leading antiprohibitionists, such as Chicago mayor Anton Cermak.[86]

Before the convention opened, the resolutions committee wrestled with the prohibition problem. Pierre du Pont, Pauline Sabin, William Stayton, and Fred Clark as well as other wets and drys presented their views to the committee. Sentiment reportedly was growing rapidly within the party for a platform endorsement of repeal. A subcommittee, heavily weighted with Roosevelt supporters, was ordered to draft a prohibition plank. This subcommittee presented a plan written by two Roosevelt backers, Cordell Hull and A. Mitchell Palmer, which endorsed submitting the prohibition question to the states but did not pledge party nominees to support repeal.[87] Once again Roosevelt was seeking to skirt the prohibition issue.

When Chairman Raskob called the convention to order on June 27, he departed from the usual practice of recalling past party glories and urging harmony. Instead, he pled fervently for a platform pledging party congressional candidates to submit repeal to state conventions. Condemning the Republican prohibition plank as deceitful, Raskob asked Democrats to be true to Jeffersonian traditions of states' rights and home rule.[88] As he had for two years, Raskob in his last public appearance as party chairman pressed for a Democratic commitment to repeal.

In the resolutions committee, support for a strong repeal plank increased steadily, fueled by the convention's warm reception of Raskob's and keynote speaker Alben Barkley's calls for repeal. A group within the resolutions committee, led by Senator David I. Walsh of Massachusetts and Governor William A. Comstock of Michigan, proposed a plank explicitly endorsing repeal of the Eighteenth Amendment and also favoring interim modification of the Volstead Act. The United Repeal Council urged adoption of an almost identical plank. When the platform drafters recessed on June 28, they were divided between the Walsh and Hull planks. The following day, they voted 35 to 17 for the Walsh version.[89]

While the prohibition fight preoccupied the resolutions committee, the fortunes of Franklin Roosevelt were declining. Roosevelt entered the convention with a substantial majority, though less than two-thirds, of the delegates. An unsuccessful effort to end the party rule requiring a two-thirds majority for nomination made it appear that Roosevelt lacked enough votes to win, caused his support to dwindle, and encouraged several other serious candidates. Then Shouse supporters accused Roosevelt of bad faith for breaking his agreement on the permanent chairmanship. On a roll call, the Roosevelt candidate, Senator Thomas Walsh, defeated Shouse by only 626 to 528.[90] Roosevelt's position appeared further eroded. With a floor battle over the prohibition plank imminent, Roosevelt seemed in danger of losing the nomination to Al Smith, John Nance Garner, Newton D. Baker, or Albert C. Ritchie, all of whom had endorsed repeal of the Eighteenth Amendment.

On June 29, in a tumultuous five-hour session, Democrats debated the prohibition issue before galleries packed with supporters of wet Chicago mayor Anton Cermak. Senator Gilbert M. Hitchcock of Nebraska presented the platform. When he read the sentence, "We advocate the repeal of the Eighteenth Amendment," most of the 20,000 people in the convention hall erupted into twenty-five minutes of parading, cheering, and vigorous applause. The Crusaders unfurled a huge "End Prohibition" banner. The *New York Times* called it "the first spontaneous demonstration of joy that has been seen in Chicago this convention year." The plank, which Hitchcock was finally allowed to finish reading, demanded that Congress immediately pass a repeal amendment to be submitted to state conventions, that in event of repeal the federal government help protect states against liquor imports in violation of their laws, and that, pending repeal, Congress modify the Volstead Act to legalize and tax the manufacture and sale of beer. Cordell Hull then offered his minority plank; it met a cold reception. In the ensuing debate, a parade of speakers urged delegates to endorse repeal emphatically. Al Smith received an emotional ten-minute ovation when he appeared to speak. Jouett Shouse recalled Raskob's and his efforts to rebuild the party and said "the outcome of this platform as presented by the majority to this convention is all the reward that either he or I ask at the hands of the party."[91]

Recognizing the convention's mood and fearing further deterioration of their strength, Roosevelt's forces abandoned the Hull plank. The word went out that delegates pledged to FDR were free to vote as they pleased. When the roll was called, delegates stood 934¾ to 213¾ in favor of the majority plank. Only eight states preferred the Hull plank.[92] Raskob's years of agitation and rising repeal sentiment had produced an unmistakable Democratic commitment to repeal.

With the prohibition plank settled to their satisfaction, a major wet objection to Roosevelt's nomination disappeared. The party was now publicly pledged to repeal regardless of its candidate. No longer could FDR's nomination be blocked on the basis of the prohibition issue. This was perhaps the only basis on which a successful anti-Roosevelt coalition could have been built. No other candidate had sufficient support to challenge the New York governor, and when Roosevelt reached an accommodation with John Nance Garner, the nomination was his.

In his moment of victory, Roosevelt sought to reassure the antiprohibitionists, blithely ignoring his former position (a not uncommon Roosevelt practice which never failed to exasperate his foes). "I congratulate this convention for having had the courage, fearlessly, to write into its declaration of principles what an overwhelming majority here assembled really thinks about the 18th Amendment. This convention wants repeal. Your candidate wants repeal. And I am confident that the United States of America wants repeal."[93] The nominee, however, granted little public recognition to Raskob's party rebuilding efforts which had put it in good shape for the 1932 presidential contest. This added to the bitterness which the outgoing national chairman felt toward the victory of a man whom he distrusted, whose positions he disliked, and against whom he had struggled. Raskob considered Roosevelt a radical, sensing in the New York governor's position on prohibition a greater tolerance of federal activity than he could accept. Nevertheless, Raskob hosted a national committee dinner for FDR at the close of the convention and, eager for a Democratic victory in the fall, later contributed $25,000 to Roosevelt's campaign.[94]

His almost obsessive concern with prohibition proved at once Raskob's great strength and glaring defect as Democratic chairman. His beliefs had led him to devote enormous energy and funds to building up the party after the disaster of 1928. At the same time, they had caused him to neglect other issues, in particular the economy, which offered the party its best chance in years to turn the Republicans out of office. Raskob favored tariff reduction and other Democratic economic reform proposals; despite his background he made no noticeable effort as chairman to advance business's special interests. Nevertheless, he clearly judged politicians more on their position on prohibition than on their economic policies. Furthermore, Raskob forsook the national chairman's traditional role as party harmonizer. His business experience emphasized rational, orderly problem solving by those in authority, not compromise to balance or avoid offending various political interests. His preoccupation with repeal had led him into conflict with Roosevelt, the presidential candidate most likely to run well in all parts of the country. Had the Democrats lost in 1932, Raskob would have borne a major portion of the responsibility. Even though the organization and issues he prompted helped achieve victory, the party chairman displayed little sensitivity to the complexities of partisan politics. Judged as a crusader, Raskob succeeded; but measured as a party leader, he proved a mixed blessing.

The conventions over, the parties and the antiprohibitionists looked ahead to the fall elections. The parties were now completely polarized on national prohibition. Coast-to-coast networks had broadcast both parties' convention debates and decisions for millions to hear. AAPA leaders who had condemned the Republican position on repeal praised the Democratic plank unstintingly. Pierre du Pont warmly approved the Democrats' action. Henry Curran called it "a sound, honest plank."[95] As the result of a four-year process in which members of the Association Against the Prohibition Amendment had played a significant part, the Republican party became publicly identified as dry and the Democrats as wet. Franklin Roosevelt, who may still have worried about the effect it would have upon his election prospects, declared that on the prohibition question "the two parties offer the voters a genuine choice this year."[96] Given this partisan division, the 1932 election results would presumably provide the nation's verdict on the fate of national prohibition.

9 REPEAL!

It was as if someone were opening a bottle of champagne. At first the cork moved slowly and only under great pressure. But once it reached a certain point, the cork literally exploded out of the neck. More than a dozen years had elapsed before those seeking to overturn national prohibition gained the support of a major political party. Only eighteen months later, they reached their goal. The final stage in the complicated process, state approval of a new amendment, was completed more quickly than in any previous constitutional change in the nation's history. The rapidity of repeal surprised observers far more than the popping of champagne corks in celebration when the United States lifted its liquor ban.

Repeal's speedy progress resulted from popular enthusiasm, Democratic party support, sustained antiprohibitionist pressure, and fortunate timing. The 1932 campaign led politicians to consider the landslide Democratic victory a mandate for repeal. Congress quickly adopted a resolution, approved by the Association Against the Prohibition Amendment and its allies, proposing a new constitutional amendment to abolish the old. Since over forty legislatures were then meeting, and foresighted leaders of the Voluntary Committee of Lawyers had drafted the necessary bills to place in legislators' hands, most states could immediately create ratification machinery. By early December 1933, thirty-seven state conventions had acted, repealing a constitutional amendment for the first time ever.

Once the 1932 national party conventions ended, the various wet organizations faced the question of how to proceed. The Women's Organization for National Prohibition Reform saw no problem. It had already resolved at its spring convention to support the party and presidential candidate that stood unequivocally for repeal.[1] Five days after the Democrats adjourned in Chicago, eighty members of the WONPR's national executive committee from twenty-five states met on Long Island and agreed unanimously to endorse the Democratic prohibition plank. Nearly two dozen Republican members hesitated to support the Democratic nominee, but the majority insisted that a president's great influence over legislation made a candidate endorsement vital. Mrs. Henry Joy, who presided, declared that the only way to reach the organization's goal was to support candidates who favored repeal, and that, although she had been a Republican all her life, she would vote for Franklin Roosevelt. A few women refused to vote for FDR, and a handful resigned, but most stood firmly behind the organization.[2] Announcement of the WONPR position earned front-page newspaper coverage and put Pauline Sabin on the cover of *Time* magazine.[3] The women's prompt action further cemented the image of partisan differences which emerged from the conventions.

The men's repeal societies hesitated to follow the women's lead. Two days after the WONPR meeting, forty leaders of the Crusaders met in Cleveland. While they commended the Democratic plank, they declined to endorse either candidate.[4] President Fred Clark in fact complained to Pierre du Pont about the WONPR's failure to consult other members of the United Repeal Council before proceeding.[5] The Republican Citizens Committee Against National Prohibition meanwhile beseeched their party's leaders to abandon the platform "straddle" and come out clearly for repeal so as to not force wet organizations and an electorate "overwhelmingly for repeal" to vote against the GOP. The committee's leaders, Raymond Pitcairn and Robert Cassatt, displayed considerable anguish at having to choose between their party and a satisfactory policy on what they considered the dominant issue of the campaign.[6]

The Association Against the Prohibition Amendment considered its situation in the 1932 campaign quite delicate. The Democrats had overwhelmingly adopted a thoroughly satisfactory platform declaration on repeal, while the Republican convention had equivocated. The association had forged strong ties to the Democrats and clearly needed to cooperate with that party. "This is our great opportunity," wrote Benedict Crowell. "This is the decisive year. If President Hoover is reelected, it will be a great victory for the drys and will be so proclaimed. Our cause will be set back for years." On the other hand, he said, "if Governor Roosevelt is elected, it will be a great wet victory and will probably force the Republican party over to our side next year."[7] At the same time, however, amending the Constitution required tremendous political support, and leading antiprohibitionists felt they could ill afford to alienate those Republicans, among them 40 percent of the delegates to the just-concluded convention, who favored repeal.[8]

The AAPA's distrust of the Democratic presidential candidate further complicated the situation. Franklin Roosevelt had vacillated on prohibition throughout his career and at the convention had backed the conservative Hull plank until the last moment. The Democratic nominee, AAPA leaders felt, had broken a promise on the choice of permanent convention chairman, and some felt he might foresake his pledge to support the repeal plank as well.[9] H. L. Mencken, for instance, wondered whether Roosevelt's denunciation of the saloon during his acceptance speech to the convention was an attempt "to pull some of the teeth of the repeal plank."[10] Furthermore, John

Raskob and Jouett Shouse, the leading wet agitators within the Democratic national committee, were relieved of their party posts with few thanks for their four-year labor. This ingratitude upset Captain Stayton.[11]

The association sought to resolve its dilemma by emphasizing its preference for the Democratic position while avoiding offense to wet Republicans. In late July executive committee chairman Pierre du Pont announced:

> The oft-stated policy of the Association Against the Prohibition Amendment with reference to political affiliations has not changed. In general, our members expect to support candidates for office, regardless of party, who have declared themselves in favor of repeal of the Eighteenth Amendment.
>
> The Democratic platform is clear-cut and supports the aims of the Association Against the Prohibition Amendment. Therefore, we should find in the Democratic Party those candidates who will propose and recommend repeal without qualification.
>
> While the Republican platform does not meet our aims, it must be remembered that 40 percent of the delegates to the Republican convention voted for submission of repeal. Therefore, we should also find in the Republican Party candidates who will likewise propose and recommend repeal without qualification.[12]

This carefully worded statement refrained altogether from mentioning the presidential contest. Irénée du Pont explained that the executive committee felt that Congress bore responsibility for initiating repeal. The president had no power in the matter except his influence. If elected, Hoover, seeing prohibition's unpopularity, might yet back repeal. A blanket endorsement of the Democratic ticket would serve no good purpose if it produced no advantage and only estranged wet Republicans.[13]

Regardless of the AAPA's cautious official position, which the United Repeal Council at Pierre du Pont's request soon adopted as its own, wet organizations displayed many signs that they nevertheless preferred the Democrats. The WONPR endorsement came first. Later in the summer, the AAPA gained nationwide attention when its executive committee replaced Henry Curran as president with Jouett Shouse.[14] Few Democrats in the country were better known as critics of Herbert Hoover and his policies than the former Democratic official.

Although early in 1932 the executive committee agreed to extend Henry Curran's contract as AAPA president, due to expire a year later, some grumbling about his leadership could be heard.[15] Curran seldom left his New York office, which placed the burden of maintaining direct contact with members upon seventy-one-year-old Captain Stayton. "This seems a great pity," Pierre du Pont confided to Charles Sabin, "but I do not know how the difficulty can be remedied, as the Major [Curran] does not seem to have the knack of visiting and accomplishing by that method whereas the Captain is extremely active."[16] Curran made too little progress, others felt, and seemed tactless; he found it difficult to get along with Fred Clark of the Crusaders and Matthew Woll of the AFL committee, as well as Stayton, Benedict Crowell, and the AAPA's chief fund-raiser, William P. Smith. In May the executive committee began seriously discussing a change and even interviewed a possible replacement.[17] After the Democratic convention, John Raskob suggested the possibility of obtaining Jouett Shouse's services. The executive committee responded enthusiastically and, without Curran's knowledge, approached Shouse in late July. After a brief negotiation, Shouse accepted.[18] Pierre du Pont broke the news to Curran on August ninth. Conditions had changed, du Pont said, likening the situation to Curran's own replacement of Captain Stayton as president four years earlier.[19] James Wadsworth and Charles Sabin urged that Curran be kept on as vice-chairman of the board. But Curran felt bitter at what he considered ungrateful and behind-the-back treatment. He and Shouse found working together difficult. After three months, when Pierre du Pont hinted that it might be appropriate, Curran was ready to sever his connection with the AAPA altogether.[20]

Curran later implied that his precipitous ouster had occurred because the du Ponts wanted a job for Shouse.[21] This suggests one possible reason for the reorganization, but Curran's personal shortcomings, his Republican background, the changing character of the repeal crusade, the need to work more closely with the Democratic party, and Shouse's demonstrated talents all seem more important factors. In announcing the change on August 17, Pierre du Pont credited Curran's "constant attacks" on national prohibition with "materially hastening" the change in public attitude. However, said du Pont, now that Democrats unconditionally and Republicans with reservations recognized that a cure must be found, different work confronted the association. State organizations must be created and candidates supported to insure an unqualified return to state liquor control. Du Pont ascribed to Shouse the capacity to work with both parties, which would help bring all opponents of the Eighteenth Amendment together. Given Shouse's four years of lambasting the Republican party, this description raised a few eyebrows. But Shouse proved both an effective president and a popular one, except among drys concerned about his political ability. They sarcastically suggested that the new AAPA head drop the "h" from his last name.[22]

In accepting the AAPA office, Shouse acknowledged and endorsed the association's long-standing principles. "The Association was founded on the theory that the police power embodied in the XVIII Amendment never belonged in the Federal Constitution and should be eliminated." They must, he said, guard against further improper attempts at federal control in any proposed substitute for national prohibition. "The American people are desirous of finding a way out of the present difficulties, not of shifting to

Jouett Shouse, 1929   Prints and Photographs Division, **Library of Congress**

others that might prove equally annoying." A return to state liquor control, Shouse agreed, offered the only sane solution.[23] From the start, the new president sounded the same themes the association had always stressed.

Shouse turned the focus of AAPA activity from mobilizing public opinion to a more specific effort to influence political leaders and insure an unqualified repeal of the Eighteenth Amendment. He moved association headquarters from New York to Washington, closed the research office, hired a newspaperman, Robert Barry, to supervise publicity, and concentrated on organizing support for repeal in each state.[24] Most importantly, the new president reinforced impressions of partisan differences on prohibition. In a well-publicized September speech, Shouse condemned the Republicans for hedging on prohibition, proposing a new amendment which would keep the federal government involved in the liquor problem, and allowing party candidates to take whatever position they desired. In contrast, he praised the Democratic plank without reservation. Shouse said the AAPA would not hesitate to support Republican candidates willing to declare for outright repeal, but he made clear the association's general Democratic preference.[25]

Republican leaders began to realize soon after their convention that their political problems on prohibition remained. Within days, Senator William Borah denounced the platform's prohibition plank, saying that it favored repeal rather than just a referendum opportunity and offered insufficient protection for states which wished to remain dry. The White House replied that it had discussed the need for a return to state liquor control with Borah and national chairman Simeon Fess before the convention, and that both senators had approved the proposed plank.[26] The controversy made it appear that platform writers had tried, albeit unsuccessfully, to suit the Senate's most powerful drys. Hoover's summer mail reflected uncertainty as to the president's position, and discontent on the part of wets and drys alike.[27] In his speech formally accepting renomination, Hoover tried to clarify matters. Each state, he said, should have the right to deal with the liquor question as it wished, "subject to absolute guarantees in the Constitution of the United States to protect each state from interference and invasion by its neighbors, and that in no part of the United States shall there be a return of the saloon system with its inevitable political and social corruption and its organized interference with other states."[28] Hoover sought to attract repeal advocates by proposing that states be able to decide whether to allow liquor sales, and temperance crusaders by retaining federal power to protect dry states and prohibit saloons. He succeeded in pleasing no one. The president failed to convince wets that his position was as attractive as his opponent's, and he angered many drys. He believed he was demonstrating a consistent interest in finding a workable means of promoting temperance, but most observers thought he was shifting ground. Nothing Hoover subsequently said during the campaign improved his image with antiprohibitionists or helped him with drys.[29]

Franklin Roosevelt, a sensitive observer of public opinion, made his strongest statement yet in favor of repeal during an August 28 speech in Sea Girt, New Jersey. Intemperance in a modern, mechanized society imperiled everyone, he told an audience of one hundred thousand. Rather than combating intemperance, prohibition encouraged its spread. "We have depended too largely upon the power of government action," Roosevelt continued. He reiterated the AAPA's long-standing complaint: "The experience of nearly one hundred and fifty years under the Constitution has shown us that the proper means of regulation is through the States, with control by the Federal Government limited to that which is necessary to protect the States in the exercise of their legitimate powers." The candidate particularly indicted prohibition on economic grounds. "We threw on the table as spoils to be gambled for by the enemies of society the revenue that our government had theretofore received, and the underworld acquired unparalleled resources thereby. . . . The only business of the country that was not helping to support the government was in a real sense being supported by the government." Not only did this lead to disrespect for law and corruption of enforcement agencies, Roosevelt went on, "Unquestionably our tax burden would not be so heavy nor the forms that it takes so objectionable if some reasonable proportion of the unaccounted millions now paid to those whose business had been reared upon this stupendous blunder could be made available for the expense of government." No wet ever made a stronger argument for repeal to relieve the depression. Roosevelt finished by saying that Hoover and the Republicans continued to be evasive, ambiguous, and insincere, claiming to support repeal while insisting on federal power to protect dry states and prevent saloons. The Republican position, said FDR, was to "sound dry to the drys and wet to the wets." By contrast, the Democratic plank, which he accepted "one hundred per cent," spoke plainly, clearly, and honestly for repeal. "On this subject the two parties offer the voters a genuine choice this year." Roosevelt never again devoted as much of a campaign speech to prohibition, but after using such unmistakable terms to the huge crowd at Sea Girt, he scarcely needed to.[30]

Wet organizations campaigned actively in the fall of 1932, concentrating on congressional races. Only the WONPR worked specifically for Roosevelt. The AAPA spent more on congressional contests than ever before, over $300,000 between June 1 and November 1, almost one quarter of what the Democratic national committee spent. While it leaned toward Democrats, the association endorsed candidates from both political parties who advocated unqualified repeal. In the California Senate race, for instance, the AAPA endorsed Republican Tallant Tubbs over Democrat William G. McAdoo. McAdoo and some others regarded this as retribution for

McAdoo's contribution to FDR's nomination. The AAPA replied that because of his well-known dry record McAdoo's commitment to repeal was uncertain despite his pledge to support his party's platform. Tubbs on the other hand had belonged to the AAPA for years. While there were a few other Republican endorsements, the AAPA generally backed Democrats for House and Senate seats.[31]

Antiprohibition arguments in the 1932 campaign differed little from the past. In late September, the AAPA issued its major campaign document, *32 Reasons for Repeal*. The forty-page pamphlet first insisted that federal power should be confined to interstate and international affairs while states retained full control of purely local matters. Putting a police regulation in the Constitution had upset this balance and destroyed such Bill of Rights protections as those against double jeopardy and unreasonable search and seizure. If communities could choose their own methods of regulating liquor, they could respond to local conditions and employ one of several more effective foreign systems. *32 Reasons* went on to summarize AAPA research-department conclusions about the specific social and economic costs of national prohibition: extensive corruption, widespread crime, enormous enforcement expenses, and the loss of one billion dollars in annual government revenue. The pamphlet concluded by reporting various indications of rising repeal sentiment. At the same time, the Crusaders distributed a book entitled *The New Crusade* containing a wide variety of arguments against prohibition but stressing the need to restore law and order as well as temperance. The VCL worked at educating lawyers attending the American Bar Association convention; Pauline Sabin generated magazine publicity; and Jouett Shouse delivered major addresses in Baltimore, Detroit, and St. Paul, emphasizing the economic relief obtainable through repeal.[32]

Some wets felt that the other antiprohibition societies should follow the WONPR lead, support Roosevelt outright, and criticize Hoover and the Republican plank more vigorously. Pierre du Pont maintained, however, that the AAPA and the United Repeal Council must not alienate wet Republicans whose support might be needed later. Du Pont, Shouse, and Raskob all made public statements in behalf of Roosevelt before the election, in each instance specifying that they spoke only for themselves. Du Pont and Raskob, furthermore, made large contributions to Roosevelt's campaign. They clearly wished for a Democratic victory, though their doubts about Roosevelt's dedication to repeal persisted.[33] Antiprohibitionist caution in the autumn of 1932, however, in no way diminished the by now deeply implanted impression that a vote for the Democrats was a vote to put an end to the Eighteenth Amendment.

On November 8, Franklin Roosevelt and the Democratic party scored one of the great electoral triumphs of American political history. Roosevelt polled nearly twenty-three million votes to his opponent's less than sixteen million, and carried forty-two states to Hoover's six. In the Congress, which had been evenly divided, Democrats gained a 310 to 117 House majority and a 60 to 35 Senate advantage. Four years earlier, Hoover had received 58.2 percent of the ballots; now he got just 39.6 percent. Undoubtedly the economic depression bore principal responsibility for the rejection of Hoover, but prohibition played a part as well. With both parties offering vague and cautious economic plans, prohibition appeared to be one issue in 1932 on which party positions were clearly distinguishable.[34] Its importance in the election became evident in various ways.

The election increased wet strength in Congress even more dramatically than it shifted party power. Despite the Democratic landslide, a few repeal-espousing Republicans, like James Wadsworth of New York and Everett Dirksen of Illinois, won their first election to the House of Representatives. Wadsworth, who defeated both a Democrat and an independent dry candidate, clearly profited from changing attitudes toward prohibition in his conservative, western–New York district since his defeat for the Senate six years earlier in a similar three-sided contest. The *New York Times* calculated that the Seventy-third Congress would have 343 wet Representatives and 61 wet Senators.[35] Wet support in the House had previously reached a peak of 187 votes on the Beck-Linthicum resolution, and the Senate had always been drier. Of the more than one hundred Congressmen turned out in 1932, some —such as Wesley L. Jones of Washington, Reed Smoot of Utah, and James E. Watson of Indiana—were among the most influential dry Senators. Quite a few surviving incumbents had reversed earlier positions and come out for repeal during the campaign.

Eleven states held referendums on prohibition issues at the November election. The results vividly demonstrated the strength of repeal sentiment. Voters abolished state prohibition laws in Arizona, California, Colorado, Louisiana, Michigan, New Jersey, North Dakota, Oregon, and Washington. In every instance, wets won by a considerable margin, including two-to-one in Michigan and California, and over four-to-one in New Jersey. Furthermore, two out of three Wyoming voters and six out of seven Connecticut voters petitioned Congress for repeal of the Eighteenth Amendment.[36]

Whatever part advocacy of repeal actually contributed to the Democratic landslide, politicians and other contemporary observers gave it major credit for the outcome. They thought the prohibition issue had determined many votes. This belief proved crucial to the process of abolishing the Eighteenth Amendment. The election of 1932 was widely interpreted as a voter directive for repeal. Those involved in antiprohibition agitation quickly labeled it so. Jouett Shouse, for the AAPA, declared the mandate "overwhelming."[37] The WONPR assessed the returns and proclaimed, "The citizens of the United States through the instrument of the ballot made it quite clear and definite on November 8th that they do not want National Prohibition."[38] Representative James Beck called the election "a clear mandate to Congress to end, as soon as possible, the tragic folly of Federal prohibition."[39] Soon signs appeared that many of Beck's colleagues in the House concurred.

Within minutes of the convening of the lame-duck session of the Seventy-second Congress on December 5, 1932, House Democratic majority leader Henry T. Rainey introduced a resolution proposing a new constitutional amendment repealing the Eighteenth Amendment. Rainey and Speaker John Nance Garner, the vice-president-elect and author of the resolution, obtained a suspension of House rules to allow its immediate consideration. In the forty minutes allowed for debate, proponents repeatedly stressed that the election had registered an unmistakable mandate for immediate repeal as called for in the Democratic platform. On a roll call, the resolution won the support of 272 members, 85 more than had voted for the Beck-Linthicum resolution only nine months earlier. Clearly the election had caused dozens of representatives who had previously supported national prohibition to reverse their position. The Garner resolution fell six votes short of the two-thirds needed for House passage, but among its 144 opponents were 81 lame ducks (70 Republicans and 11 Democrats) who would soon be unable to block repeal.[40]

The December 5 House vote dramatically underscored the November election's effect on congressional thinking. Even before newly elected representatives could replace the old, the previously dry, expiring House had nearly mustered a two-thirds repeal plurality. James Beck believed that if Garner had not tried to force the resolution down the members' throats on the first day of the session, the wets would have picked up enough votes to win. At the AAPA board of directors annual meeting the following day, a jubilant mood prevailed. Directors sensed imminent victory, and speaker after speaker insisted that the American people would accept no less than complete, unqualified repeal of the Eighteenth Amendment.[41]

Following the vote, Garner himself expected no further action until the meeting of the new Congress, with its overpowering wet majority. The seventy-third Congress was not scheduled to convene until December 5, 1933, though an earlier special session appeared likely. However, agitation continued for action before the old Congress expired March 3. Representatives of the AAPA and WONPR visited nearly every senator to urge prompt passage of the proper sort of repeal resolution. Over forty state legislatures were then in session and most would not meet again for a year or more. These legislatures would have to either ratify a repeal amendment themselves or establish state ratification conventions. If Congress submitted a repeal resolution by February, before the scheduled adjournment of various state legislatures, Shouse estimated that as much as two years might be saved in the repeal process.[42]

On January 9, 1933, the Senate Judiciary Committee reported out a repeal resolution drafted by Republican Senator John J. Blaine of Wisconsin. Blaine, who had won his Senate seat in 1926 with AAPA support, was about to retire after having lost a 1932 primary. His proposed new constitutional amendment followed the Republican platform in providing an end to national prohibition but obligating the federal government to protect dry states against liquor imports, and in granting Congress concurrent power with the states to regulate or prohibit the sale of intoxicants to be consumed on the premises where sold, in other words, power to forbid saloons. The Blaine resolution also called for ratification of this new amendment by state legislatures. The senator ignored both 1932 platforms as well as personal appeals from the head of the Wisconsin AAPA and Judge William Clark, author of the original 1930 *Sprague* decision on convention ratification procedures, that the people be allowed to express their opinions directly by electing convention delegates. Publicly, Blaine explained that state legislatures could act quickly, while the convention method would take four years or more, impose heavy expenses on the states, and, with repeal inevitable, prove unnecessary. Privately, he added that he thought drys would have a better chance to block repeal with convention ratification.[43]

The Association Against the Prohibition Amendment and the Women's Organization for National Prohibition Reform demonstrated in this situation that they were more concerned with ending federal involvement in liquor control once and for all than immediately abolishing national prohibition. Pauline Sabin announced that nothing short of complete repeal would be accepted by her group.[44] One AAPA director wrote Stayton, calling the Senate resolution "a subterfuge inspired by the Anti-Saloon League, the W.C.T.U., and the religious politicians to preserve prohibition at its worst." He continued graphically, "This counterfeit proposition of the Senate Committee shows that we have only scotched the snake, and not killed it. Let us never sleep until we have smashed its head and laid it dead on the national highway."[45] Jouett Shouse objected as vehemently if less colorfully to the Blaine resolution, saying it merely modified the Eighteenth Amendment and further extended federal police powers in the attempt to prevent saloons from reappearing. This was not what had been advocated in the Democratic platform and overwhelmingly endorsed at the polls, the AAPA president said. "Unless and until there is offered a clear cut resolution providing for outright repeal of the Eighteenth Amendment and returning unrestricted control over the liquor problem to the different states without an attempt at continued exercise of jurisdiction by the federal government," Shouse declared, "it were infinitely better that the Eighteenth Amendment should stand."[46] Raymond Pitcairn, as secretary of the United Repeal Council, wrote to Judiciary Committee chairman George Norris that his committee evidently had "no conception of the enormous resentment with which the electorate regard this so-called repeal resolution, which is a fraud [and] an outrage to enlightened public opinion conceded to have become a mandate of the people at the November elections."[47]

In a speech to the Kentucky WONPR and later in a national radio address, Shouse argued that the proposed amendment would continue asserting federal power and maintain the present system's evils. Authorizing federal protection of dry states was superfluous, he said, given the Constitution's commerce clause and the still-valid 1914 Webb-Kenyon act. However, if it would reassure states desiring to remain dry, he was willing to see the clause included. The section granting federal power to prohibit the saloon, however, Shouse strenuously opposed. "It would mean a continuance of huge general expenditures to maintain an army of snoopers and snipers," he charged. "It would mean a continuance of the reign of racketeering and crime, of bribery and corruption, of federal interference in the lives and habits of the people."[48] Shouse urged all AAPA members to impress upon their senators the need to amend the Blaine resolution.[49]

Some wets agreed with Blaine that ratifying conventions posed more problems than they were worth and that state legislatures could now be depended upon to approve repeal.[50] After their experiences with *Hawke v. Smith* and *U.S. v. Sprague* and their strenuous efforts to convince both parties to endorse submission of any new amendment to convention ratification, however, AAPA leaders had no intention of abandoning this goal of constitutional referendum when individual rights were involved. Shouse assailed Blaine's plan to send a repeal amendment to state legislatures. He repeated wet fears that rural dry areas enjoyed disproportionate representation in many legislatures. In such states a few drys could delay or block the popular will; a mere 132 senators properly distributed in thirteen states could defeat ratification altogether. Recalling both parties' endorsements of convention ratification, Shouse insisted that their pledges be kept.[51]

Until mid-February, prospects for early congressional action seemed stalemated. Two-thirds of the Republican-controlled Senate Judiciary Committee continued to support the Blaine resolution, opposed by anti-prohibition organizations and the House Democratic leadership. Meanwhile, a Huey Long filibuster tied up the Senate. It appeared that the session might come to its end March 3 before any action could be taken on prohibition. Although wet organizations, fearing a lost opportunity, kept pressing for prompt action, Shouse confessed to being very discouraged at this point.[52]

The congressional situation changed abruptly when Senator Joseph T. Robinson, the Democratic majority leader and Alfred E. Smith's staunchly dry 1928 running mate, decided to push for immediate implementation of the Democratic platform pledge. Robinson began exerting his considerable influence on behalf of submitting unqualified repeal to state ratification conventions. Shouse considered Robinson's decision the deciding factor in the congressional battle.[53] Senator Morris Sheppard of Texas, author of the

Eighteenth Amendment, frantically tried to prevent consideration of the repeal resolution. His one-man filibuster soon collapsed as repeal supporters served notice that they intended to keep the Senate in continuous session until the issue came to a vote. On February 16, senators led by Robinson easily amended the Blaine resolution 45 to 15 to provide for convention ratification. They then managed to strike out the antisaloon provision by the close vote of 33 to 32. Once amended to suit antiprohibitionists and Democratic leaders, the repeal resolution read:

> 1. The eighteenth article of amendment to the Constitution of the United States is hereby repealed.
> 2. The transportation or importation into any State, Territory, or possession of the United States for delivery or use therein of intoxicating liquors, in violation of the laws thereof, is hereby prohibited.
> 3. This article shall be inoperative unless it shall have been ratified as an amendment to the Constitution by conventions in the several States, as provided in the Constitution, within seven years from the date of the submission hereof to the States by the Congress.

No more congressional obstacles confronted the repeal resolution. The Senate quickly adopted it by a vote of 63 to 23. Four days later, the House of Representatives approved it 289 to 121, sending the resolution on to the states.[54] Partisan positions had shifted noticeably since 1917, when Democrats and Republicans had supported the Eighteenth Amendment in virtually identical proportions. By 1933 a majority in each party favored repeal, but Democrats by a much larger margin than Republicans. The Twenty-first Amendment won approval from 79 percent of Democrats and 67 percent of Republicans in the Senate, as well as 85 percent of Democrats and 55 percent of Republicans in the House. Of nineteen Senators present for both votes, only one, James Lewis of Illinois twice voted wet. Nine Democrats and four Republicans switched from dry to wet.[55] After two and a half months, the congressional log-jam had suddenly broken, and the first of the two great constitutional hurdles in the amending process had been surmounted.

Passage of the repeal resolution precipitated great confusion. In the nearly 150 years since the Constitution's original ratification, Congress had never submitted an amendment to state conventions. Constitutional scholars disagreed as to whether Congress or the individual states' legislatures possessed the authority to set up these conventions. Neither existing federal nor state law contained any provisions for them. Former Attorney General A. Mitchell Palmer argued that the duty lay with Congress, while James Beck placed the responsibility on the states.[56] The states were uncertain how to proceed. As early as January 1933, the California legislature asked Congress to enact a law covering delegate selection, scheduling, conduct of elections and conventions, and payment of expenses incurred. New Mexico, on the other hand, declared that any attempt by Congress to prescribe the rules governing conventions would be null and void in that state.[57] When Congress failed to reach a consensus after much debate, observers anticipated a long delay while the Supreme Court resolved the procedural issues.[58]

At this point the Voluntary Committee of Lawyers made its major contribution to repeal. Committee and AAPA leaders had begun discussing drafting convention legislation during the 1932 party conventions in Chicago. Since November, VCL chairman Joseph H. Choate, Jr., had been exploring the question of whether Congress or the states had power to establish conventions with Palmer, Beck, and others. Choate himself agreed with Palmer that Congress possessed such authority, but a January poll of selected VCL members, distinguished members of the bar from across the country, found that 40 percent disagreed.[59] Near the end of January the VCL executive committee decided that to avoid losing vital time in case Congress did not provide for conventions, it would be wise to pursue state action. Congress could later override the states if it chose. They acted as much from fear of the consequences of delay as from certainty of state prerogatives. Urged on by the AAPA, Choate with assistance from Columbia University law professor Noel T. Dowling hastily drafted a model bill for state legislatures to use in establishing ratification conventions. While several members reviewed the draft, supporters in each state were alerted and asked to initiate action on convention legislation since a bill would soon be forthcoming. Jouett Shouse asked state AAPA leaders to support the VCL effort.[60] Members of both the association and the lawyers committee across the country immediately agreed to cooperate.[61] With deadlines for filing bills fast approaching in some states, wets had convention bills introduced by title, the substance to await arrival of the VCL model. Completed only days before congressional passage of the repeal resolution, the model convention bill was quickly brought to every sitting legislature by VCL and AAPA representatives. The VCL executive committee wrote all forty-eight governors, explaining the bill's "exhaustive consideration" by legal experts, stressing its simplicity and slight expense, and recommending its use. Shouse urged legislators to modify the proposal if need be, but to take action on it at once.[62] The provision of a detailed plan for creating ratification conventions, along with well-marshalled arguments on the right of states to proceed rather than await congressional action, reduced state legislative indecision and delay to a minimum.

The VCL had been concerned with insuring that state conventions operate as much as possible like referendums. One attorney involved in the early stages of drafting legislation, Arthur W. Machen, Jr., of Baltimore, wrote to Choate, "The only thing in which I am interested is the underlying idea of making the members of the convention the same sort of figure-heads that presidential electors have become, and of submitting the question of repeal or continuance of the Eighteenth Amendment to a state-wide popular vote."[63] Choate and his colleagues determined that convention delegates should be elected at large to avoid gerrymandered districts which, like rural-dominated state legislatures, might favor drys. One slate of delegates pledged to repeal and one opposed would be selected on the basis of nominating petitions with the greatest number of signatures. Conventions themselves would thereby merely ratify the voters' choice. Some concern about the political reception and constitutionality of this approach led the VCL to include a third unpledged slate and to add an alternative draft, providing for delegates elected from congressional districts, as well as a clause rendering state legislation compatible if Congress chose to pass a convention act.[64]

All but a handful of states quickly and smoothly made the necessary arrangements for conventions, generally along the lines suggested by the Voluntary Committee of Lawyers. Of forty-three states which established conventions (only Georgia, Kansas, Louisiana, Mississippi, and North Dakota failed to do so, confirming wet fears that dry state legislatures represented a possible stumbling block to repeal), eleven acted within a month, thirty-nine within four months, of Congress's action submitting the repeal resolution. The VCL had clearly allayed confusion and speeded the process. Choate remained in frequent contact with VCL representatives in the individual states as their legislatures considered the matter. He answered constitutional and procedural questions, offered encouragement, and suggested ways of dealing with particular state problems. Twelve states followed the model bill almost exactly, at least eight others used it with minor modification, several more adapted portions, and many of the rest incorporated its ideas. Twenty-five states chose their convention delegates at large, fourteen selected them by district, and four combined the methods. In the absence of congressional direction, the VCL measure provided guidelines for the states, although practically every convention had its own peculiar features.[65]

So that elections would serve as referendums on prohibition, nearly every state provided for separate slates of delegates pledged to favor or oppose the proposed new amendment. Eight states provided for an unpledged slate as well, but only Wyoming made no mention of delegate preferences. Wyoming arranged for delegates to be chosen at precinct and county meetings, leaving the convention free to act as a truly deliberative body. Alabama, Arkansas, and Oregon required delegates to vote in accordance with a referendum on the amendment held at the same time as the delegate election. Arizona offered the surest sign that conventions were expected to reflect the voters' choice. There, if a delegate failed to hold to the position stated on his nominating petition, he would "be guilty of a misdemeanor, his vote not considered, and his office deemed vacant."[66]

With the repeal battle shifting to the states, all of the wet organizations continued their efforts. Despite the momentum generated by the 1932 election, the lame-duck Congress's unexpectedly swift and decisive endorsement of the repeal resolution, and the rapid provision for ratification conventions by most states, antiprohibitionists expected a struggle to carry three-fourths of the states. Drys, on the other hand, seemed to feel the battle was over, since they put up only dispirited and, by their earlier standards, very modest resistance. The Voluntary Committee of Lawyers fended off dry litigation designed to overturn convention laws in seven states. Given the uncertainties regarding the new ratification process, defenders of prohibition hoped to succeed in this desperate counterattack. Joseph Choate provided calm, reassuring counsel to local VCL representatives in Alabama, Maine, Missouri, New York, Pennsylvania, Ohio, and Vermont. Ultimately none of these dry efforts proved very threatening.[67] The Association Against the Prohibition Amendment campaigned for ratification primarily through its state divisions, playing a central role in several states in drawing up slates of prorepeal convention delegates. The association's publicity campaign, though at least equivalent to that of the drys, was not as thorough as it would have liked, for the lack of funds which had plagued it throughout the depression became more acute after the 1932 elections persuaded many that the victory was won. However, large contributions from Pierre and Irénée du Pont, Edward S. Harkness, and John Raskob, as well as many smaller donations (3,488 between $1 and $100 in 1933), enabled the AAPA to pour a quarter of a million dollars into the 1933 repeal campaign. Much of the local campaigning was carried out by the Women's Organization for National Prohibition Reform and, in some states, the Crusaders.[68]

The Delaware WONPR, for instance, brought its full force to bear in the May 1933 election of convention delegates. A typical state division of the organization, the Delaware WONPR grew to nearly 7,300 members in a state with about a quarter million residents. In previous years the women had held public meetings throughout the state, distributed literature, obtained newspaper publicity, and lobbied for repeal with state and federal legislators. Now they helped choose a slate of seventeen repeal delegates (including two of their own members), circulated nominating petitions in every election district, canvassed, and arranged newspaper advertisements and twice-daily radio speeches. Finally, together with the local branch of the Crusaders, they drove sympathetic voters to the polls.[69] Such efforts were rewarded. Delaware voted four to one for repeal, and even the most rural, supposedly the driest, county produced a two to one wet margin.

The AAPA continued to broadcast its arguments against national prohibition during the state campaigns. Jouett Shouse emphasized the economic advantages of repeal. The enactment of prohibition, he said, had eliminated the liquor industry—the country's largest single taxpayer and the employer of hundreds of thousands of citizens. Repeal of the Eighteenth Amendment, Shouse asserted, would easily restore a billion dollars a year in federal

Eleutherian Mills Historical Library

Repeal campaign car, Wilmington, Delaware, 1932

revenue, without taking additional money from the American people's pockets, by simply diverting into legitimate channels a gigantic underworld business. James Wadsworth, another frequent AAPA spokesman, indicted prohibition for producing crime, corruption, and violations of the constitutional rights of individuals. He renewed the association's call for a return to local self-government and urged fellow Republicans not to let Democrats receive all the credit for responding to the popular demand for repeal. "This is not a question merely of beverages, beers, wines, spirits," Wadsworth insisted. "It is a question of sound constitutional government, and political decency which goes with it."[70]

The Roosevelt administration, taking office March 4, threw its support behind the repeal drive. On March 13, in one of his first requests to a special session of Congress, the new president asked that the Volstead Act be modified to legalize 3.2 percent beer in the interim before repeal. Roosevelt stressed the need for additional government revenue which a beer tax would bring.[71] Congress eagerly complied, and on April 7 much of the country cheered the arrival of legal, though rather weak beer. State law permitted 3.2 beer in nineteen states as of that day, and several other states moved quickly to make provision for it as soon as possible. A shiny new beer truck bearing a huge sign, "President Roosevelt, the first real beer is yours," delivered two cases to the White House at 12:04 A.M. on the morning of the seventh while a crowd of eight hundred cheered outside the gates. H. L. Mencken and Al Smith, following ceremonial tastings, proclaimed the new beer satisfactory. Baltimore and Milwaukee, St. Louis and St. Paul, Cincinnati and San Francisco celebrated, and in New York, "Everywhere one went, in hotels, restaurants, clubs, homes, and even in some speakeasies, people were drinking the new beer and smiling."[72] According to Joseph Dublin, editor of *Brewery Age,* brewers sold over a million barrels of 3.2 beer in the first twenty-four hours. How rapidly beer drinkers consumed that quantity is anyone's guess. The United States Brewers Association, concerned that too much drinking might hand dry propagandists some new ammunition and damage chances for ratification of repeal, attempted to slow the flow by delaying deliveries. Surprisingly, arrests for drunkenness actually dropped, perhaps an indication of police tolerance of the celebration and, as likely, a measure of the potency of the beverage being so enthusiastically consumed.[73] Although the Eighteenth Amendment remained in force and only the Volstead Act definition of an intoxicant changed, many Americans considered the return of beer on April 7 as ending prohibition and gave Franklin Roosevelt credit for its demise.

The return of beer raised the often-expressed hope that repeal would help solve the depression. An Associated Press survey after a week of 3.2 beer sales found that the federal government had already collected over $4,000,000 from barrel taxes and license fees. States and municipalities also

received substantial revenue. Legalization of beer provided quick employment for an estimated twenty thousand brewery workers and created tens of
thousands of related jobs, from waiting tables to making barrels and pret-
zels, it was reported. Roosevelt emphasized repeal's economic value again in
May when he proposed new liquor taxes to take effect upon termination of
the Eighteenth Amendment. During the summer, the president, aided by
Democratic national chairman James A. Farley, continued to boost repeal.[74]

The ratification process went swiftly forward.[75] Michigan on April 3 became the first state to elect convention delegates. Voters favored the repeal
slate three to one. A week later the Michigan convention met in the chamber
of the House of Representatives in Lansing and by a vote of ninety-nine to
one ratified the repeal amendment. In rapid order, Wisconsin, Rhode
Island, New Jersey, Wyoming, New York, Delaware, and Illinois delivered
even stronger endorsements of repeal, ranging from 78 to 89 percent voter
approval, and unanimous convention decisions, except in New Jersey where 2
dry delegates held out against 202 wet ones.

On June 6 Indiana registered the first sizable dry vote, 312,120 out of
869,182 ballots cast and 83 out of 329 delegate seats, but nevertheless a solid
64 percent wet popular majority. By the end of June, sixteen states had
expressed a preference for repeal, and none for prohibition. Three states that
had scheduled their elections for mid-July were thought to be dry strong-
holds, so when Alabama and Arkansas each voted 59 percent in favor of
repeal, and the following day Tennessee eked out a 51 percent repeal majority, Jouett Shouse exultantly declared the battle won and predicted ratification's completion within the year. Before October drew to a close, fourteen
more states fell in line, and only once, in Idaho, did the wet majority slip
below 60 percent. Thirty-three states had by then held ratification conventions or arranged to do so during November.

On November 7, 1933, elections in six more states assured that repeal
would be ratified by more than the necessary thirty-six states within the year.
Maine, Ohio, Pennsylvania, and Utah chose repeal by majorities ranging
from 60 percent in Utah to 76 percent in Pennsylvania. Strangely, the only
two states to vote against repeal held their elections on this same day. South
Carolina rejected repeal by 52 percent, while in the largest dry vote all year,
71 percent in North Carolina chose not to hold a convention. But with four
more conventions certain to ratify the new amendment on December 5 or 6,
the struggle was virtually over.

Between April and November 1933, thirty-seven states held elections on
the question of retention or repeal of national prohibition. Nearly twenty-one
million Americans went to the polls to express their preference. No less than
fifteen million, 72.9 percent of those voting, favored repeal. Nevada and
Wyoming chose delegates in precinct meetings and county conventions, with
no tabulation of the popular vote. Both state conventions voted unanimously

for repeal. Montana did not elect convention delegates until its 1934 primary; on August 6, 1934, by a vote of forty-five to four, they added their approval of the already ratified Twenty-first Amendment. Nebraska, Oklahoma, and South Dakota declined to hold delegate elections after repeal was certain, while Georgia, Kansas, Louisiana, Mississippi, and North Dakota did not adopt convention legislation.

The lop-sided majority for repeal represented all sections of the country. The delegate elections approximated the February roll calls in Congress which found 70 percent of the House and 73 percent of the Senate favoring repeal. Urban northeast and Great Lakes congressmen voted overwhelmingly wet, while representatives of the more sparsely populated Great Plains and Far West divided more evenly. Southern congressmen, who had voted heavily for prohibition in 1917, for the most part chose repeal in 1933. The popular vote showed a similar pattern, with the West somewhat wetter and the South drier than their congressional delegations, but almost everywhere a clear majority for repeal.

The repeal plurality in Connecticut, Rhode Island, New York, and New Jersey exceeded 85 percent; in Massachusetts and Maryland 80 percent; and in Pennsylvania and Delaware 75 percent. In the Midwest, Illinois, Michigan, Wisconsin, and Missouri all recorded 75 percent or more in the wet column; and Ohio, home of the Anti-Saloon League, registered 71 percent for repeal. Iowa, Minnesota, Colorado, Utah, Oregon, and Washington all posted repeal majorities of between 60 and 68 percent, while in Arizona, New Mexico, and California the antiprohibition vote was 76 or 77 percent. Several southern states did not hold conventions, but with the exceptions of the Carolinas and Tennessee, those states which voted produced wet majorities of 59 percent or more. Sectional distinctions appear, but they pale in light of the dimensions of the wet landslide.

Precise, sophisticated, precinct-by-precinct quantitative analyses of these special elections—the kind which have contributed so much to better understanding of presidential voting patterns—are, unfortunately, not possible because only aggregate returns are available. The AAPA, however, distinguished the returns of each state's principal urban areas from the balance of the state and found surprisingly little difference between them despite the usual assumptions about wet cities and dry countryside. In most states the repeal plurality fell off outside the metropolitan areas, but only Utah, Tennessee, and the Carolinas recorded a dry majority there. In Virginia, outside the state's major urban centers, the vote was 60 percent wet; in West Virginia, Indiana, and Arkansas, 58 percent; in Vermont, 64 percent; in Iowa and Colorado, 60 percent; in Alabama, 52 percent; in Idaho, 57 percent; and in Ohio, 63 percent. In quite a few states, the most sparsely populated counties did return dry majorities, but everywhere the heavy wet vote extended far beyond the city limits.

The brief, formal state ratification conventions merely validated decisions made at the polls. With the exception of South Carolina, where voters chose a full slate of at-large delegates opposed to repeal, and Indiana, where one-fourth of the district delegates were elected on the basis of their opposition to repeal, hardly a delegate objected to ratification in the conventions. In only eight conventions were negative votes cast at all. So perfunctory were the actions of the conventions in carrying out voters' wishes that the question arose as to whether a simple, direct referendum would not have been more sensible and economical.

Still, state convention proceedings provide some insight into delegates' thinking and the influence of the Association Against the Prohibition Amendment, the Women's Organization for National Prohibition Reform, and other antiprohibition organizations. In the first place, many AAPA and WONPR leaders served as delegates and convention officers. His fellow delegates elected Pierre du Pont chairman of the Delaware convention. The Michigan convention chose Mary Alger, head of the state WONPR, as president pro tempore; and in both Kentucky and Missouri, WONPR leaders served as temporary convention chairmen. State AAPA leaders chaired the Colorado, Connecticut, Florida, Kentucky, Minnesota, Texas, and Wisconsin conventions, and in California the head of the association was elected honorary president of the convention. In at least five states, Colorado, Florida, Minnesota, Texas, and Utah, WONPR officials were named convention secretary. In Pennsylvania, where four of the fifteen delegates were AAPA directors, W. W. Montgomery received the honor of presenting the repeal resolution. Delegates to the New York convention included James Wadsworth, Henry Curran, and Grayson Murphy of the AAPA, Pauline Sabin and several others from the WONPR, Joseph H. Choate, Jr., Selden Bacon, and Frederic R. Coudert of the Voluntary Committee of Lawyers, as well as those prominent allies of the wet organizations, Nicholas Murray Butler, Elihu Root, and Al Smith. The New York convention, packed with ex-governors, politicians, and other prominent citizens, chose Smith as president, Root as honorary president, Wadsworth as vice-president, and Pauline Sabin as chairman of the resolutions committee. Throughout the country, the AAPA and WONPR were well represented in the ratifying conventions.

Some of the conventions merely met, chose officers, ratified the proposed amendment, and adjourned. New Hampshire completed its work in a breathtaking seventeen minutes. A number, however, passed resolutions or listened to explanations of the reasons behind the repeal vote. Speakers often mentioned the need to provide new sources of tax revenue and stimulate business activity in the face of the country's desperate economic situation. Most frequently, however, they defined the need for repeal in terms long used by the AAPA: the need to restore local self-government, to protect individual rights, and to put an end to crime, intemperance, and social decay. "This convention, in casting its vote against the Amendment, is declaring the strong opposition of our people to any amendment of our National Constitution that denies to the several states the control of the habits, customs and privileges of its own citizens," announced Illinois Governor Henry Horner.[76] Other speakers in states as diverse as Connecticut, Kentucky, Maryland, Ohio, Utah, and Virginia agreed that the Eighteenth Amendment erred by usurping each state's right to govern its local affairs. At the New York convention, James Wadsworth proclaimed the battle for repeal well worth the effort "because it was waged for a fundamental principle of government."[77] One Florida delegate declared, "The tragic error we are engaged in correcting...came from a misconception of the very essence of the federal principle...on which our federal government was founded, as well as the yet more potent promptings of human nature," while another called repeal the most important demonstration of the American people's determination to have a free and democratic government "since our forefathers threw the British tea overboard in Boston Harbor."[78]

In the course of various conventions, speakers commented on the significance of the ratification process being used. No means now existed of knowing whether the people would have ratified the Eighteenth Amendment, Governor Stanley C. Wilson of Vermont remarked, "but we do know that if this method is adopted of providing for an amendment to the Constitution, there can be no question about how the people feel as to the amendment."[79] State senate president Emerson L. Richards, presiding at the New Jersey convention, praised "this ancient form of popular expression—the convention" as "the greatest weapon for the correction of the evils of government."[80] "In this day of Fascism and Sovietism and the subjugation of people to the domination of the State or a man," said Leonard Weinberg, chairman of the Maryland convention's resolutions committee, "this marks a rededication of the people of America to the principles of Democracy."[81]

Speaker after speaker insisted that individual freedoms could not be altered through constitutional amendment except with the people's direct concurrence—possible only through ratification of amendments by convention. No one referred directly to the 1919 Ohio ratification controversy, the *Hawke v. Smith* or *Sprague* decisions, and the interest thus generated in the convention system; but Sidney Stricker, Ohio vcL leader and chairman of the resolutions committee at his state's ratification convention, alluded to them. He told the Ohio delegates that "tyranny and intolerance" could not be imposed by a minority and that "a law-abiding people" now enjoyed "a government of free institutions responsive to the will of the people."[82] To Stricker and many other delegates, the conventions of 1933 represented the discovery of a better, more democratic method of revising the Constitution. To eighty-nine-year-old Elihu Root, the convention simply provided a pleasant vindication. "Nobody seemed to remember that it was his duty to hate anybody else, and that made the occasion both novel and refreshing."[83]

On December 5, 1933, state conventions in Pennsylvania, Ohio, and Utah maneuvered to be the thirty-sixth to ratify the new Twenty-first Amendment. Utah won the honor by drawing out its proceedings until three hours after Pennsylvania and then Ohio completed action. A nationwide radio audience could hear the final roll call which ended at 3:32 P.M., mountain time. Only 288 days had passed since Congress had sent the proposed amendment to the states.[84] President Roosevelt proclaimed the Eighteenth Amendment repealed and urged that temperance mark the return of legal liquor sales. The board of directors of the Association Against the Prohibition Amendment, meeting that evening in New York, rejoiced.[85] They had reached their goal. The hitherto impossible had been achieved. For the first time in its history, the republic had rescinded an amendment to the Constitution!

10 CHAMPAGNE AND SOUR GRAPES

A few hours after Pennsylvania, Ohio, and Utah's conventions completed ratification of the Twenty-first Amendment, 170 directors of the Association Against the Prohibition Amendment from across the country gathered for a dinner at New York City's Waldorf Astoria Hotel. Once the directors assembled, waiters wheeled in a hammered-silver, six-gallon punch bowl, brimming with cocktails. With the bowl were a matching tray, two ladles, and twenty-four elegant silver goblets. An inscription on the side of the bowl read:

TO

Capt. William Henry Stayton
who from November 12, 1918, until December 5, 1933
led the Association Against the Prohibition Amendment

FROM

The Directors of that Association
as a mark of their affection and appreciation
on the occasion of their Victory Dinner
held in New York City, December 5, 1933

Everyone present as well as many absent directors had contributed to this gift for board chairman Stayton. In addition, executive committee chairman Pierre du Pont had arranged for each director to receive a cocktail glass inscribed to commemorate the occasion. President Jouett Shouse toasted the seventy-two-year-old, white-haired captain "as the founder not merely of an association but the organizer of a group which has had a profound constructive effect upon the economic and social life of America." Then with great relish the group initiated the goblets and glasses by enjoying their first legal drinks in fourteen years.[1]

Champagne, scotch whiskey, and mutual congratulations continued to flow throughout a long evening of celebration, with Stayton and du Pont receiving most of the accolades. The executive committee planned to formally dissolve the AAPA at the end of the festivities, but a number of directors, perhaps overflowing with feelings of camaraderie, achievement, or power, objected. At a board meeting the next morning, however, no one resisted further, and the oldest antiprohibition society officially disbanded.[2]

More than a month earlier, the Voluntary Committee of Lawyers had suspended its activities. On December 5, treasurer Harrison Tweed simply wrote a personal check for $6.66 to balance an overdrawn bank account and closed the VCL's books.[3] The Women's Organization for National Prohibition Reform had agreed in September to go out of existence once repeal was achieved. Over 300 women from thirty-six states gathered at the Mayflower Hotel in Washington on December 7 for the WONPR's last meeting, a subdued victory dinner in deference to the recently widowed Pauline Sabin. A few weeks later a delegation presented her with a small Renoir landscape as a tribute to her leadership of their society. Finally, a committee used $30,000 of the WONPR's leftover funds to establish a graduate fellowship in political science to be administered by Barnard College and, in memory of Charles Sabin, donated the remaining $5,000 to the New York City Boys' Club for citizenship education.[4] Of the major wet groups, only the weakest, the Crusaders, planned to continue to promote temperance and defend the Constitution, but it rapidly withered.[5] However they chose to wind up their affairs, each of these important antiprohibition organizations disbanded with a feeling of great satisfaction.

As the repeal societies prepared to depart the scene, their leaders expressed to each other and the country their sense of significant accomplishment. Captain Stayton repeatedly praised Pauline Sabin and her organization for abolishing defeatism over the possibility of repeal.[6] Jouett Shouse and Irénée du Pont congratulated Joseph H. Choate for the VCL's role in the rapid state convention ratification.[7] AAPA directors prepared for Stayton a year-long desk calendar beginning December 5, 1933, with congratulatory messages on each page. These brief, hand-written comments suggest their assessment of repeal and the association's role. For instance: December 5, "Your great day of victory! You have restored to the states their rights and to the people of the United States you have made clear the method by which they themselves may govern. What greater good could man accomplish! Pierre S. du Pont." January 2, "Every liberty loving citizen of the U.S. should feel grateful for your successful efforts in removing from our laws that blot on our Constitution. L. H. Baekeland." April 28, "When the history of our victorious struggle against constitutional desecration and legislative tyranny, as exemplified by the 18th Amendment and the Volstead act, is written your name should be emblazoned upon its pages as the proven leader of a great army of patriotic Americans. C. O'Conor Goolrick."[8]

Jouett Shouse summarized the antiprohibition movement's self-image in a national radio address on the evening of November 7, 1933, after elections that day in several states had assured adoption of the Twenty-first Amendment. He attributed victory primarily to the efforts of the AAPA and WONPR. He gave special credit to Captain Stayton and also to Al Smith,

John Raskob, Pierre du Pont, Henry Curran, and Pauline Sabin. While acknowledging their help in the campaign's final stages, Shouse pointedly objected to claims that Franklin Roosevelt and James Farley bore principal responsibility for repeal. The AAPA and its allies, laboring "through the long years of discouragement when the cause of repeal was unpopular, when the motives of those advocating it were maligned, when a successful result seemed well nigh impossible," deserved credit "for having brought about the most remarkable change in national sentiment and the most far-reaching social reform thus far recorded in the evolution of the American people." The very politicians who had long avoided the issue and were finally compelled to act by a mighty wave of public opinion, he commented indignantly, now were trying to take credit. "I deprecate and condemn the selfish attempt of certain politicians to arrogate to themselves the entire credit for the success of a movement in which they have played small part indeed in its crucial stages and toward the consummation of which their efforts were withheld until the overwhelming popularity of the movement had been assured."[9]

Many journalists agreed with Shouse's view of repeal and extolled the wet organizations. Stayton's role in particular drew notice.[10] His friend H. L. Mencken called him "the hero of the day" and went on to say, "He was bearing the heat and burden of the day at a time when nine-tenths of all the politicians were skulking. He has done the American people a vast service, and I only wish I could hope that they will not forget it."[11] A more objective observer, Arthur Krock of the *New York Times*, in a lengthy article gave the AAPA credit for forcing an outright repeal plank through the 1932 Democratic convention, electing a wet majority to the Seventy-third Congress, pushing an acceptable repeal resolution through the lame-duck Congress, and accelerating state ratification by at least two years. Captain Stayton and the AAPA, the article continued, convinced an overwhelming national majority that repeal could be achieved and then moved Congress and the states to take action. The association, said Krock, was passing out of existence "with a consciousness of a constructive social task excellently performed."[12]

Thus, repeal leaders had ample reason to believe that lasting acclaim would be theirs. After all, they were being told and were telling each other, while cautious professional politicians had hesitated, they had correctly perceived and expressed the popular will, mobilized the electorate, and achieved a significant victory against enormous odds. They had engineered a tremendous political reversal, aided an ailing economy, set the country on the path to temperance, and redeemed dearly held constitutional principles. They felt certain of historical recognition.

However, the antiprohibitionists' moment of exhilaration and glory faded rapidly, even though repeal brought better control of alcoholic beverages, an end to bootlegging and speakeasies, and sizable revenues for state and federal government. For both contemporaries and later historians, the ongoing problems of the depression and the Roosevelt administration's struggles to cope with it quickly overshadowed repeal. Before long, prohibition came to be generally remembered as an absurd and costly mistake, "the noble experiment" whose repeal was inevitable; forgotten were the initial widespread optimism and support for creating a temperate nation by law and then the tremendous obstacles to removing that law from the Constitution once it had proved unsatisfactory. Also, subsequent events blackened the reputation of the repeal movement's leadership. Any one of these factors could easily blur hindsight, and together they consigned the organized wets to historical oblivion. Under these circumstances, placing prohibition repeal and its leading advocates in better perspective becomes both worthwhile and difficult.

The return of liquor itself generally produced the temperate drinking, law observance, and economic stimulus for which its advocates had hoped. Repeal itself provoked less of a celebratory public binge than the return of 3.2 beer eight months earlier. Whereas large quantities of beer could be brewed and made available very rapidly, supplies of wine and liquor could only expand gradually because of the time needed to age or import them. In 1936, when stocks of wine and spirits had reached levels judged adequate to meet demand, consumption remained significantly below preprohibition rates. Unquestionably, some people now drank who had been unable to afford bootlegger's prices or unwilling to violate the law. Nevertheless, according to estimates based on federal liquor tax payments, the most comprehensive and reliable indicator, per capita consumption of alcohol from 1936 through 1941 was only 60 percent of what it had been in 1911–15, the last comparable period before widespread state prohibition.[13] Once the legal liquor business was fully established, most bootleggers and speakeasies could not compete profitably, and so abandoned the effort. In 1940 the legal manufacture and sale of alcoholic beverages generated, according to the Distilled Spirits Institute's estimate, 1,229,000 jobs and a billion dollars in wages. Federal, state, and local tax and license receipts amounted to another one billion dollars.[14] Certainly many problems of individual alcohol abuse remained, but the return of legal drinking proved as successful as it did because both state and federal governments took pains to assure that it would be so.

Antiprohibition organizations were called upon to propose a postrepeal liquor regulation system and were criticized for not doing so.[15] Jouett Shouse declared that the AAPA was adhering to long-standing beliefs. "The whole basis upon which the repeal fight has been waged is the theory that each state should handle the matter of liquor control in such way as seems best to its citizens and as meets its needs and conditions. We must not depart from that basic principle," he continued. "It is none of my business, it is none of your business what liquor laws may be adopted by a state of which we are not residents."[16] Joseph Choate explained that the VCL did not prepare a liquor control bill because its executive committee "was satisfied that conditions in the various states were so diverse that no single system would satisfy any considerable number of them."[17]

Though they refused in principle to propose any one national solution, wets offered assistance to individual states as they considered what to do. The AAPA called attention to models provided by its various studies of foreign systems of alcoholic beverage control, and the WONPR summarized even more foreign approaches, fifty in all, in two publications. James W. Wadsworth spent two hours testifying before the New York State Liquor Control Board while it considered the matter of regulations. He urged careful consideration of the Swedish private-monopoly and the Quebec government-monopoly systems. The governor of Delaware appointed Pierre du Pont chairman of a five-member committee to draw up a state liquor control act. The plan, drafted and adopted with minor amendments by the legislature within two months, authorized a state commission either to operate a monopoly or license private retailers. Only beer was to be available for consumption where purchased. The anticipated large initial capital investment caused eventual rejection of the Quebec-style monopoly approach. The governor then named Pierre du Pont Delaware's first liquor commissioner. Elsewhere other AAPA members offered assistance to their state officials.[18]

Nearly every state moved quickly to establish statewide alcoholic beverage regulations. This contrasted sharply with preprohibition practice, when controls remained largely in local hands and a chaotic jumble of approaches resulted. With states proceeding independently, each system of control developed its individual characteristics, but some general patterns emerged. The majority of states, twenty-five by 1936, established agencies to license and regulate private sale. Some states seemed primarily concerned with tax collection, while others established very exact and detailed requirements as to how the trade should be conducted. Most regulated hours of sale, location with respect to schools and churches, advertising, and the physical characteristics of retail outlets. At the same time, a second group of fifteen states decided to sell distilled spirits through government stores. About half of these established government monopolies, while the others also licensed private retailers. The states which took on the liquor business themselves tended to be those bordering Canada and able to closely observe its example, or else those where a third or more the voters in 1933 had opposed repeal. Legislators in states which decided to operate liquor stores shared a concern that private business would exploit liquor sales. They desired strict control over the trade more than they feared the precedent of state takeover of a formerly private business. Eight states chose to continue banning liquor sales as of 1936, but every state except Alabama and Kansas allowed the sale of beer. By 1940, 3.2 beer was available everywhere, and only Kansas, Mississippi, and Oklahoma barred liquor sales. Seventeen states had undertaken at least some government sales by then, while the other twenty-eight had placed the business in the hands of licensed retailers.[19]

Nothing in the reestablishment of legal drinking caused more concern than the return of the saloon. Temperance advocates from T. S. Arthur, the author of the 1854 *Ten Nights in a Bar-room,* to the leaders of the Anti-Saloon League focused attention on the saloon as the symbol of the corrupting influence of the liquor business. Many antiprohibitionists viewed the saloon as a social and political center of dubious virtue and agreed that its return should be prevented. Following repeal, fifteen states prohibited all liquor sales for consumption at the place of purchase, and most others restricted on-premise consumption to hotels, restaurants, and clubs where food accompanied the drink. At first only nine states licensed retail establishments to sell drinks without food. Even here strict requirements often applied: no Sunday sales, no sales to minors or intoxicated persons, no treating, gambling, dancing, disorderly conduct, or concealment of the interior from the street. Some states insisted that patrons be served seated at tables rather than standing at the bar, presumably because the latter position encouraged overindulgence and other unseemly behavior. The ownership or control of retail outlets by brewers or distillers—so-called "tied houses"— was almost universally prohibited on the grounds that such arrangements in the past had put pressure on the proprietor to encourage consumption at any cost. Jouett Shouse, for one, questioned efforts to entirely eliminate the sale of liquor by the drink. If, at least in large cities, people could not legally and openly buy a single drink without having to purchase food as well, he predicted that they would continue to patronize speakeasies.[20] Yet states regarded the saloon as a danger and closely monitored those which were allowed.

The old saloon did not reappear either in name or form, although gradually more states permitted liquor sale by the drink. In the first place, retailers thought it bad business and worse politics to call their establishments saloons and chose to label them taverns, bars, or something else. Far more important, state regulation and policing by image-conscious brewers prevented the reappearance of many saloon conditions, while other changes encouraged home consumption instead. Before 1920 most beer and liquor was packaged in barrels and kegs, too easily spoiled or too costly for home consumption. Improvements in bottling technology by the soft drink industry during prohibition, and the widespread introduction of home refrigerators made it possible to keep beer at home. Soon after repeal, the development of canned beer and nonreturn bottles, together with new advertising approaches, further stimulated home consumption. While in 1934, draught beer accounted for three-fourths of all beer sales, by 1941 package sales captured a majority of the market. The proportion of distilled liquor consumed at home increased as well, in part because the federal government, seeking to insure that nothing escaped taxation, required that all spirits destined for retail sale be packaged in nonreusable bottles no larger than one gallon. When it became as convenient and inexpensive to imbibe spirits at home, fewer people went to the saloon. Wine had always been consumed primarily in the home. Such factors insured that the saloon—or whatever the public drinking establishment was now to be called—would never regain its pre-1920 position.[21] American drinking practices and social patterns, especially in urban areas, would therefore differ markedly from those of the era before national prohibition. The saloon as principal neighborhood gathering place, information exchange, paycheck cashing service, employment bureau, and political club had disappeared forever.

The federal government settled on limited regulation of the liquor trade after repeal, but not until after the Roosevelt administration had attempted a more active role and given serious consideration to even fuller participation. The rush of states to ratify the Twenty-first Amendment caught administration leaders by surprise. In October 1933 the White House hastily formed an interdepartmental wine and spirits committee to recommend a federal policy. The committee met with Roosevelt and his cabinet on November 9, two days after state elections had assured repeal within a month, and again alone with the president a week later. Roosevelt and several close advisors, including Agriculture Secretary Henry Wallace, Interior Secretary Harold Ickes, Commerce Secretary Daniel Roper, and "brain trust" advisor Rex Tugwell, appeared to favor a federal government monopoly of the wholesale liquor trade with close regulation of the retail business. The interdepartmental committee wanted to establish strict federal control over imports in order to persuade producing nations to accept more American surplus agricultural products in return for the right to increase wine and liquor shipments to the United States. On the other hand, the committee viewed complete federal control of the liquor business as an "immense and troublesome task."[22]

Eventually the interdepartmental committee persuaded Roosevelt to establish a Federal Alcohol Control Administration under the National Recovery Administration. This plan, which the president ordered into effect on December 4, allowed private business to obtain permits to engage in the liquor trade under the terms of codes of fair competition drafted by the government. These codes, which were to encourage self-regulation by the industry, covered everything from labeling and advertising to production and pricing, from restrictions on relationships between manufacturers, wholesalers, and retailers to prevention of shipment of liquor into a state in violation of its laws. Roosevelt appointed Joseph H. Choate to head the federal alcohol agency, and the former VCL leader monitored the liquor industry in a relaxed fashion until the Supreme Court declared the NRA unconstitutional in 1935. The attempt to negotiate reciprocal import agreements proved unsuccessful, as foreign nations failed to cooperate and demand for wine and liquor imports became irresistible. The federal government gradually adopted a policy of concerning itself primarily, indeed after 1935 almost exclusively, with collection of liquor taxes. Regulation of the business fell almost entirely to the states.[23]

The initial federal plan for the liquor industry became known just as the AAPA was preparing to disband. A highly suspicious executive committee authorized Jouett Shouse to make a statement at the December 5 victory dinner expressing concern about the codes "which give autocratic authority to a Federal agency to exercise the power of life and death over the industry, which enable the Federal Government to limit production and to fix prices in any arbitrary manner." Shouse recalled the demand of repeal groups that liquor control be returned to the states. "If I have any knowledge of the motives which animated the people of America in voting for repeal of the Eighteenth Amendment, one of the strongest was the desire to throw off the yoke of Federal liquor domination." In the liquor industry code written by federal officials, Shouse saw "possible danger of corruption and of political favoritism far beyond the opportunities created by the Eighteenth Amendment." The appointment of Joseph Choate to chair the Federal Alcohol Control Administration provided reassurance, but Shouse nevertheless insisted that the codes be modified. "Otherwise there may be ultimately fastened upon the people of America a degree of Federal autocracy which exceeds in its potentialities the pernicious practices associated with attempted enforcement of the Eighteenth Amendment." Three days later, speaking in Philadelphia, Shouse repeated this message, complaining particularly that the industry involved had not been allowed to participate in the code writing, as was common practice under the NRA. He pointedly warned that "it may well be that the people of America will once more be compelled to register their protest against Federal control of the liquor industry."[24] AAPA fears about the degree of control which federal officials might try to exercise over the alcoholic beverage business proved to be exaggerated, but their instant expression revealed a great deal about how they viewed themselves and the Roosevelt administration.

Antiprohibitionist leaders felt that they had won the repeal fight because the American people shared their view that traditional constitutional arrangements, especially a limited degree of federal authority, ought to be continued. When all other issues were stripped away in the 1933 repeal convention elections, they believed, voters had overwhelmingly vindicated this principle. Now they began to see the very thing they had fought—centralization in federal hands of authority to deal with local affairs—returning in the shape of Franklin Roosevelt's New Deal. Roosevelt, they felt, had never appreciated their objections to national prohibition, had sought to ignore them, and was now proceeding in a contrary direction.

Rather than disband altogether, AAPA leaders decided to maintain a small Washington office under Stayton's direction, ostensibly to advise states on liquor control, but also to monitor administration policies on a broad front. "Recent emergency legislation and action have raised grave Constitutional doubts and problems analogous to those which have formed the basis of our work, and have led some of our Directors to suggest that our group should, in some proper fashion, be held together for a time, even after repeal of the Eighteenth Amendment," Stayton explained. The AAPA executive committee authorized this successor organization, Repeal Associates, because of concern that "Federal regulation and control might possibly become an entire refutation of the basis upon which repeal of the Eighteenth Amendment was sought by our Association." Stayton and the others worried that the new administration might be thinking of "an attempt at a continuance of Federal and State functions."[25] Repeal Associates, with an original executive committee composed entirely of former AAPA leaders, Pierre du Pont (chairman), Robert Cassatt, Benedict Crowell, Grayson Murphy, Ralph Shaw, William Stayton, and James Wadsworth, itself did little besides publish a quarterly journal.[26] Nevertheless, it helped keep together for the time being a core of like-minded antiprohibitionists ready to launch other efforts to defend their viewpoint on governmental matters.

By the spring of 1934, some repeal leaders, among them John Raskob, the du Pont brothers, Jouett Shouse, William Stayton, and James Beck, were becoming upset with what they regarded as the increasingly radical course of the New Deal. They began discussing, among themselves and with a few others, the creation of a new national organization to call for "a return to the Constitution."[27] Goaded on by Raskob especially, during the summer they made arrangements and on August 22 announced formation of the American Liberty League. The Liberty League practically reincarnated the Association Against the Prohibition Amendment. Jouett Shouse served as league president, Captain Stayton as secretary, and Grayson Murphy as treasurer. A small executive committee directed the Liberty League's affairs; its members included Shouse, Irénée du Pont, James Wadsworth, and Pauline Sabin as well as two former Democratic presidential nominees who had both been friendly to the AAPA, John W. Davis and Alfred E. Smith, and the only Republican to defeat Smith for the New York governorship, Nathan L. Miller. Raskob often met with this committee but preferred not to hold office. The Liberty League also established a larger national advisory board of prominent individuals to enhance its stature. This too contained many names from the repeal campaign, such as Representative James M. Beck, Mrs. Henry B. Joy and Mrs. James Ross Todd of the WONPR, Frederic R.

Coudert, Jr., of the vcl, Edward F. Hutton, board chairman of General Foods Corporation and one of the Crusaders' leading financial backers, and Samuel Harden Church, Edward S. Harkness, Henry B. Joy, and Ralph Shaw of the aapa. Pierre, Irénée, and Lammot du Pont and John Raskob became the Liberty League's heaviest contributors. Stayton used the aapa and wonpr membership rolls to solicit members, while Sabin, Shouse, and Raskob were delegated to enlist the Crusaders as well. Although Al Smith, John W. Davis, and many of the prominent businessmen who joined had not been directly involved in an antiprohibition organization, the Liberty League's leadership, membership, organizational structure, publicity techniques, and doctrines nevertheless bore a striking resemblance to those of the aapa.[28]

Liberty League president Shouse went to the White House late on the afternoon of August 15, 1934, for a private meeting he had requested with Franklin Roosevelt. He told Roosevelt that a powerful, nonpartisan group was being formed "to defend and uphold the Constitution of the United States and to gather and disseminate information that (1) will teach the necessity of respect for the rights of persons and property as fundamental to every successful form of government, and (2) will teach the duty of governments to encourage and protect individual and group initiative and enterprise, to foster the right to work, earn, save and acquire property, and to preserve the ownership and lawful use of property when acquired." According to Shouse, Roosevelt replied that he could "subscribe to that one hundred per cent" and, in Shouse's presence, told his press secretary to issue a statement of hearty approval when the league's establishment was announced.[29] Nine days later, however, after the league had proclaimed its existence and received considerable initial attention, Roosevelt struck a much different note, one to which he would adhere thereafter whenever he spoke of the Liberty League. Dismissing its stated constitutional concerns, he told a press conference that the league appeared to lay too much stress on protection of property and too little on protection of the average citizen. Roosevelt reportedly repeated a remark made to him that the league's tenets seemed to be "love thy God but forget thy neighbor," and God in this case appeared to be property.[30] The president's comments reinforced the hostility and distrust which league leaders had felt toward him since the repeal campaign. Open warfare between the White House and the American Liberty League now began.

For the next two years, the Liberty League and the administration battled. On both sides the weapons were vitriol and scorn; the tactics, protestations of wounded virtue and escalating criticism of the opposition. The league issued a more than one-a-week barrage of pamphlets, radio broadcasts, leaflets, and bulletins, presenting statements by its leaders or reports by its research staff. Its attack concentrated on aspects of the New Deal, such as the nra and the Agricultural Adjustment Administration, which shifted governmental responsibility, in the league's eyes usurping congressional functions and placing legislative power in the hands of the bureaucratic structures of the executive branch. Roosevelt's criticism of the Supreme Court's overturning of the NRA and AAA provoked an impassioned defense from the league of the Court's constitutional privileges and responsibilities. Roosevelt appeared set on building an omnipotent presidency, the league charged. Other measures involving large expenditures for relief drew fire for violating the 1932 platform pledge of a balanced budget and for creating huge deficits, stimulating inflation, and requiring higher taxes, all of which would hamper business and retard recovery.[31]

James Wadsworth expressed a typical league view in 1935 when he wrote, "The common man is beginning to understand that these experiments launched, presumably, for his benefit have not only failed to benefit him financially but have resulted in robbing him of a large portion of that liberty which the Constitution seeks to guarantee to him. I feel very much about the issue as I did about the eighteenth amendment, except that I realize that it is far greater in its ramifications." He told his former Senate and repeal-crusade colleague, William Cabell Bruce, "We must of course bring to the common man the seriousness of some of the experiments but we must forever pound upon the fundamentals involved regardless of the price of wheat or cotton or the slaying of hogs, etc. These last are but incidents." Wadsworth was doing his part. "I mentioned some of these incidents last night over the radio, but I repeated as best I could the assertion that from the beginning these experiments were intended as the first great steps toward the complete transformation of our government and that as such they must be resisted else the transformation will be achieved and our liberties lost."[32]

The climax of the assault came at a dinner of 2,000 Liberty Leaguers in Washington, January 25, 1936. Al Smith leveled a savage blast at the New Deal for turning class against class, establishing presidential autocracy with the aid of an army of bureaucrats, failing to carry out the 1932 Democratic platform, and introducing socialism. "The young brain trusters caught the Socialists in swimming and they ran away with their clothes" was one of the few of Smith's lines that had a light touch. His peroration was somber and apocalyptic: "There can only be one capitol, Washington or Moscow. There can be only one atmosphere of government, the clear, pure, fresh air of free America, or the foul air of communistic Russia. There can be only one flag, the Stars and Stripes or the flag of the godless union of the Soviets. There can be only one national anthem, 'The Star-Spangled Banner' or the 'Internationale.' There can be only one victor. If the Constitution wins, we win."[33]

The Roosevelt administration challenged the Liberty League from its inception, ignoring its constitutional arguments and focusing on its economic concerns. The president's August 1934 press conference remarks begat caustic references by other administration spokesmen to wealthy league members' selfish motives.[34] In his state of the union address on January 3, 1936, Roosevelt described his critics as "unscrupulous money-changers" who "steal the livery of great national constitutional ideals to serve discredited special interests." These forces of "entrenched greed," Roosevelt suggested, bore responsibility for the nation's economic collapse.[35] He returned to the same themes in June during his speech accepting renomination: "These economic royalists complain that we seek to overthrow the institutions of America. What they really complain of is that we seek to take away their power. In vain they seek to hide behind the Flag and the Constitution."[36]

Roosevelt and his aides treated the Liberty League as a serious threat, especially in the winter of 1935-36, when the president's popularity reached an all-time low, when he was being severely criticized from both right and left, and when a difficult reelection campaign appeared to lie ahead. The White House knew that leaders of the league were the same people who had mustered far more support for prohibition repeal, both in the 1932 Democratic convention and the 1933 repeal elections, than FDR and his staff, usually astute judges of voter preferences, had expected. Using the same appeals to defend the Constitution against the New Deal which had proved so successful against national prohibition, could they again mobilize support? Having underestimated this group once, Roosevelt certainly did not want to make the same mistake twice.

James Farley, as Roosevelt's campaign manager, thought enough of the Liberty League threat to hire a full-time publicist for the Democratic national committee to do nothing but plan attacks on the league, or as he would label it, "the millionaire's union."[37] Throughout the campaign, the administration chose to concentrate its attention on the league as the source of Republican funds and ideas rather than criticize the party directly. The tactic of identifying the league as a group of selfish, wealthy businessmen who wished to return to pre-1932 conditions and of spotlighting them as the primary foe helped rally the left and wavering moderates to the New Deal. The administration continued to flail the Liberty League during the summer and fall of 1936, even though by then the league had clearly failed to generate a following.

The memory of the repeal episode not only helps explain Roosevelt's uncharacteristically vocal and harsh response to his critics, it also provides a rationale for the Liberty League's rather unusual behavior during 1936. Despite great unhappiness with New Deal policies and the way administration spokesmen behaved toward it, the league declined to sever all ties to the Democratic party and openly make common cause with the Republicans. For all of Al Smith's celebrated talk of "taking a walk" and Republican campaign contributions by several individuals prominent in the league, including the du Pont brothers, the league could not bring itself to officially support the Landon-Knox ticket. The league's former antiprohibitionists held fresh and vivid memories of how unsympathetically Republicans had treated their calls for a revival of traditional constitutional values and in contrast how much support had surfaced in the Democratic party between 1928 and 1932.

Memories of how earlier defeats at Democratic hands had been followed, despite Roosevelt's opposition, by their great platform victory in 1932 undoubtedly kindled the hopes of Liberty League veterans of the repeal crusade. League leaders made it clear that they believed the Democrats had temporarily fallen under the sway of an unrepresentative clique and might heed their voices of reason once again. On the eve of the 1936 Democratic convention, delegates received an appeal signed by Al Smith and four other prominent league members. The letter urged the convention to revive the economy by taking the hand of the government off business and balancing the federal budget and to preserve the constitutional separation of powers by preventing the president from making the Congress a rubber stamp or intimidating the judiciary. This "would necessarily involve the putting aside of Franklin D. Roosevelt and the substitution of some genuine Democrat."[38] Even later, on August 5, when the league stated that it would endorse neither party and neither candidate, it declared, "The League is neither an adjunct nor an ally of the Republican party." The league's own principles, it said, "harmonized" with the "excellent platform" adopted by the Democrats in 1932, but not "the New Deal party which for the moment' has usurped control of the party of Jefferson, Jackson, Cleveland, and Wilson."[39] Roosevelt's renomination by acclamation and his subsequent landslide reelection with over 60 percent of the popular vote shattered Liberty League illusions that they more accurately represented the Democratic party and the American people than the man in the White House.

The American Liberty League badly misjudged the extent of its own influence and the changes in issues, conditions, and political circumstances between 1932 and 1936. Their exhilarating victory in overturning the Eighteenth Amendment had led Liberty League organizers to make unwarranted assumptions that they accurately reflected popular concerns about constitutional principles and could again summon a large following. The bulk of repeal voters may not have shared the organized wets' motives, but at least they shared a common goal. When the league continued to preach the same ideas in the midst of a different and much greater crisis, it offered nothing of appeal to people whose overriding concern was obtaining economic relief and who were indifferent about constitutional niceties. In light of the depressed nation's grave economic and social problems, an organization which spoke in terms of preserving constitutional forms and limiting federal initiatives appeared to most people as crass, unfeeling, self-centered, and elitist. The wealth and status of many prominent league members only strengthened popular resentment under the circumstances.

Obviously repudiated, the Liberty League sank quickly from view following the 1936 election. The du Ponts, Raskob, Shouse, and Stayton along
with most of their allies thereafter avoided politics. Three months after his
reelection, Roosevelt launched an assault on the Supreme Court, which had
been overturning New Deal legislation. The Liberty League did not rouse
itself to criticize Roosevelt's court-packing plan, although this issue would
certainly have drawn its fire earlier. Shouse later claimed this was deliberate
strategy to let administration supporters feel free to oppose the proposal
rather than force them to defend the president against attack. If so, the
league displayed more restraint and tactical flexibility than ever before.
Buoyed by his great victory, Roosevelt clearly did not worry that the Liberty
League could mount a conservative constitutional defense with the strength
to rebuff him. Ironically, others filled the departed leaguer's places, using
many of its familiar anticentralization arguments in opposing the court reorganization bill, and the bill floundered. The most striking rejection of
Roosevelt's conception of expanded executive authority occurred in the
absence of those most clearly identified as its critics.

The transformation of the antiprohibition movement into a shrill, em-
bittered, and ineffectual political splinter group distorted its historical
image. The Roosevelt administration's use of the Liberty League as a political whipping boy further blackened that reputation. Prohibitionists were
happy to blame their defeat on a little group of insensitive opponents of the
public welfare, skillful propagandists and political manipulators who had
considered only their own selfish financial interests. The image of the Liberty
League having been interposed, no one disputed such charges. The Association Against the Prohibition Amendment found itself discredited and soon
largely forgotten. The Women's Organization for National Prohibition
Reform, one of the first significant postsuffrage mass political activities of
American women, fell into obscurity as well.

The severe condemnation by New Dealers and prohibitionists of those who
had led the prohibition repeal movement provides no more accurate a
picture of the character and influence of the organized wets than does the
lavish praise they received during the December 1933 ratification celebra-
tions. Given the importance of the change in national policy which the repeal
of the Eighteenth Amendment represented, their influence and motives merit
a fairer appraisal. Several important facts emerge. The major antiprohibition societies, although they may have had little in common with the average
citizen and no feeling for his real concerns, nevertheless created a set of
unusual circumstances which allowed popular opinion on the Eighteenth
Amendment to be expressed in a politically effective fashion. Furthermore,
the prohibition episode, and wet groups' role in it, reshaped partisan politics
and attitudes toward constitutional reform. Finally, the wet organizations
influenced America's postrepeal pattern of liquor regulation.

The general public's widespread dissatisfaction with national prohibition became evident at least by the mid-1920s. Public opinion on the dry law cannot be precisely measured, but the flow of illicit liquor, the reluctance of legislators and voters in state referendums to authorize enforcement measures, and the declining strength of temperance organizations all provide signs of the popular mood. With discontent increasing, some alert politicians took up repeal on their own as a popular and rewarding cause. Urban and ethnic political leaders such as Anton Cermak and Adolph J. Sabath in Chicago, Fiorello LaGuardia and Al Smith in New York, David I. Walsh in Boston, and a handful of others saw value in opposing prohibition. But with the constitutional amending requirements creating the widespread belief that repeal was politically impossible, most legislators avoided the subject. Public unhappiness needed a vehicle, a means of visibly, measurably demonstrating its strength before it would be taken seriously. The first significant contribution of the wet organizations, then, lay in their making opposition to prohibition tangible. By articulating basic objections to the liquor ban and showing that large numbers of responsible citizens held such views, the AAPA made repeal an issue to be earnestly considered rather than dismissed as hopeless fantasy or the province of law-breakers. The WONPR demonstrated that not all women were dry and thus that women did not automatically render repeal unreachable.

The reasoning of the mass of Americans who rejected the Eighteenth Amendment did not, of course, necessarily follow that of the leaders of repeal organizations. Undoubtedly a wide variety of motives were involved. Traditional explanations which focus solely on ethnic, religious, or urban-versus-rural concerns do, however, appear too narrow. Also excessively restrictive are explanations which look no further than the desire for a drink or the economic distress of the great depression.

A mood of crisis, a feeling of threat, a fear of social disintegration permeated the criticism which antiprohibition organizations aimed at the liquor ban. They did not view the world of the 1920s with the complacency and satisfaction often thought to characterize popular attitudes during that decade. Instead, the sense of a society in turmoil, teetering between anarchy and authoritarianism, gripped them. Among the vast number of voters who endorsed repeal in 1933, as among the wet leadership, could be found many old-stock, middle-class Americans who opposed changes which disrupted their stable social and political world. The nearly three-fourths of the electorate which eventually voted to abolish national prohibition was much larger than the proportion of the population which used alcoholic beverages before or after 1933. Thus a desire for a return to tried and trusted governmental arrangements of the past must have played a part in popular thinking.

William Stayton, John Raskob, Pauline Sabin, the du Ponts, and most of their colleagues represented a social and business elite, but they generally lacked political experience or sophistication. These novices in politics felt certain that states' rights and decentralized, limited government were important in their own right. Such principles protected social, political, and economic relationships from which they benefitted and which they sincerely felt were good and healthy for America. Social upheaval, loss of respect for law, and destruction of assumed constitutional protections loomed to them as foremost among the unacceptable costs of national prohibition. Wet leaders could claim as much old-stock, middle-class respectability as drys, and they were prepared to defend their vision of traditional American values just as righteously as temperance crusaders. Antiprohibitionists diverged from the law's supporters principally in their unwillingness to accept the progressive notion of using federal power to reshape social patterns and individual behavior. They would accept strict regulation and even government operation of the liquor industry, providing it were carried out at the state or local level where the people directly affected, or at least people of standing in the community like themselves, could determine policies to be followed. In agitating for an end to the Eighteenth Amendment, they did not simply seek their own economic betterment, as often charged. Organized wets did offer economic reasons for repeal during the depression, but arguments which appeared during the final stages of the campaign and in an understandable context should not have their importance exaggerated. Their personal backgrounds in business, law, and government led antiprohibitionist leaders much earlier to a shared distrust of federal activism with its concomitant loss of local decision-making power. Economic considerations assuredly played a part in shaping these strongly Jeffersonian attitudes, but such ideas took on a life of their own, to be advanced without reference to any economic sources.

Single-minded pressure exerted by antiprohibition societies on the major political parties, and especially their role in pasting a wet label on the Democratic party, eventually proved very significant. Their persistent efforts finally obtained a means for popular opposition to national prohibition, whatever its motivation, to express itself. The Great Depression generated new arguments and enthusiasm for repeal, but unless both voters and politicians perceived alternatives at the polls in 1932, the depression might not have contributed much to repeal. However, Republican-Democratic polarization on the repeal issue coincided with a depression election. When voters threw out a dry Republican administration and installed a Democratic president and Congress, observers considered it not only a demand for new economic policies but also for repeal. Legislators moved quickly once they perceived the public verdict. The differentiation of the two parties on prohibition was taking place regardless of the depression, but the juxtaposition produced one of those rare situations where the electoral mandate seemed unmistakable. Very likely, repeal was only possible under such circumstances. At the very least, it was dramatically hastened by them.

Finally, the vcl and the aapa shaped and greatly speeded the repeal process once it was underway. Ever since 1919 wet leaders had been sensitive to the significance of the procedure which Congress had selected for ratification of an amendment, and they successfully demanded use of the untried state-convention method. By pressing for congressional submission of a repeal amendment before the 1933 lame-duck session ended, then by working out confusing legal technicalities so that ratification conventions could be held quickly, antiprohibition leaders reduced the time required to ratify the Twenty-first Amendment by many months, probably years. No constitutional amendment had ever run the ratification gauntlet so quickly, even though all others used the less complicated method of legislative approval.

The extraordinary achievement of altering the Constitution led to the overestimation of repeal leaders' power and influence. They themselves misjudged the extent to which the public shared their commitment to traditional forms and principles of government. Frightened by steps taken by the New Deal to relieve economic and social distress, these former wets remained blind to the changing nature of their society and the fact that not all were as well served as they by the existing system. The aapa and wonpr had elicited tremendous electoral support for ending the federal liquor ban, but, as the Liberty League episode demonstrated, they failed to comprehend that many voters simply used channels which they had provided and did not also subscribe to all their particular motives for seeking repeal. When more basic matters of social and economic well-being arose, traditional constitutional arrangements simply were not important. Prohibition repeal's success in rolling back the onrushing tide of federal centralization and activism during the 1930s eventually appeared a unique triumph to its greatest advocates.

Yet the antiprohibition leadership may have accomplished more than they realized. Repeal and the continued presence of its principal architects impressed Franklin Roosevelt. During the New Deal's early years, when many significant legislative programs were being developed, the president seemed wary of the American Liberty League. The extent to which Roosevelt's assessment of the political situation between 1933 and 1936 shaped his behavior and tempered his reform proposals cannot be measured precisely, but his confidence and boldness definitely increased as soon as the 1936 verdict was delivered and the Liberty League collapsed. Had it not been for the national prohibition episode, the course of the New Deal might have been different.

In the final analysis, then, what did the repeal of the Eighteenth Amendment and passage of the Twenty-first Amendment signify? In the first place, it represented a reaction against some progressive ideas of law-making. National prohibition came to be generally regarded as a serious mistake. The failure to halt widespread consumption of alcoholic beverages simply by passing a federal law forbidding their use helped discredit the view that society could be reformed and uplifted simply through passage of the proper statutes. The prohibition episode helped legislators and reformers recognize that laws must be voluntarily accepted by the vast majority of those affected in order to succeed. Changes in commonplace social and cultural patterns could not be imposed otherwise. Enforcing a widely unpopular law on an uncooperative public had proved impossible. After prohibition, American lawmakers became cautious about launching another major attempt to reshape individual behavior. The New Deal, for instance, setting a pattern of reform which would persist for decades, confined itself to efforts to remold the institutions of finance, commerce, industry, and government so as to improve people's economic, social, and political opportunities. Roosevelt's influential advisor Rex Tugwell acknowledged that "the New Deal is attempting to do nothing to people and does not seek at all to alter their way of life, their wants and desires."[40] If behavior modification occurred as a result of government action, it was an indirect result of legislation with more limited aspirations. The soaring progressive sense of the possibilities of legislation was dampened, if never totally extinguished.

A more specific reaction against progressive tendencies took place as the prohibition episode also changed twentieth-century attitudes about amending the Constitution of the United States. After a century during which the Constitution had been amended only three times, numerous progressive amendments were passed or proposed during the 1910s. Direct election of Senators, a federal income tax, and women's suffrage gained approval in the same decade as national prohibition. Reaction against the antiliquor amendment blunted enthusiasm for further constitutional innovation, including the proposed amendment prohibiting child labor which gained Congressional approval in 1924 but languished in state legislatures thereafter. The prohibition experience helped set some limits, although imprecise ones, to the amending power. Moreover, the view gained acceptance that ordinary legislation did not belong in the Constitution, even if the goal was to put it beyond the reach of a simple majority. The pace of amendment slowed again.

Prohibition also clarified some relationships between the Constitution and democracy. The Founding Fathers had deliberately made constitutional change difficult by putting it beyond the reach of a simple majority. The procedure employed for the first time in ratifying the Twenty-first Amendment demonstrated that citizens could be directly involved in a constitutional reform. The quasi-referendum convention ratification system showed itself to be fairly easy to implement, and, most importantly, it produced a general satisfaction for once that the Constitution reflected the popular will. Nevertheless, Congress, which authorized convention ratification only under extreme pressure in 1933, has not chosen to repeat the process since.

While the history of prohibition repeal demonstrated the difficulty of overturning a constitutional provision and the massive, sustained effort required, it also showed that the venerable charter could be changed—and rapidly. Only twenty years elapsed from the time the Anti-Saloon League first proposed constitutional prohibiton of alcoholic beverages to its passage and subsequent removal from the Constitution. The amending procedure posed no insurmountable obstacle—or defense—when an aroused majority wanted something badly and found means to express their wishes. Those who consider the Constitution and Bill of Rights an absolute protection of their interests should carefully consider the implications of this.

On another front, the reaction against national prohibition helped bring about one of the great shifts in American partisan politics: the emergence of the Democratic party as the nation's normal governing party after nearly a century of minority status. Prohibition brought to political consciousness a group of men and women who turned to the Democrats because of the prohibition issue, who helped rebuild the party after its 1928 defeat, and who helped label it the party of repeal. The great masses who turned to the Democrats in the 1920s and early 1930s, becoming the well-spring of its continued power, were attracted in part by the party's position on repeal. Ironically, the leaders of the antiprohibition movement rapidly became disenchanted with the Democratic administration they helped elect. Nevertheless, bonds they helped forge persisted long after their goal was reached, and the men and women of the Association Against the Prohibition Amendment, the Women's Organization for National Prohibition Reform, and the Voluntary Committee of Lawyers were forgotten.

Finally, ratification of the Twenty-first Amendment marked the admission that another in the more-than-century-long series of efforts to deal with the serious social problem of alcoholic beverage abuse had failed. Organized opponents of national prohibition showed concern for creating a temperate society and establishing more effective control over the liquor traffic, but they foreclosed certain approaches to a solution. They contended, and an overwhelming number of Americans eventually went on record as agreeing, that federally compelled abstinence offered neither a desirable nor a workable solution. In the process, they rejected a compromise often suggested during the 1920s, that is, modification of prohibition to allow beer and wine while continuing to outlaw more potent distilled spirits. There can be no certainty as to how well such a restriction would have worked, since neither the drys who insisted on a total alcohol ban in the Volstead Act nor the wets who demanded absolute repeal gave it a chance to be tested. Furthermore, by their opposition to federal solutions, the wets bear, willingly of course, considerable responsibility for the fragmented pattern of liquor control which emerged in the United States after repeal. To be sure, the antiprohibitionists cannot be held responsible for the abuse of intoxicants which went on before, during, and after prohibition, but they may have discredited one method of encouraging moderation which perhaps could have been effective on a national basis.

The problem of alcohol remains unsolved. The enormous number of drunk driving accidents and the several million alcoholics in the United States today bears bleak testimony to that unhappy fact. According to a 1977 poll, 71 percent of Americans drank alcoholic beverages and no fewer than 18 percent reported that liquor had been the cause of trouble in their family.[41] Of numerous approaches to liquor regulation tried by different states since 1933, not one has proved an unqualified success in producing temperate drinking. The ideal balance has yet to be struck between helping those who would misuse alcohol and respecting the desires of those who would use it sensibly and with pleasure. Nevertheless, it remains reasonably certain that a sweeping national prohibition of alcoholic beverages will never again be tried. During World War II, mere hints of a new attempt drew scornful comments and prompted instant widespread opposition. Constitutional prohibition of alcoholic beverages will no more be the future route to a temperate society than it proved to be in the years between 1919 and 1933. "The long path across the desert," as Warren G. Harding once described national prohibition,[42] will not be trod again.

NOTES

PREFACE TO THE FIRST EDITION

1. (Chicago: Willett, Clark, 1940), p. 26.
2. (Francestown, N.H.: Alcohol Information Press, 1943).
3. (New York: Alcohol Information Committee, 1930).
4. Dobyns' view of the AAPA persists in otherwise careful works of scholarship such as Andrew Sinclair's, *Prohibition: The Era of Excess* (Boston: Little, Brown, 1962), pp. 338-39; Norman H. Clark, *Deliver Us From Evil: An Interpretation of American Prohibition* (New York: W. W. Norton, 1976), pp. 200-201; and Paul A. Carter, *Another Part of the Twenties* (New York: Columbia University Press, 1977), pp. 92-95.
5. *The Age of Reform: From Bryan to F.D.R.* (New York: Alfred A. Knopf, 1955), pp. 289-90.
6. Peter H. Odegard, *Pressure Politics: The Story of the Anti-Saloon League* (New York: Columbia University Press, 1928).
7. Joseph R. Gusfield, *Symbolic Crusade: Status Politics and the American Temperance Movement* (Urbana: University of Illinois Press, 1963).
8. Sinclair, *Era of Excess*, p. 5.

INTRODUCTION

1. Pierre S. du Pont to Samuel Rea, February 1, 1928, Pierre S. du Pont Papers, Eleutherian Mills Historical Library, Wilmington, Delaware; *Washington Post,* December 13, 1927.
2. Ernest H. Cherrington, "American Prohibition," address to the 18th International Congress Against Alcoholism, Tartu, Estonia, July 26, 1926, in *Anti-Saloon League Year Book, 1926* (Westerville, Ohio: American Issue Press, 1927), pp. 14-15.
3. Associated Press dispatch, September 24, 1930, quoted in Charles Merz, *The Dry Decade* (Garden City, N.Y.: Doubleday, Doran, 1931), p. 297.
4. Speech in Denver, Colorado, June 25, 1923, *New York Times,* June 26, 1923, pp. 1, 12.

CHAPTER 1

1. Numerous explanations for the adoption of the Eighteenth Amendment have been put forth. The long, steady development of overwhelming popular support for prohibition provided the theme for two dry spokesmen, the Anti-Saloon League's Ernest H. Cherrington, *The Evolution of Prohibition in the United States of America: A Chronological History of the Liquor Problem and the Temperance Reform in the*

United States from the Earliest Settlements to the Consummation of National Prohibition (Westerville, Ohio: American Issue Press, 1920), and the Prohibition party's D. Leigh Colvin, *Prohibition in the United States: A History of the Prohibition Party and of the Prohibition Movement* (New York: George H. Doran, 1926). An influential contrary view, that the reform was put over by a highly organized, politically effective minority, was suggested by political scientist Peter H. Odegard, *Pressure Politics: The Story of the Anti-Saloon League* (New York: Columbia University Press, 1928), and expanded upon by Jack S. Blocker, Jr., *Retreat from Reform: The Prohibition Movement in the United States, 1890-1913* (Westport, Conn.: Greenwood, 1976). A journalist, Charles Merz, in *The Dry Decade* (Garden City: Doubleday, Doran, 1931), supported the view that the law was the product of minority agitation, but he attributed its passage to the influence of the World War I atmosphere. Sociologist Joseph R. Gusfield, *Symbolic Crusade: Status Politics and the American Temperance Movement* (Urbana: University of Illinois Press, 1963), credited prohibition to the desire of a declining middle-class elite to obtain a legal imprimatur on its life style, while Andrew Sinclair, *Prohibition: The Era of Excess* (Boston: Little, Brown, 1962), emphasized the influence of rural, Protestant, nativist prejudices against cities and their recent immigrant populations. The view that prohibition enjoyed broader support and became an integral part of early twentieth-century progressive political and social reform was put forth in James H. Timberlake, *Prohibition and the Progressive Movement, 1900-1920* (Cambridge: Harvard University Press, 1963), and reaffirmed by Norman H. Clark, *Deliver Us from Evil: An Interpretation of American Prohibition* (New York: W. W. Norton, 1976).

2. The best discussion of the early temperance and prohibition movements is John Allen Krout, *The Origins of Prohibition* (New York: Alfred A. Knopf, 1925).

3. There is no study of the prohibition movement during the last half of the nineteenth century to compare with Krout's work on the period up to 1851. For information on this later period see Blocker, *Retreat from Reform,* and Sinclair, *Era of Excess.*

4. Odegard, *Pressure Politics,* and Blocker, *Retreat from Reform,* together provide an excellent picture of the Anti-Saloon League.

5. *Prohibition and the Progressive Movement,* p. 148.

6. Ibid., p. 2; Lewis L. Gould, *Progressives and Prohibitionists: Texas Democrats in the Wilson Era* (Austin: University of Texas Press, 1973); Norman H. Clark, *The Dry Years: Prohibition and Social Change in Washington* (Seattle: University of Washington Press, 1965); Paul E. Issac, *Prohibition and Politics in Tennessee, 1885-1920* (Knoxville: University of Tennessee Press, 1965); James A. Burran, "Prohibition in New Mexico, 1917," *New Mexico Historical Review* 48 (April 1973): 133-49; Robert A. Hohner, "The Prohibitionists: Who Were They?" *South Atlantic Quarterly* 68 (Autumn 1969): 491-505; Gilman M. Ostrander, *The Prohibition Movement in California, 1848-1933,* University of California Publications in History, vol. 57 (Berkeley: University of California Press, 1957); and G. K. Renner, "Prohibition Comes to Missouri, 1910-1919," *Missouri Historical Review* 62 (July 1968): 363-97.

7. This view of progressivism is most effectively explored in Robert H. Wiebe, *The Search for Order, 1877-1920* (New York: Hill and Wang, 1967), and Paul Boyer,

Urban Masses and Moral Order in America, 1820-1920 (Cambridge: Harvard University Press, 1978), especially chaps. 13 and 14.

8. *The Course of American Democratic Thought: An Intellectual History Since 1815* (New York: Ronald Press, 1940), p. 332.

9. *The Decline and Revival of the Social Gospel: Social and Political Liberalism in American Protestant Churches, 1920-1940* (Ithaca: Cornell University Press, 1956), p. 32.

10. *Why Prohibition!* (New York: George H. Doran, 1918), pp. 48-49.

11. Ibid., pp. 71-73, 84.

12. George Elliot Howard, "Alcohol and Crime: A Study in Social Causation," *American Journal of Sociology* 24 (July 1918): 61-64.

13. Timberlake, *Prohibition and the Progressive Movement,* pp. 60-65.

14. Ibid., pp. 7-8.

15. Ibid., p. 163.

16. Ibid., pp. 174, 180.

17. Ibid., pp. 176-78.

18. Ibid., p. 175.

19. Merz, *Dry Decade,* pp. 307-8; Cherrington, *The Evolution of Prohibition,* pp. 321-64; Blocker, *Retreat from Reform,* pp. 238-40. Other states where voters approved dry laws included Arizona, Florida, Idaho, Kentucky, Michigan, Minnesota, Montana, Nebraska, Nevada, New Mexico, Oregon, South Carolina, South Dakota, Virginia, and Washington.

20. Joseph P. Tumulty, *Woodrow Wilson as I Know Him* (Garden City, N.Y.: Doubleday, Page, 1921), p. 409; Seward W. Livermore, *Politics Is Adjourned: Woodrow Wilson and the War Congress, 1916-1918* (Middletown, Conn.: Wesleyan University Press, 1966), pp. 48-52, 181-82; *Congressional Record* 58 (66th Cong., 1st sess.): 7602; Gene Smith, *When the Cheering Stopped: The Last Years of Woodrow Wilson* (New York: William Morrow, 1964), pp. 81-112.

21. Ohio, *Annual Report of the Secretary of State, 1919,* pp. 255-56; *Akron Beacon Journal,* November 7, 1918; *Hawke v. Smith,* appellate case file 27337, Records of the Supreme Court of the United States, Record Group 267, National Archives.

22. *Hawke v. Smith* appellate file; Ohio, *Annual Report of the Secretary of State, 1920,* pp. 313-14. At the same election, voters chose to retain the state prohibition law, 496,786 to 454,933.

23. *Hawke v. Smith* appellate file.

24. *Davis v. Hildebrant,* 241 U.S. 565; *Hawke v. Smith* appellate file.

25. William Howard Taft, "Can Ratification of an Amendment to the Constitution Be Made to Depend on a Referendum?" *Yale Law Review* 29 (June 1920): 822-23; John R. Meers, "The California Wine and Grape Industry and Prohibition," *California Historical Society Quarterly* 46 (1967): 26-27; Clark, *Dry Years,* p. 142.

26. *Hawke v. Smith,* 253 U.S. 221, 229-30.

27. *National Prohibition Cases,* 253 U.S. 350.

28. Will Rogers, *Rogers-isms: The Cowboy Philosopher on Prohibition* (New York: Harper, 1919), p. 29.

29. *New York Times,* January 6, 1920, p. 1; *Ruppert v. Caffey,* 251 U.S. 264.

30. *National Prohibition Cases,* 253 U.S. 350, 354–56.

31. Philip C. Jessup, *Elihu Root,* 2 vols. (New York: Dodd, Mead, 1938), 2:478; *National Prohibition Cases,* 253 U.S. 350, 361–67.

32. Elihu Root to Everett P. Wheeler, November 22, 1919, and to Lewis L. Clarke, December 20, 1919, Elihu Root Papers, Library of Congress.

33. Jessup, *Root,* 2:476–80.

34. Quoted in Nicholas Murray Butler, *Across the Busy Years,* 2 vols. (New York: Scribner's, 1939–40), 2:333–34. Root's oral argument does not appear in the official report of the case (253 U.S. 350).

35. *National Prohibition Cases,* pp. 350–51.

CHAPTER 2

1. Don S. Kirschner, *City and Country: Rural Responses to Urbanization in the 1920s* (Westport, Conn.: Greenwood, 1970), p. 41.

2. *New York Times,* January 16, 1920, p. 1.

3. Merz, *Dry Decade,* p. 52. William G. McLoughlin, Jr., *Billy Sunday Was His Real Name* (Chicago: University of Chicago Press, 1955), pp. 277–78.

4. Vera Efron, Mark Keller, and Carol Gurioli, *Statistics on Consumption of Alcohol and on Alcoholism* (New Brunswick, N.J.: Rutgers Center of Alcohol Studies, 1974), p. 4.

5. Wiebe, *The Search for Order,* p. 301.

6. Merz, *Dry Decade,* pp. 65–70, 258–62, and Sinclair, *Era of Excess,* pp. 197–206, provide good summaries of the sources of illicit liquor and are the sources for most of the following information.

7. Ostrander, *The Prohibition Movement in California,* pp. 178–81; Meers, "The California Wine and Grape Industry," pp. 27–29; E. Clemens Horst, "The Happy Grape Growers," *Outlook and Independent,* March 12, 1930, pp. 407–8, 433.

8. Ross Wilson, *Scotch: The Formative Years* (London: Constable, 1970), pp. 298–99.

9. "National Prohibition Act," 41 *U.S. Statutes at Large,* pt. 1, pp. 308–17.

10. U.S., National Commission on Law Observance and Enforcement, *Report on the Enforcement of the Prohibition Laws of the United States,* 71st Cong., 3d sess., House Document 722 (Washington: GPO, 1931), p. 17.

11. Archibald E. Stevenson, *States' Rights and National Prohibition* (New York: Clark, Boardman, 1927).

12. Charles Merz, *Dry Decade,* chaps. 4 and 11, pictured Congress and the states as unwilling to enforce the law. More recently, Joseph Gusfield (*Symbolic Crusade,* p. 120) proceeds from the same assumption to argue that drys were less concerned about enforcement than confirmation of their own social status by putting laws on the books which reflected their own cultural patterns. To say that drys viewed existing law enforcement agencies as adequate to the task in no way discredits Gusfield's conclusions regarding their underlying motivation.

13. Gusfield, *Symbolic Crusade,* pp. 134–35.

14. Efron, Keller, and Gurioli, *Statistics on Consumption of Alcohol,* p. 4. Some attempts have been made to estimate prohibition-era consumption rates or to infer them from figures on arrests for drunkenness, hospitalization for alcoholism, or

cirrhosis of the liver. While such statistics also show a decline in drinking, they are too subject to uncertain influences to have much value. See Clark Warburton, *The Economic Results of Prohibition* (New York: Columbia University Press, 1932); and J. C. Burnham, "New Perspectives on the Prohibition 'Experiment' in the 1920's," *Journal of Social History* 2 (Fall 1968): 60.

15. Martha Bensley Bruere, *Does Prohibition Work? A Study of the Operation of the Eighteenth Amendment Made by the National Federation of Settlements, Assisted by Social Workers in Different Parts of the United States* (New York: Harper, 1927).

16. Irving Fisher and H. Bruce Brougham, *The "Noble Experiment"* (New York: Alcohol Information Committee, 1930), pp. 115-16.

17. Ernest A. Dewey, "Cocktails in Kansas," *Commonweal,* February 5, 1930, pp. 384-86; Bruce Crawford, "Citadel of Enforcement: Prohibition in the Small Town," *Outlook and Independent,* March 26, 1930, pp. 488-89, 516; James E. Hansen II, "Moonshine and Murder: Prohibition in Denver," *Colorado Magazine* 50 (Winter 1973): 1-23; Larry D. Englemann, "A Separate Peace: The Politics of Prohibition Enforcement in Detroit, 1920-1930," *Detroit in Perspective* 1 (Autumn 1972): 51-73.

18. Representative Edward Voigt to Halbert L. Hoard, March 11, 1921, Halbert L. Hoard Papers, Wisconsin State Historical Society, Madison, Wisconsin. An analysis of contemporary publications which confirms the widespread image of lawlessness is Louise Duus, "There Ought To Be a Law: A Study of Popular American Attitudes toward 'The Law' in the 1920's," (Ph.D. diss., University of Minnesota, 1967), esp. p. 155.

19. Humbert S. Nelli, *The Business of Crime: Italians and Syndicate Crime in the United States* (New York: Oxford University Press, 1976), pp. 211-12.

20. Ibid., p. 207. Along with Mark Haller, who read a paper, "Bootlegging in Chicago: The Structure of an Illegal Enterprise," at the 1974 meeting of the American Historical Association, Nelli has pioneered in the examination of bootlegging as a business.

21. Nelli, *The Business of Crime,* pp. 164-75.

22. Izzy Einstein, *Prohibition Agent No. 1* (New York: Frederick A. Stokes, 1932).

23. Quoted in Eric F. Goldman, *Rendezvous with Destiny: A History of Modern American Reform.* (New York: Vintage, 1956), p. 245.

24. *Notes on Democracy* (New York: Alfred A. Knopf, 1926), p. 256. An excellent discussion of Mencken's use of the prohibition issue can be found in Andrew C. McLaughlin, "Satire as a Weapon against Prohibition. 1920-1928: Expression of a Cultural Conflict," (Ph.D. diss., Stanford University, 1969), chap. 2. See also William Manchester, *Disturber of the Peace: The Life of H. L. Mencken* (New York: Harper, 1951); and M. K. Singleton, *H. L. Mencken and the American Mercury Adventure* (Durham: Duke University Press, 1962).

25. Garth Jowett, *Film: The Democratic Art* (Boston: Little, Brown, 1976), p. 192.

26. Review of *Wine of Youth, New York Times,* August 11, 1924, p. 16.

27. Edgar Dale, *The Content of Motion Pictures* (New York: Macmillan, 1935), pp. 167-69.

28. A good starting point for studying motion pictures of the period is *The New York Times Film Reviews, 1913-1968,* vol. 1 (New York: New York Times, 1970).

More specialized but also quite useful is James Robert Parish and Michael R. Pitts, *The Great Gangster Pictures* (Metuchen, N.J.: Scarecrow, 1976).

29. Lorenzo Martin, "Kentuckian Live Wire of U.S. Treasury Department," Louisville, Kentucky, *Courier Journal*, October 3, 1920, in May-October, 1920, scrapbook, Jouett Shouse Papers, University of Kentucky Library, Lexington, Kentucky.

30. Robert K. Murray, *The Harding Era: Warren G. Harding and His Administration* (Minneapolis: University of Minnesota Press, 1969), p. 403.

31. Warren G. Harding to Walter E. Edge, August 17, 1921, Warren G. Harding Papers, microfilm edition, Ohio Historical Society, Columbus.

32. Murray, *The Harding Era*, pp. 16, 404-7; presidential files, Harding Papers.

33. *New York Times*, June 26, 1923, p. 12.

34. U.S., Department of Justice, *Report Submitted to President Coolidge by Attorney General H. M. Daugherty concerning Prohibition Litigation throughout the United States, covering the Period January 16, 1920, to June 16, 1923* (Washington: GPO, 1923), pp. 1-2.

35. Merz, *Dry Decade*, pp. 154-56, 332-33; Sinclair, *Era of Excess*, pp. 211-12.

36. Prohibition correspondence file, Calvin Coolidge Papers, Library of Congress.

37. Richard N. Kottman, "Volstead Violated: Prohibition as a Factor in Canadian-American Relations," *Canadian Historical Review* 43 (June 1962): 106-26; Robert L. Jones, *The Eighteenth Amendment and Our Foreign Relations* (New York: Thomas Y. Crowell, 1933); Donald R. McCoy, *Calvin Coolidge: The Quiet President* (New York: Macmillan, 1967), p. 303.

38. Merz, *Dry Decade*, pp. 76-78, 84.

39. U.S., House of Representatives, Committee on the Judiciary, *Prohibition Legislation, 1921: Hearings*, 67th Cong., 1st sess., serial 2 (Washington: GPO, 1921); Charles L. Dana et al., "The Medical Profession and the Volstead Act." *Journal of the American Medical Association* 76 (June 4, 1921): 1592-93; Bartlett C. Jones, "The Debate over National Prohibition, 1920-1933," (Ph.D. diss., Emory University, 1961), pp. 105-6; *Congressional Record* 61 (67th Cong., 1st sess.): 3135, 4742.

40. Murray, *The Harding Era*, pp. 404-5; Merz, *Dry Decade*, p. 163.

41. Merz, *Dry Decade*, p. 329.

42. Sinclair, *Prohibition*, pp. 351, 358.

43. Merz, *Dry Decade*, pp. 233.

44. Henry F. Pringle, *The Life and Times of William Howard Taft*, 2 vols. (New York: Farrar and Rinehart, 1939), 1:375, and 2:861, 981; Alpheus T. Mason, *William Howard Taft: Chief Justice* (New York: Simon and Schuster, 1964), p. 224.

45. Pringle, *Taft*, 2:982.

46. Ibid., pp. 981-83, 988.

47. *United States v. Lanza*, 260 U.S. 377.

48. *Carroll et al. v. United States*, 267 U.S. 132. Justices McReynolds and Sutherland dissented.

49. *Everard's Breweries v. Day*, 265 U.S. 545.

50. *Lambert v. Yellowley et al.*, 272 U.S. 581; Jones, "Debate over National Prohibition," pp. 109-15. Justice Brandeis delivered the Court's opinion, Taft, Holmes, Van DeVanter, and Sanford concurring. Justices Sutherland, McReynolds, Butler, and Stone dissented.

51. Forrest Revere Black, *Ill-Starred Prohibition Cases: A Study in Judicial Pathology* (Boston: Richard G. Badger, 1931), pp. 70–80.

52. *Olmstead et al. v. United States,* 277 U.S. 438; Mason, *Taft,* p. 256.

53. *Olmstead et al. v. United States,* 277 U.S. 485.

54. Mason, *Taft,* pp. 227, 259.

CHAPTER 3

1. The only detailed study of resistance to the prohibition crusade is Nuala McGann Drescher, "The Opposition to Prohibition, 1900–1919: A Social and Institutional Study," (Ph.D. diss., University of Delaware, 1964).

2. *National Prohibition Cases,* 253 U.S. 350, 361–62.

3. Ostrander, *The Prohibition Movement in California,* p. 183.

4. Sinclair, *Era of Excess,* pp. 152–53; Drescher, "Opposition to Prohibition," pp. 176–78.

5. Stanley Baron, *Brewed in America: A History of Beer and Ale in the United States* (Boston: Little, Brown, 1962), p. 302, argues that brewers' efforts to influence elections were no worse than those of the drys.

6. Timberlake, *Prohibition and the Progressive Movement,* pp. 157–58, 164–65, 179; Baron, *Brewed in America,* pp. 304–5.

7. Timberlake, *Prohibition and the Progressive Movement,* p. 179.

8. Merz, *Dry Decade,* pp. 208–9.

9. Timberlake, *Prohibition and the Progressive Movement,* pp. 92–94.

10. Drescher, "Opposition to Prohibition," pp. 274–78, 296–99.

11. Ibid., pp. 329–32; *New York Herald Tribune,* April 7, 1930.

12. Baron, *Brewed in America,* pp. 313–15; Thomas C. Cochran, *The Pabst Brewing Company: The History of an American Business* (New York: New York University Press, 1948), pp. 325–35; William L. Downard, *The Cincinnati Brewing Industry: A Social and Economic History* (Athens: Ohio University Press, 1973), pp. 132–34; August A. Busch to Pierre S. du Pont, March 2, 1929, Pierre S. du Pont Papers. Because of their visibility, few previously legitimate producers were in a position to engage in bootlegging.

13. Irving Bernstein, *The Lean Years: A History of the American Worker, 1920–1933* (Boston: Houghton Mifflin, 1960), p. 85.

14. Drescher, "Opposition to Prohibition," pp. 245–46; Howard E. Jensen, "Propaganda and the Anti-Prohibition Movement," *South Atlantic Quarterly* 32 (July 1933): 258–59.

15. Biographical information, unless otherwise indicated, comes from "William H. Stayton," *Repeal Review* 7 (July–September, 1942): 3; *Who Was Who in America* (Chicago: A. N. Marquis, 1950), 2:505; and interviews with Stayton's two granddaughters, Mrs. Merle A. Roemer and Mrs. John H. C. Forbes, in July, 1973.

16. William H. Stayton service record, Records of the Bureau of Naval Personnel, Record Group 24, National Archives.

17. Quoted in H. L. Mencken, "Man Who Really Busted Prohibition Gives All Credit to Opposite Sex," Baltimore *Sun,* October 30, 1932.

18. Boyden Sparkes and Samuel Taylor Moore, *The Witch of Wall Street: Hetty Green* (Garden City, N.Y.: Doubleday, 1948), pp. 233–36, 257–59.

19. Stayton manuscripts and clippings in the possession of Mrs. John H. C. Forbes;

Armin Rappaport, *The Navy League of the United States* (Detroit: Wayne State University Press, 1962), pp. 17, 76, and note 99, p. 229.

20. William H. Stayton public letter to Burton A. George, "A Reply to Rep. Dan V. Stephens of Nebraska who supports the Tavenner-Hohenzollern Bill," Stayton Papers.

21. Mencken, "Man Who Busted Prohibition."

22. Dayton E. Heckman, "Prohibition Passes: The Story of the Association Against the Prohibition Amendment," (Ph.D. diss., Ohio State University, 1939), p. 12.

23. U.S., Senate, Committee on the Judiciary, *Lobby Investigation: Hearings before a Subcommittee,* 71st Cong., 2d sess., 4 vols. (Washington: GPO, 1931), p. 4131; U.S., Senate, Special Committee Investigating Expenditures in Senatorial Primary and General Elections, *Senatorial Campaign Expenditures: Hearings,* pt. 1, June 9 to July 7, 1926, 69th Cong., 1st sess. (Washington: GPO, 1926), p. 1231; Dudley Nichols, "Total Abstainer, Captain W. H. Stayton, Leads 726,000 People in Militant Fight against the Prohibition Amendment," New York *World,* July 11, 1926, editorial section.

24. Mencken, "Man Who Busted Prohibition."

25. Ibid.; Senate Special Committee, *Campaign Expenditures,* pp. 1223, 1232.

26. Mencken, "Man Who Busted Prohibition."

27. Senate Special Committee, *Campaign Expenditures,* p. 1223.

28. Nichols, "Captain Stayton."

29. William H. Stayton printed circular, October 2, 1919, in Stayton to John J. Raskob, December 5, 1919, John J. Raskob Papers, Eleutherian Mills Historical Library.

30. Nichols, "Captain Stayton"; Senate Special Committee, *Campaign Expenditures,* p. 1223.

31. Nichols, "Captain Stayton"; Mencken, "Man Who Busted Prohibition."

32. Certificate of Formation of the Association Against the Prohibition Amendment, December 31, 1920, Association Against the Prohibition Amendment [hereafter AAPA] Papers, Library of Congress.

33. The best studies of the Anti-Saloon League are Odegard, *Pressure Politics,* and Blocker, *Retreat from Reform.*

34. Stayton circular, October 2, 1919; AAPA, "Statement of Facts," July 15, 1920, Raskob Papers; *New York Times,* May 1, 1921, sec. 8, p. 1.

35. *New York Times,* May 1, 1921, sec. 8, p. 1.

36. *St. Louis Post-Dispatch,* November 21, 1922; G. C. Hinckley to John J. Raskob, March 26, 1924, Raskob Papers; Senate Special Committee, *Campaign Expenditures,* p. 1234.

37. Senate Special Committee, *Campaign Expenditures,* p. 1504; William H. Stayton to Irénée du Pont, March 11, 1925, Irénée du Pont Papers, Eleutherian Mills Historical Library; Nichols, "Captain Stayton" (Grayson M.-P. Murphy, a leading member of the AAPA, gave Nichols the information on Stayton's personal contributions).

38. Senate Special Committee, *Campaign Expenditures,* pp. 1235–37, 1269, 1476–77, 1480–81; Nichols, "Captain Stayton"; *New York Times,* August 20, 1922, sec. 6,

p. 8; luncheon program, Molly Pitcher Club, October 17, 1922, M. Louise Gross Papers, New York Public Library; Ostrander, *The Prohibition Movement in California*, p. 184; AAPA of Southern California, *The Minute Man* 1 (December 1924), Stayton Papers; Heckman, "Prohibition Passes," p. 42; AAPA, *Anti-Saloon League Grip Broken* (Washington, 1926), Eleutherian Mills Historical Library pamphlet collection.

39. Heckman, "Prohibition Passes," pp. 36–37; AAPA, "Reports Made to the Clerk of the House of Representatives as per the 'Federal Corrupt Practices Act 1925,'" vol. 1, Records of the House of Representatives, Record Group 233, National Archives; AAPA, "Report to Members, December, 1927," AAPA Papers.

40. William H. Stayton to William Green, June 22, 1925, copy in the Samuel Gompers Letterbooks, vol. 329, pp. 403–5, Library of Congress. Green refused to participate.

41. Senate Special Committee, *Campaign Expenditures*, p. 1499; *New York Times*, August 20, 1922, sec. 6, p. 8; U.S., House of Representatives, Committee on the Judiciary, *Proposed Modification of the Prohibition Laws to Permit the Manufacture, Sale, and Use of 2.75 Per Cent Beverages: Hearings*, 68th Cong., 1st sess.; serial 39 (Washington: GPO, 1924), pp. 220–25; M. Louise Gross to members and friends of the Women's Committee for Repeal of the 18th Amendment, [December, 1931] and to Pierre S. du Pont, April 8, 1928, Women's Organization for National Prohibition Reform [hereafter WONPR] Papers, Alice Belin du Pont file, Pierre S. du Pont Papers; Gross Papers.

42. Heckman, "Prohibition Passes," pp. 280–81; Senate Special Committee, *Campaign Expenditures*, p. 1484.

43. Senate Special Committee, *Campaign Expenditures*, p. 1234.

44. Heckman, "Prohibition Passes," pp. 362–63.

45. U.S., Senate, Committee on the Judiciary, *Lobby Investigation: Hearings before a Subcommittee*, 71st Cong., 2d sess., 4 vols. (Washington: GPO, 1931), p. 4170.

46. *New York Times*, May 1, 1921, sec. 8, p. 1; William H. Stayton to John J. Raskob, December 5, 1919, and June 5, 1920, and AAPA membership card in Raskob's name dated June 26, 1922, Raskob Papers; Irénée du Pont to G. C. Hinckley, November 22, 1922, Irénée du Pont Papers; Senate Special Committee, *Campaign Expenditures*, pp. 1253–68.

47. James W. Prothro, *The Dollar Decade: Business Ideas in the 1920's* (Baton Rouge: Louisiana State University Press, 1954), p. 35.

48. Jensen, "Propaganda and the Anti-Prohibition Movement," p. 255; Roy A. Haynes, *Prohibition Inside Out* (Garden City, N.Y.: Doubleday, Page, 1923), p. 180; U.S., House of Representatives, Committee on the Judiciary, *The Prohibition Amendment: Hearings*, 71st Cong., 2d sess.; serial 5 (Washington: GPO, 1930), p. 93. Most of the smaller antiprohibition organizations left few, if any, records and simply cannot be studied thoroughly. This is disappointing, but not tragic, since they appear to have had little or no influence.

49. Quoted in Heckman, "Prohibition Passes," pp. 256–57.

50. *New York Times*, April 7, 1922, pp. 1, 2.

51. William H. Stayton, "Our Experiment in National Prohibition: What Progress

Has It Made?" in T. Henry Walnut, ed., *Prohibition and Its Enforcement,* Annals of the American Academy of Political and Social Science, vol. 109 (Philadelphia, 1923), pp. 26, 30-31.

52. Samuel Harden Church, "The Paradise of the Ostrich," *North American Review* 221 (June 1925): 626.

53. Henry S. Priest, "The Eighteenth Amendment an Infringement of Liberty," in Walnut, *Prohibition and Its Enforcement,* p. 40.

54. Ransom H. Gillett, "Address to the Economic Club of Boston, March 6, 1923," *Consensus* 8 (April 1923): 3-32.

55. Ransom H. Gillett and John Haynes Holmes, *Repeal of the Prohibition Amendment,* The Reference Shelf, vol. 1, no. 11 (New York: H. W. Wilson, 1923), pp. 8-14, 46.

56. Fabian Franklin, "An Anti-Prohibition Movement," *Weekly Review* 4 (May 28, 1921): 505.

57. Fabian Franklin, *What Prohibition Has Done to America* (New York: Harcourt, Brace, 1922), pp. 8-9, 24-29.

CHAPTER 4

1. Stevenson, *States Rights and National Prohibition,* p. 126.

2. Ibid., p. 126; note 74, p. 152; and note 113, pp. 156-57. The pervasive nature of the belief during the 1920s in the futility of a repeal campaign is thoroughly documented in Jones, "Debate over National Prohibition," chap. 1. For one prominent example, see Howard Lee McBain, *Prohibition: Legal and Illegal* (New York: Macmillan, 1928), pp. 16-20.

3. Clarence Darrow, "The Ordeal of Prohibition," *American Mercury,* August 1924, p. 419. He confirmed this pessimistic appraisal in private correspondence (Darrow to Halbert L. Hoard, October 15, 1924, Hoard Papers.

4. James W. Wadsworth, Jr., "Amending the Constitution," transcript of a speech at the National Republican Club Lincoln dinner, February 12, 1923, James W. Wadsworth, Jr., Papers, Library of Congress (Senator Wadsworth and Democratic Congressman Finis J. Garrett of Tennessee, the House minority leader, sponsored a constitutional amendment to insure voter participation in the amending process. They despaired of reversing past amendments, but hoped to prevent further "revolutionary change." Hearings were held, but neither house of Congress ever voted on the Wadsworth-Garrett resolution.); House Judiciary Committee, *Proposed Modification of the Prohibition Law,* p. 37; William Green to William H. Stayton, June 24, 1925, vol. 327, pp. 723-97; and to Joseph F. Obergfell, July 11, 1925, vol. 329, pp. 395-96, Gompers Letterbooks; Walter Lippmann, "Our Predicament under the Eighteenth Amendment," *Harper's Magazine,* December 1926, p. 56; *New York Times,* May 12, 1922, p. 18.

5. John C. Gebhart, "Movement against Prohibition," *Annals of the American Academy of Political and Social Science* 163 (September 1932): 177; Harry B. Kirtland, "Address of May 20, 1924," Hoard Papers; Moderation League of Minnesota to Calvin Coolidge, October 17, 1923, Coolidge Papers; Clarke A. Chambers, *Seedtime of Reform: American Social Service and Social Action, 1918-1933* (Minneapolis: University of Minnesota Press, 1963), p. 39.

6. *New York Times,* April 7, 1922, pp. 1, 2.

7. Ibid., April 29, 1922, p. 14.

8. W. H. Stayton to John J. Raskob, November 3, 1925, Raskob Papers.

9. *New York Times,* May 12, 1922, p. 18.

10. Senate Special Committee, *Senatorial Campaign Expenditures,* pp. 1500–01.

11. Merz, *Dry Decade,* p. 202.

12. Gillett, "Address to the Economic Club of Boston," p. 32.

13. Henry F. Pringle, *Alfred E. Smith: A Critical Study* (New York: Macy-Masius, 1927), pp. 320–28.

14. Ibid., pp. 318–19; Matthew and Hannah Josephson, *Al Smith: Hero of the Cities* (Boston: Houghton Mifflin, 1969), pp. 292–95. The debate over the repeal filled the New York papers for weeks. For the many pressures on Smith as well as his wavering attitudes, see *New York Tribune,* May 6, 20, 29, 30, and 31, 1923.

15. *New York Times,* June 1, 1923, pp. 1, 2.

16. Pringle, *Smith,* p. 328.

17. *New York Times,* June 2, 1923, pp. 1, 2. For varied reactions to the signing, see the June 2, 1923, editorials in the *Times,* the *New York Tribune,* and the New York *World,* as well as the June 3 editorial in the *Des Moines Register.* The White House received a flood of mail protesting the repeal from all over the country (Harding Papers).

18. *New York Times,* June 10, 1924, p. 8.

19. *St. Louis Post-Dispatch,* November 20, 1922; G. C. Hinckley to John J. Raskob, March 26, 1924, Raskob Papers. The same slogan was used as the title of a 1922 AAPA pamphlet.

20. For example, Stayton to Raskob, November 3, 1925, Raskob Papers.

21. Samuel Gompers to Woodrow Wilson, December 14, 1917, and to W. H. Hawkins, September 1, 1920, in House Judiciary Committee, *Proposed Modification of the Prohibition Law,* pp. 26–28.

22. Ibid., p. 66.

23. Green to Stayton, June 24, 1925, and to Obergfell, July 11, 1925, Gompers Letterbooks.

24. *New York Tribune,* April 7, 1922; *New York Times,* August 13, 1922, sec. 2, p. 4; *St. Louis Post-Dispatch,* November 20, 1922; Archibald Hopkins and Gorton C. Hinckley to Calvin Coolidge, January 17, 1924, Coolidge Papers; *New York Times,* January 22, 1924, p. 8; *Washington Post,* June 11, 1924; *New York Times,* June 23, 1924, p. 6; AAPA, *Anti-Saloon League Grip Broken* (Washington, 1925); *New York Times,* March 15, 1925, p. 19; Senate Special Committee, *Campaign Expenditures,* pp. 1500–01.

25. *Bulletin of the Association Against the Prohibition Amendment* 1 (February 26, 1924); *New York Times,* January 28, 1924, p. 2.

26. Heckman, "Prohibition Passes," pp. 25, 290.

27. *Bulletin of the AAPA* 1 (June 10, 1924).

28. House Judiciary Committee, *Proposed Modification of the Prohibition Law,* pp. 8–16.

29. Ibid., p. 36, 45–46, 61, 68.

30. Ibid., pp. 77–83, 156.

31. Ibid., pp. 220-25, 198-203, 238-68.

32. *Chicago Tribune,* April 22, 1924; *Des Moines Register,* April 22, 1924; *New York Times,* April 22, 1924, pp. 1, 5; *Washington Post,* April 22, 1924.

33. *Congressional Record* 67 (69th Cong., 1st sess.): 832-42.

34. *Bulletin of the AAPA* 7 (June 17, 1926).

35. U.S., Senate, Committee on the Judiciary, *The National Prohibition Law: Hearings before the Subcommittee on Bills to Amend the National Prohibition Act.* 69th Cong., 1st sess., 2 vols. (Washington: GPO, 1926), pp. 39-40.

36. Ibid., pp. 278-79.

37. Ibid., pp. 64-66, 461-62.

38. *Washington Post,* April 17, 1926, pp. 1, 4.

39. Senate Judiciary Committee, *The National Prohibition Law,* pp. 94-128, 178-207. Buckner, a prominent New York attorney who practiced with Elihu Root when he wasn't serving as U.S. attorney (1925-27), offered the same appraisal to the Economic Club of New York (Martin Mayer, *Emory Buckner* [New York: Harper and Row, 1968], pp. 196-98).

40. U.S., Senate, Committee on the Judiciary, report of the subcommittee, May 31, 1926, papers relating to hearings on the national prohibition law, file S. 33-69th, Records of the Senate, Record Group 46, National Archives.

41. Donald B. Johnson and Kirk H. Porter, compilers, *National Party Platforms, 1840-1972* (Urbana: University of Illinois Press, 1973), p. 229.

42. Lawrence W. Levine, *Defender of the Faith: William Jennings Bryan: The Last Decade, 1915-1925* (New York: Oxford University Press, 1965), pp. 162-66.

43. *Cleveland Plain Dealer,* June 11, 1924; *Washington Post,* June 11, 1924; *New York Times,* June 11, 1924, p. 3; Republican National Committee, *Republican Campaign Text-book 1924* (n.p.: 1924), p. 93.

44. *New York Times,* June 8, 1924, p. 8.

45. Ibid., June 10, 1924, p. 8.

46. Ibid., June 23, 1924, p. 6.

47. Ibid., June 28, 1924, p. 2.

48. AAPA, "The Anti-Prohibition Campaign: Progress and Prospects" [August, 1924], Irénée du Pont Papers.

49. William H. Harbaugh, *Lawyer's Lawyer: The Life of John W. Davis* (New York: Oxford University Press, 1973), p. 248.

50. *New York Times,* July 23, 1924, p. 15, and July 24, 1924, p. 3.

51. Ibid., May 7, 1923, p. 4, and May 22, 1923, p. 3.

52. Arthur T. Hadley, "Law Making and Law Enforcement," *Harper's Magazine,* November 1925, pp. 641-46.

53. "Nullification by Consent," *New Republic,* June 16, 1926, pp. 101-2; Jerome D. Greene, "The Personal Problem," *Atlantic Monthly,* October 1926, pp. 526-28; "Enforcement, Repeal, and Nullification," *World's Work,* November 1926, pp. 5-6.

54. Lippmann, "Our Predicament under the Eighteenth Amendment," pp. 55, 56.

55. Clarence Darrow and Victor S. Yarros, *The Prohibition Mania* (New York: Boni and Liveright, 1927), pp. 177-87, 201-2, 213-14; Brand Whitlock, *The Little Green Shutter* (New York: D. Appleton, 1931); Robert C. Binkley, "The Ethics of Nullification," *New Republic,* May 1, 1929, pp. 297-300; Wainwright Evans, "The

Sanctity of the Law," *Outlook and Independent,* June 19, 1929, pp. 283-86; Schuyler C. Wallace, "Nullification: A Process of Government," *Political Science Quarterly* 45 (September 1930): 347-58; Harry Elmer Barnes, *Prohibition versus Civilization: Analyzing the Dry Psychosis* (New York: Viking, 1932).

56. John A. Ryan, "A Catholic Economist and Theologian on Prohibition," *Fortnightly Review* 23 (April 1, 1916): 100-101; idem, "Are Our Prohibition Laws 'Purely Penal'?" *Ecclesiastical Review* 70 (April 1924): 404-11; idem, "Do the Prohibition Laws Bind in Conscience?" *Catholic World,* May 1925, pp. 145-57; idem, *Declining Liberty and Other Papers* (New York: Macmillan, 1927); idem, "The Evolution of an Anti," *Commonweal,* June 26, 1929, pp. 211-12; Francis L. Broderick, *Right Reverend New Dealer John A. Ryan* (New York: Macmillan, 1963).

57. William H. Stayton to Coleman du Pont, September 27, 1925, Irénée du Pont Papers.

58. Julian Codman, "Must Congress Enforce an Amendment?" *Independent,* June 12, 1926, pp. 683-84, 699.

59. "Final Returns in The Digest's Prohibition Poll," *Literary Digest,* September 9, 1922, pp. 11-13. Statisticians judged that the proportion of those voting for modification that actually favored repeal but considered it impossible approximated the percentage of voters for repeal as against those for enforcement (Walter F. Willcox, "An Attempt to Measure Public Opinion about Repealing the Eighteenth Amendment," *Journal of the American Statistical Association* 26 [September 1931]: 244-56).

60. *New York Times,* November 9, 1922; p. 3; and November 11, 1922, p. 1; Merz, *Dry Decade,* p. 334.

61. "Booze Is the Victor," *Collier's,* October 10, 1925, pp. 8-9.

62. *New York Times,* November 4, 1926, p. 1; Merz, *Dry Decade,* p. 334; Kirschner, *City and Country,* pp. 91-94.

63. House Judiciary Committee, *The Prohibition Amendment,* pp. 62-63; Hearst Temperance Contest Committee, *Temperance—or Prohibition?* (New York: New York American, 1929).

64. *New York Tribune,* April 7, 1922; *New York Times,* June 17, 1922, p. 15, November 19, 1925, p. 5, and February 23, 1926, pp. 1, 16; *St. Louis Post-Dispatch,* November 20, 1922; *Washington Post,* January 22, 1924; AAPA of Southern California, *The Minute Man* 1 (December 1924); Senate Special Committee, *Campaign Expenditures,* pp. 1473-77.

65. David Burner, *The Politics of Provincialism: The Democratic Party in Transition, 1918-1932* (New York: Alfred A. Knopf, 1968), p. 97.

CHAPTER 5

1. James W. Wadsworth, Jr., to Lewis G. Stapley, March 7, 1926, Wadsworth Papers.

2. *New York Times,* January 16, 1920, p. 1.

3. Merz, *Dry Decade,* pp. 329-32.

4. Edward Robb Ellis, *A Nation in Torment: The Great American Depression, 1929-1939* (New York: Capricorn, 1971), p. 70.

5. Irving Fisher, *Prohibition at Its Worst* (New York: Macmillan, 1926).

6. William H. Stayton to Halbert L. Hoard, May 8, 1926, Hoard Papers.

7. Henry Bourne Joy to Herbert F. Perkins, June 6, 1928, to *Detroit News,* March 29, 1925, Henry Bourne Joy Papers, Michigan Historical Collections, University of Michigan, Ann Arbor.

8. Joy to Carl W. Riddick, National Republican Constructive League, December 30, 1925, Joy Papers.

9. Joy, "Prohibition against Human Nature," *North American Review* 221 (June 1925): 609, 611.

10. AAPA, Corrupt Practices Act Reports.

11. Joy to Thomas H. Brennan, Deputy Prohibition Administrator, December 16, 1926, to Representative Clarence MacLeod, January 25, 1927, to Brennan, December 21, 1927, to J. W. Murphy, August 29, 1928, Joy Papers.

12. Joy to William V. Hodges, February 10, 1927, Joy Papers.

13. AAPA, Corrupt Practices Act Reports; Joy to Frederick W. Peabody, January 11, 1927, and to Arthur E. Wood, president of the Detroit Republican Club, December 22, 1927, Joy Papers.

14. House Judiciary Committee, *The Prohibition Amendment,* pp. 135-37, 314.

15. AAPA, Committee of Fifty poster [1925], Raskob Papers; Wadsworth to Stapley, March 7, 1926, and to James M. Grey, August 31, 1926, Wadsworth Papers.

16. Martin L. Fausold, *James W. Wadsworth, Jr.: The Gentleman from New York* (Syracuse: Syracuse University Press, 1975), pp. 1-12.

17. Ibid., pp. 12-156; Wadsworth, "The Reminiscences of James W. Wadsworth," unpublished memoirs, Oral History Research Office, Columbia University, 1952, pp. 20-21; Alden Hatch, *The Wadsworths of the Genesee* (New York: Coward-McCann, 1959), p. 215. In 1920 suffragists opposed Wadsworth for voting against the Nineteenth Amendment, the American Legion for opposing the soldier's bonus, and the AFL for voting to return American railroads to private ownership following World War I.

18. Wadsworth, "Public Contentment," speech at dinner in his honor, New York City, February 20, 1920, "The 18th Amendment and the Volstead Act," speech to the New York State American Legion convention, September 14, 1923, Wadsworth Papers.

19. Wadsworth, "Amending the Constitution," speech of February 12, 1923, Wadsworth Papers.

20. Fausold, *Wadsworth,* p. 416.

21. Wadsworth, "Public Contentment."

22. Wadsworth, "The 18th Amendment."

23. Wadsworth, "Amending the Constitution," and to John A. Richardson, July 3, 1923, Wadsworth Papers.

24. Fausold, *Wadsworth,* pp. 182-98; Claude G. Bowers, "The Reminiscences of Claude Bowers," unpublished memoirs, Oral History Research Office, Columbia University, 1957, pp. 57-58; J. Joseph Huthmacher, *Senator Robert F. Wagner and the Rise of Urban Liberalism* (New York: Atheneum, 1968), pp. 50-53.

25. Wadsworth, speech to Republican Businessmen's dinner, New York City, August 4, 1926, and speech at Madison Square Garden, October 30, 1926, Wads-

worth Papers; Wadsworth, "Reminiscences," p. 347.

26. Wadsworth, campaign speech, Binghamton, New York, September 4, 1926, Wadsworth Papers.

27. Fausold, *Wadsworth*, p. 199; Huthmacher, *Wagner*, p. 53.

28. Wadsworth to Miss Helen Richardson, December 14, 1926, Wadsworth Papers.

29. Wadsworth, "Reminiscences," p. 362.

30. By far the most impressive and useful study of Pierre's generation of du Ponts is Alfred D. Chandler, Jr., and Stephen Salsbury, *Pierre S. du Pont and the Making of the Modern Corporation* (New York: Harper & Row, 1971). Other helpful works are John K. Winkler, *The Du Pont Dynasty* (New York: Reynal & Hitchcock, 1935); Max Dorian, *The du Ponts: From Gunpowder to Nylon*, trans. Edward B. Garside (Boston: Little, Brown, 1962); and William H. A. Carr, *The du Ponts of Delaware* (New York: Dodd, Mead, 1964).

31. Pierre S. du Pont to Stuyvesant Fish, May 24, 1922, Pierre S. du Pont Papers; Carter Field, "Captain Bill Stayton—Guiding Spirit of the 'Little Group of Millionaires,' " *Life*, July 24, 1931, p. 15; Irénée du Pont to G. C. Hinckley, November 27, 1922, and August 22, 1924, to William H. Stayton, September 25, 1925, and December 2, 1925, to Frank Haley, October 2, 1925, to G. T. Barnhill, February 26, 1926, and April 6, 1926, to William S. Prichett and nine others, February 9, 1926, and to H. G. Haskell, February 18, 1926; Irénée du Pont AAPA membership cards, 1922-25; minutes, "mass meeting" committee, February 16, 1926; Irénée du Pont Papers.

32. Irénée du Pont to William Allen White, July 3, 1926, Irénée du Pont Papers. The letter was not sent.

33. Irénée du Pont to Frank Haley, October 2, 1925, Irénée du Pont Papers.

34. Irénée du Pont to William S. Prichett *et al.*, February 9, 1926, Irénée du Pont Papers.

35. Irénée du Pont to G. C. Crawford, April 3, 1928, Irénée du Pont Papers.

36. Irénée du Pont to Dr. Layton Grier, June 3 and 9, 1926, to Rt. Rev. Philip Cook, June 21 and July 13, 1926, Irénée du Pont Papers.

37. Irénée du Pont to Rev. J. H. Whedbee, July 28, 1926, Irénée du Pont Papers.

38. Irénée du Pont to William Allen White, July 3, 1926, Irénée du Pont Papers.

39. Pierre S. du Pont to Isabel Darlington, April 17, 1926, Pierre S. du Pont Papers; G. C. Hinckley to Halbert L. Hoard, June 21, 1928, Hoard Papers.

40. Chandler and Salsbury, *Pierre S. du Pont*, pp. 430, 534-64.

41. Chandler and Salsbury trace Pierre du Pont's business career in great detail and with penetrating insight.

42. Chandler and Salsbury, *Pierre S. du Pont*, pp. 459, 563-64.

43. Pierre S. du Pont to Paul B. Belin, June 12, 1924, exhibit 162, *U.S. v. E. I. du Pont de Nemours and Company, General Motors Corporation, et al.*, Eleutherian Mills Historical Library.

44. Statement by Stayton during the summer of 1933 to Heckman, "Prohibition Passes," pp. 206-7; Carter Field, "Captain Stayton," p. 15; Irénée du Pont to Stayton, March 31, 1925, Irénée du Pont Papers; Pierre S. du Pont to Mrs. Ella P.

Cordray, March 16, 1925, to G. W. Crabbe, March 25, 1925, and to P. H. Callahan, May 22, 1928; Stayton to Pierre du Pont, November 11, 1926, Pierre S. du Pont Papers.

45. Pierre S. du Pont to Mrs. Ella D. Cordray, March 20, 1925, Pierre S. du Pont Papers. He made much the same argument to P. H. Callahan, May 22, 1928, and in "Eighteenth Amendment Not a Remedy for the Drink Evil," *Current History* 28 (April 1928): 17-22.

46. Pierre S. du Pont, "A Business Man's View of Prohibition," radio address broadcast by the National Broadcasting Company, December 15, 1929, reprinted as a pamphlet by the AAPA, AAPA Papers. George E. Thompson, Pierre S. du Pont's private secretary, in a March 24, 1975, interview with the author recalled this as a particular concern of his employer.

47. John P. Nields to Pierre S. du Pont, February 2, 1926, Pierre S. du Pont Papers.

48. Pierre S. du Pont, "Eighteenth Amendment Not a Remedy," p. 19. See also Pierre S. du Pont to Phillips Lee Goldsborough, May 3, 1928, Pierre S. du Pont Papers, and "Why I Am Against Prohibition," *Liberty,* November 13, 1928, pp. 13-14.

49. Pierre S. du Pont to Ella D. Cordray, March 16, 1925.

50. Chandler and Salsbury, *Pierre S. du Pont,* pp. 396-97.

51. Pierre S. du Pont, "Why I Am Against Prohibition," pp. 13-14.

52. Roy Haywood Lopata, "John J. Raskob: A Conservative Businessman in the Age of Roosevelt," (Ph.D. diss., University of Delaware, 1975), p. 13.

53. A Raskob biography remains to be written. This paragraph and the ones following draw upon Henry F. Pringle, "John J. Raskob: A Portrait," *Outlook,* August 22, 1928, pp. 645-49, 678; *New York Times,* October 16, 1950, p. 27; Chandler and Salsbury, *Pierre S. du Pont,* pp. 39, 313, 435-37, 450-56, 460, 491, 508, 536; and Lopata, "Raskob," chaps. 1 and 3.

54. John J. Raskob to R. N. Holsaple, November 14, 1928, Raskob Papers.

55. William H. Stayton to John J. Raskob, October 2, 1919; John J. Raskob, AAPA membership card, June 26, 1922; unsigned, handwritten memorandum of contributions to the AAPA, February, 1926, through February, 1930, Raskob Papers. Raskob gave $750 in 1926, $100 in 1927, and then in March, 1928, began contributing thousands of dollars a year to the AAPA.

56. John J. Raskob to P. H. Callahan, June 4, 1928, printed and distributed as *The Raskob-Callahan Correspondence,* Raskob Papers.

57. Ibid.

58. AAPA, Corrupt Practices Act Reports.

59. Senate Judiciary Committee, *The National Prohibition Law.*

60. *Washington Post,* April 25, 1926.

61. Senate Special Committee, *Senatorial Campaign Expenditures,* pp. 1248-57, 1504; *Chicago Tribune,* July 7, 1926; New York *World,* July 2, 1926; *New York Times,* July 7, 1926, p. 1.

62. Minutes of meeting of AAPA policy committee, November 15, 1927, reprinted in Senate Judiciary Committee, *Lobby Investigation,* p. 4145.

63. *Milwaukee Sentinel,* September 1, 4, and 5, 1926; *Milwaukee Journal,* Sep-

tember 1, 1926; [Madison] *Wisconsin State Journal,* September 1 and 3, 1926; *New York Times,* September 3, 1926, p. 3, and September 4, 1926, p. 4.

64. *New York Herald-Tribune,* June 30, 1926; Franklin D. Mitchell, *Embattled Democracy: Missouri Democratic Politics, 1919–1932* (Columbia: University of Missouri Press, 1968), pp. 94–101; *St. Louis Post-Dispatch,* November 6, 1926.

65. Grayson M.-P. Murphy to James W. Wadsworth, Jr., April 28, 1926, marked "Personal and Confidential," Wadsworth Papers.

66. Heckman, "Prohibition Passes," p. 13.

67. Wadsworth to Grayson M.-P. Murphy, May 12, 1926, Wadsworth Papers.

68. William H. Stayton to Pierre S. du Pont, November 1, 1927, Pierre S. du Pont Papers; Fausold, *Wadsworth,* pp. 221–22; *New York Herald-Tribune,* November 29, 30, 1927.

69. Wadsworth to Grayson M.-P. Murphy, December 2, 1927, Wadsworth Papers.

70. *Washington Post,* December 13, 1927; *New York Herald-Tribune,* December 13, 1927; Wadsworth to James M. Beck, December 22, 1927, James M. Beck Papers, Firestone Library, Princeton University; William H. Stayton to Henry B. Joy, December 3, 1927, Joy Papers.

71. Pierre S. du Pont to Samuel Rea, February 1, 1928, Pierre S. du Pont Papers; Fausold, *Wadsworth,* p. 223; "Draft Report of Sub-Committee on Program," and Julian Codman to Pierre S. du Pont, December 27, 1927, Pierre S. du Pont Papers.

72. "Report [of committee on organization] to Meeting of January 6, 1928;" Pierre S. du Pont to Samuel Rea, February 1, 1928, Pierre S. du Pont Papers.

73. Chandler and Salsbury, *Pierre S. du Pont;* Pierre S. du Pont to Charles H. Sabin, August 10, 1932, Irénée du Pont Papers; Executive Committee of the Board of Directors, *Report to the Directors, Members and Friends of the Association Against the Prohibition Amendment for the Year 1928* (Washington: AAPA, 1929),˙pp. 1–2; Pierre S. du Pont to Samuel Rea, February 1, 1928, Pierre S. du Pont Papers; AAPA executive committee minutes, January 4, 1929, and July 8, 1930, Irénée du Pont Papers. Most AAPA executive committee minutes can be found in the Irénée and Pierre S. du Pont Papers.

74. Henry H. Curran, *Pillar to Post* (New York: Scribner's, 1941), pp. 285–86; Curran to James W. Wadsworth, Jr., March 14, 1924, and Wadsworth to Grayson M.-P. Murphy, May 12, 1926, Wadsworth Papers; Henry F. Pringle, "Wet Hope," *The New Yorker,* June 14, 1930, pp. 23–25.

75. AAPA executive committee minutes, April 17, 1928, Irénée du Pont Papers; Executive Committee, *AAPA Report for 1928,* p. 2; [Jouett Shouse], *Annual Report of the President of the Association Against the Prohibition Amendment for the Year 1933* (Washington: AAPA, 1934), p. 3.

76. Executive committee to Irénée du Pont, February 20, 1928; William H. Stayton to Irénée du Pont, March 20 and April 25, 1928; Irénée du Pont to Henry H. Westinghouse and Paul W. Litchfield, March 22, 1928; Westinghouse to Irénée du Pont, March 28, 1928; Litchfield to Irénée du Pont, March 26, 1928; AAPA executive committee minutes, April 17, 1928, Irénée du Pont Papers. *New York Times,* April 23, 1928, p. 48.

77. Pierre S. du Pont to Henry H. Curran, March 19, 1928, Irénée du Pont to Curran, March 20, 1928, Pierre S. du Pont to Curran, May 31, 1928, and Irénée du

Pont to Curran, June 29, 1928, Irénée du Pont Papers; John J. Raskob to Curran, May 29, 1928, and to Charles H. Sabin, March 22, 1928, Raskob Papers; Senate Judiciary Committee, *Lobby Investigation,* p. 4140; AAPA, Corrupt Practices Act Reports.

78. AAPA executive committee minutes, 1928–33, Irénée du Pont Papers; AAPA, Cash Receipts and Expenditures, 1928–33, Pierre S. du Pont Papers (separate expenditures by state affiliates added slightly to annual totals reflected in Corrupt Practices Act reports. When it disbanded in December 1933, the association left Pierre du Pont holding an unpaid $75,489 loan); Odegard, *Pressure Politics,* p. 181.

79. *New York Times,* April 23, 1928, p. 48; Haynes, *Prohibition Inside Out,* p. 183; Pierre S. du Pont, "Comments on a Pamphlet Entitled 'Brewers and Billionaires Conspire Against the Working Class,'" March 28, 1931, Pierre S. du Pont Papers.

80. Dobyns, *The Amazing Story of Repeal,* p. ix; Clark, *Deliver Us From Evil,* pp. 200–201; Carter, *Another Part of the Twenties,* p. 94.

81. Odegard, *Pressure Politics,* p. 208.

82. AAPA, Corrupt Practices Act Reports. Henry H. Curran to John J. Raskob, February 18, 1931, to Edward S. Harkness, May 29, 1931, and Raskob to Curran, March 4 and 26 and July 6, 1931, Raskob Papers, suggests that a number of directors made larger contributions in 1931 than the corrupt practices reports indicated.

83. AAPA, finance department schedule for 1929, Pierre S. du Pont Papers.

84. AAPA, Cash Receipts and Expenditures, 1930–33.

85. Senate Judiciary Committee, *Lobby Investigation,* p. 3957; Executive Committee of the Board of Directors, *Annual Report to the Directors, Members and Friends of the Association Against the Prohibition Amendment for the Year 1930* (Washington: AAPA, 1931), p. 16; U.S., Senate, Committee on the Judiciary, *Modification or Repeal of National Prohibition: Hearings,* 72d Cong., 1st sess. (Washington: GPO, 1932), pt. 1, pp. 12–13.

86. Odegard, *Pressure Politics,* pp. 183, 190.

87. "Resolution offered by the Executive Committee of the Association against the Prohibition Amendment to the Board of Directors of the Association assembled in meeting on April 17, 1928, for their preliminary consideration, pending a further meeting of the board," Raskob Papers; AAPA board of directors minutes, May 28, 1928, in William Stayton to Irénée du Pont, June 6, 1928, Irénée du Pont Papers; Executive Committee, *AAPA Report for 1928,* p. 7.

CHAPTER 6

1. *Washington Post,* June 12, 1928.

2. "Statement made by Major Henry H. Curran, President of the Association Against the Prohibition Amendment, before the Republican National Convention, June, 1928," press release, Irénée du Pont Papers; *New York Times,* June 13, 1928, p. 3.

3. *Official Report of the Proceedings of the Nineteenth Republican National Convention, 1928* (New York: Tenny Press, 1928), pp. 172–73; *New York Times,* June 13, 1928, p. 3, June 14, 1928, p. 1, June 15, 1928, p. 4; *Washington Post,* June 19, 1928.

4. Herbert Hoover, "Address Accepting the Nomination," August 11, 1928, *Public Papers of the Presidents of the United States: Herbert Hoover, 1929* (Washington:

GPO, 1974), p. 511.

5. Herbert Hoover, *American Individualism* (Garden City, N.Y.: Doubleday, Page, 1922), p. 37. For more on Hoover's thinking, see Joan Hoff Wilson, *Herbert Hoover: Forgotten Progressive* (Boston: Little, Brown, 1975), especially pp. 87–88, 159–60.

6. *Christian Science Monitor* interview, March 13, 1925; address to YMCA convention, October 26, 1925, public statements file, Herbert Hoover Papers, Herbert Hoover Presidential Library, West Branch, Iowa.

7. Herbert Hoover to William Borah, *New York Times,* February 24, 1928, p. 1; "Address Accepting Nomination," p. 511. For a different view of Hoover, see David Burner, *Herbert Hoover: A Public Life* (New York: Alfred A. Knopf, 1979), pp. 203, 218–20.

8. *Washington Post,* June 19 and 28, 1928; *New York Times,* June 29, 1928, p. 1; *Official Record of the Proceedings of the Democratic National Convention, 1928* (Indianapolis: Bookwalter-Ball-Greathouse, 1928), pp. 184–85, 200–204.

9. *New York Times,* June 30, 1928, p. 1; *Proceedings of the Democratic Convention, 1928,* pp. 266–86.

10. Pringle, "Raskob," pp. 645–49.

11. *The Raskob-Callahan Correspondence* (n.p., June 1928). See chapter 5 for Raskob's argument. Raskob had also just written a letter condemning prohibition to Undersecretary of the Treasury Ogden L. Mills, July 2, 1928, "National Prohibition," Secretary's Correspondence, 1919–32, U.S. Department of the Treasury, Record Group 56, National Archives.

12. Minutes of a meeting of the Democratic National Committee, July 11, 1928, *Proceedings of the Democratic Convention, 1928,* pp. 437–44.

13. Pringle, "Raskob," p. 646. Al Smith later confirmed this in his autobiography, *Up to Now* (New York: Viking, 1929), p. 382.

14. Alfred E. Smith, "Address Accepting Nomination," August 22, 1928, *Proceedings of the Democratic Convention, 1928,* pp. 275–77; Sinclair, *Era of Excess,* p. 302.

15. John J. Raskob to Thomas F. Ryan and Bernard Baruch, October 17, 1928, John J. Raskob Papers; David Burner, *The Politics of Provincialism: The Democratic Party in Transition, 1918–1932* (New York: Alfred A. Knopf, 1968), p. 200; John J. Raskob to Irénée du Pont, July 19, 1928, Raskob Papers.

16. John J. Raskob to Coleman du Pont, August 17, 1928, Defendants Trial Exhibit GM 20, *U.S. v. du Pont, et al.*

17. Pierre S. du Pont to John J. Raskob, August 11, 1928, Pierre S. du Pont Papers; Coleman du Pont to Pierre S. du Pont, August 15, 1928, Defendants Trial Exhibit GM 19, *U.S. v. du Pont, et al.*

18. Pierre S. du Pont to Lammot du Pont, August 25, 1928, Pierre S. du Pont Papers.

19. Pierre S. du Pont to W. S. Pole, August 29, 1928, Pierre S. du Pont Papers.

20. Henry H. Curran, press release, August 27, 1928, Irénée du Pont Papers.

21. William H. Stayton to Henry B. Joy, June 28, 1928, Joy Papers; William H. Stayton to Irénée du Pont, November 1, 1928, and Irénée du Pont to Henry B. Joy, December 24, 1929, Irénée du Pont Papers; unidentified newspaper clipping, Oc-

tober 4, 1928, Wadsworth Papers.

22. Virginius Dabney, *Dry Messiah: The Life of Bishop Cannon* (New York: Alfred
A. Knopf, 1949); Michael S. Patterson, "The Fall of a Bishop: James Cannon, Jr.,
versus Carter Glass, 1909–1934," *Journal of Southern History* 39 (November 1973):
497.

23. Quoted in J. Joseph Huthmacher, *Massachusetts People and Politics, 1919–
1933* (Cambridge: Harvard University Press, 1959), p. 155.

24. Kirschner, *City and Country*, p. 50; Robert Moats Miller, *American Protestants and Social Issues, 1919–1939* (Chapel Hill: University of North Carolina Press,
1958), p. 51.

25. Burner, *Politics of Provincialism*, p. 217.

26. Ibid., pp. 218–42; Ruth Silva, *Rum, Religion, and Votes: 1928 Re-examined*
(University Park: Pennsylvania State University Press, 1962); John W. Allswang, *A
House for All Peoples: Ethnic Politics in Chicago, 1890–1936* (Lexington: University
Press of Kentucky, 1971); Allan T. Lichtman, "Critical Election Theory and the
Reality of American Presidential Politics, 1916–40," *American Historical Review* 81
(April 1976): 317–51.

27. "Was the Election a Victory for Prohibition?" *Literary Digest*, November 24,
1928, pp. 14–15; "Protestant Press Call It a Dry Victory," *Literary Digest*, December
8, 1928, pp. 28–29; *Current History* 29 (December, 1928), pp. 367–81; William
Ogburn and Nell Talbot, "A Measurement of the Factors in the Presidential Election
of 1928," *Social Forces* 8 (December 1929): pp. 175–83; Roy V. Peel and Thomas C.
Donnally, *The 1928 Campaign: An Analysis* (New York: Richard R. Smith, 1931),
pp. 58–59; Sinclair *Era of Excess*, p. 353; Senate Judiciary Committee, *Lobby
Investigation*, pp. 3941–43.

28. Herbert Hoover, "Inaugural Address," March 4, 1929, *Public Papers of
Herbert Hoover, 1929*, pp. 2–3; John A. Ryan, "Who Shall Obey the Law?" *Com-
monweal*, April 3, 1929, p. 617; Carlton M. Sherwood, "The Drys Rally to Hoover,"
Christian Herald, March 23, 1929, reprint file, Hoover Papers; *New York Times*,
March 9, 1929, p. 1.

29. AAPA executive committee minutes, November 27, 1928, Pierre S. du Pont
Papers.

30. Special Advisory Committee of the Social Science Research Council, *Sources of
Information Concerning the Operation of the Eighteenth Amendment* (n.p., 1928),
p. 3, Committee on Prohibition, Records of the National Commission on Law
Observance and Enforcement, Record Group 10, Washington National Records
Center, Suitland, Maryland; House Judiciary Committee, *The Prohibition Amend-
ment*, p. 343.

31. Executive Committee, *AAPA Report for 1928*, p. 24.

32. Unsigned memoranda, "An Analysis of the Work of the Research Department" and "An Analysis of the Publication and Information Service of the Association Against the Prohibition Amendment," Irénée du Pont Papers. Before 1928,
AAPA publications took a variety of forms, including small pamphlets and flyers,
short-lived newspapers (*The Minute Man*, c. 1922, and *Bulletin of the Association
Against the Prohibition Amendment*, c. 1923), and reprints of news articles (the
irregular *Clip Sheet*). Most of these have been lost, but a few appear among the

papers of members and in the Library of Congress's compilation, Association Against the Prohibition Amendment, *Bulletins, Pamphlets, and Miscellaneous Printed Materials, 1923-1933.*

33. Executive Committee, *AAPA Report for 1928,* p. 25; AAPA executive committee minutes, April 4, 1928, Irénée du Pont Papers; Special Committee of Social Science Research Council, *Sources of Information,* pp. 1-4; House Judiciary Committee, *Prohibition Amendment,* p. 343; "Analysis of Research Department"; *New York Times,* December 31, 1928, p. 1.

34. "Analysis of Research Department" and "Analysis of Publication and Information Service." The research department assisted, with both information and funds, the publication of Rheta Childe Dorr, *Drink: Coercion or Control?* (New York: Frederick A. Stokes, 1929); Henry Alan Johnston, *What Rights Are Left?* (New York: Macmillan, 1930); and Millard Tydings, *Before and After Prohibition* (New York: Macmillan, 1930); see Henry Curran to Irénée du Pont, December 6, 1929, and AAPA executive committee minutes, April 29 and September 1, 1930, Irénée du Pont Papers. The department also cooperated in the writing of articles and in at least one case prepared an article signed by an executive committee member: James W. Wadsworth, Jr., "The Death Toll of Enforcement," *North American Review* 229 (March 1930): 257-62; see Senate Judiciary Committee, *Lobby Investigation,* pp. 3914-16.

35. William H. Stayton, memorandum to Henry B. Joy, T. W. Phillips, and the executive committee, September 10, 1928, and Phillips to Stayton, August 29, 1928, Irénée du Pont Papers.

36. AAPA, *Scandals of Prohibition Enforcement* (Washington, March 1, 1929). This pamphlet and several others were reprinted in *Official Records of the National Commission on Law Observance and Enforcement,* 71st Cong., 3d sess.; Senate document 307, vol. 5 (Washington: GPO, 1931).

37. Quoted in *Scandals,* p. 1.

38. *New York Times,* May 13, 1929, p. 1; AAPA, *Cost of Prohibition and Your Income Tax,* 2d ed. (Washington, July, 1930).

39. "Analysis of Publication and Information Service."

40. AAPA, *Canada Liquor Crossing the Border* (Washington, July, 1929). The AAPA report was confirmed and elaborated upon by Jones, *The Eighteenth Amendment and Our Foreign Relations,* and Kottman, "Volstead Violated," pp. 106-26.

41. "Analysis of Publication and Information Service."

42. AAPA, *Measuring the Liquor Tide,* 1st ed. (Washington, August, 1929), 2d ed. (Washington, June, 1930).

43. AAPA, *Reforming America With a Shotgun: A Study of Prohibition Killings* (Washington, November 1929).

44. AAPA, *Prohibition Enforcement: Its Effect on Courts and Prisons* (Washington, December, 1930).

45. Executive Committee, *AAPA Report for 1928,* pp. 25-27; Senate Judiciary Committee, *Lobby Investigation,* pp. 3834-42.

46. AAPA, *The Quebec System: A Study of Liquor Control* (Washington, November, 1928); AAPA, *Government Liquor Control in Canada* (Washington, October, 1929); AAPA, *The Last Outpost of Prohibition in Canada: Nova Scotia and Prince*

Edward Island (Washington, December, 1929); AAPA, *The Quebec System,* p. 36.

47. AAPA, *The Bratt System of Liquor Control in Sweden* (Washington, January, 1930); AAPA, *England's Solution of the Liquor Problem* (Washington, September, 1930); AAPA, *Temperance by Taxation: How Denmark Does It* (Washington, March, 1932); AAPA, *Finland's Prohibition: An Echo of Volsteadism* (Washington, June, 1930); and AAPA, *Norway's Noble Experiment* (Washington, April, 1931).

48. "Analysis of Publication and Information Services"; Senate Judiciary Committee, *Lobby Investigation,* pp. 4012-13; Henry H. Curran to Allan V. Junkin, February 1, 1932, Irénée du Pont Papers; Pierre S. du Pont, statement over WDEL, Wilmington, Delaware, November 3, 1930, Pierre S. du Pont Papers; [Henry H. Curran], memorandum of Mr. [Pierre] du Pont's remarks on a plan for state control of liquor manufacture and sale, March 8, 1929, Pierre S. du Pont to Eldridge R. Johnson, November 1, 1929, Henry Curran to Pierre S. du Pont, January 20, 1930, Pierre S. du Pont to Henry Curran, January 27, 1930, Pierre S. du Pont Papers; Pierre S. du Pont to AAPA directors, April 1, 1929, William H. Stayton to John J. Raskob, July 10, 1929, August 12, 1929, and January 8, 1930, Raskob Papers; "Minutes of round-table meeting of certain directors of the AAPA held in New York City, November 12th and 13th, 1929," Irénée du Pont Papers; Pierre S. du Pont to Rev. E. H. Derrickson, July 1, 1926, to W. Cabell Bruce, August 30, 1926, memorandum "Some Attractive Features of the Quebec Plan of Drink Control," October 26, 1926, to William H. Stayton, December 28, 1926, to Eldridge R. Johnson, January 11, 1929, Pierre du Pont Papers; Pierre S. du Pont, *Plan for Distribution and Control of Intoxicating Liquors in the United States* (n.p., September, 1930).

49. Hoover, "Address Accepting Nomination," p. 511; National Commission on Law Observance and Enforcement, *Report on the Enforcement of the Prohibition Laws of the United States,* 71st Cong., 3d sess., House document 722 (Washington: GPO, 1931), p. iii; Hoover, "Inaugural Address," pp. 2-4.

50. Herbert Hoover, "Remarks at the First Meeting of the National Commission on Law Observance and Enforcement," May 28, 1929, *Public Papers of Herbert Hoover, 1929,* pp. 159-60; Peel and Donnelly, *The 1932 Campaign,* p. 5.

51. George W. Wickersham, address before Boston Chamber of Commerce, March 12, 1931, National Commission of Law Observance and Enforcement file, Newton D. Baker Papers, Library of Congress; Commission minutes and research reports, Records of the National Commission on Law Observance and Enforcement; *Official Records of the National Commission on Law Observance and Enforcement,* vol. 3, *Hearings;* Gene E. and Elaine H. Carte, *Police Reform in the United States: The Era of August Vollmer, 1905-1932* (Berkeley: University of California Press, 1975), p. 67; *New York Times,* July 17, 1929, pp. 1, 2, and January 14, 1930, p. 1; Herbert Hoover, "Special Message to Congress Proposing Administrative Reforms in Federal Law Enforcement and Judicial Machinery," January 13, 1930, *Public Papers of Herbert Hoover, 1930,* pp. 21-23.

52. William S. Kenyon and Herbert Hoover, July 28, 1930, National Commission on Law Observance and Enforcement file, Hoover Papers.

53. House Judiciary Committee, *Prohibition Amendment,* p. 136.

54. Ibid., pp. 343-60.

55. Herbert Hoover, "Message to the Congress Transmitting Report of the Na-

tional Commission on Law Observance and Enforcement," January 20, 1931, *Public Papers of Herbert Hoover, 1931,* pp. 29-31. An advanced text was issued on January 19.

56. National Commission on Law Observance and Enforcement, *Report on Prohibition,* p. 83.

57. Hoover, "Message Transmitting Report," p. 30.

58. Pierre S. du Pont to Henry Curran, January 21, 1931, Pierre S. du Pont Papers.

59. "Confusion Worse Confounded," *Nation,* February 4, 1931, p. 116; "Four Aspects of the Wickersham Report," *New Republic,* February 4, 1931, p. 312; J. Frederick Essary, "Blowing the Lid Off the Wickersham Report," *Liberty,* August 29, 1931, pp. 13-16.

60. National Commission on Law Observance and Enforcement, *Report on Prohibition,* pp. 89-162.

61. For a sample of their comments, see Sinclair, *Era of Excess,* pp. 365-66.

62. Summaries of editorial comments on the law-enforcement commission report, January 23, 24, and 26, 1931, presidential press relations file, Hoover Papers.

63. Walter Lippmann, "The Great Wickersham Mystery," *Vanity Fair,* April 1931, pp. 41-42.

64. "Confusion Worse Confounded," p. 116.

65. Peter H. Odegard, "Mr. Hoover's 'Noble Experiment,'" *Nation,* July 29, 1931, p. 103.

66. Quoted in Sinclair, *Era of Excess,* p. 366. See also "The Talk of the Town," *The New Yorker,* January 31, 1931, pp. 9-10.

67. *New York Times,* January 21, 1931, p. 18.

CHAPTER 7

1. Executive Committee, *AAPA Report for 1928,* pp. 10-11; *New York Times,* June 29, 1928, p. 4.

2. Merz, *Dry Decade,* p. 334; Huthmacher, *Massachusetts People and Politics,* pp. 156, 188.

3. [Madison] *Capital Times,* March 30 and 31, April 1 and 3, 1929; *Chicago Tribune,* April 4, 1929; *Washington Post,* April 4, 1929.

4. AAPA executive committee minutes, March 19 and April 5, 1929, Irénée du Pont Papers; [Madison] *Capital Times,* March 26, 27, and 31, 1929; Senate Judiciary Committee, *Lobby Investigation,* p. 4173.

5. "The Huge Poll's Final Report: All Records Outdone," *Literary Digest,* May 24, 1930, p. 7.

6. Willcox, "An Attempt to Measure Public Opinion," pp. 244-56.

7. "Prohibition Repeal—Practical Politics," *New Republic,* June 11, 1930, p. 84; Edward S. Martin, "The Editor's Easy Chair," *Harper's Magazine,* August 1930, p. 378.

8. *New York Herald-Tribune,* April 7, 1930.

9. House Judiciary Committee, *The Prohibition Amendment,* pp. 1243-44; idem, *Proposing an Amendment to the Constitution of the United States in Lieu of the Eighteenth Amendment: Hearings,* 70th Cong., 1st sess., serial 21 (Washington: GPO, 1928); William H. Stayton to Pierre S. du Pont, September 11, 1928, Pierre S.

du Pont Papers. The Federal Dispensary Tax Reduction League appears to have disappeared by the summer of 1930.

10. William H. Stayton to Irénée du Pont, May 22, 1928; AAPA executive committee minutes, November 9, 1928, and February 7, 1929, William P. Smith to Irénée du Pont, April 29 and July 19, 1929, Irénée du Pont Papers; Stayton to H. G. Seer, July 30, 1928, and to AAPA Directors, November 19, 1931, Raskob Papers.

11. Biographical information on Pauline Morton Sabin, unless otherwise noted, comes from Dorothy Ducas, "In Miniature: Mrs. Charles H. Sabin, Lady into Tiger," *McCall's*, September 1930, p. 4; "Ladies at Roslyn," *Time*, July 18, 1932, pp. 8–10; Wilmington, Delaware, *Star*, July 31, 1932; Milton MacKaye, "The New Crusade," *The New Yorker*, October 22, 1932, pp. 20–24; Grace C. Root, *Women and Repeal: The Story of the Women's Organization for National Prohibition Reform* (New York: Harper, 1934); *New York Times*, March 9, 1929, and December 29, 1955.

12. MacKaye, "New Crusade," p. 21.

13. Wilmington *Star*, July 31, 1932.

14. *New York Times*, November 16, 1926, p. 3; Root, *Women and Repeal*, p. 4; Wilmington *Star*, July 31, 1932; Pauline Morton Sabin, "I Change My Mind on Prohibition," *Outlook*, June 13, 1928, p. 254.

15. *Wilmington Star*, July 31, 1932.

16. House Judiciary Committee, *The Prohibition Amendment*, pp. 41–42.

17. *New York Herald-Tribune*, April 4, 1929.

18. "Ladies at Roslyn," p. 9.

19. Sabin, "I Change My Mind," p. 272.

20. Root, *Women and Repeal*, p. 3; *New York Times*, April 4, 1929, pp. 1, 2; *New York Herald-Tribune*, April 4, 1929.

21. Root, *Women and Repeal*, pp. 3–6; *New York Times*, May 10, 1929, p. 56; "Minutes of the Organization Meeting of the Women's Organization for National Prohibition Reform, held at the Drake Hotel, Chicago, Illinois, May 28, 1929," WONPR Papers. A note on appellations: The women of the WONPR referred to each other and themselves by their husbands' names, and they used the masculine form in official titles. Therefore, despite subsequent trends, they are referred to in forms of address they themselves would recognize.

22. *New York Times*, May 10, 1929, p. 56, and May 29, 1929, p. 3; Root, *Women and Repeal*, pp. 6–11; *Chicago Tribune*, May 29, 1929; *Des Moines Register*, May 29, 1929; *New York Herald-Tribune*, May 29, 1929.

23. Senate Judiciary Committee, *Lobby Investigation*, p. 4061 (The national WONPR did not levy dues, rather it allowed each state to set its own policies and asked that 10 percent of income be turned over to the national office for its use. Most states apparently set very low dues or relied entirely upon donations. The organization never seems to have suffered financial woes); MacKaye, "New Crusade," p. 22; "An Address made by Mrs. Charles H. Sabin at a meeting of the Massachusetts Branch of the National Civic Federation in Boston, November 18th, 1929," WONPR Papers; Pauline Morton Sabin, "Women's Revolt against Prohibition," *Review of Reviews* 80 (November 1929): 86–88; Transcript, Women's Organization for National Prohibition Reform First Annual Convention, April 23–24, 1930, WONPR Papers.

24. *The Amazing Story of Repeal,* pp. 105-6.

25. MacKaye, "New Crusade," p. 22.

26. AAPA executive committee minutes, November 9, 1928, and January 4, 1929, Irénée du Pont Papers.

27. Gross Papers.

28. Transcript, WONPR first convention, WONPR Papers.

29. Franklin Chase Hoyt, "The Effect of Prohibition in Juvenile Court Work," (New York: WONPR, n.d.), Pamphlets on Prohibition in the United States, Library of Congress.

30. Grace Robinson, "Women Wets," *Liberty,* November 1, 1930, p. 30.

31. Transcript, WONPR first convention, WONPR Papers.

32. Ibid.

33. "Report of Second Annual Conference of Women's Organization for National Prohibition Reform," WONPR Papers; Root, *Women and Repeal,* p. 56; WONPR program of victory dinner, Washington, D.C., December 7, 1933, WONPR Papers; Senate Judiciary Committee, *Modification or Repeal of National Prohibition,* pt. 1, pp. 12-13.

34. WONPR national executive committee minutes, September 28-29, 1932, WONPR Papers.

35. WONPR, press releases, summaries of state reports, April 15, 1931, and April 7, 1933, and victory dinner program, WONPR Papers.

36. Wadsworth, "Reminiscences," p. 358.

37. MacKaye, "New Crusade," p. 22.

38. WONPR, press releases, summaries of state reports, April 15, 1931, and April 7, 1933. For more information on state activities, especially those of the Delaware branch, see David E. Kyvig, "Women against Prohibition," *American Quarterly* 28 (Fall 1976): 465-82.

39. WONPR national executive committee minutes, February 29, 1932, WONPR Papers.

40. Sinclair, *Era of Excess,* p. 343. The idea of sociel status as key to women's involvement in temperance movements comes from Gusfield, *Symbolic Crusade,* pp. 129-30 and *passim.*

41. Margaret Culkin Banning, "Anti-Prohibitionette," *Vogue,* September 1, 1930, p. 82; "Ladies at Roslyn," pp. 8-10; Ducas, "Lady into Tiger," p. 4; Isabel Leighton, "A Charming Aristocrat," *Smart Set,* March 1930, pp. 36-37; Robinson, "Women Wets," pp. 30-35; MacKaye, "New Crusade," pp. 20-25; Anna Steese Richardson, "Grandmother Goes Wet," *Forum,* June 1931, pp. 365-68; Jefferson Chase, "The Sabines Ravish the Senators," *Vanity Fair,* August 1931, pp. 42, 80.

42. Banning, "Anti-Prohibitionette," p. 82.

43. WONPR, press releases, summary of state reports, April 7, 1933, "Who's Who at the Conference of the Women's Organization for National Prohibition Reform, Mayflower Hotel, Washington, D.C., April 14-15, 1931," WONPR Papers.

44. WONPR national executive committee minutes, January 1931, WONPR Papers.

45. See especially Robinson, "Women Wets," pp. 30-35; Richardson, "Grandmother Goes Wet," pp. 365-68.

46. George Westervelt, summary of account, July 1, 1927, to October 18, 1928,

Harrison Tweed file, Voluntary Committee of Lawyers Papers, Collection on Legal Change, Wesleyan University, Middleton, Connecticut; Clement E. Vose, *Constitutional Change: Amendment Politics and Supreme Court Litigation since 1900* (Lexington, Mass.: D.C. Heath, 1972), p. 102; *New York Times*, December 11, 1927, p. 27; Account book, October 18, 1928, to August 6, 1929, Tweed file, VCL Papers.

47. *New York Times*, January 23, 1929, p. 2; Frances C. Smith to Joseph H. Choate, Jr., November 19, 1942, Joseph H. Choate, Jr., file, VCL Papers.

48. "Joseph Hodges Choate," in *Harvard College Class of 1897: Fiftieth Anniversary Report, 1897-1947* (Cambridge, Mass.: Harvard University Press, 1947), p. 119.

49. *New York Times*, March 14, 1929, p. 2; VCL statement of finances, January 22, 1929, to April 30, 1930, and H. P. Rhudy, memorandum on finances, April 9, 1931, Tweed file, VCL Papers; Vose, *Constitutional Change*, pp. 103-5, 128-33.

50. *New York Herald-Tribune*, January 23, 1929.

51. Frederic R. Coudert, *The Repeal of the Eighteenth Amendment and the Restoration of Our Constitution* (n.p., March 1931), Raskob Papers.

52. Henry Alan Johnston, "The Eighteenth Amendment is Void," *Century Magazine*, April 1928, pp. 641-53; Sterling E. Edmunds, "Mining and Sapping Our Bill of Rights," *Virginia Law Review* 16 (November 1929): 1-39; House Judiciary Committee, *The Prohibition Amendment*, pp. 390-94; George Gordon Battle, *The South— And the Eighteenth Amendment* (n.p.: Voluntary Committee of Lawyers, 1931), Eleutherian Mills Historical Library pamphlet collection; *New York Herald-Tribune*, January 23, 1929; Vose, *Constitutional Change*, p. 104; Executive Committee, *AAPA Report for 1930*, p. 8; VCL, report of executive committee, May 30, 1930, Choate file, VCL Papers; William P. MacCracken, Jr., Secretary, to members of the American Bar Association, July 1, 1930, National Commission on Law Observance and Enforcement file, Hoover Papers; U.S., Senate, Committee on Manufactures, *Amendment of the Prohibition Act: Hearings before a Subcommittee*, 72d Cong., 1st sess. (Washington: GPO, 1932), pp. 198-99; *New York Times*, November 19, 1930, pp. 1, 3.

53. Fred G. Clark Oral History, Hoover Library; Jackson-Babbitt, Inc., *The New Crusade* (Cleveland: Crusaders, Inc., 1932), pp. xi-xxi.

54. House Judiciary Committee, *The Prohibition Amendment*, p. 226; "Prohibition: United Wets," *Time*, November 7, 1932, p. 16; "Prohibition and Illiteracy," *Commonweal*, May 27, 1931, p. 89; Jackson-Babbitt, *The New Crusade, passim;* Senate Judiciary Committee, *Lobby Investigation*, pp. 4102-3; Tom S. Hines, Jr., "Mississippi and the Repeal of Prohibition," *Journal of Mississippi History* 24 (January 1962): 19.

55. AAPA executive committee minutes, September 24, October 18, and December 4, 1929, January 8, November 14, and November 25, 1930, January 27, April 7, June 16, and September 22, 1931, Irénée du Pont Papers; William H. Stayton to Henry B. Joy, Joy Papers; Stayton, notes on May 10, 1932, executive committee meeting, agenda for executive committee meeting, August 16, 1932, Benedict Crowell to Pierre S. du Pont, August 23, 1932, Pierre S. du Pont Papers; Fred G. Clark Oral History, Hoover Library; John C. Gebhart, describing the organized national repeal movement in 1932, barely mentioned the Crusaders in "Movement against Prohibition," pp. 177-78.

56. Merz, *Dry Decade*, p. 233.

57. Samuel Crowther, *Prohibition and Prosperity* (New York: John Day, 1930), pp. 4-5.

58. Ibid., pp. 18-21, 23-59. Similar arguments were made by Herman Feldman, *Prohibition: Its Economic and Industrial Aspects* (New York: D. Appleton, 1927); Fisher, *Prohibition at Its Worst;* Fisher and H. Bruce Brougham, *Prohibition Still at Its Worst* (New York: Alcohol Information Committee, 1928); J. C. Penny, "The Economic Results in the Enforcement of the Eighteenth Amendment," address to the annual meeting of the Citizens Committee on One Thousand, February 7, 1930, Gifford Pinchot Papers, Library of Congress.

59. Ernest H. Cherrington, general secretary of the World League against Alcoholism, quoted in October 8, 1929, *Congressional Record* 71 (71st Cong., 1st sess.): 4367.

60. Sixty thousand copies of the first edition of *Does Prohibition Pay?* (Washington, October, 1930) were distributed, and total newspaper circulation of stories based on the pamphlet reached 25,466,000, according to "An Analysis of the Publication and Information Service of the Association Against the Prohibition Amendment, March 19, 1931," Irénée du Pont Papers. For examples, see *New York Times,* October 2, 1930, p. 3, and May 25, 1931, pp. 1, 2.

61. *New York Times,* June 10, 1931, p. 22; "Intemperance of Prohibition," *Commonweal,* November 5, 1930, pp. 5-6; C. T. Revere, "Prohibition: Its Effect on Taxation," *Review of Reviews* 85 (April 1932): 37; Clark Warburton, *The Economic Results of Prohibition* (New York: Columbia University Press, 1932), pp. 5, 259-63.

62. *New York Times,* June 29, 1931, p. 12; AAPA, *Prohibition and the Deficit* (Washington, January 1932).

63. Roscoe W. Vinning, Superintendent of the Anti-Saloon League of Delaware, form letter, June 24, 1930, Irénée du Pont Papers.

64. Senate Judiciary Committee, *Lobby Investigation,* pp. 4165-66; Irénée du Pont to H. Lawton Blanchard, October 27, 1930, Irénée du Pont Papers.

65. Irénée du Pont to Ruter W. Springer, December 17, 1930, Irénée du Pont Papers.

66. Irénée du Pont to Roscoe W. Vinning, July 18, 1930, Irénée du Pont Papers.

67. The clearest examples of this are found in Dobyns, *The Amazing Story of Repeal;* and Gordon, *The Wrecking of the Eighteenth Amendment.* Even the survey of prohibition by Sinclair, *The Era of Excess,* accepts this view.

68. Henry H. Curran to AAPA members, October 16, 1931, Irénée du Pont Papers.

69. Irénée du Pont to Blanchard, October 27, 1930, Irénée du Pont Papers.

70. "Report of second annual conference of WONPR," WONPR Papers.

71. Watson Washburn to Herbert Hoover, May 31, 1931, "National Prohibition," Secretary's Correspondence, 1919-32, U.S., Department of the Treasury, Record Group 56, National Archives.

72. *Official Records of the National Commission on Law Observance and Enforcement,* vol. 3, *Hearings,* pp. 151-56.

73. See, for example, Malvern Hall Tillitt, *The Price of Prohibition* (New York: Harcourt, Brace, 1932), p. 100; and an editorial, "Prohibition and Prosperity," *New York Times,* August 30, 1931, sec. 3, p. 1.

74. Labor's National Committee for Modification of the Volstead Act, *Report of*

the First National Conference (Washington, 1931), Pamphlets on Prohibition in the United States, Library of Congress; Senate Committee on Manufactures, *Amendment of the Prohibition Act,* p. 260.

75. Donald J. Lisio, *The President and Protest: Hoover, Conspiracy, and the Bonus Riot* (Columbia: University of Missouri Press, 1974), pp. 43–45; and Roger Daniels, *The Bonus March: An Episode of the Great Depression* (Westport, Conn.: Greenwood, 1971), p. 51. Lisio and Daniels differ in their views of the ultimate outcome of the bonus agitation, the Bonus March on Washington in 1932, but both provide useful accounts.

76. AAPA executive committee minutes, April 7, 1931, Irénée du Pont Papers; *New York Times,* September 25, 1931, pp. 1, 2, and September 26, 1931, p. 18.

77. Senate Committee on Manufactures, *Amendment of the Prohibition Act,* p. 142.

78. Odegard, *Pressure Politics,* pp. 226–43; *New York Times,* January 30, 1924, pp. 1, 6; Joint Legislative Committee, *Face the Facts,* vol. 2 (February 6 and April 3, 1926), AAPA Miscellaneous Printed Material, Library of Congress; Executive Committee, *AAPA Report for 1929,* p. 27.

79. Baltimore *Evening Sun,* April 30, 1934, quoted in Patterson, "The Fall of a Bishop," p. 493.

80. Patterson, "The Fall of a Bishop," pp. 493–518. Also see Dabney, *Dry Messiah,* for a critical biography, and James Cannon, Jr., *Bishop Cannon's Own Story: Life as I Have Seen It,* ed. Richard L. Watson, Jr. (Durham: Duke University Press, 1955), for a self-defense.

81. Sinclair, *Era of Excess,* p. 339.

82. William H. Stayton to Irénée du Pont, May 22, 1928, Robert Athey to Irénée du Pont, August 27, 1928, William P. Smith to Irénée du Pont, April 3 and 29 and July 19, 1929, Stayton to executive committee, November 19, 1931, Irénée du Pont Papers; AAPA executive committee minutes, May 14, 1929, and April 7, 1931, J. H. Hawkins to Pierre S. du Pont, February 5, 1930, and William M. Smith to Pierre S. du Pont, October 24, 1931, Pierre S. du Pont Papers; Stayton to H. G. Seer, July 30, 1928, and to AAPA directors, November 19, 1931, Raskob Papers.

CHAPTER 8

1. William L. Marbury, "The Limitations upon the Amending Power," *Harvard Law Review* 33 (December 1919): 223–35; Justin DuPratt White, "Is There an Eighteenth Amendment?" *Cornell Law Quarterly* 5 (January 1920): 113–27; Everett V. Abbot, "Inalienable Rights and the Eighteenth Amendment," *Columbia Law Review* 20 (February 1920): 183–95; Charles K. Burdick, "Is Prohibition Lawful?" *New Republic,* April 21, 1920, pp. 245–48; D. O. McGovney, "Is the Eighteenth Amendment Void because of Its Contents? *Columbia Law Review* 20 (May 1920): 499–518.

2. *New York Times,* December 17, 1930, p. 23. Other legal scholars, at least one of them prompted by Bacon, had begun to reconsider the ratification question at about the same time. See George H. Williams, "Article V of the Constitution," *Constitutional Review* 12 (April 1928): 69–83; Lester B. Orfield, "The Scope of the Federal Amending Power," *Michigan Law Review* 28 (March 1930): 550–85; Henry W. Taft,

"Amendment of the Federal Constitution: Is the Power Conferred by Article V Limited by the Tenth Amendment?" *Virginia Law Review* 16 (May 1930): 647–58; George Washington Williams, "Are There Any Limitations upon the Power to Amend the United States Constitution?" *Temple Law Quarterly* 5 (June 1931): 554–61.

3. Selden Bacon, *The Tenth Amendment, Its Supreme Importance and Its Effect on the XVIII Amendment* (New York, 1930), Eleutherian Mills Historical Library pamphlet collection. See also Selden Bacon, "How the Tenth Amendment Affected the Fifth Article of the Constitution," *Virginia Law Review* 16 (June 1930): 771–91.

4. *New York Times,* December 17, 1930, p. 23.

5. AAPA executive committee minutes, April 1, 1930, Irénée du Pont Papers; Senate Judiciary Committee, *Lobby Investigation,* p. 4004; William H. Stayton to Henry B. Joy, April 1, 1930, Joy Papers.

6. William H. Stayton to AAPA directors, July 8, 1930, and to John J. Raskob, November 10, 1930, Raskob Papers.

7. *United States v. Sprague,* 44 F. 2d 967; *New York Times,* December 17, 1930; pp. 1, 21; "Prohibition: William Sprague Decision," *Time,* December 29, 1930, pp. 8–9; "No Eighteenth Amendment for Judge Clark," *Literary Digest,* December 27, 1930, p. 6; Joseph P. Pollard, "The Rebel on the Bench," *North American Review* 131 (March 1931): 227–34; Pollard, *The Road to Repeal: Submission to Conventions* (New York: Brentano's, 1932).

8. *New York Times,* December 17, 1930, pp. 1, 21, February 25, 1931, pp. 1, 21; Pollard, *Road to Repeal,* pp. 177–81; *United States v. Sprague,* 282 U.S. 716; "Judge Clark Overruled," *Outlook and Independent,* March 11, 1931, p. 359.

9. *U.S. v. Sprague,* 44 F. 2d 967.

10. Selden Bacon to William H. Stayton, December 29, 1930, Pierre S. du Pont Papers.

11. National Commission on Law Observance and Enforcement, *Report on the Enforcement of the Prohibition Laws of the United States,* p. 45.

12. Ibid., pp. 135, 156, 162; "Judge Clark and the Constitution," *New Republic,* December 31, 1930, p. 178; "Judge Clark's Decision," *Nation,* December 31, 1930, p. 722; "Repeal the Eighteenth Amendment," *Nation,* May 4, 1932, p. 502; "Vox Pop: Can It Bring Repeal," *World's Work,* January 1932, p. 28.

13. Pierre S. du Pont to John J. Raskob, January 14, 1931, Raskob Papers.

14. William H. Stayton to Henry B. Joy, May 14, 1931, Joy Papers.

15. Henry B. Joy to Arthur E. Wood, December 5, 12, and 19, 1929; newspaper clippings, most dated December 15, 16, or 17, 1929, scrapbook 35, Joy Papers; *New York Times,* May 17, 1930, p. 19.

16. Quoted in Morton Keller, *In Defense of Yesterday: James M. Beck and the Politics of Conservatism* (New York: Coward-McCann, 1958), p. 197.

17. Ibid., pp. 128–29; James M. Beck, *The Constitution of the United States* (New York: George H. Doran, 1922); and Beck, *The Vanishing Rights of the States* (New York: George H. Doran, 1926).

18. Beck, *The Constitution,* p. 280.

19. Keller, *In Defense of Yesterday,* pp. 207–8.

20. *Congressional Record,* February 7, 1930, 72 (71st Cong., 2d sess.): 3257–62;

Senate Judiciary Committee, *Lobby Investigation,* pp. 4177–78.

21. Executive Committee, *AAPA Report for 1930,* p. 6; Dwight W. Morrow, *For Repeal of the Eighteenth Amendment: Address Given in Newark, N.J., May 15, 1930* (n.p.: AAPA, 1930); AAPA, *Information for Members* (New York, July 1930), p. 1; *New York Times,* September 6, 1930; Executive Committee, *AAPA Report for 1930,* pp. 2–3. For Morrow's view of the campaign, see Harold Nicolson, *Dwight Morrow* (New York: Harcourt, Brace, 1935), pp. 377–81.

22. AAPA, *Information for Members,* p. 1; *New York Times,* July 15, 1930, p. 14, and August 3, 1930, p. 2. Irwin F. Greenburg, "Pinchot, Prohibition and Public Utilities: The Pennsylvania Election of 1930," *Pennsylvania History* 40 (January 1973): 21–35, while questionable on some details, is a useful attempt to make sense of this complex election.

23. Church had been trying to interest the AAPA in his efforts to develop the Liberal party as a new national third party with a platform stressing states rights, reduction of war debt claims, and prohibition repeal. Pennsylvania AAPA chairman Robert K. Cassatt wrote to Church in May 1930 to say his group had appropriated the Liberal Party label for its campaign against Pinchot; he hoped Church didn't object because this differed from Church's national plan. Church continued to try to obtain support. Pierre du Pont encouraged him until December 1931, then concluded that the Democrats embodied all that Church desired. Samuel Harden Church, *A New Political Party: An Address before the Association Against the Prohibition Amendment at the Metropolitan Club, New York City, February 4, 1930* (n.p., n.d.), Eleutherian Mills Historical Library pamphlet collection; *New York Times,* February 5, 1930, p. 17; AAPA executive committee minutes, February 5, 1930, Irénée du Pont Papers; Senate Judiciary Committee, *Lobby Investigation,* pp. 4199–4200; Pierre S. du Pont to Samuel Harden Church, February 14, March 25, April 28, and December 29, 1930, August 8 and December 7, 1931, to Harry Atwood, April 30, 1930, and Cassatt to Church, May 24, 1930, Pierre S. du Pont Papers.

24. *New York Times,* November 11, 1930, p. 1, November 13, 1930, p. 1; John L. Nethers, "'Driest of Drys': Simeon D. Fess," *Ohio History* 79 (Summer–Autumn, 1970): 187–88; TRB, "Washington Notes," *New Republic,* February 4, 1931, p. 321; "The Wickersham Report," *Commonweal,* February 4, 1931, p. 369; [Robert S. Allen and Drew Pearson], *Washington Merry-Go-Round* (New York: Horace Liveright, 1931), pp. 268–70, 289–91.

25. Executive Committee, *AAPA Report for 1930,* p. 6. Other states where Democrats endorsed repeal were New Hampshire, Vermont, Rhode Island, Connecticut, Delaware, Maryland, Wisconsin, North Dakota, and Washington.

26. Carter Field, "Life in Washington," *Life,* November 7, 1930, p. 14.

27. *New York Times,* January 19, 1929, p. 2, February 3, 1929, p. 2, and March 8, 1929, p. 25.

28. Burner, *The Politics of Provincialism,* p. 199.

29. John J. Raskob as told to James C. Derieux, "Rich Men in Politics," *Colliers,* March 5, 1932, p. 54.

30. Marie Chatham, "The Role of the National Party Chairman from Hanna to Farley," (Ph.D. diss., University of Maryland, 1953), pp. 247–48; Thomas S. Barclay, "The Publicity Division of the Democratic Party, 1929-1930," *American*

Political Science Review 25 (February 1931): 68-72; Cornelius P. Cotter and Bernard C. Hennessy, *Politics without Power: The National Party Committees* (New York: Atherton, 1964), p. 72. Chairman Robert McCombs talked of a permanent national headquarters in 1915, and Cordell Hull briefly began one in the early twenties, but no sustained organization preceded Raskob's. The Republicans followed suit in the mid-thirties.

31. Robert Cruise McManus, "Raskob," *North American Review* 231 (January 1931): 10-15; Barclay, "The Publicity Division," pp. 68-70; Charles Michelson, *The Ghost Talks* (New York: G. P. Putnam's Sons, 1944), pp. 15-16, 141; Claude G. Bowers, *My Life* (New York: Simon and Schuster, 1962), p. 224; Ray V. Peel and Thomas C. Donnelly, *The 1932 Campaign: An Analysis* (New York: Farrar & Rinehart, 1935), p. 112; John J. Raskob to Henry Curran, March 4, 1931, Raskob Papers; Lopata, "Raskob," pp. 101-16.

32. Scrapbooks, 1916-28; clippings from the New York *Morning Telegraph,* October 14, 1917, La Crosse, Kansas, *Republican,* July 4, 1918, Kingsley, Kansas, *Graphic,* October 11, 1928, Shouse Papers.

33. Michelson, *The Ghost Talks,* pp. 135-36.

34. *New York Times,* February 14, 1930, p. 2; March 13, 1930, p. 6; March 14, 1930, p. 22; March 31, 1930, p. 4; April 5, 1930, p. 18; and May 22, 1930, p. 2; U.S., Senate, Committee on the Judiciary, *Lobbying and Lobbyists: Partial Report,* 71st Cong., 2d sess., Senate Report 43, pt. 8, May 21, 1930 (Washington: GPO, 1930); Senate Judiciary Committee, *Lobby Investigation,* pp. 3676-96.

35. Leslie J. Stegh, "A Paradox of Prohibition: Election of Robert J. Bulkley as Senator from Ohio, 1930," *Ohio History* 83 (Summer 1974): 170-82.

36. John J. Raskob to Frederic R. Coudert, March 9, 1931, and to P. M. Abbott, March 12, 1931, Raskob Papers; Proceedings of Democratic national committee meeting, March 5, 1931, *Official Report of the Proceedings of the Democratic National Convention, 1932* (n.p., n.d.), p. 448; Jouett Shouse to John J. Raskob, January 21, 1931, marked *Personal and Confidential,* Raskob Papers; Jouett Shouse to Daniel C. Roper, November 15, 1930, and address in Miami, Florida, February 6, 1931, Shouse Papers; Shouse, "Watchman, What of the Night?" *Atlantic Monthly,* February 1931, p. 257; John J. Raskob, speech, March 5, 1931, *Proceedings of the Democratic Convention, 1932,* pp. 408-11; *Proceedings of the Democratic Convention, 1928,* p. 277; Pierre S. du Pont, "Memorandum...on a Plan for State Control of Liquor," March 8, 1929, Pierre S. du Pont Papers; minutes of meeting of certain directors of the AAPA, November 12 and 13, 1929, Irénée du Pont Papers; Pierre S. du Pont to Nicholas Murray Butler, January 6 and 13, 1930, Nicholas Murray Butler Papers, Columbia University.

37. Jouett Shouse to John J. Raskob, January 21, 1931, and Joseph P. Tumulty to Raskob, January 21, 26, and February 6, 1931, Raskob Papers; Shouse, Miami Address.

38. William E. Leuchtenburg, *Franklin D. Roosevelt and the New Deal* (New York: Harper & Row, 1963), p. 5; Arthur M. Schlesinger, Jr., *The Crisis of the Old Order, 1919-1933* (Boston: Houghton Mifflin, 1957), pp. 282, 386-87.

39. Raskob favored corporate assumption of greater responsibility for social well-being, the voluntary sharing of prosperity with workers in an industrial democracy

superior to socialist schemes. His "welfare capitalism" included a "workingman's trust" (an investment program for workers based on small monthly stock purchases for retirement income and worker ownership of corporations), a shorter work week (in which increased leisure would encourage consumption), public works programs (especially highway construction to stimulate employment), and lower tariffs to encourage trade (Lopata, "Raskob," pp. 124-42).

40. Unsigned memorandum, donations, 1926-30, Raskob Papers; AAPA contributions from national directors, 1931-33, Irénée du Pont Papers; John J. Raskob to Coleman du Pont, August 17, 1928, Defendants' Trial Exhibits no. GM 20, *U.S. v. du Pont et al.*

41. John J. Raskob to Governor Albert C. Ritchie, November 5, 1931, Raskob Papers; James Levin, "Governor Albert C. Ritchie and the Democratic Convention of 1932," *Maryland Historical Magazine* 67 (Fall 1972): 282-83.

42. Frank Freidel, *Franklin D. Roosevelt: The Ordeal* (Boston: Little, Brown, 1954), pp. 56, 161-63, 246-47, 253-55; James MacGregor Burns, *Roosevelt: The Lion and the Fox* (New York: Harcourt, Brace, & World, 1956), p. 73; Alfred B. Rollins, Jr., *Roosevelt and Howe* (New York: Alfred A. Knopf, 1962), p. 228; John J. Raskob to Franklin D. Roosevelt, October 10, 1928, Raskob Papers.

43. Frank Freidel, *Franklin D. Roosevelt: The Triumph* (Boston: Little, Brown, 1956), pp. 141-45; Jouett Shouse to Frances Perkins, March 23 and 27, 1959, Shouse Papers; Franklin D. Roosevelt to Robert F. Wagner, September 9, 1930, *The Public Papers and Addresses of Franklin D. Roosevelt* (New York: Random House, 1938), 1:319-21; AAPA, press release, November 5, 1930, Shouse Papers.

44. James A. Farley, *Behind the Ballots* (New York: Harcourt, Brace, 1938), pp. 73-74; Michelson, *The Ghost Talks,* p. 137.

45. John J. Raskob, speech, March 5, 1931, *Proceedings of Democratic Convention, 1932,* pp. 406-7; Jouett Shouse to John W. Davis, February 28, 1931, Shouse Papers; *New York Times,* March 6, 1931, p. 17.

46. *New York Times,* March 3, 1931, p. 1; Farley, *Behind the Ballots,* pp. 74-76; Freidel, *The Triumph,* pp. 179-82; Proceedings, March 5, 1931, *Proceedings of Democratic Convention, 1932,* p. 399.

47. John J. Raskob to Franklin D. Roosevelt, March 31, 1931, to Jouett Shouse, August 31, 1931, Shouse to Raskob, August 29, 1931, to Roosevelt, September 2, 1931, Raskob Papers.

48. Farley, *Behind the Ballots,* pp. 75-76; John J. Raskob to Frederic R. Coudert, March 9, 1931, to Samuel Harden Church, March 9, 1931, Raskob Papers.

49. Scrapbooks for March 4, 5, and 6, 1931, Shouse Papers.

50. John J. Raskob to the members of the Democratic national committee, April 4, 1931, Raskob Papers (the italics are Raskob's).

51. "Mr. Raskob's Suggestions," *Commonweal,* April 15, 1931, p. 647; "Raskob on Solid Ground," *Outlook and Independent,* April 15, 1931, p. 516; "The New Raskobian Uproar," *Literary Digest,* April 25, 1931, p. 12; and "Chairman Raskob's Convictions," *Review of Reviews* 83 (May 1931): 28; *New York Times,* September 31, 1931, p. 3.

52. John J. Raskob, "Questionnaire," undated, Raskob Papers (the italics are Raskob's). See also *New York Times,* November 23, 1931, p. 1.

53. *New York Times,* November 24, 1931, p. 1; *Washington Post,* November 23, 24, 1931.

54. *New York Times,* November 24, 1931, p. 1; December 14, 1931, p. 1.

55. John J. Raskob to members of the Democratic national committee, January 5, 1932, copy released to the press, Shouse Papers; *New York Times,* January 9, 1932, p. 10, January 10, 1932, p. 1; Carter Field, "The Political Status of Prohibition," *Life,* March 1932, p. 11.

56. *New York Times,* February 21, 1932; pp. 1, 3; Friedel, *The Triumph,* pp. 254–55.

57. Alfred E. Smith, "A New Way Out of Prohibition," *Liberty,* January 23, 1932, pp. 6–11.

58. Senate Committee on Manufactures, *Amendment of the Prohibition Act;* Senate Judiciary Committee, *Modification or Repeal of National Prohibition.*

59. Pierre S. du Pont to James H. Beck, January 14, 1932, and Beck to Pierre S. du Pont, January 16, 1932, Irénée du Pont Papers; J. Charles Linthicum to members of the House of Representatives, January 21, 1932, Beck Papers; *New York Times,* March 14, 1932, p. 2; March 15, 1932, p. 1.

60. "The Great Prohibition Poll's Final Week," *Literary Digest,* April 30, 1932, pp. 6–7; Claude E. Robinson, "That Great 'Wet Landslide': A Critical Inquiry into the *Literary Digest* Poll," *New Republic,* April 13, 1932, pp. 224–27; [Shouse], *AAPA Report for 1933,* p. 21.

61. Charles Stelzle to Pierre S. du Pont, June 22, 1932, Pierre S. du Pont Papers. For Stelzle's earlier opinions, see chapter 1.

62. *New York Times,* June 7, 1932, pp. 1, 12.

63. Pierre S. du Pont to John D. Rockefeller, Jr., June 10, 1932, Pierre S. du Pont Papers.

64. Henry H. Curran to members of Congress, December 12, 1931, Pierre S. du Pont Papers; *New York Times,* April 25, 1932, p. 3; Henry H. Curran to Republican convention delegates, May 28, 1932, Pierre S. du Pont Papers. President Hoover's secretary received Curran's letter and wrote on it, "No acknowledgment" (Curran to Walter H. Newton, May 28, 1932, president's secretary's file, Hoover Papers).

65. Pierre S. du Pont to James A. Farley, May 24, 1932, in Farley to John J. Raskob, June 1, 1932, Raskob Papers; *New York Times,* June 27, 1932, p. 11; Voluntary Committee of Lawyers, press release, May 31, 1932, Choate file, vcl Papers.

66. *New York Times,* June 8, 1932, pp. 1, 2.

67. William H. Stayton to Pierre S. du Pont, April 25 and May 5, 1932, Grayson M.-P. Murphy to Henry Curran, May 23, 1932, Henry Curran to Pierre S. du Pont, June 1, 1932, Pierre S. du Pont Papers.

68. TRB, "Washington Notes," *New Republic,* March 30, 1932, p. 180.

69. Field, "The Political Status of Prohibition," pp. 11, 50; Wilson, *Herbert Hoover,* pp. 159–60; Bronson Cutting to Theodore Joslin, May 6, 1932; George Martin to Joslin, May 12 and 14, 1932, Joslin to Martin, May 13 and 16, 1932, Joseph H. Choate, Jr., to Herbert Hoover, May 28, 1932, presidential subject file; John H. Morehead to Hoover, July 23, 1931, Hoover to Morehead, August 3, 1931, Charles D. Hilles to Joslin, November 2, 1931, Joslin to Hilles, November 3, 1931, Walter H.

Newton to Morehead, November 12, 1932, and Morehead to Newton, November 19, 1932, John H. Morehead individual file, Hoover Papers.

70. Republican Citizens Committee Against National Prohibition, report for December 18, 1931, to May 31, 1932, in AAPA, Corrupt Practices Act Reports; Raymond Pitcairn to Chevalier Jackson, February 6, 1932, enclosed in Jackson to secretary to President Hoover, February 29, 1932, "Prohibition" official file, Hoover Papers; Pitcairn to Henry B. Joy, March 14, 1932, Joy Papers.

71. *Chicago Tribune,* June 14, 1932; *New York Times,* June 14, 1932, p. 1.

72. Prohibition correspondence, 1929-33, presidential subject file, Hoover Papers.

73. H. L. Mencken's convention reports in the Baltimore *Sun* were collected and reprinted as *Making a President: A Footnote to the Saga of Democracy* (New York: Alfred A. Knopf, 1932), p. 36.

74. Henry H. Curran to Irénée du Pont, June 1, 1932, Irénée du Pont Papers; *New York Times,* June 13, 1932, p. 11.

75. *New York Times,* June 14, 1932, p. 1; June 15, 1932, pp. 1, 13.

76. Wadsworth, "Reminiscences," p. 369; *New York Times,* June 16, 1932, p. 1; Herbert Hoover to James R. Garfield, January 14, 1933, presidential personal file, Hoover Papers; Peel and Donnelly, *The 1932 Campaign,* p. 90; Mencken, *Making a President,* pp. 50-51.

77. *Official Report of the Proceedings of the Twentieth Republican National Convention, 1932* (New York: Tenny Press, 1932), pp. 119-21.

78. Mencken, *Making a President,* p. 74.

79. *Proceedings of the Republican Convention, 1932,* pp. 126-60; *New York Times,* June 16, 1932; p. 1; Peel and Donnelly, *The 1932 Campaign,* p. 86-87; Mencken, *Making a President,* pp. 72-73.

80. "Republicans and Prohibition," *New Republic,* June 22, 1932, p. 141.

81. *New York Times,* June 16, 1932, p. 14.

82. *New York Herald-Tribune,* June 16, 1932.

83. Peel and Donnelly, *The 1932 Campaign,* p. 65.

84. Statement of Robert Jackson, "Proceedings of Committee on Arrangements, Democratic National Committee, April 4, 1932," Shouse Papers.

85. "Statement of Jouett Shouse concerning Robert Jackson and the compromise at the Arrangements Committee meeting, May 31, 1932," Raskob Papers; Jouett Shouse memorandum, "The Chicago Convention of 1932," March 20, 1959, Shouse Papers; Michelson, *The Ghost Talks,* pp. 7-8.

86. *New York Times,* June 6, 1932, p. 1; June 8, 1932, p. 1; Alex Gottfried, *Boss Cermak of Chicago: A Study of Political Leadership* (Seattle: University of Washington Press, 1962), pp. 299-301.

87. *New York Times,* June 21, 1932, p. 1; June 22, 1932, p. 1; June 25, 1932, p. 1; June 26, 1932, p. 1.

88. *Proceedings of Democratic Convention, 1932,* p. 10.

89. Ibid., pp. 10, 34-37; *New York Times,* June 28, 1932, p. 1; June 29, 1932, pp. 1, 17; June 30, 1932, p. 15.

90. *New York Times,* June 28, 1932, p. 1; *Proceedings of Democratic Convention, 1932,* pp. 125-26, 135.

91. *Proceedings of Democratic Convention, 1932,* pp. 146-78; *New York Times,*

June 30, 1932, pp. 1, 14, 17; Gottfried, *Cermak,* p. 303.

92. *New York Times,* June 30, 1932, p. 15; Farley, *Behind the Ballots,* p. 128; *Proceedings of Democratic Convention, 1932,* pp. 188-92.

93. *Proceedings of Democratic Convention, 1932,* p. 378.

94. William H. Stayton to John J. Raskob, July 6, 1932, Raskob to Stayton, July 7, 1932, to Jouett Shouse, July 7, 1932, and to Harry Flood Byrd, July 5, 1932, Raskob Papers; *New York Times,* July 3, 1932, p. 10; *Proceedings of Democratic Convention, 1932,* pp. 595-98. At this dinner, Roosevelt praised the efforts of "my very good and old friend" Raskob as chairman, along with the work of Shouse and Michelson.

95. Peel and Donnelly, *The 1932 Campaign,* pp. 86-87, 195. *New York Times,* July 1, 1932, p. 14.

96. *New York Times,* August 28, 1932, p. 20.

CHAPTER 9

1. Women's Organization for National Prohibition Reform, press release, "Resolutions adopted at WONPR conference, April 13, 1932," WONPR Papers.

2. Minutes, WONPR national executive committee meeting, July 6, 1932, WONPR Papers; *New York Times,* July 8, 1933, p. 1, July 10, 1933, p. 11, July 11, 1933, p. 3, July 14, 1933, p. 6.

3. *New York Times,* July 8, 1933, p. 1; *Time,* July 18, 1932.

4. "Ladies at Roslyn," *Time,* July 18, 1932, pp. 9-10.

5. Fred G. Clark to Pierre S. du Pont, July 22, 1932, Pierre S. du Pont Papers.

6. Raymond Pitcairn to Henry L. Stimson (copies to the president, cabinet officers, and Republican members of Congress), June 19, 1932, to Ogden L. Mills, June 20 and July 15, 1932, Robert K. Cassatt to Mills, July 15, 1932, "National Prohibition" file, secretary's correspondence, 1919-32, U.S., Department of the Treasury, Record Group 56, National Archives.

7. Benedict Crowell to Pierre S. du Pont, July 7, 1932, Pierre S. du Pont Papers.

8. Pierre S. du Pont to A. M. Paonessa, September 6, 1932, to Frederick H. Allen, September 23, 1932, to Raymond Pitcairn, November 9, 1932, Pierre S. du Pont Papers.

9. Jouett Shouse to Newton D. Baker, July 7, 1932, and to Frances Perkins, March 27, 1959, Shouse Papers; Wadsworth, "Reminiscences," p. 372.

10. *Baltimore Sun,* July 5, 1932, reprinted in Mencken, *Making a President,* p. 176.

11. William H. Stayton to John J. Raskob, July 6, 1932, Raskob Papers.

12. *New York Times,* July 22, 1932, p. 2.

13. Irénée du Pont to Samuel Harden Church, July 29, 1932, Irénée du Pont Papers.

14. Pierre S. du Pont to Ralph M. Shaw, August 29, 1932, Pierre S. du Pont Papers; Scrapbook, August 6 to September 17, 1932, Shouse Papers.

15. Pierre S. du Pont to John J. Raskob, January 21, 1932, Raskob Papers; Henry Curran agreement file, Pierre S. du Pont Papers. An even earlier hint of discontent appeared in Pringle, "Wet Hope," p. 25.

16. Pierre S. du Pont to Charles Sabin, November 25, 1931, Pierre S. du Pont Papers.

17. William P. Smith to Pierre S. du Pont, March 23, 1932, Pierre S. du Pont to Charles Sabin, May 13, 1932, and to Benedict Crowell, May 19, 1932, Grayson M.-P. Murphy to Pierre S. du Pont, May 31, 1932, Pierre S. du Pont to Murphy, June 3, 1932, to William B. Burruss, June 1 and July 7, 1932, and to executive committee, September 6, 1932, William H. Stayton to Pierre S. du Pont, September 8 and 13, 1932, Pierre S. du Pont Papers.

18. Jouett Shouse to Pierre S. du Pont, July 29, 1932, Pierre S. du Pont to Robert K. Cassatt, August 4, 1932, and to Shouse, September 10, 1932, Pierre S. du Pont Papers; Shouse, "The Eighteenth Amendment," undated memorandum [probably late 1950s], Shouse Papers.

19. Pierre S. du Pont to Robert K. Cassatt, Benedict Crowell, Irénée du Pont, Charles Sabin, William H. Stayton, and James W. Wadsworth, August 10, 1932, Irénée du Pont Papers.

20. James W. Wadsworth, Jr., to Pierre S. du Pont, August 4, 1932, Irénée du Pont Papers; William H. Stayton to Pierre S. du Pont, September 13, 1932, Pierre S. du Pont Papers; Curran, *Pillar to Post*, pp. 335–37; Pierre S. du Pont to Henry Curran, November 7 and 10, 1932, Curran to Pierre S. du Pont, November 9, 1932, Pierre S. du Pont Papers.

21. Curran, *Pillar to Post*, pp. 335–37.

22. Pierre S. du Pont to Irénée du Pont, August 17, 1932, Irenee du Pont Papers; *New York Times*, August 18, 1932, pp. 1, 2; Pierre S. du Pont to L. H. Baekeland, August 24, 1932, and to Dunlevy Milbank, August 26, 1932, Pierre S. du Pont Papers; Scrapbook, August 6 to September 17, 1932, Shouse Papers.

23. Jouett Shouse, statement on becoming AAPA president, August 17, 1932, Shouse Papers.

24. AAPA executive committee minutes, August 29, 1932, Irénée du Pont Papers; [Jouett Shouse], *Annual Report of the President of the Association Against the Prohibition Amendment for the Year 1932* (Washington, 1933), p. 19; Heckman, "Prohibition Passes," pp. 23–24.

25. Jouett Shouse, "How the Repeal of the Prohibition Amendment Will Improve Business," address to the Advertising Club of Baltimore, September 14, 1932; scrapbook, August 8 to September 17, 1932, Shouse Papers.

26. *New York Times*, June 21, 1932, pp. 1, 12; [Herbert Hoover] memorandum on dinner with Borah, April 10, 1932, [c. April 11, 1932]; memorandum "Messrs. Robbins, Garfield, and Van Valkenberg report as to Senator Borah's position," June 10, 1932; E. A. Van Valkenburg, statement to Associated Press, Philadelphia, June 21, 1932, "Prohibition: Borah," presidential subject file; Hoover to James R. Garfield, January 14, 1933, presidential personal file, Hoover Papers; Herbert Hoover, *Memoirs: The Great Depression, 1929–1941* (New York: Macmillan, 1952), pp. 318–20.

27. For example, R. A. Robinson to president's secretary, July 9, 1932, prohibition correspondence, presidential subject file, Hoover Papers.

28. Herbert Hoover, "Address Accepting the Republican Presidential Nomination," August 11, 1932, *Public Papers of Herbert Hoover, 1932–33*, pp. 372–74.

29. Herbert Hoover to Daniel A. Poling, chairman, Allied Forces for Prohibition, August 22, 1932, and telegram to Edward C. Stokes, November 2, 1932, public

statements file; J. M. Beatty to presidential secretary Lawrence Richey, October 17, 1932, prohibition correspondence, presidential subject file; James R. Garfield to Hoover, October 19, 1932, presidential personal file, Hoover Papers; *New York Times,* August 25, 1932, p. 9, October 6, 1932, p. 2, November 3, 1932, p. 1.

30. Franklin D. Roosevelt, speech at Sea Girt, New Jersey, August 27, 1932, *Public Papers,* 1:684–92; *New York Times,* September 24, 1932, pp. 1, 17, October 2, 1932, p. 33.

31. Jouett Shouse to Halbert L. Hoard, November 3, 1932, Hoard Papers; *New York Times,* November 5, 1932, p. 5, September 15, 1932, p. 20, September 28, 1932, p. 11, September 29, 1932, p. 12, October 1, 1932, p. 8; AAPA executive committee minutes, October 21, 1932, Pierre S. du Pont Papers.

32. AAPA, *32 Reasons for Repeal* (Washington, 1932); Jackson-Babbitt Inc., *The New Crusade;* Hugh Satterlee to Mrs. H. P. Rhudy, September 1, 1932, Choate file, VCL Papers, Pauline Sabin, "Why American Mothers Demand Repeal," *Liberty,* September 10, 1932, pp. 12–14; Milton MacKaye, "New Crusade," pp. 20–24; Jouett Shouse, speeches to Advertising Club of Baltimore, September 14, 1932, to meeting sponsored by Minnesota branches of the WONPR and AAPA, St. Paul, September 28, 1932, and to rally sponsored by WONPR and Crusaders, Detroit, October 29, 1932, Shouse Papers.

33. Raymond Pitcairn to Pierre S. du Pont, October 13, 1932, W. W. Montgomery to Pierre S. du Pont, October 25, 1932, Pierre S. du Pont to Robert K. Cassatt, September 9, 1932, and to Raymond Pitcairn, November 9, 1932, Pierre S. du Pont Papers; Scrapbook, September 17 to October 30, 1932, Shouse Papers; Pierre S. du Pont to Irénée du Pont, November 4, 1932, Irénée du Pont Papers; *New York Times,* November 5, 1932, p. 5; Michelson, *The Ghost Talks,* p. 39; Schlesinger, *The Crisis of the Old Order,* p. 421; Pierre S. du Pont to Joseph H. Leib, September 16, 1932, to Rev. Philip Cook, October 14, 1932, Pierre S. du Pont Papers.

34. For example, see Albert C. Ritchie, "The Democratic Case," *Saturday Evening Post,* October 29, 1932, pp. 3–5, 62–64.

35. *New York Times,* November 10, 1932, p. 1.

36. Ibid., November 10, 1932, p. 9; [Shouse], *AAPA Report for 1932,* pp. 8–12.

37. *New York Times,* November 10, 1932, p. 9.

38. WONPR, National Information Service Bulletin no. 9, "The People Speak," November 30, 1932, WONPR Papers.

39. James M. Beck, press release, November 13, 1932, Beck Papers.

40. *Congressional Record* 76 (72d Cong., 2d sess.): 6–13; *New York Times,* December 6, 1932, p. 1.

41. James M. Beck to A. Mitchell Palmer, December 5, 1932, Beck Papers; Transcript, proceedings of AAPA board of directors annual meeting, December 6, 1932, Shouse Papers; *New York Times,* December 7, 1932, p. 17.

42. John Nance Garner to Halbert L. Hoard, January 19, 1933, Hoard Papers; [Shouse], *AAPA Report for 1933,* pp. 15–16.

43. *New York Times,* January 10, 1933, pp. 1, 2; William Clark to John J. Blaine, December 27, 1932, J. J. Seelman to Blaine, January 26 and February 13, 1933, John J. Blaine Papers, Wisconsin State Historical Society, Madison; *Congressional Record* 76 (72d Cong., 2d sess.): 4005; John J. Blaine to J. J. Seelman, January 30 and

February 15, 1933, Blaine Papers.

44. *New York Times,* February 14, 1933, p. 2.

45. Samuel Harden Church to William H. Stayton, January 10, 1933, Raskob Papers.

46. AAPA press release, January 10, 1933, Raskob Papers; see also *Congressional Record* 76 (72d Cong., 2d sess.): 1622.

47. Raymond Pitcairn to George W. Norris, January 21, 1933, Choate file, VCL Papers.

48. Jouett Shouse, speech, "The Status of Prohibition Repeal," January 17, 1933, Louisville, Kentucky, reprinted as pamphlet (Washington, 1933), AAPA Papers. Also excerpted in [Shouse], *AAPA Report for 1933,* p. 12.

49. Jouett Shouse to AAPA directors, January 24, 1933, Raskob Papers.

50. For example, Webb Rice to Joseph H. Choate, Jr., November 28, 1932, and Lucien H. Boggs to Choate, December 2, 1932, Choate file, VCL Papers.

51. Shouse, "Status of Prohibition Repeal."

52. *New York Times,* January 10, 1933, pp. 1, 2, January 26, 1933, p. 1, February 6, 1933, p. 1; [Shouse], *AAPA Report for 1933,* pp. 15–16.

53. [Shouse], *AAPA Report for 1933,* p. 16.

54. *New York Times,* February 15, 1933, p. 1, February 16, 1933, pp. 1, 14; *Congressional Record* 76 (72d Cong., 2d sess.): 4058, 4169, 4179, 4231, and 4516.

55. M. B. Hamilton, "Lest We Forget," *American Mercury,* May 1933, pp. 40–58, provides a useful tabulation of the voting.

56. Vose, *Constitutional Change,* pp. 112–15.

57. Everett Somerville Brown, ed., *Ratification of the Twenty-first Amendment to the Constitution of the United States: State Convention Records and Laws* (Ann Arbor: University of Michigan Press, 1938), p. 515.

58. *Congressional Record* 76 (72d Cong., 2d sess.): 4139–40, 4148–68, 4515, 4524–25; *New York Times,* February 26, 1933, sec. 8, p. 5.

59. William H. Stayton to Pierre S. du Pont, July 22, 1932, Pierre S. du Pont to Raymond Pitcairn, December 1, 1932, Pierre S. du Pont Papers; Joseph H. Choate, Jr., to Sidney G. Stricker, January 11, 1933, to Ralph M. Shaw, January 26, 1933, to A. Mitchell Palmer, January 30, 1933, Choate file, VCL Papers.

60. Joseph H. Choate, Jr., to Thomas F. Cadwalder, March 10, 1933, Choate file, VCL Papers; [Shouse], *AAPA Report for 1933,* pp. 17–18; Noel T. Dowling to Joseph H. Choate, Jr., January 31, 1933; Joseph H. Choate, Jr., to Robert C. Cummings, John T. Dooling, Abraham S. Gilbert, and C. E. Moore, February 2, 1933; Mrs. Charles B. Smith to Sterling E. Edmunds, February 2, 1933; Jouett Shouse to Joseph H. Choate, Jr., February 3, 1933, Choate file, VCL Papers.

61. For example, Joseph J. Daniels to VCL executive committee, February 4, 1933, George W. Abberger to Jouett Shouse, February 4, 1933, Choate file, VCL Papers.

62. Jouett Shouse to Joseph H. Choate, Jr., February 8, 1933; Joseph H. Choate, Jr., to Jouett Shouse, February 11, 1933, Choate file, VCL Papers; [Shouse], *AAPA Report for 1933,* p. 18; VCL executive committee to governors, February 24, 1933, Choate file, VCL Papers; *New York Times,* February 21, 1933, p. 12.

63. Arthur W. Machen, Jr., to Joseph H. Choate, Jr., January 30, 1933, Choate file, VCL Papers.

64. Joseph H. Choate, Jr., to John Godfrey Saxe, Arthur W. Machen, Jr., and Abraham S. Gilbert, February 3, 1933, Choate file, VCL Papers; Noel T. Dowling, "A New Experiment in Ratification," *American Bar Association Journal* 19 (July 1933): 383-87.

65. Brown, *Ratification of the Twenty-first Amendment,* pp. 515-700; Joseph H. Choate, Jr., correspondence, February-April, 1933, Choate file, VCL Papers.

66. Brown, *Ratification of the Twenty-first Amendment,* p. 526.

67. Joseph H. Choate, Jr., correspondence, April-November, 1933, Choate file, VCL Papers; AAPA executive committee minutes, September 19, 1933, Pierre s. du Pont Papers. See also Vose, *Constitutional Change,* pp. 121-26. Ironically, one unsuccessful dry effort was to compel a referendum on the convention law in Ohio, the state where they won their suit overturning the 1919 referendum rejecting prohibition.

68. J. J. Seelman to Halbert L. Hoard, March 6, 1933, Hoard Papers; James W. Wadsworth, Jr., to Alfred E. Smith, March 24, 1933, to Charles D. Hilles, May 24, 1933, Wadsworth Papers, Stayton to John J. Raskob, April 10, 1933, and Raskob to Stayton, April 11 and 24, 1933, Raskob Papers; William H. Stayton to Irénée du Pont, April 5, 1933, Irénée du Pont Papers; Stayton to John J. Raskob, April 19, 1933, "Contributions from National Directors, January 1-November 30, 1933," R. J. Dillon to Raskob, December 14, 1933, Raskob Papers; William H. Stayton, memorandum to the executive committee, March 24, 1933, Irénée du Pont Papers; [Shouse], *AAPA Report for 1933,* p. 36; Heckman, "Prohibition Passes," p. 34.

69. Jeannette Eckman to Mrs. Solon Jacobs, June 26, 1933; Alice Belin du Pont to George T. Barnhill, May 20, 1933; [Jeannette Eckman], "Delaware W.O.N.P.R. History," (unpublished manuscript, September, 1933), WONPR Papers. See also Kyvig, "Women against Prohibition," pp. 477-78.

70. *New York Times,* February 21, 1933, p. 18; James W. Wadsworth, Jr., to Frederick H. Gillett, March 8, 1933, Wadsworth Papers; J. J. Seelman to Halbert L. Hoard, March 23, 1933, Hoard Papers; [Shouse], *AAPA Report for 1933,* p. 19; Jouett Shouse, speech at joint AAPA-WONPR meeting, New Haven, Connecticut, May 15, 1933, Shouse Papers; James W. Wadsworth, Jr., radio address to New York voters, "Finishing the Job of Repeal," [May 19, 1933], speech, Knoxville, Kentucky, July 14, 1933, to Reed Smoot, September 30, 1933, speech to the WONPR, "Repeal on the Way," undated, Wadsworth Papers.

71. Franklin D. Roosevelt, message to Congress, March 13, 1933, *Public Papers,* 2:66-67.

72. *New York Times,* April 8, 1933, p. 1; *Time,* April 17, 1933, p. 13.

73. *New York Times,* April 7, 1933, pp. 1, 2; April 8, 1933, p. 1; April 16, 1933, p. 12; April 17, 1933, p. 1.

74. *New York Times,* April 16, 1933, p. 12; April 17, 1933, p. 1; Franklin D. Roosevelt, message to Congress, May 17, 1933, *Public Papers,* 2:202-4; Franklin D. Roosevelt to Leon McCord, Democratic national committeeman for Alabama, July 8, 1933, ibid., pp. 272-73; Stephen Early to Reginald F. Bourke, August 11, 1933, official file, Franklin D. Roosevelt Papers, Franklin D. Roosevelt Library, Hyde Park, New York; Farley, *Behind the Ballots,* p. 222.

75. The best sources of information on state ratification are [Shouse], *AAPA*

Report for 1933, pp. 18–27, for election returns; and Brown, *Ratification of the Twenty-first Amendment,* pp. 3–511, for convention proceedings. The following paragraphs draw on both.

76. Brown, *Ratification of the Twenty-first Amendment,* pp. 112.

77. Ibid., p. 305.

78. Ibid., pp. 69, 71.

79. Ibid., pp. 432–33.

80. Ibid., pp. 280–81.

81. Ibid., p. 196.

82. Ibid., p. 330.

83. Elihu Root to Harry D. Yates, July 31, 1933, Root Papers.

84. Convention ratification proved no more time-consuming than legislative action. Indeed, not until 1971, when the Twenty-sixth Amendment, lowering the voting age to eighteen, was approved by thirty-eight state legislatures in only 100 days, was an amendment much more quickly accepted. The Twelfth Amendment was ratified in 190 days in 1803–4, but required the approval of only twelve states. The Twenty-third Amendment was ratified by thirty-eight states in 291 days in 1960–61. All other amendments took longer to be ratified, anywhere from 11 to 47 months. U.S., Senate, *Proposed Amendments to the Constitution of the United States of America,* 91st Cong., 1st sess., Senate Document 91–38 (Washington: GPO, 1969), pp. 76–89.

85. Franklin D. Roosevelt, proclamation, December 5, 1933, *Public Papers,* 2:510–12; *New York Times,* December 6, 1933, p. 3.

CHAPTER 10

1. [Shouse], *AAPA Report for 1933,* p. 42; *New York Times,* December 6, 1933, p. 3; Irénée du Pont to Bailey, Banks, and Biddle Co., October 20, 1933, to AAPA treasurer, December 12, 1933, Irénée du Pont Papers; Irénée du Pont to AAPA directors, October 24, 1933, Raskob Papers; Pierre S. du Pont to Jouett Shouse, November 29, 1933, Pierre S. du Pont Papers.

2. [Shouse], *AAPA Report for 1933,* pp. 3, 43; *New York Times,* December 7, 1933, p. 18.

3. Francis Clarke Smith to VCL executive committee, October 11, 1933, Choate file; VCL check book, August 11, 1932, to December 5, 1933, Tweed file, VCL Papers.

4. WONPR executive committee minutes, September 26 and December 7, 1933; victory dinner program, December 7, 1933; Mrs. Christian R. Holmes and Mrs. Mabel Jacques Eichel to Mrs. Pierre S. du Pont, November 11, 1933; unsigned form letter, January 24, 1934; surplus funds committee minutes, April 17, 1934; Dean Virginia C. Gildersleeve to Mrs. Pierre S. du Pont, May 21, 1934, WONPR Papers.

5. Crusader file, postpresidential subject files, Hoover Papers.

6. Mencken, "Man Who Really Busted Prohibition"; Wilmington, Delaware, *Star,* June 25, 1933.

7. Irénée du Pont to Joseph H. Choate, Jr., April 10, 1933, Jouett Shouse telegram to Choate, November 8, 1933, Choate file, VCL Papers. The files of Choate, Pierre and Irénée du Pont, John Raskob, and Jouett Shouse are all filled with congratulatory messages during the months of November and December 1933.

8. "Good Mornings" to William H. Stayton, Stayton Papers in the possession of

Mrs. John H. C. Forbes.

9. Jouett Shouse, "The Repeal Victory," radio address on N.B.C., 10:45 to 11:00 p.m., November 7, 1933, Shouse Papers.

10. See, for example, *Washington Herald*, September 5, 1933; Baltimore *Sun* and *New York Times*, November 8, 1933; *New York Mirror*, November 12, 1933; and *Philadelphia Inquirer*, December 6, 1933.

11. Baltimore *Sun*, December 6, 1933.

12. *New York Times*, December 31, 1933, sec. 4, p. 1.

13. Though consumption jumped 25 percent during World War II, thereafter it remained very stable for fifteen years. During the 1960s per capita consumption gradually increased, but not until 1970 did it reach preprohibition levels. By this time Americans were drinking more wine and spirits than in 1911-15, and less beer. Efron, Keller, and Gurioli, *Statistics on Consumption of Alcohol;* E. M. Jellinek, "Recent Trends in Alcoholism and in Alcohol Consumption," *Quarterly Journal of Studies on Alcohol* 8 (July 1947): 1-43; Leonard V. Harrison and Elizabeth Laine, *After Repeal: A Study of Liquor Control Administration* (New York: Harper, 1936), p. 1.

14. John E. O'Neill, "Federal Activity in Alcoholic Beverage Control," *Law and Contemporary Problems* 7 (Autumn 1940): 570.

15. For example, Stanley Walker, "Open or Secret Saloons?" *New York Herald-Tribune Magazine*, March 26, 1933, pp. 3, 9; Frank E. Gannett to James W. Wadsworth, Jr., October 17, 1933, Wadsworth Papers.

16. Shouse, "The Repeal Victory."

17. Joseph H. Choate to William F. Riley, November 6, 1933, Choate file, VCL Papers.

18. Grace C. Root, ed., *Thirty-seven Liquor Control Systems of Today* (n.p., 1932) and *More Liquor Control Systems of Today* (n.p., March, 1933), WONPR Papers; James W. Wadsworth, Jr., to Frank E. Gannett, October 23, 1933, Wadsworth Papers; Delaware Liquor Commission, *Report* (June 14, 1933, to December 1, 1934), Pierre S. du Pont Papers.

19. Harrison and Laine, *After Repeal;* George A. Shipman, "State Administrative Machinery for Liquor Control," *Law and Contemporary Problems* 7 (Autumn 1940): 600-620.

20. Shouse, "The Repeal Victory."

21. Carl W. Badenhausen, "Self-Regulation in the Brewing Industry," *Law and Contemporary Problems* 7 (Autumn 1940): 689-95; Baron, *Brewed in America*, pp. 324-28; O'Neill, "Federal Alcoholic Beverage Control," pp. 578-79.

22. Herbert Feis, *1933: Characters in Crisis* (Boston: Little, Brown, 1966), pp. 334-35; Harold L. Ickes, *The Secret Diary of Harold L. Ickes: The First Thousand Days, 1933-1936* (New York: Simon and Schuster, 1954), p. 118; Henry Alan Johnston to John S. Wise, Jr., November 28, 1933, Choate file, VCL Papers.

23. Feis, *Characters in Crisis*, pp. 135-40; O'Neill, "Federal Alcoholic Beverage Control," pp. 571-82; Harrison and Laine, *After Repeal*, pp. 16-41; Baron, *Brewed in America*, p. 325.

24. [Shouse], *AAPA Report for 1933*, pp. 38-40.

25. William H. Stayton to AAPA directors, November 27, 1933, Jouett Shouse to

John J. Raskob, December 12, 1933, Raskob Papers; Repeal Associates, report, May 28, 1934, Pierre S. du Pont Papers.

26. Repeal Associates, directed by Captain Stayton until his death in 1942, never had more than a couple thousand members and never had a large budget, but it managed to survive until 1965, publishing *Repeal Review,* a journal filled with critiques of prohibition and expanding federal government, nostalgic recollections of the repeal movement, and obituaries for prominent AAPA members.

27. Irénée du Pont to Pierre S. du Pont, July 10, 1934, Pierre S. du Pont to William H. Stayton, August 3, 1934, Pierre S. du Pont Papers.

28. American Liberty League executive committee and board of directors minutes, August 23 to December 18, 1934, in William H. Stayton to executive committee, January 15, 1935, Jouett Shouse to James W. Wadsworth, Jr., June 18, 1935, Wadsworth Papers; George Wolfskill, *The Revolt of the Conservatives: A History of the American Liberty League, 1934–1940* (Boston: Houghton Mifflin, 1962), pp. 55–72; Robert J. Comerford, "The American Liberty League," (Ph.D. diss., St. Johns University, 1967), pp. 1–60; Keller, *In Defense of Yesterday,* pp. 256–60; Harbaugh, *Lawyer's Lawyer,* pp. 344–48.

29. Jouett Shouse, "Memorandum for the personal files of Jouett Shouse relating to the substance of conversation had with President Roosevelt at the White House, Wednesday afternoon, August 15, 1934," August 16, 1934, Shouse Papers.

30. *New York Times,* August 25, 1934, p. 1.

31. Jouett Shouse, *The Return to Democracy,* radio speech, July 1, 1935, reprinted as pamphlet (Washington: American Liberty League, 1935); Wolfskill, *Revolt of the Conservatives,* pp. 65–67, 102–18; Frederick Rudolph, "The American Liberty League, 1934–1940," *American Historical Review* 56 (October 1950): 19–33.

32. James W. Wadsworth, Jr., to William Cabell Bruce, March 30, 1935, Wadsworth Papers.

33. *New York Times,* January 26, 1936, pp. 1, 36.

34. Wolfskill, *Revolt of the Conservatives,* pp. 30–33.

35. Roosevelt, "Annual Message to the Congress," January 3, 1936, *Public Papers,* 5:13–14.

36. Roosevelt, "Acceptance of the Renomination for the Presidency," June 27, 1936, *Public Papers,* 5:234.

37. Wolfskill, *Revolt of the Conservatives,* p. 212.

38. *New York Times,* June 22, 1936, pp. 1, 2.

39. Ibid., August 6, 1936, p. 11.

40. Rexford G. Tugwell, *The Battle for Democracy* (New York: Columbia University Press, 1935), p. 319.

41. *New York Times,* February 13, 1977, p. 35.

42. Warren G. Harding to O. S. Rapp, December 26, 1917, Harding Papers.

BIBLIOGRAPHY

The most valuable resources for this study proved to be the collections of the Eleutherian Mills Historical Library in Wilmington, Delaware. The papers of Pierre and Irénée du Pont and John Raskob in that repository contain a great deal of useful, unpublished information concerning the ideas and activities of many leading anti-prohibitionists as well as the positions, tactics, finances, membership, and other affairs of the Association Against the Prohibition Amendment. The correspondence, memoranda, minutes, reports, and other materials in these three large collections are especially important since no significant body of William H. Stayton's papers have survived and since the AAPA's organizational records, located at the Library of Congress, consist mainly of publications and clippings for the years 1928 through 1933. Within the Pierre du Pont collection, furthermore, is the only significant body of material thus far located on the Women's Organization for National Prohibition Reform. Without the extensive holdings of the Eleutherian Mills Library, it would be exceedingly difficult to draw a detailed portrait of the organized repeal movement.

Several other sources added particular insight into the repeal process. Archival materials which proved especially worthwhile included the papers of Herbert Hoover at the Hoover Presidential Library, Jouett Shouse at the University of Kentucky, James W. Wadsworth, Jr., at the Library of Congress, and the Voluntary Committee of Lawyers at Wesleyan University. The publications of the AAPA were very helpful. Transcripts of various congressional hearings, most notably several held in 1926 and 1930, provided an extremely useful if incomplete and occasionally distorted picture of the AAPA and to a lesser degree the WONPR and other wet groups. Everett Somerville Brown's 1938 compilation of state convention legislation and transcripts of ratification conventions was extraordinarily valuable.

Although the above-mentioned materials played a central role in this study, a variety of other resources contributed as well. These included archival holdings, public documents, newspapers, interviews, dissertations, and both contemporary and retrospective articles and books. The following is a comprehensive list of materials directly consulted in the course of this inquiry.

PRIMARY SOURCES
ARCHIVES AND MANUSCRIPT COLLECTIONS
Association Against the Prohibition Amendment Papers. Library of Congress.
Association Against the Prohibition Amendment. "Reports Made to the Clerk of the House of Representatives of the United States as per the 'Federal Corrupt Practices

Act 1925.'" Records of the House of Representatives. Record Group 233, National Archives.

Baker, Newton D., Papers. Library of Congress.

Beck, James M., Papers. Princeton University Library. Princeton, New Jersey.

Blaine, John J., Papers. Wisconsin State Historical Society. Madison, Wisconsin.

Butler, Nicholas Murray, Papers. Columbia University Library. New York.

Coolidge, Calvin, Papers. Library of Congress.

Du Pont, Irénée, Papers. Eleutherian Mills Historical Library. Wilmington, Delaware.

Du Pont, Pierre S., Papers. Eleutherian Mills Historical Library. Wilmington, Delaware.

Gross, M. Louise, Papers. New York Public Library. New York.

Harding, Warren G., Papers. Ohio Historical Society. Columbus, Ohio.

Hoard, Halbert Louis, Papers. Wisconsin State Historical Society. Madison, Wisconsin.

Hoover, Herbert, Papers. Herbert Hoover Presidential Library. West Branch, Iowa.

Joy, Henry Bourne, Papers. Michigan Historical Collections, University of Michigan. Ann Arbor, Michigan.

Kading, Charles A., Papers. Wisconsin State Historical Society. Madison, Wisconsin.

Pinchot, Gifford, Papers. Library of Congress.

Raskob, John J., Papers. Eleutherian Mills Historical Library. Wilmington, Delaware.

Ritchie, Albert C., Papers. Maryland Historical Society. Baltimore, Maryland.

Roosevelt, Franklin D., Papers. Franklin D. Roosevelt Library. Hyde Park, New York.

Root, Elihu, Papers. Library of Congress.

Root, Mrs. Edward Wales, Papers. Library of Congress.

Shouse, Jouett, Papers. University of Kentucky Library. Lexington, Kentucky.

Stayton, William H., Papers. In possession of Mrs. John H. C. Forbes, Fallston, Maryland.

U.S., Bureau of Naval Personnel. Records. Record Group 24, National Archives.

U.S., Department of the Treasury. Secretary's Correspondence, 1919-32, "National Prohibition." Record Group 56, National Archives.

U.S., National Commission on Law Observance and Enforcement. Records of the Commission. Record Group 10, Washington National Records Center. Suitland, Maryland.

U.S., Senate, Committee on the Judiciary. "Lobbying," File 71A-F15, Files of the Committee. Record Group 46, National Archives.

————. "Papers Relating to Hearings before a Subcommittee on Proposed Amendments to the National Prohibition Law," File S.33-69th. Record Group 46, National Archives.

U.S., Supreme Court. Appellate Case Files. Record Group 267, National Archives.

U.S. v. E. I. du Pont Nemours and Company, General Motors Corporation, United States Rubber Company, Christiana Securities Company, Delaware Realty and Investment Corporation, Pierre S. du Pont, Lammot du Pont, Irénée du Pont, defendants. Eleutherian Mills Historical Library. Wilmington, Delaware.

Voluntary Committee of Lawyers, Inc., Papers. Collection on Legal Change. Wesleyan University. Middletown, Connecticut.

Wadsworth, James W., Jr., Papers. Library of Congress.

Women's Organization for National Prohibition Reform Papers, in Alice Belin du Pont files, Pierre S. du Pont Papers. Eleutherian Mills Historical Library. Wilmington, Delaware.

INTERVIEWS AND ORAL HISTORIES

Bowers, Claude G. "The Reminiscences of Claude Bowers." Oral History Research Office, Columbia University, 1957.

Forbes, Mrs. John H. C. Interview with author. Fallston, Maryland. July 27, 1973.

Roemer, Mrs. Merle A. Interview with author. Millington, Maryland. July 26, 1973.

Thompson, George E., Sr. Interview with author. Wilmington, Delaware, March 24, 1975.

Wadsworth, James W. "The Reminiscences of James W. Wadsworth." Oral History Research Office, Columbia University, 1952.

PUBLIC DOCUMENTS

Association Against the Prohibition Amendment. *Bulletins, Pamphlets, and Miscellaneous Printed Materials.* Library of Congress, 1923-33.

Brown, Everett Somerville, ed. *Ratification of the Twenty-first Amendment to the Constitution of the United States: State Convention Records and Laws.* University of Michigan Publications, Law, vol. 7. Ann Arbor: University of Michigan Press, 1938.

Executive Committee of the Board of Directors. *Annual Report to the Directors, Members and Friends of the Association Against the Prohibition Amendment for the Year 1928.* Washington: AAPA, 1929. Issued under this title from 1929 through 1931 and as [Jouett Shouse] *Annual Report of the President of the Association Against the Prohibition Amendment for the Year 1932* and for 1933.

Johnson, Donald B., and Porter, Kirk H., compilers. *National Party Platforms, 1840-1972.* Urbana: University of Illinois Press, 1973.

Official Report of the Proceedings of the Democratic National Convention, 1924. Indianapolis: Bookwalter-Ball-Greathouse, 1924.

Official Report of the Proceedings of the Democratic National Convention, 1928. Indianapolis: Bookwalter-Ball-Greathouse, 1928.

Official Report of the Proceedings of the Democratic National Convention, 1932. n.p., n.d.

Official Report of the Proceedings of the Eighteenth Republican National Convention, 1924. New York: Tenny Press, 1924.

Official Report of the Proceedings of the Nineteenth Republican National Convention, 1928. New York: Tenny Press, 1928.

Official Report of the Proceedings of the Twentieth Republican National Convention, 1932. New York: Tenny Press, 1932.

Pamphlets on Prohibition, Temperance, Liquor Problem, Liquor Traffic, etc., in the United States. 8 vols. Library of Congress, 1855-1933.

Public Papers and Addresses of Franklin D. Roosevelt. Vols. 1, 2, and 5. New York: Random House, 1938.

Public Papers of the Presidents of the United States: Herbert Hoover, 1929-33. 4 vols. Washington: GPO, 1974-77.

Republican National Committee, *Republican Campaign Text-book 1924.* n.p., 1924.

U.S., Department of Justice. *Report Submitted to President Coolidge by Attorney General H. M. Daugherty concerning Prohibition Litigation throughout the United States, Covering the Period January 16, 1920, to June 16, 1923.* Washington: GPO, 1923.

U.S., House of Representatives, Committee on Alcoholic Liquor Traffic. *Survey of Alcoholic Liquor Traffic and the Enforcement of the Eighteenth Amendment: Hearings before the Subcommittee.* 68th Cong., 2d sess. Washington: GPO, 1925.

U.S., House of Representatives, Committee on the Judiciary. *Prohibition Legislation, 1921: Hearings.* 67th Cong., 1st sess., Serial 2. Washington: GPO, 1921.

————. *The Prohibition Amendment: Hearings.* 71st Cong., 2d sess., Serial 5. Washington: GPO, 1930.

————. *Proposed Modification of the Prohibition Law to Permit the Manufacture, Sale, and Use of 2.75 Per Cent Beverages: Hearings.* 68th Cong., 1st sess., Serial 39. Washington: GPO, 1924.

————. *Proposing an Amendment to the Constitution of the United States in Lieu of the Eighteenth Amendment: Hearings.* 70th Cong., 1st sess., Serial 21. Washington: GPO, 1928.

U.S., House of Representatives, Committee on Ways and Means. *Modification of Volstead Act: Hearings.* 72d Cong., 2d sess. Washington: GPO, 1932.

U.S., National Commission on Law Observance and Enforcement. *Enforcement of the Prohibition Laws: Official Records of the National Commission on Law Observance and Enforcement Pertaining to Its Investigation of the Facts as to the Enforcement, the Benefits, and the Abuses under the Prohibition Laws, both before and since the Adoption of the Eighteenth Amendment to the Constitution.* 71st Cong., 3d sess., Senate Document 307. 5 vols. Washington: GPO, 1931.

————. *Report on the Enforcement of the Prohibition Laws of the United States.* 71st Cong., 3d sess., House Document 722. Washington: GPO, 1931.

U.S., Senate, *Proposed Amendments to the Constitution of the United States of America.* 91st Cong., 1st sess., Senate Document 91-38. Washington: GPO, 1969.

U.S., Senate, Committee on the Judiciary. *Lobby Investigation: Hearings before a Subcommittee.* 71st Cong., 2d sess. 4 vols. Washington: GPO, 1931.

————. *Lobbying and Lobbyists: Partial Report, Submitted by Mr. Robinson of Indiana.* 71st Cong., 2d sess., Senate Report 43, pt. 8, May 21, 1930. Washington: GPO, 1930.

————. *Modification of Volstead Act: Hearings before a Subcommittee on an Act to Provide Revenue by the Taxation of Certain Nonintoxicating Liquor, and For Other Purposes.* 72d Cong., 2d sess. Washington: GPO, 1933.

————. *Modification or Repeal of National Prohibition: Hearings before a Subcommittee on Bills and Joint Resolutions Relative to the Prohibition Act.* 72d Cong., 1st sess. Washington: GPO, 1932.

————. *The National Prohibition Law: Hearings before the Subcommittee on Bills to*

Amend the National Prohibition Act. 69th Cong., 1st sess. 2 vols. Washington: GPO, 1926.

U.S., Senate, Committee on Manufactures. *Amendment of the Prohibition Act: Hearings before a Subcommittee.* 72d Cong., 1st sess. Washington: GPO, 1932.

U.S., Senate, Special Committee Investigating Expenditures in Senatorial Primary and General Elections. *Senatorial Campaign Expenditures: Hearings,* pt. 1, June 9 to July 7, 1926. 69th Cong., 1st sess. Washington: GPO, 1926.

U.S., Treasury Department, Bureau of Prohibition. *Digest of Supreme Court Decisions Interpreting the National Prohibition Act and Willis-Campbell Act.* Washington: GPO, 1929.

NEWSPAPERS

Akron Beacon Journal, 1918.
Baltimore *Sun,* 1924, 1932-33.
Boston Evening Transcript, 1921-30.
Boston Globe, 1924.
Boston Herald, 1928.
Chicago Tribune, 1922-33.
Cleveland Plain Dealer, 1924.
Des Moines Register, 1922-33.
[Madison] *Capital Times,* 1929, 1933.
[Madison] *Wisconsin State Journal,* 1926.
Milwaukee Journal, 1926, 1929, 1933.
Milwaukee Sentinel, 1926.
New York Evening Post, 1927.
New York Herald-Tribune, 1922-33.
New York Mirror, 1933.
New York Times, 1918-33.
New York *World,* 1922, 1926.
Philadelphia Inquirer, 1933.
St. Louis Post-Dispatch, 1922, 1926.
Washington Herald, 1933.
Washington Post, 1921-33.
Wilmington *Star,* 1932.

ARTICLES

Abbot, Everett V. "Inalienable Rights and the Eighteenth Amendment." *Columbia Law Review* 20 (February 1920): 183-95.

"Advertising the Drought." *Commonweal,* April 30, 1930, p. 725.

Agar, Herbert. "Prohibition and Democracy: A Plea for Limiting the Franchise." *English Review* 52 (May 1931): 556-66.

Agnew, B. J. "A Saloon-Keeper's Son." *American Mercury,* January 1925, pp. 42-47.

Asbury, Herbert. "The Father of Prohibition." *American Mercury,* November 1926, pp. 344-48.

Bacon, Selden. "How the Tenth Amendment Affected the Fifth Article of the Constitution." *Virginia Law Review* 16 (June 1930): 771-91.

Banning, Margaret Culkin. "Anti-Prohibitionette." *Vogue,* September 1, 1930, p. 82.

Barclay, Thomas S. "The Bureau of Publicity of the Democratic National Convention, 1930-32." *American Political Science Review* 27 (February 1933): 63-65.

———. "The Publicity Division of the Democratic Party, 1929-1930." *American Political Science Review* 25 (February 1931): 68-72.

Battle, George Gordon. "The Effect of Prohibition on Crime." *North American Review* 221 (June 1925): 601-7.

Binkley, Robert C. "The Ethics of Nullification." *New Republic,* May 1, 1929, pp. 297-300.

"Booze Is the Victor." *Collier's,* October 10, 1925, pp. 8-9.

Burdick, Charles K. "Is Prohibition Lawful?" *New Republic,* April 21, 1920, pp. 245-48.

"Campaign Captains." *Time,* November 10, 1930, pp. 16-17.

"Chairman Raskob's Convictions." *Review of Reviews* 88 (May 1931): 28.

Chase, Jefferson. "The Sabines Ravish the Senators." *Vanity Fair,* August 1931, pp. 42, 80.

Church, Samuel Harden. "The Paradise of the Ostrich." *North American Review* 221 (June 1925): 625-31.

Clapper, Raymond. "Happy Days." *American Mercury,* January 1927, pp. 25-29.

Codman, Julian. "Must Congress Enforce an Amendment?" *Independent,* June 12, 1926, pp. 683-84, 699.

"Confusion Worse Confounded." *Nation,* February 4, 1931, pp. 116-17.

Crawford, Bruce, "Citadel of Enforcement: Prohibition in the Small Town." *Outlook and Independent,* March 26, 1930, pp. 488-89, 516.

Crowther, Samuel. "Everybody Ought to be Rich: An Interview with John J. Raskob." *Ladies Home Journal,* August 1929, pp. 9, 36.

Dana, Charles L. *et al.* "The Medical Profession and the Volstead Act." *Journal of the American Medical Association* 76 (June 4, 1921): 1592-93.

Darrow, Clarence S. "The Ordeal of Prohibition." *American Mercury,* August 1924, 419-27.

———. "Our Growing Tyranny." *Vanity Fair,* February 1928, pp. 39, 104.

———. "Prohibition Cowardice." *Vanity Fair,* September 1928, pp. 53, 100.

———. "Tyranny and the Volstead Act." *Vanity Fair,* March 1927, pp. 45-46, 116.

Davis, Elmer. "How the Wets Won." *Current History* 34 (December 1933): 276-84.

Dewey, Ernest A. "Cocktails in Kansas." *Commonweal,* February 5, 1930, pp. 384-86.

Dowling, Noel T. "A New Experiment in Ratification." *American Bar Association Journal* 19 (July 1933): 383-87.

Ducas, Dorothy. "In Miniature: Mrs. Charles H. Sabin, Lady into Tiger." *McCall's,* September 1930, p. 4.

Du Pont, Pierre S. "Eighteenth Amendment Not a Remedy For the Drink Evil." *Current History* 28 (April 1928): 17-22.

———. "Why I Am Against Prohibition." *Liberty,* November 13, 1928, pp. 13-14.

Edmunds, Sterling E. "Mining and Sapping Our Bill of Rights." *Virginia Law Review* 16 (November 1929): 1–39.

"Enforcement, Repeal, and Nullification." *World's Work,* November 1926, pp. 5–6.

Essary, J. Frederick. "Blowing the Lid Off the Wickersham Report." *Liberty,* August 29, 1931, pp. 13–16.

Evans, Wainwright. "The Sanctity of the Law." *Outlook and Independent,* June 9, 1929, pp. 283–86.

"The Face on the Bar-room Floor." *Commonweal,* June 22, 1932, p. 199.

"Feudal Delaware." *Time,* January 31, 1927, p. 22.

Field, Carter. "Captain Bill Stayton—Guiding Spirit of the 'Little Group of Millionaires.'" *Life,* July 24, 1931, pp. 14–15.

———. "Life in Washington." *Life,* November 7, 1930, p. 14.

———. "The Political Status of Prohibition." *Life,* March 1932, p. 11.

"Final Returns in 'The Digest's' Prohibition Poll." *Literary Digest,* September 9, 1922, pp. 11–13.

"Four Aspects of the Wickersham Report." *New Republic,* February 4, 1931, pp. 311–13.

Franklin, Fabian. "An Anti-Prohibition Movement." *Weekly Review* 4 (May 28, 1921): 505.

———. "The Onward March of Repeal." *Forum* 85 (May 1931): 307–10.

Gebhart, John C. "Movement against Prohibition." *Annals of the American Academy of Political and Social Science* 163 (September 1932): 172–80.

———. "Prohibition: Statistical Studies of Enforcement and Social Effects." In *Statistics in Social Studies,* ed. Stuart A. Rice, pp. 111–49. Philadelphia: University of Pennsylvania Press, 1930.

Gillett, Ransom H. "Is Prohibition a Failure?" *Current History* 17 (October 1922): 48–54.

———. "Address to the Economic Club of Boston, March 6, 1923." *Consensus* 8 (April 1923): 3–32.

Grant. J. A. C. "The *Lanza* Rule of Successive Prosecutions." *Columbia Law Review* 32 (December 1932): 1309–31.

"The Great Prohibition Poll's Final Week." *Literary Digest,* April 30, 1932, pp. 6–7, 39.

Greene, Jerome D. "The Personal Problem." *Atlantic Monthly,* October 1926, pp. 525–28.

Hadley, Arthur Twining. "Law Making and Law Enforcement." *Harper's Magazine,* November 1925, pp. 641–48.

Hamilton, M. B. "Lest We Forget," *American Mercury,* May, 1933, pp. 40–58.

Hill, John Philip. "A State's Rights Remedy for Volsteadism." *North American Review* 221 (June 1925): 635–40.

Holland, James P. "The Workingman's View of Prohibition," *North American Review* 221 (June 1925): 611–15.

Horst, E. Clemens. "The Happy Grape Growers." *Outlook and Independent,* March 12, 1930, pp. 407–8, 433.

Howard, George Elliot. "Alcohol and Crime: A Study in Social Causation." *American Journal of Sociology* 24 (July 1918): 61–80.

"The Huge Poll's Final Report: All Records Outdone." *Literary Digest,* May 24, 1930, pp. 7-10.

"Intemperance of Prohibition." *Commonweal,* November 5, 1930, pp. 5-6.

Jensen, Howard E. "Propaganda and the Anti-Prohibition Movement." *South Atlantic Quarterly* 32 (July 1933): 254-65.

Johnston, Henry Alan. "The Eighteenth Amendment is Void." *Century Magazine,* April 1928, pp. 641-53.

———. "Prohibition: Born of War." *Outlook and Independent,* August 6, 1930, pp. 523-26, 558-59.

Joy, Henry Bourne. "Prohibition against Human Nature." *North American Review* 221 (June 1925): 608-11.

"Judge Clark and the Constitution." *New Republic,* December 31, 1930, pp. 178-79.

"Judge Clark Overruled." *Outlook and Independent.* March 11, 1931, p. 359.

"Judge Clark's Decision." *Nation,* December 31, 1930, p. 722.

Kirby, Byron C. "The Logic of Prohibition." *Scientific Temperance Journal* 39 (1930): 1-5.

Krock, Arthur. "Jefferson's Stepchildren." *American Mercury,* February 1926, pp. 129-35.

Krout, John Allen. "Glimpses of a Golden Age." *American Mercury,* June 1925, pp. 208-14.

"Ladies at Roslyn." *Time,* July 18, 1932, pp. 8-10.

Leighton, Isabel. "A Charming Aristocrat." *Smart Set,* March 1930, pp. 36-37.

Lippmann, Walter. "The Great Wickersham Mystery." *Vanity Fair,* April 1931, pp. 41-42.

———. "Our Predicament under the Eighteenth Amendment." *Harper's Magazine,* December 1926, pp. 51-56.

———. "The Popular Dogma of Law Enforcement." *Yale Review* 19 (September 1929): 1-13.

Lunt, Dudley Cammett. "The Rising Tide of Prohibition Repeal." *Scribner's Magazine,* June 1930, pp. 630-35.

McGovney, D. O. "Is The Eighteenth Amendment Void because of Its Contents?" *Columbia Law Review* 20 (May 1920): 499-518.

MacGrath, Harold. "The Retreat from Utopia." *American Mercury,* April 1926, pp. 404-11.

MacKaye, Milton. "The New Crusade." *The New Yorker,* October 22, 1932, pp. 20-24.

McManus, Robert Cruise. "Raskob." *North American Review* 231 (January 1931): 10-15.

Marbury, William L. "The Limitations upon the Amending Power." *Harvard Law Review* 33 (December 1919): 223-35.

Martin, Edward S. "The Editor's Easy Chair." *Harper's Magazine,* August 1930, p. 378.

———. "Much Ado, and More Making." *Harper's Magazine,* November 1929, pp. 785-88.

Mencken, H. L. "Man Who Really Busted Prohibition Gives All Credit to Opposite Sex." *Baltimore Sun,* October 30, 1932.

"Mr. DuPont Solves the Liquor Problem." *Christian Century,* April 16, 1930, pp. 485.

"Mr. Raskob's Suggestions." *Commonweal,* April 15, 1931, p. 647.

Moore, Samuel Taylor. "Lo, the Poor Bootlegger!" *New Outlook,* October 1933, pp. 30-33.

"The New Raskobian Uproar." *Literary Digest,* April 25, 1931, p. 12.

Nicoll, Courtlandt. "The Farce of Enforcement." *North American Review* 217 (June 1929): 641-47.

"No Eighteenth Amendment for Judge Clark." *Literary Digest,* December 27, 1930, p. 6.

"Nullification by Consent." *New Republic,* June 16, 1926, pp. 101-2.

Odegard, Peter H. "Mr. Hoover's 'Noble Experiment.'" *Nation,* July 29, 1931, pp. 102-4.

Ogburn, William, and Talbot, Nell. "A Measurement of the Factors in the Presidential Election of 1928." *Social Forces* 8 (December 1929): 175-83.

Orfield, Lester B. "The Scope of the Federal Amending Power." *Michigan Law Review* 27 (March 1930): 550-85.

Pollard, Joseph Percival. "The Rebel on the Bench." *North American Review* 231 (March 1931): 227-34.

Priest, Henry Samuel. "Prohibition and Respect for Law." *North American Review* 221 (June 1925): 596-601.

Pringle, Henry F. "John J. Raskob: A Portrait." *Outlook,* August 22, 1928, pp. 645-49, 678.

———. "Wet Hope." *The New Yorker,* June 14, 1930, pp. 23-25.

"Progressivism and Prohibition." *New Republic,* April 21, 1926, pp. 261-63.

"Prohibition and Illiteracy." *Commonweal,* May 27, 1931, p. 89.

"The Prohibition Hearing." *New Republic,* March 12, 1930, p. 87.

"Prohibition: United Wets." *Time,* November 7, 1932, p. 16.

"Prohibition: William Sprague Decision." *Time,* December 29, 1930, pp. 8-9.

"Prohibition Repeal—Practical Politics." *New Republic,* June 11, 1930, pp. 84-86.

"Protestant Press Call It a Dry Victory." *Literary Digest,* December 8, 1928, pp. 28-29.

Rapacz, Max P. "Effect of the Eighteenth Amendment upon the Amending Process." *Notre Dame Lawyer* 9 (March 1934): 313-16.

Raskob, John J., as told to James C. Derieux. "Rich Men in Politics." *Colliers,* March 5, 1932, pp. 7-8, 54.

"Raskob on Solid Ground." *Outlook and Independent,* April 15, 1931, p. 516.

Reed, James A. "The Pestilence of Fanaticism." *American Mercury,* May 1925, pp. 1-7.

"Repeal the Eighteenth Amendment." *Nation,* May 4, 1932, p. 502.

"Republicans and Prohibition." *New Republic,* June 22, 1932, p. 141.

Revere, C. T. "Prohibition: Its Effect on Taxation." *Review of Reviews* 85 (April 1932): 37.

Rice, Stuart A. "Prohibition and Statistics." *Journal of Social Forces* 3 (September 1924): 1-4.

Richardson, Anna Steese. "Grandmother Goes Wet." *Forum,* June 1931, pp. 365-68.

Ritchie, Albert C. "The Democratic Case." *Saturday Evening Post,* October 29, 1932, pp. 3-5.

Robinson, Claude E. "That Great 'Wet Landslide': A Critical Inquiry into the *Literary Digest* Poll." *New Republic,* April 13, 1932, pp. 224-27.

Robninson, Grace. "Women Wets." *Liberty,* November 1, 1930, pp. 30-35.

Ryan, John A. "Are Our Prohibition Laws 'Purely Penal'?" *Ecclesiastical Review* 70 (April 1924): 404-11.

————. "A Catholic Economist and Theologian on Prohibition." *Fortnightly Review* 23 (April 1, 1916): 100-101.

————. "Do the Prohibition Laws Bind in Conscience?" *Catholic World,* May 1925, pp. 145-57.

————. "The Evolution of an Anti." *Commonweal,* June 26, 1929, pp. 211-12.

————. "Prohibition, Pro and Con." *Catholic World,* April 1925, pp. 31-35.

————. "Who Shall Obey the Law?" *Commonweal,* April 3, 1929, pp. 616-18.

Sabin, Pauline Morton. "I Change My Mind on Prohibition." *Outlook,* June 13, 1928, pp. 254, 272.

————. "Why American Mothers Demand Repeal." *Liberty,* September 10, 1932, pp. 12-14.

————. "Women's Revolt against Prohibition." *Review of Reviews* 80 (November 1929): 86-88.

Seagle, William. "The Moral Law." *American Mercury,* December 1926, pp. 451-57.

Shouse, Jouett. "Watchman, What of the Night?" *Atlantic Monthly,* February 1931, pp. 250-58.

Skinner, George D. "Intrinsic Limitations on the Power of Constitutional Amendment." *Michigan Law Review* 18 (December 1919): 213-25.

Smith, Alfred E. "Child Labor." *New Outlook,* October 1933, pp. 11-12.

————. "A New Way Out of Prohibition." *Liberty,* January 23, 1932, pp. 6-11.

Stayton, William H. "Have We Prohibition or Only Prohibition Laws?" *North American Review* 221 (June 1925): 591-96.

————. "The Official View of the Anti-Prohibition Association." *Current History* 28 (April 1928): 4-9.

Taft, Henry W. "Amendment of the Federal Constitution: Is the Power Conferred by Article V Limited by the Tenth Amendment?" *Virginia Law Review* 16 (May 1930): 647-58.

Taft, William Howard. "Can Ratification of an Amendment to the Constitution be Made to Depend on a Referendum?" *Yale Law Review* 29 (June 1920): 821-25.

TRB. "Washington Notes." *New Republic,* February 4, 1931, p. 321.

————. "Washington Notes." *New Republic,* March 30, 1932, p. 180.

"Vox Pop: Can It Bring Repeal." *World's Work,* January 1932, p. 28.

Wadsworth, James W., Jr. "The Death Toll of Enforcement." *North American Review* 229 (March 1930): 257-62.

Walker, Stanley. "Open or Secret Saloons?" *New York Herald-Tribune Magazine,* March 26, 1933, pp. 3, 9.

Wallace, Schuyler C. "Nullification: A Process of Government." *Political Science Quarterly* 45 (September 1930): 347-58.

"Was the Election a Victory for Prohibition?" *Literary Digest,* November 24, 1928, pp. 14-15.

"Which Side 'Got the Breaks' in the Big Poll?" *Literary Digest,* May 14, 1932, pp. 8-9, 41.

White, Justin DuPratt. "Is There an Eighteenth Amendment?" *Cornell Law Quarterly* 5 (January 1920): 113-27.

"Who Killed Prohibition?" *Christian Century,* November 15, 1933, pp. 1430-32.

"The Wickersham Report." *Commonweal,* February 4, 1931, p. 369.

Willcox, Walter F. "An Attempt to Measure Public Opinion about Repealing the Eighteenth Amendment." *Journal of the American Statistical Association* 26 (September 1931): 243-61.

Williams, George H. "Article V of the Constitution." *Constitutional Review* 12 (April 1928): 69-83.

Williams, George Washington. "Are There Any Limitations upon the Power to Amend the United States Constitution?" *Temple Law Quarterly* 5 (June 1931): 554-61.

BOOKS

[Allen, Robert S., and Pearson, Drew]. *Washington Merry-Go-Round.* New York: Horace Liveright, 1931.

Anti-Saloon League Yearbook. Westerville, Ohio: American Issue Press, 1923-30.

Arthur, T. S. *Ten Nights without a Barroom.* Indianapolis: Bell, 1930.

Auerbach, Joseph S. *An Indictment of Prohibition.* New York: Harper, 1930.

Barnes, Harry Elmer. *Prohibition versus Civilization: Analyzing the Dry Psychosis.* New York: Viking Press, 1932.

Beck, James M. *The Constitution of the United States.* New York: George H. Doran, 1922.

————. *May It Please the Court.* Edited by O. R. McGuire. Atlanta: Harrison, 1930.

————. *Our Wonderland of Bureaucracy: A Study of the Growth of Bureaucracy in the Federal Government and Its Destructive Effect upon the Constitution.* New York: Macmillan, 1932.

————. *The Vanishing Rights of the States.* New York: George H. Doran, 1926.

Binkley, Robert C. *Responsible Drinking.* New York: Vanguard, 1930.

Black, Forrest Revere. *Ill-Starred Prohibition Cases: A Study in Judicial Pathology.* Boston: Richard G. Badger, 1931.

Bossard, James H. S., and Thorstein Sellin, eds. *Prohibition: A National Experiment.* Annals of the American Academy of Political and Social Science, vol. 163. Philadelphia, 1932.

Bowers, Claude. *My Life.* New York: Simon and Schuster, 1962.

Bruere, Martha Bensley. *Does Prohibition Work? A Study of the Operation of the Eighteenth Amendment Made by the National Federation of Settlements, Assisted by Social Workers in Different Parts of the United States.* New York: Harper, 1927.

Butler, Nicholas Murray. *Across the Busy Years.* 2 vols. New York: Scribner's, 1939-40.

Cannon, James, Jr. *Bishop Cannon's Own Story: Life as I have Seen It.* Edited by

Richard L. Watson, Jr. Durham: Duke University Press, 1955.

Cherrington, Ernest H. *The Evolution of Prohibition in the United States of America: A Chronological History of the Liquor Problem and the Temperance Reform in the United States from the Earliest Settlements to the Consummation of National Prohibition.* Westerville, Ohio: American Issue Press, 1920.

Colvin, D. Leigh. *Prohibition in the United States: A History of the Prohibition Party and of the Prohibition Movement.* New York: George H. Doran, 1926.

Crowther, Samuel. *Prohibition and Prosperity.* New York: John Day, 1930.

Curran, Henry H. *John Citizen's Job.* New York: Scribner's, 1924.

————. *Pillar to Post.* New York: Scribner's, 1941.

Darrow, Clarence, and Holmes, John Haynes. *Debate; Resolved: That the United States Continue the Policy of Prohibition as Defined in the Eighteenth Amendment.* New York: League for Public Discussion, 1924.

Darrow, Clarence, and Yarros, Victor S. *The Prohibition Mania: A Reply to Professor Irving Fisher and Others.* New York: Boni and Liveright, 1927.

Dorr, Rheta Childe. *Drink: Coercion or Control?* New York: Frederick A. Stokes, 1929.

Edge, Walter Evans. *A Jerseyman's Journal: Fifty Years of American Business and Politics.* Princeton: Princeton University Press, 1948.

Einstein, Izzy. *Prohibition Agent No. 1.* New York: Frederick A. Stokes, 1932.

Farley, James A. *Behind the Ballots.* New York: Harcourt, Brace, 1938.

Feis, Herbert. *1933: Characters in Crisis.* Boston: Little, Brown, 1966.

Feldman, Herman. *Prohibition: Its Economic and Industrial Aspects.* New York: D. Appleton, 1927.

Fisher, Irving. *Prohibition at Its Worst.* New York: Macmillan, 1926.

————, and Brougham, H. Bruce. *The "Noble Experiment."* New York: Alcohol Information Committee, 1930.

————. *Prohibition Still at Its Worst.* New York: Alcohol Information Press, 1928.

Fosdick, Raymond B., and Scott, Albert C. *Toward Liquor Control.* New York: Harper, 1933.

Franklin, Fabian. *The A B C of Prohibition.* New York: Harcourt, Brace, 1927.

————. *What Prohibition Has Done To America.* New York: Harcourt, Brace, 1922.

Gillett, Ransom H., and Holmes, John Haynes. *Repeal of the Prohibition Amendment.* The Reference Shelf, vol. 1, no. 11. New York: H. W. Wilson, 1923.

Gordon, Ernest. *When the Brewer Had the Stranglehold.* New York: Alcohol Information Committee, 1930.

Hapgood, Norman, ed. *Professional Patriots.* New York: Albert & Charles Boni, 1927.

Harrison, Leonard V., and Laine, Elizabeth. *After Repeal: A Study of Liquor Control Administration.* New York: Harper, 1936.

Haynes, Roy A. *Prohibition Inside Out.* Garden City, N.Y.: Doubleday, Page, 1923.

Hearst Temperance Contest Committee. *Temperance—or Prohibition?* New York: New York American, 1929.

Hennessy, Francis X. *Citizen or Subject?* New York: E. P. Dutton, 1923.

Holthusen, Henry F. *James W. Wadsworth, Jr.: A Biographical Sketch.* New York: G. P. Putnam, 1926.

Hoover, Herbert. *American Individualism.* Garden City, N.Y.: Doubleday, Page, 1922.

———. *Memoirs: The Great Depression, 1929–1941.* New York: Macmillan, 1952.

Ickes, Harold L. *The Secret Diary of Harold L. Ickes: The First Thousand Days, 1933–1936.* New York: Simon and Schuster, 1954.

Jackson-Babbitt, Inc. *The New Crusade.* Cleveland: Crusaders, Inc., 1932.

Jessup, Henry Wynans. *The Bill of Rights and Its Destruction by Alleged Due Process of Law.* Chicago: Callaghan, 1927.

Johnston, Henry Alan. *What Rights Are Left?* New York: Macmillan, 1930.

Jones, Robert L. *The Eighteenth Amendment and Our Foreign Relations.* New York: Thomas Y. Crowell, 1933.

Joy, Henry B. *Appeal to President Coolidge's 'Court of Last Resort' in Defense of the Constitution of the United States and the Bill of Rights against the XVIIIth Amendment.* Detroit: privately printed, 1930.

Koren, John. *Alcohol and Society.* New York: Henry Holt, 1916.

Lindley, Ernest K. *Franklin D. Roosevelt: A Career in Progressive Democracy.* Indianapolis: Bobbs-Merrill, 1931.

McAdoo, William Gibbs. *The Challenge: Liquor and Lawlessness versus Constitutional Government.* New York: Century, 1928.

McBain, Howard Lee. *Prohibition: Legal and Illegal.* New York: Macmillan, 1928.

Maurice, Arthur Bartlett, ed. *How They Draw Prohibition.* New York: Association Against the Prohibition Amendment, 1930.

Mencken, H. L. *Making a President: A Footnote to the Saga of Democracy.* New York: Alfred A. Knopf, 1932.

———. *Notes on Democracy.* New York: Alfred A. Knopf, 1926.

Merz, Charles. *The Dry Decade.* Garden City, N.Y.: Doubleday, Doran, 1931.

Michelson, Charles. *The Ghost Talks.* New York: G. P. Putnam's Sons, 1944.

National Wholesale Liquor Dealers Association of America. *The Anti-Prohibition Manual.* Cincinnati: National Wholesale Liquor Dealers Association of America, 1917.

Odegard, Peter H. *Pressure Politics: The Story of the Anti-Saloon League.* New York: Columbia University Press, 1928.

Pollard, Joseph Percival. *The Road to Repeal: Submission to Conventions.* New York: Brentano's, 1932.

President's Research Committee on Social Trends. *Recent Social Trends in the United States.* 2 vols. New York: McGraw-Hill, 1933.

Pringle, Henry F. *Alfred E. Smith: A Critical Study.* New York: Macy-Masius, 1927.

Reed, James A. *The Rape of Temperance.* New York: Cosmopolitan, 1931.

Rogers, Will. *Rogers-isms: The Cowboy Philosopher on Prohibition.* New York: Harper, 1919.

The Roosevelt Club Borah-Butler Debate. Boston: The Roosevelt Club, 1927.

Root, Grace C. *Women and Repeal: The Story of the Women's Organization for National Prohibition Reform.* New York: Harper, 1934.

Ryan, John A. *Declining Liberty and Other Papers.* New York: Macmillan, 1927.

———. *Questions of the Day.* Boston: Stratford, 1931.

———. *Social Doctrine in Action: A Personal History.* New York: Harper, 1941.

Scott, William Rufus. *Revolt on Mount Sinai: The Puritan Retreat from Prohibition.* Pasadena, Calif.: Logan, 1944.

Smith, Alfred E. *Up to Now.* New York: Viking, 1929.

Stelzle, Charles. *Why Prohibition!* New York: George H. Doran, 1918.

Steuart, Justin. *Wayne Wheeler, Dry Boss: An Uncensored Biography of Wayne B. Wheeler.* New York: Fleming H. Revell, 1928.

Stevenson, Archibald E. *States' Rights and National Prohibition.* New York: Clark Boardmen, 1927.

Stout, Charles Taber. *The Eighteenth Amendment and the Part Played by Organized Medicine.* New York: Mitchell Kennerly, 1921.

Tillitt, Malvern Hall. *The Price of Prohibition.* New York: Harcourt, Brace, 1932.

Tugwell, Rexford G. *The Battle for Democracy.* New York: Columbia University Press, 1935.

Tumulty, Joseph P. *Woodrow Wilson as I Know Him.* Garden City, N.Y.: Doubleday, Page, 1921.

Tydings, Millard. *Before and After Prohibition.* New York: Macmillan, 1930.

Walnut, T. Henry, ed. *Prohibition and Its Enforcement.* Annals of the American Academy of Political and Social Science, vol. 109. Philadelphia, 1923.

Warburton, Clark. *The Economic Results of Prohibition.* New York: Columbia University Press, 1932.

Whitlock, Brand. *The Little Green Shutter.* New York: D. Appleton, 1931.

Willebrandt, Mabel Walker. *The Inside of Prohibition.* Indianapolis: Bobbs-Merrill, 1929.

Windle, Charles A. *The Case against Prohibition.* Chicago: Iconoclast, 1927.

Wood, Charles S., ed. *A Criticism of National Prohibition.* Washington: Association Against the Prohibition Amendment, 1926.

SECONDARY WORKS
UNPUBLISHED

Chatham, Marie. "The Role of the National Party Chairman from Hanna to Farley." Ph.D. diss., University of Maryland, 1953.

Comerford, Robert J. "The American Liberty League." Ph.D. diss., St. John's University, 1967.

Drescher, Nuala McGann. "The Opposition to Prohibition, 1900–1919: A Social and Institutional Study." Ph.D. diss., University of Delaware, 1964.

Duus, Louise. "There Ought To Be a Law: A Study of Popular American Attitudes toward 'The Law' in the 1920's." Ph.D. diss., University of Minnesota, 1967.

Engelmann, Larry D. "O Whiskey: The History of Prohibition in Michigan." Ph.D. diss., University of Michigan, 1971.

Haller, Mark H. "Bootlegging in Chicago: The Structure of an Illegal Enterprise." Paper delivered at the American Historical Association meeting, December 29, 1974, Chicago, Ill.

Heckman, Dayton E. "Prohibition Passes: The Story of the Association against the Prohibition Amendment." Ph.D. diss., Ohio State University, 1939.

Jones, Bartlett C. "The Debate over National Prohibition, 1920–1933." Ph.D. diss., Emory University, 1961.

Lopata, Roy Haywood. "John J. Raskob: A Conservative Businessman in the Age of Roosevelt." Ph.D. diss., University of Delaware, 1975.

McLaughlin, Andrew C. "Satire as a Weapon against Prohibition, 1920-1928: Expression of a Cultural Conflict." Ph.D. diss., Stanford University, 1969.

Sexton, Robert F. "Kentucky Distillers React to Prohibition." Paper delivered at the American Historical Association meeting, December 29, 1974. Chicago, Ill.

Stegh, Leslie J. "Wet and Dry Battles in the Cradle State of Prohibition: Robert J. Bulkley and the Repeal of Prohibition in Ohio." Ph.D. diss., Kent State University, 1975.

PUBLISHED

Allsop, Kenneth. *The Bootleggers and Their Era.* Garden City, N.Y.: Doubleday, 1961.

Allswang, John M. *A House for All Peoples: Ethnic Politics in Chicago, 1890-1936.* Lexington: University Press of Kentucky, 1971.

Archer, Jules. *The Plot to Seize the White House.* New York: Hawthorn, 1973.

Asbury, Herbert. *The Great Illusion: An Informal History of Prohibition.* Garden City, N.Y.: Doubleday, 1950.

Ashby, LeRoy. "The Disappearing Dry: Raymond Robins and the Last Days of Prohibition." *North Carolina Historical Review* 51 (October 1974): 401-19.

Badenhausen, Carl W. "Self-Regulation in the Brewing Industry." *Law and Contemporary Problems* 7 (Autumn 1940): 689-95.

Bagby, Wesley M. *The Road to Normalcy: The Presidential Campaign and Election of 1920.* Baltimore: Johns Hopkins Press, 1962.

Baron, Stanley. *Brewed in America: A History of Beer and Ale in the United States.* Boston: Little, Brown, 1962.

Bauman, Mark K. "Prohibition and Politics: Warren Candler and Al Smith's 1928 Campaign." *Mississippi Quarterly* 31 (Winter 1977-78): 109-17.

Beaver, Daniel R. *Newton D. Baker and the American War Effort.* Lincoln: University of Nebraska Press, 1966.

Bergman, Andrew. *We're in the Money: Depression America and Its Films.* New York: Harper & Row, 1971.

Bernstein, Irving. *The Lean Years: A History of the American Worker, 1920-1933.* Boston: Houghton Mifflin, 1960.

Blocker, Jack S., Jr. *Retreat from Reform: The Prohibition Movement in the United States, 1890-1913.* Westport, Conn.: Greenwood, 1976.

Boyer, Paul. *Urban Masses and Moral Order in America, 1820-1920.* Cambridge: Harvard University Press, 1978.

Broderick, Francis L. *Right Reverend New Dealer John A. Ryan.* New York: Macmillan, 1963.

Burner, David. *Herbert Hoover: A Public Life.* New York: Alfred A. Knopf, 1979.

———. *The Politics of Provincialism: The Democratic Party in Transition, 1918-1932.* New York: Alfred A. Knopf, 1968.

Burnham, J. C. "New Perspectives on the Prohibition 'Experiment' of the 1920's." *Journal of Social History* 2 (Fall 1968): 51-68.

Burns, James MacGregor. *Roosevelt: The Lion and the Fox.* New York: Harcourt,

Brace & World, 1956.

Burran, James A. "Prohibition in New Mexico, 1917." *New Mexico Historical Review* 48 (April 1973): 133-49.

Byse, Clark. "Alcoholic Beverage Control before Repeal." *Law and Contemporary Problems* 7 (1940): 544-69.

Carr, William H. A. *The du Ponts of Delaware.* New York: Dodd, Mead, 1964.

Carte, Gene E. and Elaine H. *Police Reform in the United States: The Era of August Vollmer, 1905-1932.* Berkeley: University of California Press, 1975.

Carter, Paul A. *Another Part of the Twenties.* New York: Columbia University Press, 1977.

———. *The Decline and Revival of the Social Gospel: Social and Political Liberalism in American Protestant Churches, 1920-1940.* Ithaca: Cornell University Press, 1956.

Chafe, William H. *The American Woman: Her Changing Social, Economic, and Political Role, 1920-1970.* New York: Oxford University Press, 1972.

Chambers, Clarke A. *Seedtime of Reform: American Social Service and Social Action, 1918-1933.* Minneapolis: University of Minnesota Press, 1963.

Chandler, Alfred D., Jr. *Strategy and Structure: Chapters in the History of the Industrial Enterprise.* Cambridge: M.I.T. Press, 1962.

———. *The Visible Hand: The Managerial Revolution in American Business.* Cambridge: Belknap Press of Harvard University Press, 1977.

———, and Salsbury, Stephen. *Pierre S. du Pont and the Making of the Modern Corporation.* New York: Harper & Row, 1971.

Chepaitis, Joseph B. "Albert C. Ritchie in Power, 1920-1927." *Maryland Historical Magazine* 68 (1973): 383-404.

Clark, Nancy Tisdale. "The Demise of Demon Rum in Arizona." *Journal of Arizona History* 18 (Spring 1977): 69-92.

Clark, Norman H. *Deliver Us from Evil: An Interpretation of American Prohibition.* New York: W. W. Norton, 1976.

———. *The Dry Years: Prohibition and Social Change in Washington.* Seattle: University of Washington Press, 1965.

Cochran, Thomas C. *The Pabst Brewing Company: The History of an American Business.* New York: New York University Press, 1948.

Coffey, Thomas M. *The Long Thirst: Prohibition in America, 1920-1933.* New York: W. W. Norton, 1975.

Conley, Paul C., and Sorensen, Andrew A. *The Staggering Steeple: The Story of Alcoholism and the Churches.* Philadelphia: Pilgrim Press, 1971.

Cotter, Cornelius P., and Hennessy, Bernard C. *Politics without Power: The National Party Committees.* New York: Atherton, 1964.

Cramer, C. H. *Newton D. Baker: A Biography.* Cleveland: World, 1961.

Dabney, Virginius. *Dry Messiah: The Life of Bishop Cannon.* New York: Alfred A. Knopf, 1949.

Dale, Edgar. *The Content of Motion Pictures.* New York: Macmillan, 1935.

Daniels, Roger. *The Bonus March: An Episode of the Great Depression.* Westport, Conn.: Greenwood, 1971.

Dobyns, Fletcher. *The Amazing Story of Repeal: An Exposé of the Power of Propa-*

ganda. Chicago: Willett, Clark, 1940.

————. *The Underworld of American Politics*. New York: by author, 1932.

Dorian, Max. *The du Ponts: From Gunpowder to Nylon*. Translated by Edward B. Garside. Boston: Little, Brown, 1962.

Downard, William L. *The Cincinnati Brewing Industry: A Social and Economic History*. Athens: Ohio University Press, 1973.

Drescher, Nuala McGann. "Organized Labor and the Eighteenth Amendment." *Labor History* 8 (Fall 1967): 280-99.

Efron, Vera; Keller, Mark; and Gurioli, Carol. *Statistics on Consumption of Alcohol and on Alcoholism*. New Brunswick, N.J.: Rutgers Center of Alcohol Studies, 1974.

Elias, Robert H. *Entangling Alliances with None: An Essay on the Individual in the American Twenties*. New York: W. W. Norton, 1973.

Ellis, Edward Robb. *A Nation in Torment: The Great American Depression, 1929-1939*. New York: Capricorn, 1971.

Englemann, Larry D. "A Separate Peace: The Politics of Prohibition Enforcement in Detroit, 1920-1930." *Detroit in Perspective* 1 (Autumn 1972): 51-73.

Fausold, Martin L. *James W. Wadsworth, Jr.: The Gentleman from New York*. Syracuse: Syracuse University Press, 1975.

Filene, Peter G. "An Obituary for 'The Progressive Movement.'" *American Quarterly* 22 (Spring 1970): 20-34.

Franklin, Jimmie L. *Born Sober: Prohibition in Oklahoma, 1907-1959*. Norman: University of Oklahoma Press, 1971.

Freidel, Frank. *Franklin D. Roosevelt: Launching the New Deal*. Boston: Little, Brown, 1973.

————. *Franklin D. Roosevelt: The Ordeal*. Boston: Little, Brown, 1954.

————. *Franklin D. Roosevelt: The Triumph*. Boston: Little, Brown, 1956.

Friedman, Lawrence M. *A History of American Law*. New York: Simon and Schuster, 1973.

Furnas, J. C. *The Life and Times of the Late Demon Rum*. New York: Capricorn, 1965.

Gabriel, Ralph Henry. *The Course of American Democratic Thought: An Intellectual History Since 1815*. New York: Ronald Press, 1940.

Goldman, Eric F. *Rendezvous with Destiny: A History of Modern American Reform*. New York: Vintage, 1956.

Gordon, Ernest R. *The Wrecking of the Eighteenth Amendment*. Francistown, N.H.: Alcohol Information Press, 1943.

Goshen, Charles E. *Drinks, Drugs, and Do-Gooders*. New York: Free Press, 1973.

Gottfried, Alex. *Boss Cermak of Chicago: A Study of Political Leadership*. Seattle: University of Washington Press, 1962.

Gould, Lewis L. *Progressives and Prohibitionists: Texas Democrats in the Wilson Era*. Austin: University of Texas Press, 1973.

Grant. J. A. C. "Successive Prosecutions by State and Nation: Common Law and British Empire Comparisons." *UCLA Law Review* 4 (December 1956): 1-37.

Gray, James H. *Booze: The Impact of Whiskey on the Prairie West*. Toronto: Macmillan of Canada, 1972.

Greenberg, Irwin F. "Pinchot, Prohibition and Public Utilities: The Pennsylvania Election of 1930." *Pennsylvania History* 40 (January 1973): 21-35.

Gusfield, Joseph R. "Prohibition: The Impact of Political Utopianism." In *Change and Continuity in Twentieth-Century America: The 1920's,* ed. John Braeman, Robert H. Bremner, and David Brody, pp. 257-308. Columbus: Ohio State University Press, 1968.

―――. *Symbolic Crusade: Status Politics and the American Temperance Movement.* Urbana: University of Illinois Press, 1963.

Hand, Samuel B. "Al Smith, Franklin D. Roosevelt, and the New Deal: Some Comments on Perspective." *Historian* 27 (May 1965): 366-81.

Handlin, Oscar. *Al Smith and His America.* Boston: Little, Brown, 1958.

Hansen, James E., II. "Moonshine and Murder: Prohibition in Denver." *Colorado Magazine* 50 (Winter 1973): 1-23.

Harbaugh, William H. *Lawyer's Lawyer: The Life of John W. Davis.* New York: Oxford University Press, 1973.

Harrison, Brian. *Drink and the Victorians: The Temperance Question in England, 1815-1872.* London: Faber and Faber, 1971.

Hatch, Alden. *The Wadsworths of the Genesee.* New York: Coward-McCann, 1959.

Hicks, John D. *Republican Ascendancy, 1921-1933.* New York: Harper, 1960.

Hines, Tom S., Jr. "Mississippi and the Repeal of Prohibition." *Journal of Mississippi History* 24 (January 1962): 1-39.

Hofstadter, Richard. *The Age of Reform: From Bryan to F.D.R.* New York: Alfred A. Knopf, 1955.

Hohner, Robert A. "The Prohibitionists: Who Were They?" *South Atlantic Quarterly* 68 (Autumn 1969): 491-505.

Holbrook, Stewart H. *The Age of the Moguls.* Garden City, N.Y.: Doubleday, 1953.

Huthmacher, J. Joseph. *Massachusetts People and Politics, 1919-1933.* Cambridge: Harvard University Press, 1959.

―――. *Senator Robert F. Wagner and the Rise of Urban Liberalism.* New York: Atheneum, 1968.

Issac, Paul E. *Prohibition and Politics: Turbulent Decades in Tennessee, 1885-1920.* Knoxville: University of Tennessee Press, 1965.

Jackson, Kenneth T. *The Ku Klux Klan in the City, 1915-1930.* New York: Oxford University Press, 1967.

Jakoubek, Robert E. "A Jeffersonian's Dissent: John W. Davis and the Campaign of 1936." *West Virginia History* 35 (January 1974): 145-53.

Jellinek, E. M. "Recent Trends in Alcoholism and in Alcohol Consumption." *Quarterly Journal of Studies on Alcohol* 8 (July 1947): 1-42.

Jessup, Philip C. *Elihu Root.* 2 vols. New York: Dodd, Mead, 1938.

Johnson, Dorothy E. "Organized Women as Lobbyists in the 1920's." *Capitol Studies* 1 (Spring 1972): 41-58.

"Joseph Hodges Choate," in *Harvard College Class of 1897: Fiftieth Anniversary Report, 1897-1947.* Cambridge, Mass.: Harvard University Press, 1947.

Josephson, Matthew and Hannah. *Al Smith: Hero of the Cities: A Political Portrait Drawing on the Papers of Frances Perkins.* Boston: Houghton Mifflin, 1969.

Jowett, Garth. *Film: The Democratic Art.* Boston: Little, Brown, 1976.

Keller, Morton. *In Defense of Yesterday: James Beck and the Politics of Conservatism, 1861-1936.* New York: Coward-McCann, 1958.

Kingsdale, Jon M. "The 'Poor Man's Club': Social Functions of the Working-Class Saloon." *American Quarterly* 25 (October 1973): 472-89.

Kirby, Jack T. *Darkness at the Dawning: Race and Reform in the Urban South.* Philadelphia: J. B. Lippincott, 1972.

Kirschner, Don S. *City and Country: Rural Responses to Urbanization in the 1920s.* Westport, Conn.: Greenwood, 1970.

Kobler, John. *Ardent Spirits: The Rise and Fall of Prohibition.* New York: G. P. Putnam's Sons, 1976.

————. *Capone: The Life and World of Al Capone.* New York: G. P. Putnam's Sons, 1971.

Kottman, Richard N. "Volstead Violated: Prohibition as a Factor in Canadian-American Relations." *Canadian Historical Review* 43 (June 1962): 106-26.

Kraditor, Aileen S. *The Ideas of the Woman Suffrage Movement, 1890-1920.* New York: Columbia University Press, 1965.

Krout, John Allen. *The Origins of Prohibition.* New York: Alfred A. Knopf, 1925.

Kyvig, David E. "Amending the U.S. Constitution: Ratification Controversies, 1917-1971." *Ohio History* 83 (Summer 1974): 156-69.

————. "Raskob, Roosevelt, and Repeal." *Historian* 37 (May 1975): 469-87.

————. "Women against Prohibition." *American Quarterly* 28 (Fall 1976): 465-82.

Lemons, J. Stanley. *The Woman Citizen: Social Feminism in the 1920s.* Urbana: University of Illinois Press, 1973.

Leuchtenburg, William E. *Franklin D. Roosevelt and the New Deal.* New York: Harper & Row, 1963.

Levin, James. "Governor Albert C. Ritchie and the Democratic Convention of 1932." *Maryland Historical Magazine* 67 (Fall 1972): 278-93.

————. "Governor Albert C. Ritchie and the Democratic National Convention of 1924." *Maryland Historical Magazine* 66 (Summer 1971): 101-20.

Levine, Lawrence W. *Defender of the Faith: William Jennings Bryan: The Last Decade, 1915-1925.* New York: Oxford University Press, 1965.

Lichtman, Allan T. "Critical Election Theory and the Reality of American Presidential Politics, 1916-1940." *American Historical Review* 81 (April 1976): 317-51.

Lisio, Donald J. *The President and Protest: Hoover, Conspiracy, and the Bonus March.* Columbia: University of Missouri Press, 1974.

Livermore, Seward W. *Politics Is Adjourned: Woodrow Wilson and the War Congress, 1916-1918.* Middletown, Conn.: Wesleyan University Press, 1966.

Longmate, Norman. *The Waterdrinkers: A History of Temperance.* London: Hamish Hamilton, 1968.

McCarthy, Raymond G., ed. *Drinking and Intoxication: Selected Readings in Social Attitudes and Controls.* New Haven: College and University Press, 1959.

McCoy, Donald R. *Calvin Coolidge: The Quiet President.* New York: Macmillan, 1967.

McLoughlin, William C., Jr. *Billy Sunday Was His Real Name.* Chicago: University of Chicago Press, 1955.

Manchester, William. *Disturber of the Peace: The Life of H. L. Mencken.* New York:

Harper, 1951.

Mann, Arthur. *La Guardia: A Fighter against His Times, 1882-1933.* Philadelphia: J. B. Lippincott, 1959.

Markmann, Charles Lam. *The Noblest Cry: A History of the American Civil Liberties Union.* New York: St. Martin's, 1965.

Mason, Alpheus Thomas. *William Howard Taft: Chief Justice.* New York: Simon and Schuster, 1964.

May, Henry. *How Dry We Were: Prohibition Revisited.* Englewood Cliffs, N.J.: Prentice-Hall, 1963.

Mayer, Martin. *Emory Buckner.* New York: Harper & Row, 1968.

Meers, John R. "The California Wine and Grape Industry and Prohibition." *California Historical Society Quarterly* 46 (1967): 19-32.

Mennell, S. J. "Prohibition: A Sociological View." *Journal of American Studies* 3 (July 1969): 159-75.

Meriwether, Lee. *Jim Reed: "Senatorial Immortal."* Webster Groves, Mo.: International Mark Twain Society, 1948.

Miller, Robert Moats. *American Protestantism and Social Issues, 1919-1939.* Chapel Hill: University of North Carolina Press, 1958.

Mitchell, Franklin D. *Embattled Democracy: Missouri Democratic Politics, 1919-1932.* Columbia: University of Missouri Press, 1968.

Moore, Edmund A. *A Catholic Runs for President: The Campaign of 1928.* New York: Roland Press, 1956.

Morgan, David. *Suffragists and Democrats: The Politics of Women Suffrage in America.* East Lansing: Michigan State University Press, 1972.

Murphy, Paul L. *The Constitution in Crisis Times, 1918-1969.* New York: Harper & Row, 1972.

Murray, Robert K. *The Harding Era: Warren G. Harding and His Administration.* Minneapolis: University of Minnesota Press, 1969.

———. *The 103rd Ballot: Democrats and the Disaster in Madison Square Garden.* New York: Harper & Row, 1976.

Nelli, Humbert S. *The Business of Crime: Italians and Syndicate Crime in the United States.* New York: Oxford University Press, 1976.

———. *Italians in Chicago, 1880-1930: A Study in Ethnic Mobility.* New York: Oxford University Press, 1970.

Nethers, John L. "'Driest of Drys': Simeon D. Fess." *Ohio History* 79 (Summer-Autumn, 1970): 178-92.

O'Connor, Richard. *The First Hurrah: A Biography of Alfred E. Smith.* New York: G. P. Putnam's Sons, 1970.

O'Neill, John E. "Federal Activity in Alcoholic Beverage Control." *Law and Contemporary Problems* 7 (Autumn 1940): 570-99.

Ostrander, Gilman M. *The Prohibition Movement in California, 1848-1933.* University of California Publications in History, vol. 57. Berkeley: University of California Press, 1957.

Parish, James Robert, and Pitts, Michael R. *The Great Gangster Pictures.* Metuchen, N.J.: Scarecrow, 1976.

Patterson, Michael S. "The Fall of a Bishop: James Cannon, Jr., *versus* Carter Glass, 1909-1934." *Journal of Southern History* 39 (November 1973): 493-518.

Paulson, Ross E. *Women's Suffrage and Prohibition: A Comparative Study of Equality and Social Control.* Glenview, Ill.: Scott, Foresman, 1973.

Pearson, C. C., and Hendricks, J. Edwin. *Liquor and Anti-Liquor in Virginia, 1619-1919.* Durham: Duke University Press, 1967.

Peel, Roy V., and Donnelly, Thomas C. *The 1928 Campaign: An Analysis.* New York: Richard R. Smith, 1931.

———. *The 1932 Campaign: An Analysis.* New York: Farrar & Rinehart, 1935.

Pickering, Clarence R. *The Early Days of Prohibition.* New York: Vantage, 1964.

Pickett, Deets. *Then and Now: The Truth about Prohibition and Repeal.* Columbus, Ohio: School and College Service, 1952.

Pringle, Henry F. *The Life and Times of William Howard Taft.* 2 vols. New York: Farrar and Rinehart, 1939.

Prothro, James W. *The Dollar Decade: Business Ideas in the 1920's.* Baton Rouge: Louisiana State University Press, 1954.

Quinn, Larry. 'The End of Prohibition in Idaho." *Idaho Yesterdays* 17 (Winter 1974): 6-13.

Rappaport, Armin. *The Navy League of the United States.* Detroit: Wayne State University Press, 1962.

Renner, G. K. "Prohibition Comes to Missouri, 1910-1919." *Missouri Historical Review* 62 (July 1968): 363-97.

Rippa, S. Alexander. "Constitutionalism: Political Defense of the Business Community during the New Deal Period." *Social Studies* 56 (October 1965): 187-90.

Rogin, Michael P., and Shover, John P. *Political Change in California: Critical Elections and Social Movements, 1890-1966.* Westport, Conn.: Greenwood, 1970.

Rollins, Alfred B., Jr. *Roosevelt and Howe.* New York: Alfred A. Knopf, 1962.

Rosen, Elliot A. *Hoover, Roosevelt, and the Brains Trust: From Depression to New Deal.* New York: Columbia University Press, 1972.

Rudolph, Frederick. "The American Liberty League, 1934-1940." *American Historical Review* 56 (October 1950): 19-33.

Schlesinger, Arthur M., Jr. *The Crisis of the Old Order, 1919-1933.* Boston: Houghton Mifflin, 1957.

Schmeckebier, Laurence F. *The Bureau of Prohibition: Its History, Activities and Organization.* Washington: Brookings Institution, 1929.

Schwartz, Jordan A. "Al Smith in the Thirties." *New York History* 45 (October 1964): 316-30.

———. *The Interregnum of Despair: Hoover, Congress, and the Depression.* Urbana: University of Illinois Press, 1970.

Sellers, James Benson. *The Prohibition Movement in Alabama, 1702-1943.* Chapel Hill: University of North Carolina Press, 1943.

Severn, Bill. *The End of the Roaring Twenties: Prohibition and Repeal.* New York: Julius Messner, 1969.

Shipman, George A. "State Administrative Machinery for Liquor Control" *Law and Contemporary Problems* 7 (Autumn 1940): 600-620.

Silva, Ruth. *Rum, Religion, and Votes: 1928 Re-examined.* University Park: Pennsylvania State University Press, 1962.

Sinclair, Andrew. *The Available Man: The Life Behind the Masks of Warren Gamaliel Harding.* New York: Macmillan, 1965.

————. *Prohibition: The Era of Excess.* Boston: Little, Brown, 1962.

Singleton, M. K. *H. L. Mencken and the American Mercury Adventure.* Durham: Duke University Press, 1962.

Smith, Gene. *When the Cheering Stopped: The Last Years of Woodrow Wilson.* New York: William Morrow, 1964.

Sparkes, Boyden, and Moore, Samuel Taylor. *The Witch of Wall Street: Hetty Green.* Garden City, N.Y.: Doubleday, 1948.

Stegh, Leslie J. "A Paradox of Prohibition: Election of Robert J. Bulkley as Senator from Ohio, 1930." *Ohio History* 83 (Summer 1974): 170-82.

Sullivan, Mark. *The Twenties. Our Times: The United States, 1900-1925,* vol. 6. New York: Scribner's, 1935.

Swindler, William F. *Court and Constitution in the Twentieth Century: The Old Legality, 1889-1932.* Indianapolis: Bobbs-Merrill, 1969.

Timberlake, James H. *Prohibition and the Progressive Movement, 1900-1920.* Cambridge: Harvard University Press, 1963.

Tugwell, Rexford G. *The Democratic Roosevelt.* Garden City, N.Y.: Doubleday, 1957.

Vose, Clement E. *Constitutional Change: Amendment Politics and Supreme Court Litigation since 1900.* Lexington, Mass.: D. C. Heath, 1972.

Warner, Emily Smith, with Daniel, Hawthorne. *The Happy Warrior: A Biography of my Father, Alfred E. Smith.* Garden City, N.Y.: Doubleday, 1956.

Warren, Harris Gaylord. *Herbert Hoover and the Great Depression.* New York: Oxford University Press, 1959.

Wenger, Robert E. "The Anti-Saloon League in Nebraska Politics, 1898-1910." *Nebraska History* 52 (1971): 267-92.

West, Elliott. "Cleansing the Queen City: Prohibition and Urban Reform in Denver." *Arizona and the West,* Winter 1972, pp. 331-46.

Whipple, Sidney B. *Noble Experiment.* London: Methuen, 1934.

White, William Allen. *A Puritan in Babylon: The Story of Calvin Coolidge.* New York: Macmillan, 1938.

Whitener, Daniel Jay. *Prohibition in North Carolina, 1715-1945.* Chapel Hill: University of North Carolina Press, 1946.

Wiebe, Robert H. *The Search for Order, 1877-1920.* New York: Hill and Wang, 1967.

Wilson, Joan Hoff. *Herbert Hoover: Forgotten Progressive.* Boston: Little, Brown, 1975.

Wilson, Ross. *Scotch: The Formative Years.* London: Constable, 1970.

Winkler, Allan M. "Drinking on the American Frontier." *Quarterly Journal of Studies on Alcohol* 29 (June 1968): 413-45.

Winkler, John K. *The Du Pont Dynasty.* New York: Reynal & Hitchcock, 1935.

Wolfskill, George. *The Revolt of the Conservatives: A History of the American Liberty League, 1934-1940.* Boston: Houghton Mifflin, 1962.

————, and Hudson, John A. *All but the People: Franklin D. Roosevelt and His Critics, 1933-39.* New York: Macmillan, 1969.

Wood, Stephen B. *Constitutional Politics in the Progressive Era: Child Labor and the Law.* Chicago: University of Chicago Press, 1968.

INDEX